# ALTERNATIVE EUROPE

D1343457

b.2007

## AlterImage

**a new list of publications
exploring global cult and popular cinema**

# ALTERNATIVE EUROPE

## EUROTRASH AND EXPLOITATION CINEMA SINCE 1945

EDITED BY ERNEST MATHIJS & XAVIER MENDIK

**WALLFLOWER PRESS**

LONDON and NEW YORK

First published in Great Britain in 2004 by
Wallflower Press
4th Floor, 26 Shacklewell Lane, London E8 2EZ
www.wallflowerpress.co.uk

A catalogue for this book is available from the British Library.

ISBN 1-903364-93-0

Printed in Turn, Italy by Grafiche Dessi s.r.l.

# CONTENTS

# ACKNOWLEDGEMENTS

The Editors would like to thank all of the writers who contributed so much hard work to this volume. We would also like to offer our sincere thanks to Jean Rollin for contributing the foreword. Thanks also to Brian Yuzna, Jörg Buttgereit and Giovanni Lombardo Radice for their support and assistance with compiling the interview materials used in this book.

We would also like to thank Andy Black, Charlie Blake, Gwen Bouvier, Peter Brooker, Nicola Daine, Dirk Van Extergem and the staff of the Brussels International Festival of Fantastic Film, Mikel Koven, Mylene Halsall (Momentum Pictures Home Entertainment), Howard Martin (Hem Productions), Magnus Paulsson and all the staff at the Fantastisk Film Festival, Tuomas Riskala, Cristina Sagardui, George Savona and Sally Young (Cathy Beck Communications).

Dona Kercher's essay, 'Violence, Timing and the Comedy Team in Alex de le Iglesia's *Muertos de Risa*', was first published in *Post Script*, and we wish to thank Gerald Duchovny for allowing us to reprint the essay in this volume.

Finally, we offer our thanks to the staff at Wallflower Press for their continued assistance and support of the *AlterImage* book series.

The images used in the chapter 'Alternative Belgian Cinema and Cultural Identity: *S.* and the Affaire Dutroux', are courtesy of Luc Reynaert/Europartners Film. The images used in 'Jörg Buttgereit's Nekromantiks: Things to do in Germany with the Dead' and 'A Very German Post-mortem: Jörg Buttgereit and Co-writer/Assistant Director Franz Rodenkirchen Speak', are courtesy of Jörg Buttgereit (with the exception of the director's image, which is courtesy of Thomas Ecke). The images of *Place on Earth* and *Of Freaks and Men* in 'Mise-en-scènes of the Impossible: Soviet and Russian Horror Films' are courtesy of Intercinema Agency, Moscow. The images used in 'Emmanuelle Enterprises' (from the film *Emmanuelle* only) are copyright to Studio Canal Image. (The film is available on DVD in the UK from Momentum Pictures and we wish to offer our thanks for their support in finding these stills for us). The images used in the following chapters: '"The Film You Are About to See is Based on Fact": Italian Nazi Sexploitation Cinema', 'Masochistic Cinesexuality: The Many Deaths of Giovanni Lombardo Radice', 'Male Masochism, Male Monsters: An Interview with Giovanni Lombardo Radice', 'Black Sex, Bad Sex: Monstrous Ethnicity in the *Black Emanuelle* Films', 'Jean Rollin: Le Sang d'un Poète du Cinéma' and 'Trans-European Excess: An Interview with Brian Yuzna', are all courtesy of the Noir Collection and we would like to thank Andy Black for his assistance with finding illustrative material for this volume. The cover image is from *Re-Animator* (1985), directed by Stuart Gordon/produced by Brian Yuzna, and is courtesy of the Noir Collection.

The rest of the images contained in the book are the property of the production or distribution companies concerned. They are reproduced here in the spirit of publicity and the promotion of the films in question.

*Ernest Mathijs dedicates this book to Gwen*
*Xavier Mendik dedicates this book to Essie – for a more perfect, future time*

# NOTES ON CONTRIBUTORS

**CHRISTOPHER BARRY** is a freelance film reviewer/critic/essayist specialising in drive-in film and cult cinema. He has been published in American publications *Cineguide*, *Shock Cinema* and *Screen Magazine*. His articles can also be found on www.filmfodder.com and www.men360.com. He is also creator/publisher/editor/writer for the website www.skyhighpictureshow.com, which provides reviews and essays regarding drive-in films from the 1960s, 1970s and 1980s.

**LINNIE BLAKE** is Senior Lecturer in the Department of English at Manchester Metropolitan University where she teaches film studies. She is especially interested in the politics of atrocity cinema and trash culture. She has most recently published on film noir and the western, the American serial killer, George A. Romero's 1970s shockers and German horror cinema.

**GARRETT CHAFFIN-QUIRAY** received his BA and MA from the University of Southern California School of Cinema-Television. He has since sponsored film festivals, taught television and cinema history and published book, movie, video and event reviews, several scholarly essays and book chapters, and one short story in 'The Subway Chronicles'. He now lives in New York City researching various subjects and writing fiction.

**JENNIFER FAY** is Assistant Professor and Co-director of Film Studies in the English Department at Michigan State University. She has an article forthcoming in *Cinema Journal* and is completing a book on film and democratic pedagogy in American-occupied Germany.

**BENJAMIN HALLIGAN** lectures in Film in York St John College, University of Leeds. His critical biography of Michael Reeves was published by Manchester University Press in their British Filmmakers series in 2003.

**I. Q. HUNTER** is Head of Film Studies at De Montfort University, Leicester. He is co-editor of Routledge's British Popular Cinema series, for which he edited *British Science Fiction Cinema* (1999) and *British Spy Cinema* (forthcoming). Among his other publications are the co-edited books *Pulping Fictions* (1996), *Trash Aesthetics* (1997) and *Retrovisions* (2001). His recent work has focused on Paul Verhoeven, British exploitation cinema and Hammer's science fiction and fantasy films, on which he is writing a book.

**LEON HUNT** is Senior Lecturer in Film and TV Studies at Brunel University. He is the author of *British Low Culture: From Safari Suits to Sexploitation* (1998) and *Kung Fu Cult Masters: From Bruce Lee to Crouching Tiger* (2003).

**DONA M. KERCHER** is Associate Professor of Spanish and Chair of the Department of Foreign Languages at Assumption College in Worcester, Massachusetts. She has published on a group of Spanish writers and directors: Rosa Chacel, Alex de la Iglesia, Manuel Gutiérrez Aragón, Javier Marías and Gracia Querejeta. Currently she is working on Federico Luppi and transnational star discourse, and on the role of Hitchcock in Hispanic film history.

**MIKEL J. KOVEN** lectures in Film and Television Studies at the University of Wales, Aberystwyth. His main research areas are exploitation cinema, Italian horror films, folklore and film, Jewish representation in film, Holocaust cinema and Classical Hollywood. He is the author of the Pocket Essentials book on *Blaxploitation Films* (2000) and is currently working on a book-length study of the *giallo* film.

**PATRICIA MACCORMACK** is Lecturer in Communication at Anglia Polytechnic University, Cambridge. She has published mainly on Italian horror, sexuality, feminism and the work of Gilles Deleuze and Felix Guattari.

**ERNEST MATHIJS** is Lecturer in Film Studies at the University of Wales, Aberystwyth. He has written extensively on the reception of alternative and Belgian cinema (with particular topics including David Cronenberg, *Daughters of Darkness* and *Man Bites Dog*). He is the editor of *The Cinema of the Low Countries* (2004) and co-editor (with Janet Jones) of *Big Brother International: Format, Critics and Publics*, forthcoming from Wallflower Press in 2004.

**XAVIER MENDIK** is Director of the Cult Film Archive at University College Northampton, and general editor of the Wallflower Press book series *AlterImage*. He has published widely on European cult and exploitation cinema, and his books (as author, editor and co-editor) include Dario Argento's *Tenebrae* (2000), *Unruly Pleasures: The Cult Film and Its Critics* (2000), *Shocking Cinema of the Seventies* (2002) and *Underground U.S.A.: Filmmaking Beyond the Hollywood Canon* (2002). He is currently working on his sixth book: *Fear Theory: Case Studies in European and American Horror* (forthcoming from Wallflower Press) and has just produced his first documentary film entitled *Cabin Fever: Fear Today, Horror Tomorrow*.

**TAMAO NAKAHARA** is a PhD candidate at the University of California at Berkeley. On Nunsploitation (and related topics) she has publications forthcoming in *Exploiting Fear*, *Horror Zone* and *Kinoeye*. She is also currently editing *Born to be Bad: Production, Exhibition and Reception of Trash Cinema* with Jeffrey Karlsen.

**COLIN ODELL** and **MICHELLE LE BLANC** are freelance authors and film critics. They have numerous books, including titles on *David Lynch*, *Jackie Chan*, *Vampire Films*, *Horror Films*, *John Carpenter* and *Tim Burton* for the Pocket Essentials series. They are regular contributors to *Vector*, the critical journal of the British Science Fiction Association, www.kamera.co.uk and bookmunch.co.uk.

**MAGNUS PAULSSON** is the International Director of the Fantastisk Film Festival in Sweden, as well as being a founder and board member of the event. An established journalist and filmmaker, he has written for a variety of publications including *Kvällsposten* and *Magasin Defect* and has also worked on a number of projects for prominent media organisations including MTV Europe and SVT (Swedish National Television). He is currently a producer for the Malmö-based media company *Solid Entertainment*.

**MARCELLE PERKS** is an postgraduate student in Media Studies and lectures at Hanover University. An avid horror film fan, she has been contributing to genre magazines since 1992 and is a regular contributor to US magazine *Fangoria*. She has contributed to *The BFI Companion to Horror, British Horror Cinema, Gothic Lifestyle* and currently writes for www.kamera.co.uk, *The Guardian* online and *Gay Times*. She is currently writing her first novel and hoping to develop her interest in virology.

**TUOMAS RISKALA** has been director of programming at the Espoo Ciné International Film Festival since 2000. He is also one of the main editors of the leading Finnish film magazine, *Hohto*, and a contributor to many other film-related media publications and television productions in Finland. He has been a member of the international juries at Fantasporto: Oporto International Film Festival in Portugal, Fantastisk Film Festival in Sweden, Neuchâtel International Fantastic Film Festival in Switzerland and the New Visions jury at Sitges Internacional Festival de Cinema de Catalunya.

**ADAM RODGERS** is a freelance filmmaker as well as being a film researcher currently based at the Cult Film Archive. Having graduated with a degree in Digital Film Production he has worked on projects for the BBC and HTV and regularly contributes to assignments for independent production companies based in Yorkshire and the Midlands. Adam recently undertook the research behind the documentary *Cabin Fever: Fear Today, Horror Tomorrow*, and is currently developing a series of short dramas around a variety of contemporary social and moral themes.

**CHRISTINA STOJANOVA** is an academic, curator and writer focusing on cultural semiotics and historical representation in Central and Eastern European cinema, interwar German cinema and the cinema of Québec. She teaches at Wilfrid Laurier University, Ontario, Canada.

**DIRK VAN EXTERGEM** is one of the organisers/programmers of the Brussels International Festival of Fantastic Film. He studied Communication and Cultural Sciences at the Free University of Brussels. Already seven years working for the Festival, he stood at the founding of the Festival's parallel section, 'the 7th Orbit', which he now supervises. He is also a regular collaborater with the Cinema Nova collective.

# FOREWORD

## FOR AN ILLOGICAL AND NONSENSICAL EUROPEAN CINEMA

For me, the terms of popular cinema starkly oppose those of commercial cinema. Commercial cinema attaches value only to the profitability of the product. Popular cinema, or B-series, on the contrary, allows for the creation and development of a director's personality, even in realms of alternative or genre cinema. I decided to become a B-series auteur on purpose, at a time when young cineastes predominantly drew on the *nouvelle vague*, with its very fashionable pseudo-modern style. My spirit was more influenced by surrealism: the films of Buñuel, Franju, the paintings by Magritte, Paul Delvaux, and the collages of Max Ernst. The latter seemed to me to refer directly to *Fantomas*, to Feuillade, to the episodic and to the famous serials. Every week, after coming out of school, we would go to the Cineac Cinema (found in the former Montparnasse train station). Here, we would watch strange and popular films and serials such as Tom Mix in *The Miracle Rider*, *Mysterious Doctor Satan*, *Zorro Fighting Legion* or *Nyoka and the Tiger Men*. The projections of these films were often interrupted by the public address system of the train station, announcing the arrival or departures of trains. Travellers entered or exited the cinema theatre as if they were in a waiting lobby. If there was ever such a thing as Dadaist cinema session, then the screenings at the Cineac were it!

My first film, *Le viol du Vampire* (*Rape of the Vampire*) carries that same spirit. The same goes for the ones that followed, especially for *Requiem for a Vampire*, up until my last film *La fiancée de Dracula* (*Dracula's Fiancee*), which pays homage to the great serial maker, Gaston Leroux. *Rape of the Vampire* is nothing else than a film announcing the 1990s, an improvised serial, a surrealist collage, a dadaist way of making cinema.

Ever since my debut film I have tried to add a certain emotion to my screenplays, a sense of tragedy that mixes with humour, a voluntary lyricism. I have tried to acquire a sort of poetry that is irrational through its realistic oratory, where the imagination turns the simple cobblestones of Paris in the year 1913 into a strange and baroque environment, solely because they allow a connection to *Fantomas* and Feuillade. The images and dialogues of my films, like the images and texts of my books, attach themselves to the idea that they can become, or are, a cinema of the imaginary. A cinema which permits the gaze to travel along a pair of glimming shoes, upwards along the body of a man dressed in a tuxedo, his hand holding a gun, to settle upon a face fixed on the camera. Accompanied by ritualistic music (Maurice Jarre), the man takes his gun along his masked guests, who startle at its passage. This is of course, the cinema of Franju's *Judex*.

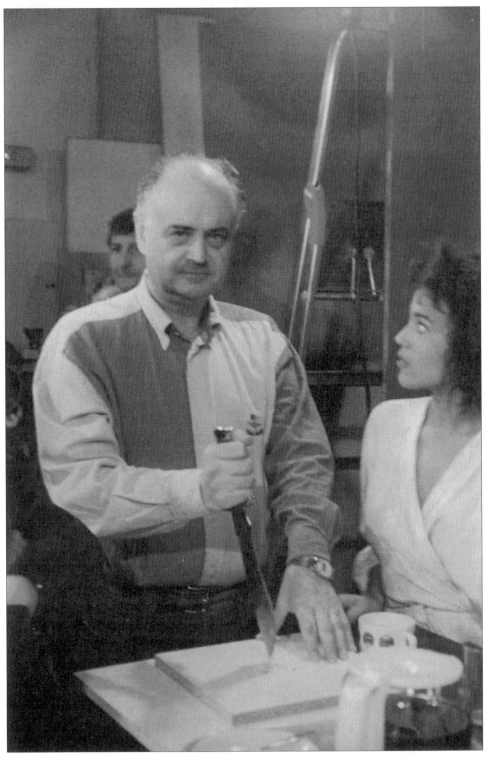

**FIGURE 1** Jean Rollin on the set of *Killing Car*

For me, a cinema which permits these meanderings is the only real cinema. It is the European cinema I want to make and write about. It is also the type of cinema that *Alternative Europe* discusses. In this cinema, nothing is more normal than a woman coming out of a clock at the last stroke of midnight; nothing more normal than a coffin on a bed; walking in a garden and hearing the cry of the female vampire; two clown-girls trying to escape across a field. What else? This is the kind of cinema which permits a half-smile at the sight of a naked woman; a blind man drowning in the sea; the naked corps of Dracula's fiancée covered by roses; the clock becoming Dracula's grave. Indeed, 'the Presbyterian house has lost nothing of its appeal; the garden nothing of its clarity and shadows' (Gaston Leroux in *The Mystery of the Yellow Chamber*). I tried to use this phrase, these premises, in all of my films.

I will leave it for you to decide if I have succeeded.

Jean Rollin
April 2004

# INTRODUCTION
# MAKING SENSE OF EXTREME CONFUSION:
# EUROPEAN EXPLOITATION AND UNDERGROUND CINEMA

Ernest Mathijs and Xavier Mendik

## ALTERNATIVE EUROPEAN CINEMA: TWO PERSPECTIVES AND A CHALLENGE

Recent years have seen a small but significant global surge of activity in the study of alternative cinema. Conferences, research projects and various publications around the meaning of cult and the appeal of horror and trash, added to plans for new specific courses around cult and alternative cinema, have raised questions as to how alternative cinema has been dealt with on an academic level. These lines of enquiry have undoubtedly introduced fresh new perspectives in the study of what constitutes 'the alternative' in media arts studies. This volume aims to contribute to this discussion by focusing on European alternative cinema.

There is hardly a more difficult object of media study than European cinema. Although seemingly evident by its geographical boundaries, from the Atlantic to the Urals, from the Arctic Circle to the Mediterranean, its cultural, aesthetic, economical, political and ideological demarcations are far from clear. European cinema cannot be pinned down to a small number of production strategies, or reduced to a limited series of intentions or ideological perspectives; it does not even fit barriers of language or nations. It cannot be defined through audience and reception practices, nor through its range of textual meanings. There are no straightforward genres to hold on to, no uncontested canon, not even an undisputed series of countries (Flemish cinema? Yiddish cinema? Turkish cinema? Yugoslavian cinema?), people (Alfred Hitchcock, Luc Besson, Paul Verhoeven?) or texts (*Stranger Than Paradise? Buena Vista Social Club?*). As a result, pitching this vague concept against other, often more clearly delineated, subjects of cinema studies, such as Hollywood, or perspectives like feminism (European cinema is too masculine), postcolonialism (European cinema is too Eurocentric – favouring the 'Old World') or liberalism (European cinema is economically protectionist) only allows for a negative definition of European film; it is what others are not.

This book aims to blow some of that vagueness away by analysing European cinema through two main perspectives: a cultural and an aesthetic one. None are new in the study of European cinema; in fact they are perhaps the most often used perspectives for analysing it. But we would like to challenge their use. First, and importantly, we want to make clear that this book sees both perspectives as intrinsically connected. We believe the relation between research into how a film works culturally, and analyses of its aesthetic nature and status cannot be separated. This does not necessarily mean we believe that good films (aesthetically) have a specific (high?) cultural impact, a view which is, still, all too common in public debates about film. As the works of Pierre Bourdieu have made clear, the cultural position of a product is always linked to (elements of) the aesthetic, but different taste perceptions and preferences can lead to different celebrations, without the one taking precedence over the other.[1] For cinema, and perhaps on a somewhat more political and ideological level, the work of Pierre Sorlin has demonstrated a similar pattern: a film's place in a culture is linked to its aesthetics, and vice-versa, without implying that 'quality' equals cultural value.[2]

Second, and following from the above, this book aims to tread outside the usual uses of cultural and aesthetic perspectives, in fact turn their use upside down. It is the theoretical brief of this volume to investigate European cinemas' capacity to *reconstruct cultural frameworks, and its resistance to canons of film aesthetics*. As will be made clear below, certain views and practices of employing these two perspectives, although useful at times, hinder a lot of research into parts of European cinema, and here we wish to address and challenge these. The words 'reconstructing' and 'resistance' are of crucial importance because they constitute an alternative to the mainstream. It is always difficult to pinpoint exactly what 'an alternative' is, but in this case we see it as the kind of films which, consciously or unwillingly, are (i) ignored inside the politically and ideologically accepted cultural frame of reference yet still (try to) construct meanings on that frame of reference; and (ii) resist, by (lack of) effort or attitude, a place within accepted canons of the popular, the artistic or the morally acceptable. Through this focus on alternative, resisting, reconstructing European cinema we hope to revive the debate on what European cinema is, how its history is written and what its role in society is. Ideologically and politically, this includes the investigation of and intervention in public discourses around 'the acceptable versus the deviant', challenging presumptions about what might (and what might not) be attempted in film, theatre, internet, performance, television, video and their academic study, thus questioning climates of inclusiveness and objectification in culture and its discourses.

## AGAINST THE 'HIGH WHITE TRADITION'

A crucial embedded belief about European cinema, described by Richard Dyer and Ginette Vincendeau, is that it is prone to a 'high white tradition', one that is interested more in highbrow canons than in popular entertainment, exploitation or the underground.[3] The twelve films Jill Forbes and Sarah Street discuss form a neat example of that canon, moving from pre-war discussions of censorship and propaganda, over post-war realist movements, into an array of new waves, to conclude with a double focus on film economics (the GATT agreement) and ideological and postmodern challenges to it (unfortunately, challenges which are all too easy recuperated within the canon).[4] Another example of this is to be found in the writings collected in Catherine Fowler's *European Cinema Reader*, which (one or two exceptions notwithstanding) concentrate exclusively on canonical discussions.[5]

It is this tradition that *Alternative Europe* wishes to challenge. We frankly wonder how it is still possible to restrict European cinema to a modernist taste-economy if, at the same time, it is recognised as a constantly shifting site aesthetically, ideologically and politically. True, in the last years efforts have been made to address this imbalance, and in particular we would want to acknowledge the already-noted work by Richard Dyer and Ginette Vincendeau as a source of inspiration here, which offered an original overview of many relevant traditions of mass-cultural entertainment previously ignored by the academy.[6] But these efforts, as other works by Elizabeth Ezra, Dimitris Eletheriotis, and Diana Holmes and Alison Smith show,[7] often consider only the popular as an alternative to the highbrow canon – still ignoring nasty and trashy European cinema (a notable exception being Dyer's later analysis of popular Italian cycles such as the peplum).[8] Our intention here is to extend the scope further into the extremes of exploitation and underground cinema.

3

## ALTERNATIVE EUROPE: EXPLOITATION AND THE UNDERGROUND AS EXTREMES

By looking at the two extreme corners of exploitation and underground film it becomes clear that something that could rightfully be labelled 'Alternative Europe', does emerge. In the one corner, there is that part of readily and unquestionably accepted European cinema (for whatever reason) that feels odd, that somehow seems to be out of place while still being celebrated. The works of Jean Cocteau, Chris Marker or Werner Herzog come ready to mind – heavily canonised, aesthetically challenging and representative of certain sensitivities but still too edgy or fanatic to be placed amongst the bulk of films. In the other corner, there is that part of European cinema many film scholars do not know exists (or consciously ignore) because it escapes scrutiny or because it is an unworthy object of study, often because it does not even set itself up as legitimate film at all. Italian cop films, German serial porn or 'video nasty' co-productions are but some examples.

The first corner is often referred to as 'underground', designating a series of texts that in a sense belong to the established repertoire, but only as antipodes consolidating the mainstream – they want to be alternative, but are often prevented of becoming obscure through their continuous canonisation. The second corner is often referred to as 'exploitation', designating a series of texts that do not belong to the recognised repertoire, mostly because they are not deemed worthy enough. This latter category of films wants to become popular, but is often prevented of becoming part of the cinema establishment because the films are continuously dismissed as cheap or irrelevant rubbish.

The dynamics between these corners, the battlefield of alternative cinema, has not gone unnoticed by scholars. Jeffrey Sconce, Joan Hawkins and Mark Betz, to name but a few, have been trying to pin down the mechanisms that operate between these supposedly separate spheres of cinema.[9] Sconce's concept of paracinema, Hawkins' notion of the artistic horrific and Betz's analysis of unusual reception practices all point to the same thing: they try to explain why some films are considered to be more (or less) alternative than others. Sometimes it is their textual organisation, their status, their controversial potential or even their reception, mostly it is a combination of all these factors. Almost always reputations are involved. As analyses of *Tenebrae* (Dario Argento, 1982), by Xavier Mendik, and *Daughters of Darkness* (Harry Kümel, 1971), by Ernest Mathijs, point out, alternative films do not allow for a clear-cut distinction between text and context; they are messy dispersible texts, existing beyond and below the usual confinements of film culture.[10]

So, all qualifications taken into account, 'alternative European cinema' encompasses everything between the odd-but-accepted and the unknown, from the almost obvious to the almost non-existing. Rather than offer an exhaustive account of all of the traditions that have hitherto remained concealed from theoretical investigation, *Alternative Europe* offers a series of key case studies gathered from major European cycles, traditions and figures. In its claim that European 'trash' and 'exploitation' cinema represents a legitimate area of intellectual study, this volume draws upon, reconsiders and extends, existing cinematic studies into the underbelly of international film.

## GUILT, CONFESSION, TESTIMONY – RESISTANCE, REBELLION, LIBERATION

Given its focus, this book's intention is to give room to a diversity of approaches and topics concerning exploitation and underground cinema. With so much work to be done on the topic, charting the territory becomes a dominant issue. We have tried to make sure that as many interesting perspectives were present, while also ensuring that the chapters enclosed all address alternative European cinema. However, while fully acknowledging the diversities of alternative European cinema, there seem to be a couple of recurring issues, above and beyond the ones that inform this book. First of all, much of alternative European cinema seems to address issues of guilt, confession and testimony. This seems to point, consciously or involuntarily, to their ability to function as sites of reconfiguration of the self, as attempts to explore possibilities of reconstructing cultural frameworks. Of course, with the massive traumas of World War Two, the rise and collapse of communism, and decolonisation only a few decades behind them, both the audiences and makers of alternative European cinema could hardly ignore it. Nor can they be blind for the scandals and upheavals in their own local contexts, be they coup attempts, serial murders or terrorism. But it seems telling that these traumas are both acknowledged through interiorisation, and expressed through excesses, offering both soft- and shock-therapy.

A second, and connected, recurrent thread appears to be that of resistance, rebellion and liberation. Alternative European cinema sets itself not just against a mainstream culture, but also against a range of ways of thinking, politically and ideologically. Arguably, alternative European cinema as discussed in this volume does not always campaign for politically correct perspectives. But at the very least it seems to be championing, almost anarchically, a call for liberty. It is that call that ultimately makes alternative European cinema worthwhile.

## OVERVIEWING THE EXTREMES OF EXPLOITATION AND UNDERGROUND CINEMA

The first chapter that exemplifies the borders around underground and exploitation cinema is on one of the most reviled cycles in European exploitation cinema. This is addressed in Mikel J. Koven's chapter '"The Film You Are About to See is Based on Fact": Italian Nazi Sexploitation Cinema'. Although the Nazi sexploitation movie would seem unashamedly commercial and cynical in its titillating depiction of German wartime atrocities, Koven's analysis reveals a fluidity between high art and popular film patterns in this field, replicating a dynamic that exists in wider patterns of the alternative European domain. As the author notes, the Nazi sexploitation film in fact consists of two related cycles: those which outline the decadent sexual tendencies of the Third Reich, and a separate sub-genre based around the sexual humiliation of concentration camp inmates. For Koven, both of these controversial cycles frequently slide between alternative (high art) and exploitation (mass cultural formats) in a complex set of cultural and historical interchanges that often remains ignored by critics of the cycle. For instance, the author offers a comparative study of Liliana Cavani's 'art-house' work *The Night Porter* (which explores the sadomasochistic relations between a fugitive Nazi guard and his former, female prisoner) and Cesare Canevari's 'exploitation' film *The Gestapo's Last Orgy*. Although these two films sit across the presumed 'legitimate' vs. 'exploitation' divide, they follow a similarly 'extreme' thematic trajectory in their accounts of the links between human desire, sexual power and humiliation. For the author, where the two films differ is in their formal structure: while Cavani's film offers multiple flashbacks around differing perspectives on the couple's concentration camp love affair, Canevari's film uses a past-tense structure merely to motivate a revenge tactic that unwinds in its closing scenes. While this may suggest that such structural differences do reiterate a high art/exploitation cinema division of formal complexity, Koven notes that the more 'debased' variants of the cycle do offer an interesting 'exploitation' of historical events as they relate to Nazi power and sexual ideology. For instance, he argues that Canevari's film offers an explicit reading of *Rassenschande* (or 'racial shame') in its contorted 'orgy numbers' between SS guards and Jewish prisoners. Equally, the author picks out Sergio Garrone's infamous video nasty *SS Experiment Camp* as providing an intriguing study of the way in which respected Jewish surgeons were exploited by Nazi medics as part of their experiments into racial difference.

While Koven analyses a cycle often seen as too controversial to legitimise within the academy, I. Q. Hunter argues that even obscure and aesthetically flawed European exploitation films tell us something about the cultures they are part of and born from. In the chapter 'Deep Inside *Queen Kong*: Anatomy of an *Extremely* Bad Film', Hunter considers Frank Agrama's 1970s British exploitation comedy starring Robin Askwith (as Ray Fay) and Rula Lenska (as Luce Habit, a feminist filmmaker). The author first analyses the film's obvious commentary on gender: Kong is female, the damsel in distress is male – and carries a macho template as Askwith is best known for his sexual (and sexist) opportunism in *Confessions of a Window Cleaner*, and the filmmaker (pun on her name intended) is a feminist. As Hunter argues, these puns not only resemble a Benny Hill sketch or 'one of the plays what Ernie Wise wrote' for the *Morecambe and Wise Show* on British television in the 1970s. They also point, like *Attack of the 50 Foot Woman* and *The Incredible Shrinking Woman*, to a clumsily articulated feminist 'message', with *Queen Kong* held up as a symbol of 'oppressed women everywhere'. Hunter puts the seriousness of this message at the centre of his argument, showing that *Queen Kong* fits into different contexts, all of which equip the film with a range of disparate meanings, sometimes contradictory. As part of British exploitation filmmaking in the 1970s, it exemplifies a period when sexploitation was one of the few thriving areas of indigenous cinema. As part of the 'ape film' and giant creature sub-genres, like *King Kong*, *Godzilla* and British imitations such as *Konga*, *Gorgo* and *Digby: The Biggest Dog in the World*, the focus is on the films' treatment of race, *Konga* and *Queen Kong* being allegories, loosely speaking, of white sexual fantasies about the black presence in Britain. The film also draws parallels between discourses of primitivism in *Queen Kong* and Hammer's prehistoric fantasies of the 1960s (*One Million Years BC*, *Slave Girls*). And with its 'message' it can be seen as British popular culture's response to feminism.

Jennifer Fay's chapter, 'The *Schoolgirl Reports* and the Guilty Pleasure of History', also discusses the 1970s, and the German series of *Schoolgirl Report* films of Ernst Hofbauer in particular. Fay argues that these films, arguably among the most successful produced in Germany during the 1970s, are usually undeservedly reproached for their excessive portrayal of teenage nudity, as well as their implicit hints of Nazi history (through scenes of torture, execution, military paraphernalia). But, although the *Schoolgirl Report* films may seem to be merely exploitative at first sight, they actually fit very well in a context of rising permissiveness and the contesting of authority occurring in Germany at this time. A crucial issue the series tackles is that of teenage female sexuality, which Fay places at the centre of cultural debates in Germany during the 1970s (noting that German soft-porn outnumbered even US production). As this chapter shows, the usual dismissal of the series refuses to acknowledge both the importance of sexuality as a site of power struggles and the significance of the vignette structure of the films as a means of questioning Germany's past. Through close analyses of key scenes of the most striking films in the series, and by focusing on the importance of confession and guilt in their narrative structure, Fay discloses how the *Schoolgirl Report* films raise a number of issues of political and cultural importance in post-war Germany. Here, Fay applies Michel Foucault's notion of the 'perpetual spirals of power and pleasure' to the 'family struggles' portrayed in these films, arguing that these act as metaphors for the difficulties many youngsters had in relating to their parents' and guardians' roles in the war. By linking the *Schoolgirl Report* films to Michael Geyer's work on post-war memory politics, Fay convincingly demonstrates how guilty memories haunt these films, their structure and their style.

Whereas Fay tackles a relatively large timeframe of analysis in her consideration of a film cycle, Dona M. Kercher focuses on the relationship of a specific European director and his ability to tap into particular crises in local cultures in a comic and disturbing way. In her chapter 'Violence, Timing and the Comedy Team in Alex de le Iglesia's *Muertos de Risa*', Kercher outlines de la Iglesia's versatile profile as one of Spain's most interesting directors (with a trademark of wild and surreal humour, grotesque violence and social subtexts). This chapter then goes on to locate his place in a local/global framework of media production. As Kercher shows through stylistic analyses of some of de la Iglesia's films, cutting-edge technology informs this director's look on reality, using special effects and virtuoso style to maximise impact. Kercher rightfully emphasises how de la Iglesia's interest in mixing genres, and his work for both Pedro Almodóvar and Andrés Vincente Gómez, also shows a curious relation with Hollywood, not unusual for Spanish directors. *Muertos de Risa*, however, demonstrates how specific cultural references and political commentary do need to be placed within local contexts to be made sense of. Kercher first criticises Marsha Kinder's view on violence in Spanish films, arguing instead for a discussion of violence in relation to comedy. Through a close analysis of both the production context (including star profiles of Santiago Segura, El Gran Wyoming and Raphael) and key sequences in *Muertos de Risa*, Kercher then analyses how the film uses a seemingly innocent doubling of comics (Nino and Bruno) to point to how cultural narratives are formed and distorted by history. As such, Kercher argues that references to both politics and local media invoke doubt as to the real circumstances of the 1981 failed coup attempt in Spain. Kercher stresses how the very structure and style of the film, both ridiculing history and commodifying it, allows for an alternative view on how events unfolded, pointing to how media can shape and criticise cultural memory.

It is ability for alternative European film to tap into contemporary social and political crises that also informs Ernest Mathijs' chapter, 'Alternative Belgian Cinema and Cultural Identity: *S.* and the Affaire Dutroux'. Here, the author uses an innovative mixture of reception theory, psychoanalytic and close textual analysis to consider the extent to which Guido Henderickx's controversial movie *S.* can be seen as a mirror to the real-life sex crimes occurring in Belgium during the 1990s. Specifically, the film's emphasis on a young woman subjected to humiliation, habitual violence and sexual abuse (before resorting to extreme violence herself) drew parallels with the infamous 'Affaire Dutroux'. Here, police and official incompetence actually assisted the campaign of the former convict Marc Dutroux, who kidnapped, abused and killed a number of young girls after being released early from prison. As a result of the shock waves that the case has produced, Mathijs discusses the notion of a 'Belgian disease' (as embodied by extreme acts of violence, sexual perversion and political corruption), which seeped into the popular imagination to optimise the nation's ills. Although Henderickx's previous works and his penchant for flashy and realistic art-house visuals had already made him a celebrated 'alternative' Belgian filmmaker, his film's ability to reflect this national malaise has often been dwarfed by domestic reviewers. Conducting an international reception account of the film's release, Mathijs noted that whereas local reviews emphasised *S.*'s more gruesome and shocking elements, overseas accounts made a more solid connection between these images and the Belgian disease. Central to this unsettling effect that the film creates are the connections it makes between the collapse of a social body (and its symbols, agents of order) and the physical body which is reduced to a series of wounds, scars and floods. For Mathijs, this indicates the extent to which *S.* is socially and psychically abject, reflecting a series of social events where the unpalatable image of the Belgian body as deviant, imperfect and violated had been controversially exposed.

Over the last ten years, a great number of theoretical advances have been made into the study of Italian exploitation and underground film (as discussions of the *giallo* genre, Dario Argento, Mario Bava, Lucio Fulci and others testify.)[11] However, in his contribution to this collection, Christopher Barry goes beyond that recognised body of texts, to unearth new examples of Italian exploitation and underground cinema and argue that they act as a crucial mirror to social and political upheaval. In

7

his chapter, 'Violent Justice: Italian Crime/Cop Films from the 1970s', Barry examines the largely untheorised genre of *poliziotteschi*, or violent police/crime films, produced in Italy between 1971 and 1979. With titles such as *The Violent Professionals*, *Violent Naples* and *Live Like a Man, Die Like a Cop*, the poliziotteschi marked a new style of Italian thriller created by emerging directors such as Enzio G. Castellari, Sergio Martino and Umberto Lenzi. These works traded on images of extreme brutality, sex and perversion, and popularised actors like Maurizio Merli whose persona was defined by a 'dirty mop of blond hair, thick bushy moustache, unruly mutton chop side burns, rose-lensed aviator shades, chipped teeth, clenched fists and a wardrobe straight out of *Shaft*'. Although these films have frequently been dismissed as emulating existing American 'rogue cop' movies such as *Dirty Harry*, Barry argues that the cycle in fact reflects historically specific social and political concerns occurring in Italy at the time. As titles such as *Violent Naples* and *Violent Rome* indicate, major areas of the country were under effectively rendered lawless by violent political extremists (such as the Red Brigade), militant groups and organised criminal gangs. As a result, Barry argues that this cycle not only reflected the inherent fear of crime experienced by ordinary citizens, but also the frustration and suspicion at the police and government structures to stem this violent tide. This ambivalence towards the forces of authority are indicated in the poliziotteschi's repeated theme of an unorthodox enforcer forced to adopt extreme measures to combat not only violent crime but also police incompetence and wider political corruption. As a result, these unconventional loners have little option but to step outside the law, as in the case of the hero of *The Violent Professionals*, forced to resign from the police force to avenge the politically motivated assassination of his superior. By echoing real life concerns about the possible collusion between the police and criminal/extremist organisations (as seen in the 1978 controversy surrounding the kidnapping and death of Aldo Moro), the poliziotteschi film remains a highly-charged cycle produced during one of the most turbulent decades in Italy's recent history.

Another author to offer an original exploration of hitherto marginal European texts is Christina Stojanova. In her chapter, '*Mise-en-scènes* of the Impossible: Soviet and Russian Horror Films', Stojanova employs psychoanalysis to discuss the relationship between film, psyche and society. Her chapter is one of the first ever to attempt to connect Russian and Soviet horror cinema to ideological and socio-psychological frameworks of the country's cultural foundations. Her discussion of themes of the horrific in Russian and Soviet links several periods through major motifs of supernatural mysticism, physical and psychological horror, and their transmutations over years and genres. Specifically, Stojanova identifies three major time frames (a Tsarist one, a Soviet period and a recent period characterised by both reflexivity and renewed nationalism). The author's framework provides a method for comparing (at least on a theoretical level) the ways in which Russian and Soviet films have used (and continue to use) horrific images and threads as a means of addressing *and* symbolically resisting official ideologies and religions. Innovatively, Stojanova uses the philosophical work of Nikolay Berdyaev as a guideline. In particular, Berdyaev's work on the origin and consequences of Russian-ness in 'The Russian Idea' (the mission of the nation in a context of strenuous co-existence of socio-psychological and ethical extremes) is deployed to reveal how exactly these cinematic horror motifs relate to larger issues of cultural representation and resistance. Through the myth and metaphor of Kitezh-grad (the sunken city), Stojanova links this philosophy to general Freudian and Lacanian perspectives. She argues that, from a psychoanalytical point of view, the Kitezh myth invites issues of death and decay, thus acting as a prime source of inspiration for all Russian horror (and of cinema in general). The films under discussion in this chapter can therefore be viewed as attempts to represent an impossible collective desire, one where implications of the Russian Idea are fixated into fantasies or 'imaginary scenarios' of a national myth. While Stojanova's chapter is organised chronologically, concentrating on recent works, her general perspective allows for a broader consideration of the idiosyncrasies of the Russian and Soviet cinematic mysticism and horror. As such it urges a view of the specificity of the Russian and Soviet perception of horror, and of its cinematic representation, in terms of its cultural, political and aesthetic aspects in a larger philosophical framework.

Arguably, the application of psychoanalysis to European exploitation cinema has provided many innovative interpretations of previously marginal texts. However, it is the search for a new methodology to explain Europe's vocabulary of the flesh that informs Patricia MacCormack's chapter, 'Masochistic Cinesexuality: The Many Deaths of Giovanni Lombardo Radice'. Here, the author provides a reading of the Italian cult exploitation actor, who appeared in a number of 'video nasties' during the 1980s under the pseudonym of John Morghan. However, as MacCormack's analysis of films such as *House on the Edge of the Park*, *Cannibal Ferox* and *City of the Living Dead* indicate, what endeared Radice to Euro-gore fans was not so much his performances in these controversial works, as his visceral and exaggerated deaths. These characteristically centred on his flesh being torn apart, as well as literal castrations, cranial penetrations with drills and even having his brains eaten by third-world cannibals. While such images are frequently dismissed as part and parcel of the 'excess' associated with Italian exploitation cinema, Radice's deaths offer an insight to the liberation of the flesh that occurs in the most degraded forms of European popular culture. As with the infamous image of Barbara Steele's violated face that dominated Mario Bava's film *The Mask of Satan*, Radice's savaged and incomplete body remains one of the most prominent symbols of suffering in European exploitation cinema. The fact that Radice's corporeal performances offer an image of the violated male body detracts from the normal gender presumptions surrounding exploitation cinema. As a result, MacCormack argues that these visions require a new method of theorising the illicit pleasures that his degraded flesh offers. Rather than see the actors' performances in light of a castrated/feminised psychoanalytic methodology, the author proposes a theory of 'cinesexuality' to explain these enticing but repulsive European representations. Drawing on Lyotard's notion of the 'great ephemeral skin', she considers the extent to which Radice's body forms an un-binarised surface that allows both actor and audience to revel in a masochistic excess that outstrips the gender presumptions governing socially sanctioned behaviour. MacCormack's novel response to the psychoanalytically dominated approaches to the study of Italian horror film provides an intriguing account of one of Europe's most iconic (and frequently punished) cult actors.

In a companion piece to the above chapter, the Italian exploitation actor Giovanni Lombardo Radice goes on to explain how his performance style and delivery contributes to a wider cultural understanding of male suffering in alternative European cinema. His comments are captured in Patricia MacCormack's chapter 'Male Masochism, Male Monsters: An Interview with Giovanni Lombardo Radice'. Here, the star reveals that his acting talents extend far beyond anything that his flamboyant on-screen deaths would indicate. As he admits in the course of the interview, his first love is theatre, a profession that he has fed and developed by taking roles in European trash movies. Although not entirely critical of the films he has worked in (citing his work with directors such as Michele Soavi and Antonio Margheriti as highlights of his 'Eurotrash' career), the interview makes clear that Radice sees differing performance styles and skills as operating across the platforms of cinema and theatre. Interestingly, Radice's admission that theatre requires a performance of the actor's total body has relevance for the way in which his physical form has been exploited in his most infamous on-screen demises. This is a point that MacCormack follows up by examining issues relating to his masochistic positioning as European exploitation cinema's icon of male suffering. In response, Radice offers some fascinating comments about the ways in which alternating states of sadism and masochism remain a common feature of Italian horror, further relating his own depictions of masculine suffering to a personal exploration of bisexuality. These points as well as Radice's own interesting interpretations of some of his own films (including an AIDS-style analysis of *Cannibal Apocalypse*), provide the interview with a fascinating overview of one of European exploitation cinema's most articulate and endearing figures.

While the films of Giovanni Lombardo Radice can be interpreted as erotising the actor's deaths, the chapter 'Barred Nuns: Italian Nunsploitation Films' moves further into disturbing images and narratives of the sexual. Here, author Tamao Nakahara discusses how specific Italian exploitation cycles depict the sexualised nun as a challenge to cultural order. As many of the original 'nun-narratives' show, they are usually locked away for fear of being socially uncontrollable. Considering a wide range of Italian 'nunsploitation' films, roughly situated between the mid- to late 1960s and the mid-1980s, Nakahara traces their cultural origins. She first discusses the social and production contexts, singling out the relationship between the all-dominant Catholic Church and the 1960s sexual revolution as a source of inspiration, while also acknowledging the significance of exploitation quickies (*filones*) as a production practice. The chapter then focuses on the importance of medieval sex comedies (especially Pasolini's *Decamerone* film), Ken Russell's *The Devils* and the story of the Nun of Monza (on which two books appeared during the 1960s) as lineages to nunsploitation. Using both close textual analysis and the work of Michel Foucault, Nakahara proceeds to identify some of the major tropes and ideological structures of these films. As Nakahara observes, there is a *double entendre* in these films in that they promise to reveal (by penetrating into the cloistered environment exclusively reserved for nuns) the 'truth' about convent life, implying that these truths are titillating and shocking. But they also assume a viewing position that allows for that shock to be recognised as something we did not want to see at all, thus saving the viewer from the accusation of being perverse. However, it is the nuns' behaviour, not the viewer's that is condemned. As Nakahara concludes, nunsploitation seems to be a logical answer to the perceived need for sexual confession often associated with Foucault's notion of 'transforming sex into discourse'. As sex is turned into a controllable narrative, it becomes controllable itself, thus allowing the reiteration of institutionalised containment of sexuality.

In his chapter, 'Emmanuelle Enterprises', Garrett Chaffin-Quiray examines one of the most influential and startling French films of the 1970s, *Emmanuelle*. He argues that Just Jaeckin's provocative film not only came to define the sexual sentiments of a decade, but it also affirmed wider international perceptions of mores and values of the nation that has produced these images.

Importantly for the context of this volume, one particular focus for this chapter is the extent to which the international reception of *Emmanuelle* fed upon existing (and often mythical) conceptions of French sexual morality and filmmaking culture. Central to the film's reputation, was the (primarily American) view that the film could be viewed as a nationalistic celebration of the intellectual and the libidinal, a view which Chaffin-Quiray critically examines. By tracing Jaeckin's influence back to the source material of Emmanuelle Arsan's novel, the author concludes that its theme of a young French architect's wife reaching a position of sexual liberation via a series of sexual encounters in Bangkok remains a 'lofty palimpsest of cheap thrills and ambitions'. It is this uneven mixture of pseudo-sophistication and titillation that is then examined in light of the film's presumed relation to national filmmaking traditions. For many, Jaeckin's film can be seen as a natural extension of established cinematic traditions such as the French New Wave. While this movement's 'celebration (rather than suppression of) sexuality' seem to fit well with *Emmanuelle* (and the other French films defined as spearheading the 'l'epoque erotique'), the structure of Jaeckin's movie seems far more conservative, with static camerawork and overdubbing replacing the freestyle techniques favoured by earlier New Wave advocates. For Chaffin-Quiray, these contradictions were minimised by the film's American reception, which promoted the film as intrinsically French in (film) tone and its representation of bourgeois/erotic experimentation as a form of sexual liberation.

In 'Black Sex, Bad Sex: Monstrous Ethnicity in the *Black Emanuelle* Films', Xavier Mendik considers the Italian sex and death series which followed hot on the heels of the success of Jaeckin's film. Mendik's consideration of the figure and films of *Black Emanuelle* is the first academic discussion of one of the most contested series of films of the 1970s and 1980s. It combines issues of sex, death and racial representation in order to reveal the extent to which the black body evokes contradictory colonial tensions relating to Italy's past. In an innovative discussion of the locales and settings of the *Black Emanuelle* films, which he labels 'travelogues of desire', this chapter shows that these depictions of sexual and monstrous Otherness is, to a certain extent, invited by exotic locations. As Mendik observes, the classical (white) Emmanuelle hardly manages to penetrate these locations, always staying the outsider. Her sexual performances remain unfinished attempts, often only satisfying a curiosity. The figure of Black Emanuelle however turns the out-of-the-ordinary sexual activities into undesirable ones. Obviously, as Mendik is quick to acknowledge, such issues of estranging indigenous features are not new, and he mentions the Mondo film as a prime example of how it has been exploited before. But he goes beyond this by also considering the place and role of Laura Gemser, the Indonesian actress playing Black Emanuelle, as constantly shifting between accepted and unacceptable sexual desires, hence turning the usually fixed notion of monstrosity into a dynamic one (local and temporal). As Mendik points out, this too can be traced back to the original *Emmanuelle* series, for whenever a non-white local is involved in the sexual act, it is described as 'revolting' or 'impure'. The *Black Emanuelle* films make explicit that unease, and turn it into the prime narrative and exploitative drive. As a result, Laura Gemser's persona almost becomes a primus locus for sexual Otherness in the postcolonial era.

For many theorists writing in this volume, European trash and underground cinema represents a unique fusion of the aesthetic sensibilities associated with the avant-garde and the visceral/erotic thrills associated with the world of exploitation. It is this eclectic mixture of experimental style and 'explicit' sexual content that is central to Colin Odell and Michelle Le Blanc's analysis of the French filmmaker Jean Rollin. In their chapter, 'Jean Rollin: Le Sang D'Un Poète du Cinema', they argue that while Rollin's erotic vampire and supernatural horror films have often been shunned by mainstream critics, they represent a 'crucial blurring of art and artifice' occurring within the so-called 'Eurotrash' domain. While Odell and Le Blanc outline the way in which Rollin draws on certain mass cultural traditions (including pulp novels of the 1930s, pop art and the 'primitive' traditions of silent cinema), they see the director's film style is far more 'painterly' than populist. Here, the authors point to Rollin's repeated use of stylistic features such as long takes and static shots, both of which allow the viewer to contemplate and scrutinise certain features represented within the film frame. Alongside the use of these stylistic features, Odell and Le Blanc also identify aspects of Rollin's *mise-en-scène* (such as his use of props) as another way in which his films balance 'the pulp aesthetic and art aesthetic with striking results'. Here, decorations, objects and interiors come to occupy as much on-screen significance as actors themselves, while the placement of both people and props in created or positioned stages points towards a self-reflexive policy of filmmaking traditionally associated with art cinema. While the authors go on to explore other aspects of Jean Rollin's experimental film style, they also address issues of sexual representation in the latter part of the chapter. For a director often associated with both erotic horror (and also some examples of hardcore pornography), it comes as little surprise that Rollin's films have frequently been dismissed on grounds of sexism. However, for Odell and Le Blanc, the director's work remains 'no more pornography than a painting by Delvaux'. For them, Rollin's female creations achieve ultimate power precisely because of their unashamed sexuality, while their male counterparts remain nothing more than two-dimensional characters.

Whereas certain cycles of Italian 'sex and death' cinema have been successfully documented and 'rescued' by 'trash' cinema theorists, Leon Hunt reassesses a marginal genre anomaly in his chapter 'Burning Oil and Baby Oil: *Bloody Pit of Horror*'. For Hunt, Massimo Puppillo's 1965 film has been relegated to the irredeemable end of Italian exploitation cinema for a number of reasons. Not only is *Bloody Pit of Horror* seen as a film that lacks a well-known auteur (like Dario Argento or Mario Bava), but its definable 'horror' elements are complicated by masculine depictions more commonly found in other Italian genres such as the Peplum (or the sword and sandal/muscleman movie). Rather than dismissing Pupillo's film as irrelevant, Hunt argues that its hybrid features can be traced to the complex patterns of film production and (regionally distinct) modes of audience reception that govern Italian genre cinema. Employing Christopher Wagstaff's influential work on the 'electrocardiogram' principle at play in Italian popular cinema, Hunt argues that this brand of popular European film works in opposition to the standards of classical Hollywood by emphasising elements of excitement, tension or titillation, rather than the narrative trajectory as a whole. As a result, strict generic boundaries are never observed in a system of cinema that frequently offered differing thrills from disparate film formulas to the distinct spectator groups that consumed these variants of popular culture. Having established the reasons behind the *Bloody Pit of Horror's* incongruous formal features, Hunt goes on to explore some of the issues of male sexuality that the Peplum's elements evoke in the film. Pointing to the inclusion of the former Mr Universe (and frequent Peplum star) Mickey Hargitay in the movie's leading role, Hunt argues that Pupillo's film offers an atypical horror characterisation of male narcissism and suffering that warrants the serious consideration offered by this lively account.

While many of the directors and icons profiled in this volume have their names firmly anchored within a nationally specific context, Brian Yuzna offers a fascinating example of an American director who has relocated to Europe because of the creative freedom offered to exploitation and underground cinema within its borders. The director, famed for productions such as *Society* and *The Dentist*, is profiled in Xavier Mendik's chapter, 'Trans-European Excess: An Interview with Brian Yuzna'. Here, the filmmaker explains the motivations behind his relocation to Spain to launch the Fantastic Factory with leading producer Julio Fernández. The Fantastic Factory can basically be defined as a 'horror Hollywood' located in Barcelona. The production house aims to draw on leading genre talent from across the world, while maintaining the nationally specific traditions of Spanish cinema. As an American director whose output has been significantly influenced by European art and genre cinema, Yuzna sees the Fantastic Factory as encompassing the business acumen of the LA approach to filmmaking, while maintaining the concept of creative integrity classically afforded to European auteurs. In the interview, Yuzna explains how this appeal to two very different filmmaking traditions has affected the structure of recent releases such as *Faust* and *Arachnid*. Beyond an examination of his duel European and American influences, this chapter also considers themes of sexuality, perversion and immorality that permeate the director's work, while some of the issues surrounding female depictions within the horror genre are also discussed. The chapter concludes with Mendik providing an update of the Fantastic Factory's Spanish progress since the interview was first conducted.

While Brian Yuzna's trans-national images of horror and excess often court controversy, some critics would argue that they are tame in comparison with the cinema of Jörg Buttgereit. This director is the focus of Linnie Blake's chapter 'Jörg Buttgereit's Nekromantiks: Things to do in Germany with the Dead'. Although frequently criticised and censored for producing films that conflate bizarre sexual practices with extreme depictions of the dead body, Blake argues that works such as *Nekromantik* and *Schramm* contain an edgy, experimental feel that reveals Buttgereit's roots in avant-garde rather than horror filmmaking. Central to her analysis, is the claim that while the director's gore epics remain outlandish and unsettling, they actually represent an extension of the more legitimate traditions of New German Cinema dominant in the 1960s and 1970s. As embodied by directors such as Werner Herzog and Rainer Werner Fassbinder, this film movement sought to bind documentary and experimental film techniques to an examination of the alienated and desolate protagonists inhabiting the post-1945 German landscape. For Blake, it is these methods as well as the movement's focus on the repression and sublimation of guilt and trauma relating to Germany's Nazi past that reappear in a brutal form in the films of Jörg Buttgereit. From his early shorts combining punk and Nazi imagery, to later works like *Nekromantik* (where a necrophile couple's activity frequently evokes concentration camp iconography), Blake argues that Buttgereit is not only digging up corpses, but the memories of a hideous past not fully acknowledged by the German nation.

As a companion piece to the above article, the controversial Jörg Buttgereit reveals the extent to which his works have become a crucial index to past issues of national and political significance. This is indicated in Marcelle Perks' article, 'A Very German Post-mortem: Jörg Buttgereit and Co-Writer/Assistant Director Franz Rodenkirchen Speak', which was specially prepared for inclusion in this volume. The interview explores a number of themes in the director's work, including his preoccupation with the mechanics of necrophilia, as well as his fascination with the cult of the serial

13

killer. What makes Perks' chapter particularly interesting is the way in which it reveals Buttgereit as reflecting and re-framing his thoughts around his own films on the basis of having read Linnie Blake's theoretical interventions. Thus, the second interview conducted with the director (after he has digested the 'Jörg Buttgereit's Nekromantiks: Things to do in Germany with the Dead' article contained in this volume), leads him to adopt a far more elaborate and reflective account of the personal and cultural influences underpinning his work. Here, Perks manages to tease out the links between Buttgereit's own relationship with his father (as embodied in his early art-house short *Mein Papi*) and the later deviant male figures that populate his more gruesome works. The author's interventions also provoke some interesting comments on the links between art-house and exploitation tendencies in Buttgereit's work, while both the director and Rodenkirchen cast light on the ability of their morbid movies to reflect Germany's uneasy relationship with its own twentieth-century past.

Although some of the chapters have analysed the European trash text in terms of reception, philosophy, politics and history, the section on the European Federation of the Fantastic Film Festivals changes that. It puts exhibitors, distributors and the 'Eurotrash consuming' public at its centre. The Federation was formed to assist with the promotion and distribution of 'difficult' European texts that often transcend the traditional divisions of art-house and commercial productions. Enclosed in this section is a unique insight into the forces that mould alternative European film production and distribution in ways that greatly differ from American and mainstream versions of the 'popular'. This section also explores the strategies that European funders and distributors use to ensure that trash and alternative cinema receive appropriate festival coverage.

These accounts are drawn from three key member countries within the European Federation of Fantastic Film Festivals: Belgium, Finland and Sweden. Writing from a practical point of view, Dirk Van Extergem's chapter provides a view behind the screens of one of Europe's hidden and (sometimes) forbidden treasures, the laid-back but highly innovative Belgian International Festival of Fantastic Film (BIFFF). Van Extergem sketches the unique position this festival occupies within the festival landscape, as a regionally subsidised event with far-reaching international connections. To give an example, the Festival was in 2000 and 2001 one of the first to link into to the new wave of extreme Asian cinema, inviting filmmakers like Kiyoshi Kurosawa and Takashi Miike when no one had really heard of them. Earlier in its history, BIFFF had done the same for David Cronenberg (who they invited in 1984, and whose until-then unseen *Videodrome* created a furore), while also honouring long-time *compagnons de route* like Dario Argento, Brian Yuzna or Lloyd Kaufman. As Van Extergem explains, this combination of innovation and loyalty has given the festival a specific reputation as a cult event, attend by a cult audience which faithfully anticipates and celebrates it each year. The participatory aspect of the cult experience is probably unique in the world; among the recurrent rites are massive shouting contests during screenings, and a 'human rafting' race in which film critics are put in a rubber life boat an carried from front to back (and back) over the heads of the audience (who have the choice to carry or drop them). BIFFF is much more than just a cult event though, and as Van Extergem goes on to argue, its strengths and problems are not unlike those of other small-scale niche festivals around the world.

Alongside BIFFF, another leading event associated with the European Federation is Finland's Espoo Ciné Festival, which is discussed by Tuomas Riskala's chapter, 'The Espoo Ciné International

Film Festival'. In his report, Riskala accounts for the growth of the Festival during the last fourteen years, while also linking the event's emergence to wider exhibition strategies in Finnish film culture. Not only has the Espoo Ciné Festival established itself as the primary showcase for contemporary European cinema within Finland, but over 80 per cent of the films shown at the event are of European origin. While Riskala is keen to acknowledge the increasing importance of non-Western fantasy cinema on Finnish film culture, his account also makes clear the educational strategies central to the festival's wider critical acceptance. As with other exhibitors' accounts outlined in this section, Riskala outlines the importance of the European Federation of the Fantastic Film Festivals on the programming, retrospective and educational strands offered by the Espoo Ciné organisers. These 'fantastic forums' are held via a series of seminars and panel discussions on both aesthetic and production-based topics that relate to the genres under review. Some of the issues included in these discussion slots have included scriptwriting, sound editing and the role of special effects in fantastic film, with visiting directors, SFX masters and technicians attending to give their professional input. Beyond a consideration of the extent to which the Federation's policies have affected the growth and structure of this Finnish event, this chapter also discusses the Festival in the context of wider national debates around censorship (particularly addressing state policies up until 2001). As Riskala notes, during this era of censorship, the Espoo Ciné Festival remained the only place to see 'dark and violent celluloid creations' that Europe had to offer. Although censorship issues have eased in recent years, he concludes that the Espoo Ciné Festival has retained an unorthodox edge, where it is able to court cinematic creativity and controversy in equal measure.

The final festival report compiled for this volume takes the form of an interview with Magnus Paulsson, the International Director of the Fantastisk Film Festival in Sweden. In his article, 'The Fantastisk Film Festival: An Overview and Interview with Magnus Paulsson', Xavier Mendik discovers that the event sets a broad remit for the types of subject matter they will exhibit. These include films that lie 'between dream and reality, the ordinary and the extraordinary, the possible and the impossible. The aim of the Festival is to help stretch the limits of the imagination, and to reinforce the intrinsic value of imagination in films.' The Festival's philosophy of not setting narrow limits on what it intends to screen partly explains its successful growth over the last eight years, something which Paulsson expands upon in his interview. As with other festivals outlined in this volume, the focus of the Fantastisk Film Festival remains the large number of European films that it screens, though as with Tuomas Riskala of Espoo Ciné, Paulsson also admits being increasingly drawn to the cult traditions that are emerging from Asia. Beyond a wide variety of quirky and off-beat productions that make it into the Festival's feature film competition, the event is marked by a progressive attitude towards documentary and fiction shorts, which are also primarily European based. As Paulsson explains, the short film can in many respects be seen as 'the perfect cinematic format' in its compression of creativity into a tightly constrained timeframe and the short selection proves to be ever popular with the Fantastisk Film Festival's audience, who vote for their own selection of favourites (alongside a panel of judges) on an annual basis. As well as outlining the factors that affect the programming of both the feature and short competitions at the Festival, Paulsson also explains the educational events that accompany the event on a regular basis. These include lectures and seminars given in conjunction with the Film Studies Department at Lund University as well as art exhibitions and musical events, all of which aim to elevate the status of the films under review. While Paulsson believes that the inclusion of these activities confirm the Fantastisk Film Festival as a 'great meeting place for open minded people', they also serve to underscore the critical dimension to film viewing that holds sway at this and other key events within the European Federation of Fantastic Film Festivals.

It still remains a matter of debate as to what extent alternative European film practice can be of any significant use in thinking about, or even intervening in, the world as it stands. Previous essays may have mentioned 'guerilla cinema' (Mathijs), 'questioning memory' (Blake, Kercher), or 'teenage disobedience' (Fay) and 'lawlessness' (Barry), but can alternative European cinema really take a practical political position? This question informs the last chapter in this book, Benjamin Halligan's 'The Tasks of the European Underground: A Letter to Luis Buñuel'. Halligan raises the question of what constitutes underground and exploitation cinema, the political use of it, its aesthetics (or lack of it) or its directness? His arguments are reminiscent of the theatre of cruelty, as propagated by Antonin Artaud, and the subsequent cinema of cruelty that André Bazin favoured.[12] It champions films that urge for immediacy, firmly rooted in what Halligan calls their experiential exploitativeness, showing instead of abstracting, attacking instead of contemplating. Throughout Halligan's letter, European alternative cinema is set up as that which cannot be commodified because, as Halligan observes particularly in *Un chien andalou* and *Los Olvidados*, it attacks the audience rather than points towards itself; it does not allow for excessive self-reflection; it just displays. It is exactly through this confrontational display, Halligan suggests, that the straightforwardness with which Buñuel's films (as opposed to the ones of Jen-Luc Godard or Michael Haneke) snap out at the viewer. However, since it does not allow for contemplation, it must hence be disregarded as useless or ethically unsound. This uselessness through immediacy, much like porn, is what constitutes the European underground and exploitation cinema. As Halligan points out, these films do not allow us a critical distance from the horrors that are shown – rather, they position themselves squarely in front of the viewer. At the same time, Halligan also calls attention to the moral discussions about cultural and social inequalities and injustices these films inevitably bring about. Even in their ugly forms, and as Halligan suggests precisely because of that form, they are often more accurate accusations than cleverly constructed campaigns. But because of their ugliness they are also morally undesirable, often inviting a counter-reaction. Building on that, and employing the works of Walter Benjamin and linking them to instances of the neutralisation of radicalness in Europe (issues also addressed by Jennifer Fay and Christopher Barry), Halligan then argues for a thorough reconsideration of what exactly the relevance of such underground and exploitation cinema can be, concluding that the roughness and in-your-face attitude of what he labels the Buñuelian underground is saved by its contemporaneity (not its timelessness).

## RESEARCHING TRASH, CULT AND ALTERNATIVE CINEMA

The essays included in this collection investigate the national traditions of European trash and exploitation from a variety of perspectives, as well incorporating filmmakers' commentaries and exhibition strategies alongside 'traditional' academic approaches. In this respect *Alternative Europe* represents part of a larger examination of global cult and popular cinema currently being undertaken at the Cult Film Archive at University College Northampton which will be published through the *AlterImage* book series. Since its inception in 2000, the Cult Film Archive has rapidly grown to become an established research centre, as well as a venue with an international reputation. From the outset, the Archive has sought to develop a critical understanding of cult, trash and underground film and its audiences for both academic and commercial projects. This is central to the Archive's belief that trash can be taken seriously, but that cult and trash cinema requires a multiplicity of interpretations that combine 'traditional' academic thought alongside an appreciation of production practices.

This philosophy of integrating academic with critical and fan-based approaches to cult and 'marginal' film forms has proven a key feature in the rapid and successful growth of the Archive, to the extent that it now enjoys important links with key academic and commercial film organisations (both nationally and internationally). In terms of its commercial links, the Archive enjoys longstanding relationships with the leading national television production companies and regularly contributes to broadcast projects in this field. The growing reputation of the Cult Film Archive has also meant that its staff have been able to draw upon exclusive interviews with key cult filmmakers from across the world and transcriptions of these works will be available in future volumes of the *AlterImage* series. Given its emphasis on analysing the links between cult film theory and production practices, the Cult Film Archive's move into documentary filmmaking is the next logical step of its rapid development. Working with noted television producers such as Howard Martin (creator of television series such as *OutTHERE* and *Shock Movie Massacre*), the Archive is currently developing a number of documentary projects around cult film and its wider social and cultural ramifications, for both broadcast and film festival purposes. The first project to be completed as part of this new venture is entitled *Cabin Fever: Fear Today, Horror Tomorrow*. The documentary analyses the success of Eli Roth's recent film against a backdrop of wider American social fears. The project was completed in December 2003 and details of its release schedule are available from the editors of this volume.

From the outset, the Cult Film Archive's mission has been to promote its research via a credible academic publisher, and this is facilitated through the long-term association we have with Wallflower Press and the *AlterImage* series. The book series reiterates the Archive's objective of integrating theoretical with critical and production accounts of cult film and its audiences. Each edition of *AlterImage* will be themed and contain 12–15 key academic articles alongside shorter critical accounts and interviews with cult filmmakers and exhibitors. Further details on future editions of the book series are available from both the editors and the publishers.

The Cult Film Archive's philosophy of 'taking trash seriously' is undoubtedly shared by a number of other academic research units, with whom we work in tandem. These include the research and conference seminar staged on an annual basis at De Montfort University by I. Q. Hunter. The Cult and Exploitation Film Research Network was set up at De Montfort University in 2003 to encourage academic research into this new field of study. Coordinated by I. Q. Hunter and colleagues at Northampton and Aberystwyth, the Network runs annual Day Schools at De Montfort University, Leicester, and will organise an international conference on Exploitation in 2007.

Another major research project concerned with the study of cult, trash and alternative cinema is the Centre for Research into Extreme and Alternative Media (CREAM), located in the Department of Theatre, Film and Television Studies at the University of Wales, Aberystwyth. CREAM functions as a nodal point for the study of cult, trash and alternative cinema, as a site where original research into the area is being undertaken, and as a voice for scholarly intervention in public discourses around alternative media arts. To the first aim, CREAM has set up a network of contacts and meeting points to enable academic communication (including, in the long run, the association with other research centers, archives and festivals in the organisation of lectures, seminars and conferences, the setting up and maintaining of academic research networks, and the dissemination of research results (including a website). The links with both De Montfort University and the Cult Film Archive are key to this.

To the second aim, CREAM works towards creating funding possibilities for individual and joint research projects in the study of extreme and alternative media of regional, national and international scope. The Centre recognises the diversity of angles and topics of its field of enquiry. Therefore, a main activity of the Centre is to function as an umbrella for projects (either individual or joint projects), of its members. This means it will support to its best ability funding applications, function as a provider of feedback, and facilitate initiatives.

To the third aim, CREAM acts as an active participant in debates about the nature, reception and public place of alternative media arts. Here, its explicit intention is to provide expert advise, take part in public debates (events, lectures, hearings, discussion panels, festivals), and generally support the visibility, dissemination and public understanding of alternative media arts.

Together, these initiatives represent a rise in academic interest in the lowbrow undercurrents of cinema that have all too often been exorcised from critical scrutiny. It is our hope, as editors, that this book may contribute to their visibility. While taking away some of the mystery, it may also help to dissipate some fear.

# CHAPTER 1

# 'THE FILM YOU ARE ABOUT TO SEE IS BASED ON DOCUMENTED FACT': ITALIAN NAZI SEXPLOITATION CINEMA

Mikel J. Koven

> The cycle of Nazi atrocity films ... are without a doubt some of the most distasteful examples
> of exploitation ever committed to film. ... It is interesting to speculate whether the sordid
> events depicted are so outrageous due to the fact that they seek to exploit events from recent
> history. ... Time can be a great healer but I doubt whether any film which revels in the misery
> of the Holocaust can ever be anything other than a highly dubious form of 'entertainment'
> which can only be viewed as an example of the lowest forms of trash culture.[1]

## THE NAZI SEXPLOITATION FILM

This chapter deals with a kind of European exploitation cinema which, as noted by Adrian Luther-Smith above, seems to defy even the most nominal categories of a 'taste' culture. This is a cinema that emerged out of a long-standing exploitation tradition, but even by those standards seems to have pushed the envelope too far. Italian exploitation cinema has always been characterised by cycles of imitations and downright rip-offs of other European and American films. A film will emerge that seems to take the national box-office, or at least receives the media's attention, and then very quickly, often before the original has reached the Italian cinema screens itself, a whole slew of imitators emerges.[2] One of the questions this chapter asks is what sparked off the cycle of Nazi sexploitation films (predominantly Italian in origin), which emerged over a brief period, 1975–77, after which the cycle quickly petered out?

One of the aspects that emerges in a study of this kind of cinema is a devolutionary trajectory running from a 'high' or artistically informed culture (which is de facto *bourgeois*) to a more *vernacular* cinema that 'reduces' the artistic and intellectual complexities of the antecedents into base forms of exploitation. Following from that, however, when these films are placed within a cinematic historiographic context,[3] a different discourse opens revealing *how* the Nazi sexploitation cinema engages with the historical period it exploits.

Omayra Cruz, one of the few scholars to have written on these films, notes:

> Although within the context of the Italian movie experience these films make perfect sense, a general outcry usually condemns them for commercialising and exploiting a 'serious' issue. How could anyone stoop so low as to bastardise the terror and tragedy of the Nazi experience for profit?[4]

Cruz identifies *Il portiere di notte* (*The Night Porter*, Italy, 1974, Liliana Cavani) as the first of these films. Or rather, that based on this one film's success, a cycle emerged which quickly degenerated into exploitation fare.[5] But in his consideration of these films, Cruz neglects *Salò o le 120 giornate di Sodoma* (*Salo*, Italy, 1975, Pier Paolo Pasolini) as being another 'high-art' precursor, particularly in its depiction of Sadean sexuality, a theme that is picked up in many of these later films. Within the same tradition, one could equally include *Salon Kitty* (Italy, 1975, Tinto Brass; and released the same year as *Salo*), which depicts a Nazi-era bordello and the decadence of the Third Reich. *Salon Kitty*, however, owes more than just a little of its *mise-en-scène* to *La Caduta degli dei* (*The Damned*, Italy, 1969, Luchino Visconti).

What emerges from a study of these films' influences and precursors is a genetic/generic code that moves downward from 'art' films like Visconti's through Brass's glossy but salacious re-working, into the Nazi sexploitation period proper. This particular thread, from *La Caduta degli dei* to *Salon Kitty*, gives way to what can be called the 'Nazi Bordello' film: high-art prototypes such as *La Caduta degli dei* and perhaps *Il portiere di notte* give way to the extreme exploitation films *Casa private per le SS* (literally 'Private House of the SS' but known in English as *SS Girls*, Italy, 1977, Bruno Mattei) and *Le Lunghe notti della Gestapo* (*Red Nights of the Gestapo*, Italy, 1977, Fabio De Agostini), with *Salon Kitty* holding a more ambivalent middle place between high- and low-cultural product. What gets picked up from *La Caduta degli dei* is the former film's decadent visual style and its emphasis on Weimar decadence and exoticism. Of course this is a superficial reading of Visconti's film, but it is the reading which Mattei and De Agostini pick up on to exploit in their films. Likewise in Brass's *Salon Kitty*, the bordello setting changes from Weimar decadence to a Nazi-era house of spies, wherein suspected enemies of the state are able to expose their treachery while in the arms of Berlin's most desirable

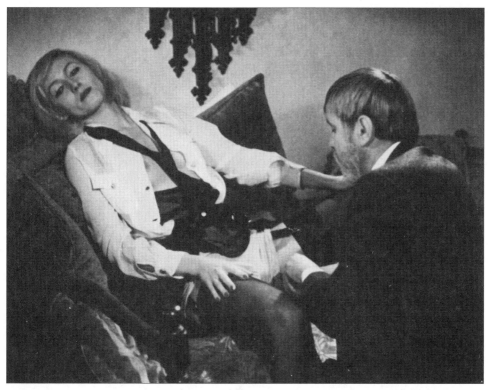

**FIGURE 2** Exploitation or an extension of art-house concerns? Fascist/erotic imagery became the motif of Nazi sexploitation cinema: *Gestapo's Last Orgy* (1976)

Aryan prostitutes. In Mattei and De Agostini's films, while the setting remains the Nazi bordello and the shadows of Weimar decadence are still in evidence, the films are more concerned with staging explicit sexuality. This is but one thread of the Nazi sexploitation film.

Another thread in Italian Nazi sexploitation cinema, and one which seems to cross a definite 'taste' line, as Luther-Smith noted above, situates the action within the concentration camp; although none of the films specifically identify their location as either a 'concentration' or 'death' camp, nor have they been given any historically authentic names such as Auschwitz, Belsen or Treblinka. The camps that are the setting for many of these films are often identified by the incongruous title of 'love camp'. 'Love Camps' are Nazi bordellos, but unlike the 'Nazi Bordello' thread, these films privilege the spectacles of rape and sexual humiliation. Frequently the films feature a group of captive and imprisoned women, forced into prostitution against their will. With the 'Nazi Bordello' films, the women are presented as more 'complicit' in their sexual exploitation. In the 'Love Camp' thread, the women, like the young people in *Salo*, have been taken by force.

The first cinematic reference to women in any kind of Nazi camp sequestered over to bordello-duty to satisfy the desires of either the camp's guards or soldiers arriving on furlough, appears to be *The Pawnbroker* (USA, 1964, Sidney Lumet). Here, in a flashback to his experiences in a concentration camp, Sol Nazerman accidentally discovers his wife held in such a bordello against her will. It is this experience in particular, the film argues, that finally destroyed Nazerman's humanity and partially explains his current alienation. As with the Nazi bordello films, we see a devolutionary trajectory from high-minded films like *The Pawnbroker*, into the more exploitation arena of *Love Camp 7* (USA, 1969, Lee Frost), really the first Nazi sexploitation film (albeit an American one). This presents, for our voyeuristic pleasures, the idea that the Nazis set up these bordellos for the entertainment of their soldiers on leave. Although both *The Pawnbroker* and *Love Camp 7* are American, yet very different kinds of films, the same idea of sexually assaulted women prisoners is in both, and this is a theme taken up by the Italian films that are the major focus of this chapter.

The difference between films *about* sexual exploitation and sexual exploitation *films* is largely in evidence through one obvious point of comparison: *L'Ultima orgia del III Reich* (*Gestapo's Last Orgy*, Italy, 1976, Cesare Canevari) directly reworks the narrative framing device of Cavani's *Il portiere di notte*: in both films a dual timeframe is demonstrated between a Nazi/concentration camp past and a present tense set a decade or so later. In *Il portiere di notte* Cavani explores the sado-masochistic relationship between Max and Lucia, a former concentration camp commandant and a young Jewish woman prisoner, both during the war and after in Vienna when their paths accidentally cross again.

**FIGURE 3** Despite their frequent definition as love camps, nazi sexploitation films reveal spectacles of sexual humiliation: *Gestapo's Last Orgy* (1976)

Likewise in *L'Ultima orgia*, where Commandant Von Starker meets up with Lise years after the war for a rendezvous on the site of the camp where Lise was imprisoned and sexually tortured by Von Starker during the war. But the comparisons end at that surface level. The same theme of power and sexual control may be seen in both films, and throughout Nazi sexploitation cinema; how that theme is presented, however, greatly differs.

Where the focus of *Il portiere di notte* is in Vienna in 1957, wherein flashbacks tie the present to the past, the opposite underlines *L'Ultima orgia* as the present tense storyline serves as a structuring device for sequences of sexual torture and rape. In Cavani's film the flashbacks are presented impressionistically, not much more than flashes of memory, and only one flashback sequence is developed in any kind of detail or length – the famous bar-room song, where Lucia is presented wearing nothing but a pair of men's trousers with braces and an SS hat, singing a German torch song *à la* Marlene Dietrich. But diegetically, Max is telling this story to a friend and embellishes it into a Salome-parable. The other flashbacks are not so much 'told' by characters as evidence of their memories. The reverse is the case in *L'Ultima orgia* where, after a lengthy set up, the present-day reunion between Von Starker and Lise is impressionistically presented in between extended sequences of rape and sexual torture.

Significantly how the flashbacks are photographed also differs: in *L'Ultima orgia* there is no subjectivity in the film's presentation. The spectator is positioned more or less objectively to the horrendous events on screen. The horrors are presented as if on some kind of Grand Guignol stage. However, Cavani demonstrates her intentions with the sexual degradation in the first few minutes of *Il portiere di notte*: the first flashback shown is Max's and we are positioned alongside him photographing the incoming prisoners awaiting registration and focusing on Lucia. The second flashback, however, is Lucia's, as we are now seeing the same moment but from the alternative perspective – among the prisoners, being blinded by the bright light of the movie camera. And whereas in Max's flashback we focus specifically on Lucia, in Lucia's 'reverse-flashback' Max is indistinct, eclipsed by the arc light of the camera. By setting up this dual perspective on the sexual exploitation within the concentration camps, Cavani is able to present flashbacks featuring rape, bondage and medical and sexual experimentation (see below) without appearing as exploitative as Canevari does in *L'Ultima orgia*, when he presents similar images (in terms of basic content) but without the subjectivity which problematise the notions of memory which are one of the central themes in Cavani's film.

The films' conclusions also underlies the differences between exploitation and 'higher-brow' cinema: in *L'Ultima orgia* Lise murders Von Starker, after having sex with him among the ruins of the concentration camp, implying that her contacting him after so many years was all a vengeful (and fully justified) ruse. In *Il portiere di notte* Max and Lucia escape from an underground cadre of former Nazi officials, whose membership had included Max himself. The cadre wanted Max to kill Lucia as she was the only survivor who could identify his war crimes, but rather than murdering her, they barricade themselves in his flat and hope the cadre will give up and go after other targets. They do not give up, Max and Lucia are shot as they attempt to escape on foot, and the final image of the film is a long-shot of the bridge where the two small figures of Max and Lucia lie dying where they stood. When phrased like that, *Il portiere di notte* sounds almost as exploitive as any action film, but it is the complexity of Max and Lucia's relationship that is the focus of the film. Rather than leaving ambiguous, as Cavani does, why Lucia would resume her relationship with Max, Canevari explains Lise's motivation as a vengeance ploy. Significantly, both Lise and Lucia die in their respective conclusions.

Although Cruz does mention above that many of these Italian exploitation films (in general as well as specifically these Nazi sexploitation films) are often derivative of American originals, his only precursor to this sexploitation cycle is *Il portiere di notte* and, as noted above, little is mentioned of other Italian influences like *Salon Kitty* or *Salo*. However, it was not *Love Camp 7*, or even *Il portiere di notte*, which sparked the cycle under consideration here, but a surprisingly successful American mainstream pornographic film, *Ilsa, She Wolf of the SS* (USA, 1974, Don Edmunds). *Ilsa*, with its emphases on women prisoners as fodder for the bordellos and men as slave sexual labour, also offers spectacles of the women prisoners used in medical experiments. The 'medical experiment' thread, along with Pasolini's *Salo*, introduced an explicit Sadean aesthetic of sexual torture, and this is what really characterises the Italian Nazi sexploitation cinema.

The vast majority of these Italian-made Nazi sexploitation films run a similar pattern of devolution from high-art, or at least 'respectable', precursors down to some of the nastiest of European cinema. As an interesting side note, although not an Italian *sex*ploitation film, one other film buzzes within the margins here: *Holocaust parte seconda: i ricordi, i deliri, la vendetta* (*Holocaust 2: The Memories, Delirium and the Vendetta*, Italy, 1980, Angelo Pannacciò). Here, as in *Il portiere di notte*, is an underground cadre, but this time of Holocaust survivors and their children, who assassinate escaped Nazis – Simon Wiesenthal as an action hero. What is significant about *Holocaust parte seconda* is that it too derives its exploitation plot from Cavani's film, albeit in reverse, and simplifies it by removing any ambiguity as to meaning or motivation. Exploitation cinema, particularly in this Italian context, is simplified cinema. Like comic book versions of literary classics these films rework/remake art cinema into something more accessible, thereby creating a more vernacular cinema. An independent American film like *The Pawnbroker* can give way to a *Love Camp 7* (also an independent American film), which can then be further tracked to films such as *Lager SSadis Kastrat Kommandantur* (literally, 'SS Camp of the Castrated Commandant' but known in English as *SS Experiment Camp*, Italy, 1976, Sergio Garrone) or *L'Ultima orgia*. These texts, although on opposite ends of the '(high/low) culture' scale, bring into play a theme of explicit visual sadism and medical experimentation. It is this last aspect, the medical experimentation theme, I now wish to turn to in more detail and relate these graphic images of pseudo-justified horror to the historical period to which the films are ostensibly referring.

## THE EXPLOITATION OF HISTORY

It is worth reiterating the question posed by Omayra Cruz above, 'How could anyone stoop so low as to bastardise the terror and tragedy of the Nazi experience?'[6] But, as I hope to have demonstrated, Cruz's 'bastardisation' is not as simple as he would have it: the Holocaust in these films is certainly simplified, certainly reduced to its most base elements, but such is the purview of exploitation cinema in general. Each of the films cited here make some direct reference to the historical period in question, in this case the Nazi era. But we need to ask *how* these Italian exploitation films simplified the representation of history?

In reference to this question, some historical documentation is needed to back up the historiography of these films. To begin with, at least one film (albeit one of the American films) makes a direct recourse to historical verisimilitude. *Ilsa, She Wolf of the SS* begins with a title card, while on the soundtrack we hear a recording of one of Hitler's Nuremberg speeches. This title card is problematic, for it brings to the fore the representation of history that these exploitation films utilise:

> The film you are about to see is based on documented fact. The atrocities shown were con-
> ducted as 'medical experiments' in special concentration camps throughout Hitler's Third
> Reich. Although these crimes against humanity are historically accurate, the characters
> depicted are composites of notorious Nazi personalities; and the events portrayed [sic] have
> been condensed into one locality for dramatic purposes. ... We dedicate this film with the
> hope that these heinous crimes will never occur again. [Signed] Herman Traeger, producer.[7]

The creation of Ilsa as a composite figure cuts to the heart of exploitation cinema, particularly historiographic exploitation. Rather than a biographical portrait, even a fictionalised one like *Schindler's List* (USA, 1993, Steven Spielberg), *Ilsa* and the Italian films discussed here reduce the historical complexities of the Holocaust into its most base and readily accessible form. If we contrast *Ilsa* with Max in *Il portiere di notte*, what is missing in the former is any of the subtleties of Dirk Bogarde's ambiguous performance in the latter: while not a 'sympathetic' or even remotely likeable character, Max is absolutely 'human' in his pettiness and in many respects embodies the Hannah Arendt description of Eichmann as 'the banality of evil'. Ilsa, on the other hand, is a cartoon depiction of 'composite' Nazi personalities, specifically Ilse Koch. Robert Wistrich gives this summary biography, which is worth quoting at length:

> Known as the 'Bitch of Buchenwald' for her sadistic cruelty and power-mad behaviour
> towards prisoners under her supervision, Ilse Koch was the wife of Karl Koch, Commandant
> of Buchenwald. ... A powerfully built, formidable nymphomaniac ... [she] was especially
> fond of horse-riding exercises [and] like[d] to ride through the camp, whipping any prisoner
> who attracted her attention. Her taste for collecting lampshades made from the tattooed skins
> of specially murdered concentration camp inmates was described as follows by a witness at
> Nuremberg: 'The finished products (i.e. tattooed skin detached from corpses) were turned
> over to Koch's wife, who had them fashioned into lampshades and other ornamental house-
> hold articles.'[8]

Even this 'historical' description of Ilse Koch, from a historical encyclopaedia-type book, reduces the complexities of a real person into its most sensational elements in order to convey the extreme behaviours of those who ran the concentration camps. But other characterisations of Ilse Koch also appear in some of the Italian sexploitation films too. For example, in *L'Ultima orgia*, Alma, the camp's lascivious second-in-command, proudly shows off a pair of gloves made from a baby's skin, and, more 'historically accurate', a lampshade made of human leather to preserve a beautiful tattoo. In the

**FIGURE 4** Exploiting real historical fact for audience titillation: *Elsa, Fraulein SS* (1977)

sequence from *L'Ultima orgia*, Alma shows Lise these grisly artefacts in a demonstration of both the Nazi's ruthless mastery over others (turning what were once human beings into artefacts), and their disregard for (apparently our) morality.

I do not wish to be misunderstood in my use of the word 'accurate': I am not for a second suggesting that these exploitation filmmakers did any kind of research, at least not as academics would understand the term. Nor am I arguing that these films offer any kind of 'truthful' historiography. In this case, although Ilse Koch is not known to have fashioned gloves out of an infant's skin, she did order prisoners with interesting tattoos to be slaughtered so she could obtain their leather, which was fashioned into lampshades. However, Ilse Koch, as notorious a historical figure as she may have been, is not dealt with in either *Ilsa* nor in *L'Ultima orgia* as any kind of motivated individual character but as a two-dimensional cartoon-like figure that is meant to represent the extremes of Nazi power. This is the entire point of exploitation cinema. Yet *what* these filmmakers got right, and what they got wrong (presumably unintentionally, in meeting the demands of exploitation cinema), is what the rest of this chapter is concerned with. Specifically: how these Italian films exploit history.

To begin with, I have been unable to find any historical verification of the 'love camp' – certainly not under that name, and exceptionally few references to women used in bordellos or for sexual favours. What few references there are to in-camp prostitution *explicitly exclude* Jewish women. For example, in Auschwitz, 'Block 10 also housed some 20 prostitutes, its only regular *non-Jewish* residents, who were available to elite prisoners as a work incentive and prophylactic against homosexual practices'.[9] Under the Third Reich, any kind of sexual activity between Jews and non-Jews was strictly forbidden, even when those Jews in question were prisoners in a concentration camp. According to the historical accounts, such a prohibition was more or less followed. Central to Nazi ideology was the concept of '*Rassenschande* (racial shame – that is, behaviour beneath the dignity of one's race)'.[10] Seen as 'sub-human' and 'racially inferior', Jews, specifically Jewish women, would have been unlikely sexual conquests. Felicja Karay, in her work on women's experiences in the forced labour-camps, notes the following:

> The Germans, most of them young bachelors, attempted to quench their libido by exploiting the Polish women in the factory, although this was explicitly prohibited. Much more dangerous were attempts to approach Jewish women, which might be construed as Rassenschande. In all three Werks [industrial-owned work camps], however, there were *rumours* of 'forbidden sexual liaisons' and the exploitation of Jewish women.[11]

'Rumour' is a word that keeps cropping up in survivor testimonies regarding sexual assaults by the SS on Jewish women. By rumour, I am not referring to the more vernacular understanding of the word, as in 'falsehood', but in a more sociological way, as a widespread, and *plausible* word-of-mouth fear. Myrna Goldenberg offers this example: 'As a beautiful, vivacious teenager, [Judith Isaacson] was troubled by persistent rumours of Jewish girls being sent to the front as prostitutes and then shot into open ditches.'[12] The seemingly fictional existence of these cinematic 'Love Camps' then is, partially, a representation of the fears that Jewish women experienced about their expected treatment at the hands of the SS.

What hypothetically emerges from this contrast between rumour and reality is a psychological paradox of the Holocaust for women: namely, that any kind of *organised* sexual assault on Jewish women was unthinkable to the Nazis, since they were not seen as human beings to begin with; whereas, from the victim's perspective, logically they would have feared sexual assault. Of course, in reality, Rassenschande would break down, but it did so in idiosyncratic ways – singular one-off events. The exception that proves the rule of Rassenschande is noted by Karay:

> Dozens of testimonies mention the Werkschultz commander Fritz Bartenschlager, who would sometimes attend selections in order to choose 'escort girls'. In October 1942, for example, five of these women were taken to a feast at his apartment, where they were ordered to serve guests in the nude and were ultimately raped by the revellers.[13]

Parties, like those of Bartenschlager, are a standard trope in all of these films, for obvious voyeuristic reasons, and are literally realised in *Ilsa*. However, it is intriguing to note that sometimes these film sequences involve diegetic willing participants (*L'Ultima orgia del III Reich*), while other films feature sequences where the women are raped and/or murdered (*Lager SSadis Kastrat Kommandantur, Ilsa, She Wolf of the SS*).

Jews are conspicuously absent from these Nazi sexploitation films as signifiers, with one notable exception. The majority of the sub-genre prefer pointed euphemisms: in *Ilsa*, the prisoners are referred to as 'inferior races', while in *Lager SSadis Kastrat Kommandantur* they are referred to as 'political criminals' – both euphemistically used for 'Jew' in the historical literature, but these filmmakers seem shy about the ethnic/racial specificity of the Nazi programmes of genocide. The exception to this is Canevari's *L'Ultima orgia*, wherein the women victims/prisoners are specified as Jews. Rassenschande is explicitly reflected in the film in one particular sequence (what Stephen Ziplow refers to as an 'orgy number').[14] In this sequence, a line of naked young German soldiers stand across a large room from a line of naked young Jewish women, while the Commandant informs the men that under Nazi ideology, since Jews are considered 'subhuman', an Aryan is forbidden to have 'sexual' relations with a Jew; however, an Aryan *is* allowed to use her merely to satisfy themselves. This is not a Third Reich legal argument I have been able to verify from historical sources, but seems designed by the requirements of the *generic* laws to lead into the 'rape/orgy' number). Again we see the process whereby the complex and subtle racial ideologies of the Third Reich are simplified in exploitation cinema.

Although the women victims/prisoners in Sergio Garrone's *Lager SSadis Kastrat Kommandantur* are designated simply as 'political criminals', one other character, referred to as a 'political enemy', is clearly signified as Jewish. The assistant camp doctor, Dr Steiner, turns out to be one Professor Abraham (an explicitly Jewish name, who later in the film is seen wearing something resembling a yarmulke and prayer shawl), a world-renowned surgeon who faked his own death during the bombing of his hospital, and took the identity of a Gentile colleague who died in the bombing. Camp Commandant, Colonel Von Klienmann (literally, 'little man', which can be read as a pointed reference to Von Kleinmann's missing penis/testicles, and this is also reflected in the literal translation of the film's title) wants an experimental testicular transplant on himself (his own were bitten off by a Red Army soldier he was raping). He discovers Steiner's real identity and blackmails the famous surgeon to conduct the operation. In exchange for this rather bizarre medical procedure, Von Klienmann promises Steiner/Abraham the identity files. Although Steiner/Abraham is operating at the Love Camp under his new identity as a Gentile, prisoner doctors at Auschwitz were allowed to assist the Nazi doctors in their surgery and research. Robert-Jay Lifton and Andrew Hackett note:

> Like other SS doctors at Auschwitz, Mengele made use of prisoner doctors. … Most were Jewish, and they were used primarily to diagnose and sometimes treat research subjects. … Mengele went so far as to set up a series of colloquia with prisoner doctors, some imported from other camps. … [T]he prisoner doctors at Auschwitz included many distinguished physicians. Most were vastly superior in skills and knowledge to the SS doctors…[15]

Garrone appears to be surprisingly historically accurate, at least within this exploitation genre context: Jewish doctors were able to assist Nazi doctors in their work; however the reality, at least at Auschwitz, was that these doctors were not able to hide their Jewish identity.

Another emergent thread within the Italian Nazi sexploitation film is the 'Medical Experiment' theme. Although the specifics of the medical experiments depicted in pictures like *Ilsa* and *Lager SSadis Kastrat Kommandantur*, as well as in films like *Il portiere di notte*, serve more to offer the audience Sadean images of (naked) women being tortured, medical experiments were also done by the Nazis, and were equally horrendous:

> Medical experimentation … was a small part of the extensive and systematic medicalised killing that was basic to the Nazi enterprise as perfected at Auschwitz. As tangible medical crimes, however, such experiments achieved considerable prominence at the Nuremberg Doctors' Trial in 1946–47. Indeed, their blending of ordinary science and extreme ideology made them emblematic of science under Germany's National Socialist regime. The considerable curiosity and notoriety aroused by research they carried out has to do with ethical questions that reach beyond Nazi doctors, and particularly with the radical Nazi reversal of healing and killing.[16]

Stories about Dr Mengele's experiments at Auschwitz of injecting blue dyes into dark-eyed subjects, and morphological dissection of twins and dwarves are well known. So too is the knowledge that the Nazis experimented with new processes of sterilisation, including experimental castrations and injections with caustic substances.[17] Lifton and Hackett note, however, that other experiments in Auschwitz's research laboratories were the stuff of horror movies:

> Experiments took place throughout the camp. In block 41 at Birkenau, for example, three noted German professors conducted surgery that entailed the exposure of leg muscles and the test application of medications. Medical students performed experimental surgery on a female hospital block, which offered the opportunity to practice whatever procedure suited their particular interests. (Sometimes a prisoner with a relevant medical condition was selected; sometimes the choice was arbitrary.) With no ethical considerations at issue, a more opportunistic surgical laboratory than Auschwitz could hardly be imagined. Beyond

convenience, a doctor could rationalise his experimentation with the thought that since his patient was ultimately condemned to death in any case, he could truly do no harm.[18]

Furthermore, 'with the help of an advanced medical student, relatively healthy Jewish inmates had toxic substances, some petroleum-based, rubbed into their arms and legs. It was hoped that the resulting infections and abscesses would provide information useful in detecting ruses by malingerers trying to avoid military service'.[19] Although the case of Dr Mengele is perhaps the better known, also at Auschwitz, Dr Wirths experimented with infectious diseases that 'might threaten the health of troops'.[20] The litany of medical atrocities reads like an outline for *Ilsa, She Wolf of the SS*; 'Camp 9' is an experimental medical camp, designed to research the effects of various extremes (air pressure, heat, cold) on soldiers, but using (naked) women for experimental purposes. Furthermore, at Camp 9, prisoners are injected with infectious diseases so Reich doctors can experiment with new drugs. As Lifton and Hackett note with regard to Auschwitz, 'the Hygienic Institute used human, rather than animal, muscle for its culture media. Animal meat was simply dearer in such an environment, even as Auschwitz substituted human guinea pigs for lab animals'.[21] Again, as with the issue of the presumed fictional 'Love Camps', the experimentation on human guinea pigs was less a Sadean desire for torture, and more the ideology which saw Jews and other non-Aryans as simply sub-human – the *equivalent* of animals. Strangely enough, apart from the experimental testicular transplant in *Lager SSadis Kastrat Kommandantur*, the other kinds of 'experiments' going on have no apparent factual appeal, unlike *Ilsa*'s: they seem to be experiments in 'arousal' and really consist of little but Aryan men raping different prisoner women in different situations. There is no attempt to explain these experiments, other than as voyeuristic 'sex numbers'.

Again and again, what we see in these Nazi sexploitation films are 'composites' of historical reality – Jewish doctors working in the camp infirmaries, specious medical experimentation, sexual assaults on women prisoners – composites which 'for dramatic purposes', as the *Ilsa* title card reads, simplify the historiographic complexities of the Third Reich. However, these Nazi sexploitation movies are merely doing what exploitation cinema has always done, namely reducing complex issues to their most basic and primal meanings. Finally, we end up back at the Luther-Smith quote cited at the outset. What perhaps *does* make these particular films feel different is their relationship to a much more recent history – often still a *living* history.

## CONCLUSION

Studies of cult and exploitation films often try to justify their interest based on kitsch or aesthetic grounds. Jeffrey Sconce's 'paracinema' attempts to explore the inherent aesthetics of the film, even when they violate academy-defined notions of taste and quality. He notes:

> By concentrating on a film's formal bizarreness and stylistic eccentricity, the paracinematic audience ... foregrounds structures of cinematic discourse and artifice so that the material identity of the film ceases to be a structure made invisible in service of the diegesis, but becomes

instead the primary focus of textual attention. It is in this respect that the paracinematic aesthetic is closely linked to the concept of 'excess'.[22]

In the Nazi sexploitation film, it is those moments of 'excess', the extreme 'numbers' depicting sex, rape and torture, which are 'the prime focus of textual attention' (in Sconce's terms). But these films do more than just offer sadomasochistic voyeuristic pleasure, for their historic specificity requires some kind of discursive consideration about the nature of their representation of the Holocaust. Clearly these films have different agendas to more 'respectable' Holocaust narrative films – *Schindler's List* or *La vita e bella* (*Life is Beautiful*, Italy, 1998, Roberto Benigni), for example – specifically in how they simplify and create their own 'composite' narratives, but the processes of reduction and explication are not dissimilar.

Space does not allow a fuller exploration of the contrast between American and European cinema – at the level of exploitation (i.e. *Ilsa, She Wolf of the SS* contrasted with *L'ultima orgia*) or art-cinema (i.e. *The Pawnbroker* contrasted with *Il portiere di notte*), or even within middle-brow, popular cinema (i.e. *Schindler's List* contrasted with *La vita e bella*). Any of those comparisons would reveal, I believe, less a direct contrast than a spectrum reflecting degrees of 'composites' between European and American exploitations of the past. Be that as it may, and to return the discussion to where it began, what emerges from studies like this is an alternative discourse to that offered by Sconce (and echoed by Hawkins).[23] Exploitation cinema is not necessarily 'alternative' or 'paracinematic' art, but a discourse of address which needs to be approached at its own level of articulation. The Italian Nazi sexploitation cycle may in fact be 'the most distasteful example of exploitation ever committed to film' – but it is also infinitely curious too, despite its disavowal to the discourses of 'art'.

# CHAPTER 2
## DEEP INSIDE QUEEN KONG: ANATOMY OF AN EXTREMELY BAD FILM

I. Q. Hunter

### INTRODUCTION: THE PLOT

A feminist director, Luce Habit (Rula Lenska), is looking for a male lead for a film she plans to make in Africa. Most British actors being too effete for her tastes ('Men are frail little beings, helpless'), she settles for a hippyish drop-out, Ray Fay (Robin Askwith of the *Confessions* films). On her boat, *The Liberated Lady*, with its crew of bikinied starlets, Luce and Ray reach the film's location, Lazanga-Where-They-Do-The-Conga, where a tribe of improbably interracial Amazons try to sacrifice Ray to their god, a 64-foot female gorilla called Queen Kong. Having fallen in love with Ray, Queen Kong is subdued with gas bombs and transported to London, where she is put on public display and forced to wear bra and panties. Outraged, she escapes with Ray, demolishes much of tourist London, and ends up on top of Big Ben. Ray saves her from the military with an impassioned speech declaring her a symbol of oppressed women everywhere. Women across Britain take to the streets in the gorilla's defence, and she and Ray are returned safely to Lazanga-Where-

They-Do-The-Conga as an unlikely happy couple. The precise nature of their relationship is left tantalisingly vague.

*Queen Kong* (1976) is a cheap, incompetent and, until recently, almost entirely unseen Anglo-Italian spoof of *King Kong* (1933), intended to cash in on the publicity for the big-budget 1976 remake. Directed by Frank [Farouk] Agrama, otherwise known to film buffs for the gore film, *Dawn of the Mummy* (1981), *Queen Kong* is chiefly notable for its obscurity. RKO and Dino De Laurentiis, who produced the official *Kong* remake, blocked the release of *Queen Kong* on the grounds of 'passing off', in a case settled out of court in 1977. The film was subsequently never seen in cinemas (except, briefly, in Italy, where copyright laws appear to have been more flexible).[1] Finally surfacing on bootleg video in 2000, *Queen Kong* acquired minor cult recognition before its legitimate DVD release, first in Japan and then in the United States.[2]

## CRACKING QUEEN KONG

Given the film's awfulness and historical insignificance, why bother to write about it at all? Certainly, with its scattering of British cult figures such as Robin Askwith, Valerie Leon and Linda Hayden, it deserves the attention of any fan of nostalgic rubbish of the 1970s. One might even take a certain nationalistic pride in Britain's producing so striking an entry in the annals of trash cinema, a category or genre otherwise colonised by American tastes and, in particular, the tiresome ideology of transgression. (Most British exploitation was not a cinema of excess and unhinged marginal expression, but one of timidity and impoverishment – suburban, middlebrow and hamstrung by censorship.)

Then again there is the 'Everest principle'. *Kong* must be conquered merely because she is there; the value of the exercise lies in being the first to bag, tag and possess her. (This completist fetish is an affliction equally of film buffs and (*mea culpa*) academics on the publish-or-perish treadmill. In spite of the DVD, *Queen Kong* is still a pretty rare and inaccessible specimen, and worth the effort of display and exploitation.) Finally, *Queen Kong* has symptomatic interest as an allegory of race, gender and national decline in the 1970s. With film and context properly aligned, *Queen Kong* casts off the shackles of mere exploitation and is revealed as a bold articulation of the political unconscious of that troubled period.

As Cynthia Erb remarks in *Tracking King Kong*, her overview of *King Kong*'s journey through popular culture, by the 1970s *King Kong* had become an established camp icon.[3] The film's sexual and racial implications were toyed with not only in parodies such as the play, *Gorilla Queen*, and *The Rocky Horror Picture Show* (1975), but also the somewhat camped-up 1976 remake directed by John Guillermin. Recognising the material as inescapably queer as well as rich in allegorical uses, it clumsily gestures towards Kong's subtextual possibilities: Kong as 'male chauvinist pig ape'; Kong as super-hippy; Kong as symbol of corporate exploitation of the Third World.[4] In opting for knowingness and camp pastiche, *Queen Kong* was in the mainstream of *Kong* lore, rather than an unexpected subversion of it. Indeed, the 1976 *Kong* is not *that* different from *Queen Kong*. Only the vast difference in the budgets squandered by each film disguises similarities of production (Agrama and De Laurentiis have roots in Italian exploitation) and creative means (the remake includes a brief, wholly unconvincing glimpse of a full-size animatronic Kong, but otherwise resorts to the same cheap effects as *Queen Kong* and other *Kong*sploitation: a man in a gorilla suit, miniature buildings and back projection).

## QUEEN KONG AS BRITISH CINEMA: CAMP AND WORLD WAR II

Although a comic romp, the most popular mode of British exploitation, *Queen Kong* is otherwise out of sync with other low-budget British films of the mid-1970s. It lurches through a number of genres – musical, science fiction, disaster film, television sitcom – but not the one most obviously hospitable to its resources and ambitions: the sex comedy. Although *Queen Kong* plays like it should be a sexploitation film, it contains not one frame of nudity. Askwith's bottom is never bared, and none of the 'Page 3' and *Benny Hill* girls in the cast strips further than her bikini. Nor is *Queen Kong* for kids, like other British 'monster on the loose' films such as *Gorgo* (1961), *Digby – The Biggest Dog in the World* (1973) and, on television, *The Goodies*' 'Kitten Kong' sketch. There are too many drug references, for one thing. *Queen Kong* seems genuinely interstitial, poised between several potential audiences but efficiently tuned into none of them. As an item of weird 'paracinema' *Queen Kong* makes sense nowadays, when niche markets flourish for camp trash with the production values of a home movie. Indeed it is a far more likely candidate for enthusiastic cult reappraisal than the 1976 *Kong*, whose reputation has not improved at all. But in the 1970s no market as such existed for camp British trash, unless it was in the waning genres of sexploitation and horror (*Horror Hospital*, 1973; *Dr Phibes Rises Again*, 1972; *The Sexplorer*, 1975).

There is one genre in British cinema, apart from comic farce, to which *Queen Kong* bears an interesting thematic relation: the science fiction film. Like many British science fiction movies, it refers back to the discourses of World War Two. While American science fiction of the 1950s and 1960s reverberated with fears of Communism, British science fiction was fixated on the imagery of war and the theme of national decline. Invasion narratives such as *The Earth Dies Screaming* (1964) and *Daleks – Invasion Earth 2050 AD* (1966) centre on occupation by Nazi-like aliens, while the Blitz is re-visualised in the 'trashing London' films at the turn of the 1960s: *Gorgo, Behemoth the Sea Monster* (1959) and *Konga* (1960) (an earlier 'giant gorilla on the loose' film).[5] These films were both a nostalgic recall of British greatness in resisting external danger, and fretful admissions that, after Suez and the end of consensus, Britain might never again muster the same resources of Blitz and Dunkirk spirit. *Queen Kong* resurrects the discourses of wartime to complement footage of London under simian siege: a radio broadcast declares that defeating the gorilla will be 'England's finest hour', while an ineffectual policeman (all the men in this film are weak and unheroic) phones his mother for advice, asking the crucial question: 'What would Churchill do now?'

If *Queen Kong* seems surreally misjudged, the reason may be that it is not 'British' at all. One must beware of describing it too eagerly as archetypal British trash or some such misleading idealist epithet. More accurately, it is a botched pastiche, by an Egyptian director and American screenwriter, of the clichés of low-brow English humour, a homage to *Carry On* precisely mistimed to coincide with the eclipse of *Carry On* by sexploitation. Eschewing cinema's superior possibilities for nudity and sexual explicitness, *Queen Kong* is reminiscent of other, more innocent continuations of traditional English low humour. The deliberate bad jokes, numerous film references and self-mocking address to the audience remind one of the plays that Ernie wrote for the *Morecambe and Wise Show* – a similarity clinched by a crocodile declaring, as Eric frequently did in the show, that we are watching 'rubbish'. Closer still is the film's resemblance to a pantomime, that peculiarly English theatrical form with its fairytale settings, excruciating puns, gender reversals, shabby special effects, topical ad libs and musical interludes – elements all present in *Queen Kong*, but not obviously conducive to box-office success. There is a case for describing the film as postmodern on account of its generic fluidity and tactic of pre-emptive self-contempt – 'We came to make a movie, we created a farce!' This anticipates what is now a standard tactic of ingratiation in deliberate trash films by the likes of Troma, Fred Olen Ray and Seduction Cinema. But such playful reflexivity is also a comic intensification of the auto-critique, in the original *Kong*, of film as sadistic spectacle and voyeuristic exploitation. Sticking with this theme, one can also read *Queen Kong* as a commentary on the state of British cinema itself in the doldrums of the 1970s – 85 humiliating minutes of what British film has been reduced to. Appropriately enough, *Queen Kong* is a self-parodying combination of the two kinds of film into which British production was largely divided: the international co-production and tacky exploitation. The scattered references to *Jaws* (1975), *The Exorcist* (1973) and *Last Konga in Lazanga* measure the unbridgeable distance between the blockbusters of the new American cinema and the desperate end of the pier stuff on screen before us (between, indeed, the remake of *King Kong* – rubbish, but a proper film – and *Queen Kong*'s cheap imitation). What is intriguing about *Queen Kong* is that it relates its own shabbiness and creative poverty not only to the British film industry but also to Britain itself in the 1970s on the cusp of punk and the Jubilee. Like *The Flesh and Blood Show* (1972) and *Terror* (1978), *Queen Kong* is exploitation as state-of-the-nation film. On the one hand, it is 'about' British weakness, male insecurity, racial insecurity and female liberation, and thus belongs with more obviously intentional and legible allegories of post-war national decline as *Juggernaut* (1974), *House of Whipcord* (1974) and *Britannia Hospital* (1981). On the other, it is a mad Freudian dreamscape, a compendium of outlandish sexual fantasies and an irresistible excuse for filthy-minded over-interpretation.

## THE SYMBOLIC GORILLA: RACE AND GENDER

This brings us to the matter of *Queen Kong* as political allegory and in particular the symbolic meaning of the gorilla herself. As an index of social fears, a giant black liberated female Other might seem so wildly over-determined as scarcely to require detailed explication. Feminism, immigration, post-Imperial decline – all are evoked as 'the monkey knocked hell out of 1000 years of English history and wiped out a year's supply of North Sea oil'. In *Konga* the rioting gorilla could, with equally minimal imagination, be read as a symbolic panic response to the post-Windrush influx of black immigrants into Britain – something completely new and mind-boggling among the familiar London landmarks.[6] Still, caution is required even with so obvious, glib and workable interpretation of a film. The imagery of apes and black people can be linked in a supple and persuasive manner, as Erb does in her readings of *King Kong*, but it is still potentially a racist reflex. So it is tentatively that in the matter of *Queen Kong*'s entanglement with racial fantasy one concludes that the gorilla represents the revenge of colonial repression. Her private race riot across London is payback for the havoc Britain wrought across Imperial Africa.

On a sliding scale of plausibility, this is a pretty straightforward reading and only mildly unscrupulous interpretative pressure yields the insight that the film is locked into racial fantasy and especially the delirious imaginings of white men about the sexual possibilities of black women. If on the one hand it is a terrifying vision of blackness out of control, on the other it is a reassuring fable about how the racial and sexual Other can be tamed by white men, in whom fear of and sexual fascination for black women are confused and intermingled.

On the face of it *Queen Kong* is 'about' feminism and the threat of women running wild. Queen Kong is a big woman, and as in *Attack of the 50 Ft Woman* (1958; the feminist television remake was 1993) and *The Incredible Shrinking Man* (1957), size is everything. Images of enormous women and pocket-sized men speak volubly of threats to patriarchy, and these are films terrified about women expanding beyond the domestic sphere. Need we delve far beneath the surface of *Queen Kong* to find this out? Not at all. The obvious symptomatic reading of the film will do quite nicely, and can be grasped in a sentence or two. As Ray says in his defence of Queen Kong, which ensures her return to Laganza (or, to keep up the hidden racial implications, benevolent repatriation) – 'You cannot destroy her, for she represents women everywhere', a cry accompanied by a montage of women liberating themselves from domestic and sexual drudgery. This satirises feminism, of course, because it is ridiculous that laddish Robin Askwith should be the spokesperson of female emancipation. And it is entirely true that as a result *Queen Kong* might be charged with appropriating and triviliasing the discourse of feminism. When Ray comments, as Queen Kong lays waste another chunk of the capital, that 'I don't know what I'm going to do with her', he, the film and the chortling audience disavow the power and meaning of her actions: she is out of control, the poor dumb animal, and in need of male protection. But, on the other hand, the feminist discourse is unmistakable *there*, openly articulated (albeit from the ample, child-bearing lips of Askwith) and diegetically effective – women momentarily throw off their chains and Queen Kong is saved. All ends happily. So, while feminism is mocked and abused in the film, its call for liberation still gets through; that the film must deal with, reproduce and bother to appropriate it is a measure, in fact, of its success. Almost without their wanting to, the filmmakers are obliged to acknowledge that because of feminism even the silliest movie about a giant female gorilla turns into a fable of women's liberation. The film makes its subtext explicit and Queen Kong is deliberately transfigured into a symbol. Unlike, say, *Digby*, in which the allegorical significance of the monstrous titular sheepdog remains elusive, *Queen Kong* knowingly presents us with a manifestation of female liberation at its most challenging, an outrageous Id monster terrorising Englishmen who, the film insists, are mostly enfeebled, confused or homosexual: 'She might have been a queen on the island, but in London half the men you meet are queens.' (Here the filmmakers buy into the popular foreign stereotype of the queer Englishman.) The result is a highly schematic vision of Britain's sexual economy in the mid-1970s: Britain is emasculated, its men sexually indeterminate and under the thumb of Mother, and women are on the verge of revolution. By the film's zero-sum logic, if women are getting more powerful, men must be turning into women or becoming homosexual (*Queen Kong* was made at the end of the glam rock period, when gender roles did seem unusually ambiguous). Britain is undergoing a gender reversal so comprehensive that even Robin Askwith has signed up for feminism. Soon the country will resemble its fantasy double, the matriarchy Lazanga.

To return to the imagery of race: why should fear of women's liberation be expressed in terms of blackness? The loaded racial interpretation of Queen Kong herself implies that symbolically she is not just a monstrous woman but a monstrous black woman – an oversized manifestation of the savage, insatiable, over-sexed black woman of the racist imagination. Most importantly, she is therefore also the untamed dark Other who lurks inside white women, which white men must disavow and keep repressed. According to Rhoda Berenstein, there is a representational affinity between blackness and white women – women (all women) are in continual danger of slipping back into blackness, which is coded as sexually excessive, uncivilised, undomesticated and beyond male control.[7] By this reading, Queen Kong is an entirely logical symbol of liberated white women. For, as Berenstein points out, in films such as *King Kong* and 1930s jungle exploitation, white women are doubled not only with black men but with apes.[8] Like them white women are hierarchically subordinate to white men. Once the hierarchy is threatened – by male weakness, for example, or female independence – white women tumble down the symbolic order to become like black women and finally apes. No longer safely under male control, they become entirely Other to the hysterical male imagination. Again, this clarifies the logic of a black ape symbolising (white) female liberation and victimhood – unleashed, all English white women would become as monstrously Other and 'un-English' as black women and apes. 'Bloody foreigners', a British Asian says of Queen Kong. 'You wouldn't see an English gorilla behaving like that.'

At the same time, as Berenstein says, the black ape in films can be a figure of desire and envy for white men. King Kong, she argues, construed as a black man, is unsettling not least because 'apes and black men also signify all the white man imagines he is but should be, as well as all he believes white women desire and resemble'.[9] Kong's strength, sexual potency (despite his invisible penis) and hypermasculinity are, to the racist white imagination, threateningly desirable and 'manly' as much as they are repulsively ape-ish. There is a similar ambivalence about Queen Kong. She is not altogether to be feared, but on some level to be welcomed and even secretly desired; the promise (or pretence) is that she can be tamed, as Ray tames her at the end of the film, and fear of her is mingled with a colonialist desire for black women's imagined sexual plenitude. Queen Kong is, after all, strong, protective, an ideal matriarch and archetypal in her iconic simplicity. In Jungian terms she is a fusion of Shadow and Anima, and her appeal strikes deep into the white male (and, specifically, postcolonial English) unconscious. Capable of swallowing a man whole – at either end – she embodies a fantasy of sexual submission that corresponds to the stereotypical Englishman's masochistic desire for punishing from a dominant matronly authority. From a certain point of view, if female liberation means women becoming more like Queen Kong – big, sexy, strapping and dark – then Ray has the right idea: give in and enjoy it. Her monstrous sexiness is celebrated in one of the film's occasional musical numbers:

> She's a queenie who ain't a weenie,
> When I'm feeling mighty spunky,
> I want to do it with my hunky monkey.

Although an ever-present theme of the English male psyche, desire for correction and control by a powerful woman found some interestingly novel and urgent forms of cultural expression in the

1970s. One striking fantasy of male insignificance and engulfment is elaborated in a text roughly contemporary to *Queen Kong*: the 'Joan Crawford' sketch on Peter Cook and Dudley Moore's 1977 album, *Derek and Clive Come Again*. The combination of misogynistic terror, helpless masochism and infantile regression makes for a suggestive parallel with *Queen Kong*:

Clive:   And I look around, and I saw someone lying on a bed. I thought 'that's a fucking familiar face'. And it was Joan Crawford.

Derek:   Gawd. Fucking hell.

Clive:   And I'm cleaning the windows, and this fucking wind blew up, tropical storm invaded the bedroom, and I was swept away by this huge gust of wind, straight up her fucking cunt.

Derek:   Oh no.

Clive:   Yeah. I went straight up through the nylon underwear, tore through the diaphragm she was wearing, and there was no exit.[10]

All this Oedipal madness raises the question: how big is Queen Kong's vagina? King Kong's erection was once calculated to be 20 inches long – impressive but not so as to make sex entirely out of the question if Fay Wray were sufficiently limber and game. What about Queen Kong, though? Ray is happy to shack up with her at the end of the film, his role some indefinable combination of acolyte, lover, colonial overlord and zookeeper. Queen Kong turns out to be the perfect woman, in whose ample symbolic form diverse fantasies of weird sex and masochistic submission are embodied and catered for. The implication is that Ray becomes a kind of human dildo. In the spirit of Derek and Clive he persistently attempts to return to the womb and thereby fulfil an Oedipal fantasy of the highest order – fucking Mother with one's entire infantile body.

## CONCLUSION

Is it, as Marxists used to say, any coincidence that a few years later, to satiate this subconscious yearning for matriarchal control and with the promise of arresting national decline, a woman should indeed come to rampage across and dominate Britain? Mrs Thatcher – mother, matron and dominatrix, the 'Great She Elephant' – was the Queen Kong of politics. Sex symbol, icon and white goddess (crucially she is bleached of Queenie's disturbing racial connotations), Mrs Thatcher spoke to and answered fantasies of desire and control submerged deep in the political unconscious, fantasies given ridiculous but comprehensive expression in an unreleased exploitation film about a 64-foot female gorilla.

# CHAPTER 3
## THE SCHOOLGIRL REPORTS AND THE GUILTY PLEASURE OF HISTORY

Jennifer Fay

### INTRODUCTION

Barbara Köster, a feminist and student activist in the German New Left, reflects on the connection between adolescent rebellion and historical consciousness in 1960s Germany:

> I was raised in the Adenauer years, a time dominated by a horrible moral conformism, against which we naturally rebelled. We wanted to flee from the white Sunday gloves, to run from the way one had to hide the fingernails behind the back if they weren't above reproach. Finally then we threw away our bras as well. … For a long time I had severe altercations with my parents and fought against the fascist heritage they forced on me. At first I rejected their authoritarian and puritanical conception of child-rearing, but soon we came into conflict over a more serious topic: the persecution of the Jews. I identified with the Jews, because I felt myself to be persecuted by my family.[1]

Köster's recollection suggests that the violent history of Nazi Germany ripples through the intimate encounters between parents and their radical offspring, and that the older generation adopts authoritarian tactics from an unreconciled past in its attempt to control and monitor the adolescent body. Quarrels over bras and soiled fingernails in this story give way to historical debate once Köster makes the connection between her parents and German history. Köster's rebellion against her parents, she explains, is animated by her own sense of shame for acts committed before her birth. For Dagmar Herzog, this statement should be read as an urgent 'flailing to free oneself from the cloying and everywhere inadequately acknowledged toxicities of the supposedly so clean post-1945 period'.[2] Perhaps more significantly, however, the charge marks a progression from adolescence into adulthood by becoming aware first of personal history and then of national history – moving, as it were, from the parents to the nation, and from the body to the state.

Recent scholarship on the German New Left reveals that this movement constructed mutually defining sexual and political positions in reference to the Judeocide. The sexual revolution, in which Köster was active, brought taboo, and presumably repressed, desires, fantasies and experiences into the public domain with the goal of confronting the *Wirtschaftwunder* generation with the past they suppressed. The liberated, nude body, free of the trappings of capitalist consumer culture, could function as a signifier of student victimisation and guilt, but also as a trope for laying bare Germany's genocidal past. If the Nazis and Adenauer adults suffered from and perpetuated sexual repression and historical amnesia, public nudity and free love represented, as Uli Linke puts it, 'a return to the authentic, the natural, the unrepressed, that is, to a way of life untainted by the legacy of Auschwitz'.[3] Confronting sex and confronting Germany's past were thus yoked in the student endeavour to bring private experience and suppressed history into the public record. Yet, the student appropriation of the Jewish victimisation was not only a provocative political gesture. The recurrence of Holocaust imagery in the New Left discourse, Herzog notes, pointed to an essential volatility, 'that the release of libido might be, not just liberatory, but rather dangerous, and that the pursuit of pleasure might lead, not to social justice, but to evil'.[4]

While the New Left found a rejoinder in the films of Rainer Werner Fassbinder, Volker Schlöndorff and Alexander Kluge, directors themselves of the left whose works spoke directly to the 'sixty-eighters', the most popular interventions in the sexual revolution were the soft-core exploitation 'Sex Report' films which began with Ernst Hofbauer's 1970 *Schulmädchen Report* and include the twelve subsequent films in the series that ended in 1980. Part documentary, part staged vignettes, the *Schoolgirl Reports* are pornographic exposés of the erotic life of Germany's middle-class adolescent girls. The films ostensibly address themselves to adults who are struggling to understand the sexual and cultural mores of the new generation, and to parents, in particular, who know practically nothing about their daughters' illicit lives. Along with his collaborators Walter Boos, writer Günther Heller, and producer Wolf Hartwig, Hofbauer, born in 1925, represented a voice of the older generation who came of age during the war and who was now ambiguously implicated in Germany's past. My interest in this series is in how it accesses the rhetoric of the sexual revolution while repackaging and eroticising the guilt associated with sexual experience.

## VOICING TEENAGE SEXUALITY IN POSTWAR GERMANY

In the pre-credit sequence of *Part One*: *Was Eltern nicht für möglich halten* (*Possibilities Parents Do Not Consider*, 1970), we follow a group of teenagers who are driving a Volkswagen Bug down Munich's Leopoldstrasse. A girl's voice-over defiantly declares:

Here we are. We, the youth of today. We are subjugated and disagreeable. Why? Because we doubt, because we have our own kind of music, and because we want a new kind of morality.

Shifting to a montage of individual schoolgirls, the voice-over continues: 'Here we are. The girls of today. We are curious and true to ourselves because our parents have lied too often.' The girl's voice is then supplanted by an authoritative, older male voice that invites us to witness first hand the new protocol of the sexual revolution, 'how it works in these new times, and how it really is.'

In the first scene of the film, a girl sneaks away from her class field trip to have sex with the school bus driver. Upon being discovered in the act by her prudish instructor, the girl is brought before the school's parent-teacher board that will decide whether or not this offence is grounds for expulsion. The rest of the film is structured around stories that the school's resident psychologist shares with the board about teenage sexuality in general. Flashbacks within flashbacks take us to the most private and intimate moments of girls' sexual awakenings. From fifteen-year-old Barbara, who confesses to carrying on an affair with her stepfather since she was twelve, to her peer Claudia who seduces an older life guard and sends him to a two-year jail sentence, each episode is relayed through a girl's own voice-over recollection as she submits details of her delinquency for scientific scrutiny and moral judgement. We then shift to documentary-style woman-on-the-street interviews where 'real' women respond to questions each of the vignettes raise. As a foil to the clearly fictional parent-teacher groups who condemn the teenage dalliances, these random respondents, in sharing their own personal experiences, often confirm the 'truth' and normalcy of the erotic encounters. In so doing they suggest that the letter of the law and the code of the classroom are both inadequate to the reality of teenage sexuality which, however criminal and immoral, is nonetheless natural.

A product of their time, the sex report films came about in response to shifts in the West German film industry. By the late 1960s the self-governing film censorship organisation, the FSK (Freiwillige Selbstkontolle der Filmwirtschaft), had liberalised its guidelines concerning acceptable film content, such that by 1972 it had ceased altogether to regulate adult films designated for audiences eighteen and older. At the same time, new laws prohibiting the glorification of violence and pornography meant that films deemed obscene could still be confiscated by the police or banned by local officials.[5] The on-the-street interviews, PTA meetings and often morally compensating endings of the *Schoolgirl Reports* offset the pornographic content with quasi-scientific appeals to sex education and documentary reportage; in this way producers might circumvent obscenity laws by making claims for the redeeming social value of the genre. This strategy explains, in part, an ambivalence in these texts that both celebrate teenage sexuality and expose the maleficence of unchecked desire.

At a time when the German film market was dominated by foreign (mostly Hollywood) films and witnessed the concomitant dwindling of film audiences, movie theatres and production financing,[6] soft-core films were inexpensive to make and easy to export. Indeed, the films in this series are important not only because they were hugely popular in Germany, but were West Germany's most profitable film exports. It is estimated that these films found 100 million viewers worldwide, out-performing the Edgar Wallace films. Moreover, the *Schoolgirl Reports* inspired a host of spin-offs including Hartwig's *Swedish Love Games*, *The Nurses Report*, *Sex in the Office* and Hofbauer's own *Hausfrau Report*.[7] To this day, the *Reports* air on German television, and the 1996 release of the *Schulmädchen* soundtrack speaks to the films' international appeal and the widespread nostalgia they invoke in their fans.

One would think that the economic importance of this series and the fact that it was representative of production trends in the 1970s when Germany became Europe's leading producer of soft-core pornography[8] would earn Hofbauer and his naughty schoolgirls a central place in post-war German film historiography. Yet the series has been either ignored,[9] summarily dismissed[10] or denounced for its address to the wrong kinds of audiences. Thomas Elsaesser, for example, laments that the pornographic turn appealed to Germany's immigrant guest workers (Italian, Greek and Turkish men) who 'ouste[d], indeed eradicate[d] the last remnants of the family audience', and the educated audiences who would support the artistic and politically trenchant efforts of the New German Cinema.[11] This unsettling language of 'eradication' aside, Elsaesser charges that the sex films siphoned resources and audiences from legitimate film projects.

These omissions and dismissals are predicated on a general disregard of genre film during the late 1960s and 1970s, and, more specifically, on the assumption that the *Schoolgirl Reports* do nothing more than tame the sexual revolution for non-political (foreign) older, male viewers. Admittedly, the commercial allure of the sex report films are the extended scenes of female masturbation, girl-on-girl petting, simulated heterosexual sex, orgies and the conspicuous display of the nude girl body. Yet these pornographic sequences are embedded in a discourse that leads us through the various regimes of power that shape and discipline sexual behaviour in ways that interrogate the relationship between sexual liberation, memory and the possibility of 'a life untainted' by German history.

## COMPULSIVE CONFESSING

In a typical episode from *Part Two: Was Eltern den Schlaf raubt* (*What Keeps Parents Awake*, 1971) a school psychologist calls fifteen-year-old Susan into her office to serve as an example to viewers of the harm that can come to girls who experiment with sex too early in life. 'You know we only want to help you,' the doctor explains, 'so you must tell me everything, every detail…' Susan is thus prompted to recount the circumstances that lead her to attempted suicide. Her first sexual forays flash across the screen as she describes her early initiation into carnal desire which fails to deliver sexual pleasure. *Immer wieder* ('over and over again') she pleads for more sex with her lovers in the unfulfilled hopes of reaching orgasm. After her parents decide to lease a room in the house, she goes to great lengths to seduce the new lodger. When finally his willpower caves, Susan's parents enter the room and discover their daughter engaged in aerobic intercourse. Susan's father, convinced of her innocence, presses charges against the lodger.

**FIGURE 5** Susan hangs herself from the attic rafters: *The Schoolgirl Reports, Part Two: What Keeps Parents Awake* (1971)

43

From the bedroom, we move to the courtroom where Susan, under oath, is compelled by the defending attorney to confess the details of her immoderate sexual past. Rather than presenting the erotic flashbacks once again, we hear her repeated confession over shots of her parents' – and especially her father's – disbelieving reaction. Charges of statutory rape are dropped, according to the law, when the girl in question has a history of promiscuity. After the trial, her father presses her for an even more detailed confession until his violent and scornful reproach drives Susan to hang herself by the rafters in the family attic. In the final shot of the flashback, the father releases Susan's limp, but still-breathing, body from her home-made noose. Now back in the psychologist's office, Susan – who earlier remarked that her favourite subject in school is German history (*Deutsche Geschichte*) – must come to terms with her transgressions by telling her story (her *Geschichte*) over and over again – (*Immer wieder!*). The repetitions of sex are transmuted into compulsions of confession.

Susan's triple confession sets in motion what Foucault describes as the 'perpetual spirals of power and pleasure'. The intensity of the confession renews the questioner's and viewer's curiosity and satisfaction, while the one who confesses, who scandalises authority, is also realising 'the pleasure that kindles at having to evade this power, flee from it, fool it, or travesty it'.[12] Indeed, early in her account, Susan flaunts the fact that her affairs occurred right under her father's nose, and that she would continue to sleep around until caught. Most of the films in this series move through cycles of breaking rules, being caught and confessing – though not always in this order – and reveal not a repression of sexuality but a play of power and pleasure which comes from making and breaking rules of sexual conduct.

Confessions also explicitly structure other vignettes in the second film, from Monika and Emi whose story is presented to us as they turn themselves in to the police, to Elke who repeats the story of her lost virginity to the 'psychologist'. In the ninth *Schoolgirl Report*, two police offers read to each other the sworn confessions of a group of teens who are brought in after suffering a near-fatal car crash. Each vignette recounts what (sexual acts) brought each student to the party that concluded with the ill-fated drag race. All of the episodes are based on someone – a parent, the psychologist, a police officer, the girls themselves – sharing a story about a girl's experimentation with illicit sex.

Of course, erotic confessional literature goes back to the seventeenth century and beyond, and the confession would appear to be a mainstay of the soft-core film genre. From Chu Hong's *Intimate Confessions of a Chinese Courtesan* (Hong Kong, 1972) to Ohara's *Wet Rope Confession* (Japan, 1979), the mere inclusion of the word in the title promises the viewer that she will be made privy to salacious secrets. Yet rarely do such films depict the act of disclosure itself. Even Hofbauer's 1970 *Confessions of a Sixthform Virgin* has little recourse to an actual confession. The very fact that such films include this word in the title speaks to the allure of a confession; that the *Schoolgirl Reports* are obsessed with, and organised around the act, however, reveals something more.

As a story and as history, the confession constitutes its teller as a social subject. It returns us to the moment when a girl loses her sexual innocence, an instant that can be avowed but not altered. In confessing, she provides the contours and causality for her story and gains a sense of herself as someone with a recognised and recognisable past. Though psychologists in the series emphasise that adolescent and even pre-pubescent sexuality is normal, the problems arise when girls move from natural, libidinal life into codified social roles of daughters, students, mothers, plaintiffs and victims for whom such acts have moral and legal consequences. The *Reports* dramatise a girl's confrontation with her past where sex is often a gateway to other offences including blackmail, drug use, shoplifting, perjury and the like – past acts for which these girls can only atone through the act of disclosure. In sum, sex as marked by the confession, by auto-narration, is an initiation into the responsibilities and limitations of adult citizenship.

## SEXUAL AND HISTORICAL AWAKENINGS

The confession is also an engagement with the causes and effects of history. As Benedict Anderson muses, individual identity, 'because it cannot be "remembered", must be narrated'. Biographies of individuals and of nations are always negotiating the suppression and inclusion of events necessary to produce a narrative palatable to the self and to the citizenry. While the individual has one birth and one death, the nation overwhelms the timeline of a single life. In order to fold our life into a narrative of nation, traumatic episodes (deaths, holocausts, wars, martyrs, assassinations) 'must be remembered/ forgotten as "our own"'.[13] Knowingly or not, Hofbauer gestures to this historical mandate at the end of the second report, in a vignette which conspicuously includes no pornographic scenes. Eighteen-year-old Barbara, who decides to bear a child out of wedlock much to her parents' stern disapproval, discovers that her parents were married some months after her birth. Not only is the parental reproof exposed as a hypocritical suppression of their own wayward past, but the daughter's radicalism is actually reproducing (as opposed to defying) her parent's history.

More importantly, this little banal story, like the others in the film, displaces larger questions of national history onto the more manageable and tame problems of the family; these are the stories that comprise what Lauren Berlant and Michael Warner call 'the amnesia archive' of collective memory. Memory, like history, 'is the amnesia you like'.[14] Significantly, the final shot of the film frames Barbara and her friends walking down Leopoldstrasse towards Munich's nineteenth-century Siegestor (Victory Arch), a memorial to Bavarian militarism that was destroyed in World War Two, and rebuilt and rededicated in 1973 as a national monument to peace. The Victory Arch functions in the opening and closing shots of this film (and in the shots that bookends the entire series) to situate these vignettes in the real space of German cities and in the narrative arc of German history which is always being remembered, forgotten and revised. The Victory Arch performs for cultural memory what the confession does for the individual. Foucault remarks that the confession exonerates and purifies the confessor. 'It unburdens him of his wrongs, liberates him, and promises him salvation.'[15]

The redemptive act of remembering and recounting sex finds its inverse in those sexual acts that are committed but suppressed. With the fourth and most interesting installment of the series, *Was Eltern oft Verzweifeln Läßt* (*What Drives Parents to Despair*, 1972), Hofbauer explores more taboo scenarios including incest, racially-charged gang rape, and sex between German girls and guest workers. In this film, he abandons the confessions, the girl-on-the-street interviews and the PTA meetings, using only a male voice-over narration to link one tale to the next. Rather than confessing and atoning for sexual indiscretions in a public forum, the youth in these episodes, we are told, pass into a normal sex life by forgetting and/or sublimating their introduction to libidinal wish fulfilment.

45

**FIGURE 6** The final shot of the film – The Victory Arch: *The Schoolgirl Reports, Part Two: What Keeps Parents Awake* (1971)

Halfway through the film we meet sixteen-year-old Barbara and her eighteen-year-old brother Wolfgang, who not only attend the same school but, due to their parents' modest incomes, share the same bedroom. As a result of these living arrangements, Barbara has become erotically fixated on her brother, particularly after she spies him having sex with another girl. Racked with guilt over her incestuous desire, Barbara has a psychedelic dream. First her father, who is constantly ordering the siblings to get undressed and go to bed oblivious that they are no longer children, commands Barbara in her dream to strip, threatening her with a kebab skewer. Pinned under her father's heaving body and on the brink of orgasm, Barbara's dream shifts. She now finds herself naked before a military tribunal where she stands accused of brotherly love. Next to her, wearing a nun's habit, is her brother's girlfriend who, judged guilty, is executed. As the soldiers fire, the wounded girl disrobes, smears her own blood across her body, and falls dead in ecstatic pleasure.

Not incidentally, the dream iconography we recognise from the décor of Barbara and Wolfgang's bedroom includes a sexy nun poster, an antique sword that hangs next to the dresser and an anti-war poster in which a solider is reeling from a bullet in a mock-up of the famous Spanish Civil War photo. We know that Barbara, a virgin, is both fixated on and scared of having sex. It thus stands to reason that she conflates the shower of bullets and blood with the girlfriend's orgasmic pleasure. But this is more than just a virgin's nightmare after falling asleep in a room filled with a phantasmagoria of objects. In Barbara's dream her father's poor judgement metamorphoses into a disturbing Oedipal scenario, one that is literally and figuratively shot through with sins of the past. In insisting that they share a room and undress for bed, the father abets this incest fantasy. Forced to have sex with her

**FIGURE 7** Barbara stands before a firing squad, condemned for brotherly love: *The Schoolgirl Reports, Part Four: What Drives Parents to Despair* (1972)

father, but sentenced to death for desiring her brother, Barbara's fantasy implicates the entire family. The girlfriend, the outsider who stands wrongly accused, is eliminated.

The violent nature of the military execution suggests that the sins of the parents run deeper and mingle in Barbara's dreamscape with the primal scene of German history – here figured as a melange of World War One and World War Two symbolism. Barbara's dream of sex is more complicated than simply losing her innocence: to know forbidden desire is to access a violent historical imaginary and to participate in the drama of guilt, shame and victimisation. Sexual awakenings always threaten to arouse the history that might otherwise sleep. In her dream, Barbara makes those acts of history her own.

Barbara's own execution in the dream jolts her back to consciousness and to a view of her brother in the shower. She lures him to bed and they make love against the backdrop of his 'why war?' poster which again links incest to military brutality. After the most satisfying sex, Wolfgang vows that this is the first and last time. The narrator confirms that Barbara will soon meet and fall in love with the man of her dreams and lead a perfectly normal life. Because Barbara is never caught with her brother, there is neither an opportunity for her to confess nor a mandate that she remember. Even Wolfgang suggests that they forget the entire ordeal. Our final image of Barbara, naked and distraught after her real and imagined incestuous sex, undercuts the possibility of a rapid rehabilitation to normalcy. Or, if Barbara goes on to lead a normal sex life, it will be forever tainted by her traumatic initiation into womanhood.

The connections between desire and criminality, confessing and forgetting, and between self knowledge and historical knowledge in these films resonated with contemporary discourses on how Germany could begin to cope with its monstrous past. Following Alexander and Margarete Mitscherlich's influential 1967 study, *The Inability to Mourn*, the West German psychotherapeutic community was beginning to consolidate its research on the psychic tolls of National Socialism. Applying the principles of psychoanalysis to the German collective unconscious, the Mitscherlichs charged that the adult population, surprisingly untroubled by feelings of guilt, remorse and shame for the atrocities committed in their name during the war, was living in an acute state of historical denial. Unable to confront their complicity with the final solution or process their grief at losing the father-figure Hitler, into whom they had collapsed their individual ego-ideals, most Germans had now broken off all 'affective bridges with the immediate past'. As a result Germans were incapable of mourning the victims of the war:

> If memory was ever admitted, it was only in order to balance one's own guilt against that of the other. Many horrors had been unavoidable, it was claimed, because they had been dictated by crimes committed by the adversary. Thus, any particular guilt attaching to oneself ends by disappearing completely. … If somehow, somewhere, one finds an object deserving of sympathy, it usually turns out to be none other than oneself.[16]

Unchecked, this cycle of dissolution would doom Germans to repeat their history – to project the surplus aggression that Hitler had harnessed onto other others. Rather than face the self-devaluation that accompanies melancholia, Germans, the study argued, choose instead to invest vast energy into forgetting.

## SEX AND FAMILY HISTORY

Perhaps more central to this film cycle, the Mitscherlichs began to investigate the aggregate effects of uncathected guilt on later generations and the apparent inability of the children to adequately process their inheritance:

> With a shrug of their shoulders the young repudiate any imputation of responsibility for the infamous behaviour of their elders. Of course, identification with the parent, and with the problems connected with the parents' sense of guilt, continues to operate unconsciously. Anyone, anywhere, who dares oppose the political views of these young people is promptly branded as a 'fascist'.[17]

Subsequent studies of post-war family dynamics, most of which were published in the 1980s, confirmed this 'second generation syndrome' – the guilt that comes with being the child or grandchild of Nazi perpetrators and collaborators. Noting that parents and grandparents hid from their children those ghastly, but formative, stories of World War Two, psychologist Sammy Speier claimed that the conjunction of historical denial and parental amnesia had, in effect, created the '"don't care" generation' who seemed to be without a past or future. The erasure of family history had produced a psychic and narrative vacuum in the subsequent generations:

> Since Auschwitz there is no longer any narrative tradition, and hardly any parents and grandparents are left who will take their children on their lap and tell them about their lives in the old days. ... Nowadays, however, the parents' and grandparents' repertoire of stories is no longer made up of 'simple' war and adventure stories, but rather of questionable, shameful, even dangerous and horrible stories, which can drive you insane.[18]

Faced with either apathy or psychosis, second generation patients abided by the 'rule of abstinence' to avert the difficult confrontation with an unreal reality. It became clear to Speier that Freud's ahistorical family romance and the universal enigma of sexual difference were alone no longer sufficient to explain the founding trauma of German citizenship:

> It is easier to talk with patients in psychoanalysis about the bedroom than about the gas chamber. However, the formula, 'that's oedipal', does not make the repressed reality of Auschwitz disappear.[19]

On the surface, generational animosity had become pointedly political, but this conflict, psychologists argued, was in fact constitutive of suppressed inherited culpability. 'In the psyches of those born after 1945', write Barbara Heimannsberg and Christoph Schmidt, 'diffuse anxiety and feelings of guilt can be the half-erased traces of the Nazi past. ... [M]any Nazi values were retained and unconsciously passed on to the next generation – as were the traumas.'[20] Driven by the quest to discover, decode and decontaminate the psychic engrams of Nazism, psychotherapists emphasised that sexuality and family dynamics were inseparable from the history that bore them, and these connections needed to be articulated through individual and group therapy. The quest for self knowledge would necessitate a confrontation with history, and historical knowledge would be bound to the story of one's own origins.

In order to comprehend their individual and national past, the children and grandchildren of Nazi-era Germans had to recover these lost family narratives, a process that always threatened to make strangers out of fathers, mothers and grandparents, and to create corrosive cycles of suspicion between the generations. While, in the immediate post-war years, children and parents colluded to put the past behind them, the public debate surrounding the 1964 Auschwitz trials in Frankfurt brought to public attention that former Nazis were comfortably ensconced in the post-war bureaucracy. Student activists took to the street to protest the Vietnam war and fascist, capitalist foreign governments. In Germany, they targeted former Nazis who held positions in the police and judicial system. Nationwide student demonstrations against the court proceedings of the 1967 Ohnesorg shooting and the assassination attempt against SDS leader Rudi Dutschke culminated in the radical terrorism of the 1970s and the protracted trials against the self-proclaimed leftist militant Fritz Teufel. The incidents of German police brutality led not a few 'sixty-eighters' to conclude that the generation who had persecuted the Jews had now turned their violent conservatism against their own children.[21]

At home, students became suspicious of their own parents. In his study of parent biographies – the posthumous stories of Nazi parents written by their children – Michael Schneider finds that what seems at first to be authors' political programme of revealing the German past through family history is 'to a much greater extent, an interest in their own beginnings'. He continues:

> The preoccupation with the political pasts of the parents, therefore, has a surrogate function, and in some cases a retaliatory one – the child strikes out against the Nazi, but is really aiming at the parent from whom he or she did not receive enough attention and love.[22]

What is interesting in Schneider's account of these biographies are the recurring patterns of discovery and blame. Children stumble upon their fathers' incriminating letters, photographs and diaries, and are forced to reconcile the discrepancy between the man at the dinner table and the one photographed in a Nazi uniform. Even when no concrete evidence presented itself, the children would look for symptoms of guilt in their parents; slips of the tongue, strange ticks and quirks made all parents suspicious in this new psychopathology of German everyday life. Repulsed by, but always seeking to discover, the 'Nazi phantom-figures of their father', this generation was haunted, like latterday Hamlets, by a kind of Nazi gothic. In Schneider's analysis, this search for criminal symptoms and will to public protest was itself symptomatic of concealed longings and subjective motivations:

> These radicalised sons and daughters of the bourgeoisie who took to the streets with flags unfurled, clenched fists and political demands, were simultaneously protesting against something else which could not be conceptualised in political or economic terms – namely, the emotional deficits from which they were suffering because of childhoods wasted in restrictive living conditions and numb joylessness.[23]

Students made their parents into political subjects in order to separate themselves from the family ties that bound them to a damning history, so that they, like their parents, might cut off the affective bridges to the past. The anti-authoritarian revolution and the politics of memory, however diffused they may have become by the 1980s, threatened to drive a permanent wedge between the generations.

If the 'sixty-eighters' had politicised their parents to the point of eviscerating family ties, and if, in some cases, politics deflected the post-traumatic dysfunctionality that plagued many middle-class homes, the *Schoolgirl Reports* recast post-war politics and family conflict in terms of adolescent sex. Read conservatively, Hofbauer's series exposes for pornographic enjoyment the sexual misdeeds of a post-war generation that was proclaiming its innocence. By displacing onto the daughters the shame and guilt more aptly associated with their fathers, these films sexually objectify their subjects and reverse the terms of familial alienation. It is not the parents whose criminal pasts make them strange and unfamiliar, but the daughters and sons who become alien the moment their pasts are revealed. So often in the series, mischievous girls are shown at the dinner table with their parents and siblings, playing the daughter role. This series puts German youth on trial revealing, and in this way containing, the politics of a more radical revolution. If older German men were the principle viewers of these films, such scenarios would have not only pornographic appeal, but would assure viewers that even self-righteous youths have something to hide. The sexually liberated body, mostly the girl body, is not delivered from German history or returned to a time before Auschwitz but is guilty of dangerous desire. Such a reading, however, presumes a homogenous audience. (Even Thomas Elsaesser writes that the youth audience – along with the guest workers – was attracted to exploitation productions. And Georg Seesslen notes that by the late 1970s, women accounted for up to 40 per cent of the audience for pornographic features.)[24] Thus, it may be more fruitful to consider how this series is mediating rather than simply foreclosing the generational and sexual politics of the 1970s.

## THE RHETORICS OF SOFT-CORE PORNOGRAPHY

Genre cinema has long been understood as a form of cultural problem – solving in that it takes up irreconcilable conflicts in society and offers improbable but satisfactory resolutions, very often delimiting problems and their solutions to those dominant culture is able to address.[25] Linda Williams' groundbreaking study of hard-core reveals that in these narratives, sex is the problem for which more, good sex is the solution. Yet, as with the musical, it is very often the other problems that are mapped on to the field of sexual difference, pleasure and displeasure that good sex serves to resolve. As Williams explains, pornography is often below the radar of film criticism, because we assume the natural fact of sex but fail to consider its rhetorical function within the film. Though pornography, like other mainstream genres, avoids the systemic roots of conflict, this genre more than others lays bare the power dynamics between the sexes from where questions of age, class and racial difference may be negotiated.[26]

As soft-core pornography, the *Schoolgirl Reports* are elusive about the fact of sex, but devote far more screen time to the discussion, assessment and judgement of problems related to good and bad sex. In *Part 6: Was Eltern gern vertuschen möchten* (*What Parents Would Gladly Hush Up*, 1973), a teenage couple is discovered having sex after school beneath the piano in the music room – an appointment, the voice-over tells us, they have been keeping for the last two weeks. The couple is subsequently brought before the parent-teacher board who, as in the first part, will hear the evidence and decide whether the students should be expelled. Outraged that they should be punished for being in love, the pair relays stories about themselves and other teens in order to compare their music-room misdemeanour to the far more outlandish sexual escapades of their peers. Soon the teachers and parents are on trial themselves. From the married fencing instructor who thrusts and parries with an amorous schoolgirl in the locker room, to the alcoholic father who prostitutes his daughter in order to pay off his debts, adults are as culpable for the misdeeds of high-school students as are the students themselves, who bribe, rape and even kill out of frustrated desire. Lest we throw up our hands at this rampant degeneracy or indiscriminately denounce all teenagers, the psychologist intervenes with tempered advice. The problems of student insolence and lawlessness, and conflicts between parents and their children, are really problems of sex. And the problem of sex can be distilled to the problem of differentiating sex from love. In or out of wedlock, within or across generations, bad sex is a product of irrational lust, and good sex is an expression of love. 'And love', the voice-over declares as the now-vindicated couple walks with their parents through the Siegestor 'is the element of life'. This extended and finally sentimental example speaks to the inherent conciliatory rhetoric of the series that attempts to solve an array of problems through the cipher of sex and to blur the boundaries between the legal and moral sense of guilt.

51

## CONCLUSION

It may be appropriate to conclude this chapter with a consideration of the *Schoolgirl Reports* series in connection with Michael Geyer's work on post-war memory politics. For Geyer, one of the principle symptoms of historical reckoning in West Germany was a conceptual melding of religious ethics and secular politics:

> Individual introspection, public tribunals to assure collectivity, critiques of hidden motives and intentions – all made up a culture of guilt and salvation. … The acknowledgement of guilt under the watchful eye of Western modernity became the measure of progress, individual and collective, in the West German politics of memory.[27]

And yet, for most Germans the actual work of remembering occurred not in the form of individual recollection; nor where memories subject to a 'tribunal of conscious in a culture of guilt'. It was rather the mass-mediated morality plays of the Holocaust in television and film that liberated Germans from their past – representations, Geyer comments

> that implicated no one in particular, but merely represented actions and non-actions, attitudes and behaviours which everyone remembered, and whose bitter consequences were now summed up in a story that led inescapably to annihilation and catastrophe.[28]

These films and television broadcasts, however, effected a transformation in their viewers 'from a pursuit of memory to a pursuit of history'. Geyer's argument suggests that the German reconciliation with history did not necessary involve actual acts of repentance; guilt and its absolution can circulate abstractly in a media-saturated image world where the popular turn to German history produced a vaguely sentimental, feminised 'culture of shame'.

Conversely, the *Schoolgirl Reports* work out the implications of the act of confessing without explicit reference to Germany's past and, in this way, participate in the post-war therapeutic public sphere. As genre-based, soft-core, trash cinema, these films negotiate in important and unassuming ways *not* the historical facts, but the affective and arousing process of remembering. In dramatising the pleasure and release that comes with the articulation of past transgressions, these films go one step further. They expose and putatively resolve and naturalise not only an erotics of guilt, but the guilty pleasure that comes with remembering one's own illicit history.

# CHAPTER 4
# VIOLENCE, TIMING AND THE COMEDY TEAM IN ALEX DE LA IGLESIA'S MUERTOS DE RISA

Dona M. Kercher[1]

## INTRODUCTION

Among current Spanish directors, Alex de la Iglesia represents the changing place of film in a multimedia global environment. This is due, in part, to his unique background. After receiving a degree in philosophy from Deusto, he drew comics for the magazine *Trokola* and various newspapers.[2] Meanwhile, he also worked as an artistic director in theatre and television productions. He has maintained a consistent technological look throughout his six feature films to date. This chapter focuses on how Alex de la Iglesia historicises the political (the local) and the technological (the global) in novel ways. Before paying attention to one of his most ambitious projects yet, *Muertos de risa* (*Dying of Laughter*, 1999), we need to underscore de la Iglesia's cinematic profile.

His most recent film, *800 Balas* (*800 Bullets*, 2002), opened to wide acclaim, displaying his trademark wild and surreal humour, grotesque violence and the social subtext of almost all of his movies. His previous film, *La comunidad* (*Common Wealth*), inaugurated the 2000 San Sebastián Film Festival, likewise to considerable acclaim. De la Iglesia's background in comics manifests itself strongly in the animated credit sequence to his 1999 black comedy *Muertos de risa*. The style of the animated line drawings recalls the work of Edward Gorey, who like de la Iglesia is known for his dark humour. The coloration sets a retro scene, evocative of the fetishised openings of Pedro Almodóvar's *Mujeres al borde de un ataque de nervios* (*Women on the Verge of a Nervous Breakdown*, 1988) or Carlos Saura's *Peppermint frappé* (1967). The sequence introduces motifs not only as a prelude to the film's story and character typology, such as in the images of the comedy team and the silhouetted go-go girls, but also as humorous icons of the creative process, as in the magic act or the black goat jumping over the typewriter keyboard. The sequence thus foreshadows the self-reflective approach of the movie. The soundtrack is circus-like, evoking a Fellini-esque fantasy mood.

## TRANSNATIONAL CULT STATUS AS A SPANISH TECHIE

Besides animation, de la Iglesia has shown interest in other new media, namely video games. He has invited web browsers to collaborate with him online to make a video game. Underscoring de la Iglesia's investment in the digital age, the alternative media 'press', the e-zine *Dossiernegro*, discusses his films in a special issue devoted to the 'directores de culto' (cult directors), John Waters, David Lynch and Alex de la Iglesia. Significantly, *Muertos de risa* was screened, and well received according to the responses on its web site, at the 2000 Montreal Fantasia Film Festival, a forum generally associated with action/kung-fu and animé pictures.

What we see in all of de la Iglesia's films are scenes that call attention to technology in ways that insert Spanish cinema onto a global scene and often critique that very media process. De la Iglesia is also unique in Spanish film history in copying special effects techniques that have themselves been breakthroughs in international cinema history, as generally defined by Hollywood industry standards. He received the Goya, the Spanish equivalent of the Oscar, for the special effects of *Día de la bestia* (*Day of the Beast*, 1995), besides winning that year for best picture. In his article on *Día de la bestia* Malcolm Compitello lauds de la Iglesia's *Modern Times* remake scene:

> In one of the best special effects ever staged in Spanish film, de la Iglesia literally hangs his protagonists on the huge neon Schweppes sign that adorns the front of the Capitol Building.[3]

In the same film, de la Iglesia uses blue screen at the moment when the Devil appears on a skyscraper and throws one of the main characters to his death. De la Iglesia's use of special effects is an important element to assess how recent Spanish cinema negotiates the national/global interface. I would argue that his films consistently are most successful, contestatory and intellectually challenging when they allude to nationally inflected images. It bears noting that the special effects in both *Acción mutante* (1992) and *Día de la bestia* might not innovate beyond Hollywood standards, but allude to well-known images of Goya's 'black paintings', respectively 'Asomodea' and 'El Gran Cabrón'. In this chapter I will analyse another example of de la Iglesia's special effects – the placing of a character into historical footage, in *Muertos de risa* – and explore how the political continues to be reread through media history.

What is most revealing about de la Iglesia's citation of cutting edge, technological innovation is the reception these gestures have had within Spain. On the one hand, one senses a certain pride that Spain has arrived, at least strongly on the European scene, as a vibrant, contemporary culture. John Hopewell forecast this:

> Thus the 'significant' cinematographic transition which has triumphed in Spain has been the appearance, development and definitive hegemony of a cinema of a European liberal style.[4]

This pride in place is evident, for instance, in Juan Manuel de Prada's enthusiastic assessment of the transformative power that *Día de la bestia* has over Madrid: 'Seldom has Madrid been portrayed in such a hallucinogenic manner metamorphosed into a city with laws at the margins of physics and reason.'[5] At the same time, the ways in which de la Iglesia employs his 'innovations' are often themselves parodic, so that what we may at first recognise as a nationalist gesture is also a critique of the process. The use of blue screen in the aforementioned climatic scene of *Día de la bestia* is a prime example. The shot is so stark that the bizarre character José Marí appears suspended in mid-air before being thrown off a building against nothing but a blue screen. Unlike the Schweppes/*Modern Times* sequence which Compitello celebrates, the effect here is campy citation of well-known uses of blue screen in Hollywood films. We recognise the special effect, but we also note an absurdity to the bare-bones use of the artifice. Overall, the use of special effects, however, positions de la Iglesia well for a young audience. In this regard his work resembles that of Alejandro Amenábar, director of *Tesis* (*Thesis*, 1996) and *Abre los ojos* (*Open Your Eyes*, 1997). Paul Julian Smith's concluding comments in a recent review of *Abre los ojos* in *Sight and Sound* could apply equally well to de la Iglesia:

> Nonetheless, Amenábar's virtuoso style and connection to the youth audience, both of which are resented by the Spanish film establishment, make him a plausible model outside of Spain for a European cinema that bridges the gap between arthouse and mainstream.[6]

## HIGH PRODUCTION VALUES, NEW GENRES, PEDRO ALMODÓVAR AND ANDRÉS VINCENTE GÓMEZ

Special effects or a virtuoso style, marks of high production values in film, do not come easily or cheaply. Indeed, de la Iglesia is known for his genre experimentation – science fiction, horror, road film, crime story – most often within a general rubric of black comedy that includes a considerable dose of gratuitous violence. Like Almodóvar, de la Iglesia is not a product of a Spanish film school. This puts him outside of the film establishment. But he is, in a sense, a product of Almodóvar. De la Iglesia's first feature film *Acción mutante* was one of the first films Almodóvar produced through his own production company El Deseo. About *Acción mutante*, José Arroyo writes:

> [I]t pushed graphic representations of sex and violence to the point of comic dis-belief, managing to be shocking and funny. Perhaps because *Acción mutante* seemed to think its every infraction of good taste was hilarious, it gained a fervent following among adolescent boys.[7]

Almodóvar's own artistic independence and extraordinary profitability within the Spanish film industry has long been asserted and at times attributed to the existence of his loyal 'family' of co-workers that is El Deseo.[8] Smith points out that having his own production company allowed Almodóvar the luxury to film sequences in order. Not all first-time directors produced by El Deseo have shared de la Iglesia's eventual triumphs; Mónica Laguna's *Tengo una casa* (1996) is one example of a youth-oriented, but artistically abysmal, film backed by El Deseo. But there is no question that the selection by Almodóvar positioned de la Iglesia for eventual recognition in a transnational context. De la Iglesia entered the market before Spanish government film subsidies had an effective special category targeted to first-time directors, and also before Eurimages, the system of European co-production support, was strongly viable for Spain. As Angus Finney argues, European film industries in the 1990s were particularly blind to the need to train film producers, instead placing emphasis in film schools on the development of directors.[9]

After *Acción mutante,* all of de la Iglesia's films were produced by Andrés Vincente Gómez, 'the top Spanish producer',[10] active in the business since 1962 and from 1994 the head of Sogotel's production unit. All these subsequent films have been co-productions. From his earliest projects, Gómez's career has been distinguished in its emphasis on foreign markets. He worked in charge of foreign markets, for example, for two years for Elías Querejeta, perhaps the most significant Spanish producer ever in terms of the artistic impact of the films he produced. Of Gómez's relationship with de la Iglesia, Antonio Santamarina Alcón writes, 'his good nose also leads him to collaborate with the most restless and promising young directors of the 1990s'.[11] Gómez produced Fernando Trueba's international success, the Oscar-winning *Belle époque* (1992) and two critical disasters aimed at an international market, *El sueño del mono loco* (*Twisted Obsession*, 1989) and the Hollywood-farce *Two Much* (1995).

De la Iglesia followed this same ill-fated pattern into Hollywood and English-language production with *Perdita Durango* (1997), generally termed a critical disaster. As Arroyo intones:

> Even if Alex de la Iglesia is one of the most interesting young directors working today, *Perdita Durango* is not the film that will convince anyone of this fact.[12]

To be fair to de la Iglesia, he picked up the *Perdita Durango* project after the Catalan director Bigas Luna pulled out of it. The script had numerous problems from the start. In an overall positive review the Spanish critic M. Torreiro of *El País* still faults the logic of the script above all, asking

> why a love relationship marked by the most absolute madness and by unstoppable passion suddenly is interrupted, and even dissolved towards the middle of the picture, when the character for whom the film is named loses her lead role.[13]

Yet, *Perdita Durango* fell flat because de la Iglesia did not know American or Mexican culture well enough. For American mainstream culture, the film lacked a great soundtrack. For Hispanic cultures, the film, especially the santería sequences, came off flat-footed. Arroyo is absolutely correct when he pans *Perdita Durango*:

The problem with *Perdita Durango* is that nobody in this Spanish-American production knows enough about the American culture (as embodied in the characters of Duane and Estelle) the film is meant to be ridiculing to tease out the subtleties and nuances that would transform mere crudity into social satire, shock and laughter.[14]

In the end what is significant about *Perdita Durango* is that it represents for Spanish cinema the continued Hollywood dominance of the world entertainment market. De la Iglesia 'tailored it' to Hollywood, to make an English-language production. In this he joined a very select group of European directors to even attempt to break into the dominant industry, which Marsha Kinder called, in a reference to Buñuel, 'the obscure object of global desire'.[15] More sinisterly, it also means that Spanish directors, after they develop strong careers in Europe, continue to be expected to interpret Hispanic culture for a US Latino market.

## MUERTOS DE RISA: A RETURN TO NATIONAL REFERENTS AND POLITICAL COMMENTARY

Unlike *Perdita Durango*, de la Iglesia's 1999 film *Muertos de risa* is rife with subtleties, evoking Spanish national history and culture. Within the course of de la Iglesia's career, this return to national referents can perhaps be read as resistance to global capitalism. Nonetheless, the commonality of interests defined in this film is different from other significant Spanish films of its same genre. *Muertos de risa* is a less regionally inflected film than *Día de la bestia*, whose main character, a Jesuit theologian, was Ur-Basque. As such it echoes Dimitris Eleftheriotis who notes a trend to 'the increasing engagement of European films with precisely the issues of identity, similarity and difference, and cultural exchange'.[16]

It is worth noting that *Muertos de risa* came on the heels of the politically incorrect comedy, *Torrente, brazo tonto de la ley* (*Torrente, the Dumb Arm of the Law*), the highest grossing Spanish film in history, in 1998. Its main character, Torrente, is an alcoholic, fascist policeman who acts out against immigrants and any rules of physical propriety. Like *Muertos de risa*, *Torrente* starred Santiago Segura; actually, *Torrente* was Segura's first film. Segura's 'neocostumbrismo subversivo' is closely associated with de la Iglesia.[17] Yet precisely the issues of pan-European 'cultural difference and exchange', as detailed by Eleftheriotis, and at the heart of *Torrente*, seem absent from de la Iglesia's *Muertos de risa*, which was released one year later (with ads featuring Segura).

*Muertos de risa* tells the story of the comedy team of Nino and Bruno. They meet in a remote, shabby nightclub in Andalucía in the waning years of the Franco regime. When they try out for a variety show, they fortuitously discover that slap humour has a cathartic effect on the audience. From then on their rise to fame as a comedy team is meteoric. *Muertos de risa* juxtaposes two decades of their lives, the 1970s and the 1990s, as it foregrounds Nino and Bruno in the media event of Spanish history. Beneath the surface of camaraderie and media adulation, the two become mortal enemies. At their reunion television special on New Year's Eve 1993, they kill each other in an on-stage bloodbath.

In part because it is rereading 1970s Spanish history and the national media monopoly of that time period, *Muertos de risa* deals with the production of a Spanish national identity *through* the media. Whereas Marie-Soledad Rodríguez has argued that Torrente's initial appearance on a stage as an actor clues the audience that *Torrente* should be perceived as parody, and further, thus defused of racist undertones,[18] *Muertos de risa* also begins with the protagonists, two comedians, moving onto a television stage, but its insistence on the place of media staging in the culture avoids the same distancing effect. Instead, it invites a serious examination of the role of the media in the formation of historical consciousness. Moreover, television history, itself still in its infancy, is advanced by the film. (Tellingly, de la Iglesia in fact had to recreate a famous episode of the television show *Directísimo* for his film because the original copy of the show had disappeared.)

Acknowledging the role of media is not new to de la Iglesia. Since *Acción mutante*, he has drawn inspiration from popular media. In *Día de la bestia*, the protagonist, a Jesuit priest, teams up with the counter-culture manager of a heavy metal record store to save civilisation by short-circuiting the birth of the Antichrist. They coerce the host of a television talk show on the occult to enlist in their cause, too. *Muertos de risa* continues the critique of the contemporary media through black humour begun in *Día de la bestia*. Whereas *Día de la bestia* was apocalyptically set to go off on Noche Buena, Christmas Eve, *Muertos de risa* takes as its zero hour Noche Vieja, New Year's Eve. In all, most Spanish critics welcomed *Muertos de risa* as the return of de la Iglesia to better timing, to his characteristic 'peculiar universes that provided in parallel an indirectly allegorical reading of the current situation'[19] after the debacle of *Perdita Durango*.

Through close analysis I intend to show how *Muertos de risa* assumes an anti-intellectual popular stance of dismissible bad taste and public spectacle to expose what Kinder, with regard to other Spanish films, has termed a distinctly Spanish 'mode of representation of violence'.[20] Recently, Malcolm Compitello has taken issue with Kinder's reading of *Día de la bestia* as merely 'a kind of an allegory of the excesses of Socialism' to argue that it plots a condemnation of a wider sort', namely that it 'contributes to an understanding of how politics is merely one part of the dynamic interplay of forces through which urbanised capital forms consciousness'.[21] I will argue with Compitello that in the way that *Muertos de risa* represents Spanish television history it likewise confronts the commodification of culture in Spain, as did de la Iglesia's previous work.

## THE CRITIQUE OF COMMODIFICATION WITHIN SPANISH CULTURAL HISTORY

*Muertos de risa* depicts Nino and Bruno's success above all as a commercial one. Clips from actual black-and-white 1970s television commercials for frozen popsicles, 'Flag Golosina' in the sequence 'La apuesta' ('The bet'), set the scene and introduced a paradigm for the subsequent sequence 'Y llegó el éxito' ('And success arrived'). The epitome of Nino and Bruno's whirlwind success is a fictitious ad for children's cupcakes, 'Pastelitos Nino y Bruno', done in contemporary Teletubbies style. On a hill full of sunflowers little girls in white dresses surround Nino and Bruno in tuxedos as they sign autographs. The representation critiques the pernicious exploitation of children through the commodification of the media star in that the camera swings around to show the backs of Nino and Bruno crawling with insects. The final image, in which their dark backs fill the frame, draws additional shock value since the commercial's dialogue is describing the cupcakes' filling, and hence implies that the children are being enticed into eating a disgusting product.

On the one hand, the superimposed beehive backs are yet another example of special effects in de la Iglesia's work. More specifically, the image recalls Dalí and Buñuel's surrealist depiction of corruption and putrefaction, which appeared in *Un perro andaluz* (*Un chien andalou*, 1928). More recently it has resurfaced in the protagonist's nightmare in Bigas Luna's film *Huevos de oro* (*Golden Balls*, 1993). The allusion to Dalí/Buñuel in *Muertos de risa* thus draws attention to the subversive, critical potential of the film. It also connects de la Iglesia's film to a particularly Spanish visual arts tradition.

Humour plays an essential role in the film. In an interview that appears as supplementary material to the DVD of *Muertos de risa*, de la Iglesia observes that Spanish comedy, unlike its American counterpart, relies particularly strongly on the comedy team. In *Refiguring Spain*, Kinder draws parallels between the unlikely duo of priest and rock store manager in *Día de la bestia*, and Don Quixote and Sancho.[22] In *Muertos de risa* the manager takes the protagonists to a wax museum to view the greats of Spanish humour, concentrating above all on Tip and Coll. Whereas the dialogue notes other comedy teams like Abbott and Costello, for an international audience, the imaginary museum of the film frames Tip and Coll as larger than life. In the 1970s Tip and Coll based their politically topical humour, both in live performances and in their columns for the weekly *Interviu*, mostly on word play. They symbolised Spain's transition to democracy and they reached their greatest popularity during Adolfo Suárez's government. It bears remembering that Suárez was himself a former head of RTVE, when it was popularly called 'el bunker' due to the extent that Franco controlled the national television network.[23] As Juan Carlos Martini writes in 1977 in his introduction to the collection *Tip y Coll Spain*,

> They have created an adult humouristic form, worthy of the Spain of today in the same way as this current Spain is (or ought to be) worthy of the humour that Tip and Coll develop, with notable elaboration, in each one of their performances, in each one of their articles, in each one of their books.[24]

In *Muertos de risa* the duality, which de la Iglesia emphasises as the basis of Spanish humour, is moreover integral to the *mise-en-scène* and the narrative form. The over-the-top polyester 1970s, seen from the moment of production in the 1990s, exaggerates the *mise-en-scène*. Bad taste is not just a matter of their sequinned twin boys dressing for the stage, in jackets whose outlandish squiggles recall television test patterns. Their stringy long hairstyles and leisure attire – for instance, Nino's peach turtleneck, gold jewellery and wide-labelled, brown window-pane suit – all of the wardrobe, is the basis for much of the film's appeal. We repeatedly laugh at ridiculously exaggerated attire on male and female bodies alike. The mid-body framing, on 'buns' and 'packages' of a celebratory conga line in the bar scene, 'Me pasó el día de juerga' ('I partied the day away'), does not let us miss the heterosexual parade of polyester. (In passing, although Bruno/el Gran Wyoming has a nude close-up of his backside in bed with the camera at the level of his body, the adolescent male fantasy is the only one satisfied through exhibitionary nudity in the film.) Still, getting retro right, a kind of visual timing, is one reason to recognise and label de la Iglesia, John Waters and David Lynch together as 'directores de culto' as does the zine *Dossiernegro*.

## DUALITY IN THE NARRATIVE: ALTERNATING VERSIONS, READING THE SHIFTS IN EMPHASIS AS MEDIA/POLITICAL HISTORY

> There are generations that remember some television programmes better than certain political events. Or they remember those events that had to do with television better.[25]

While de la Iglesia owes his cult status in part to the 'look' of his films, what lets a film such as *Muertos de risa* connect as well as it did to audiences not accustomed to Spanish films, such as at the recent Fantasia Film Festival in Montreal, is its narrative structure. In *Muertos de risa*, this is clear but by no means simplistic. Like a successful video game, it is well crafted in its complexity, and punctuated with cartoonish physical violence. Nino and Bruno's manager narrates their story from a chronological flashback of their joint murder/demise on their special reunion programme, through a linearly told rise of their career. Angel Fernández-Santos in his *El País* review was particularly scornful of the voice-over device:

> There is no way to make the merely *informative* voice of Alex Angulo one's own. When in a film we know the end from the beginning, the hook for our attention ought to be more complex and engaging.[26]

I disagree with Fernández-Santos' assessment of the effect of voice-over in this film. The documentary tone set by voice-over sustains the viewer through the general filmic concern with histories. Moreover, other filmic elements – of editing and camera position – do actively engage the viewer, even a viewer who tires of listening to Alex Angulo.

At their apogée the comedians become jealous of each other and stop performing together. Yet, although estranged, their fame lives on in syndication. In parallel sequences, each beginning with an establishing shot of their side-by-side mansions, they are portrayed living in tormented seclusion, only simulating their success to each other. While Nino goes to bed with cotton in his ears, he keeps his hired go-go dancers on the job casting shadows of a wild party on his front room shades. The simulacrum, or media image, is all that exists until Bruno literally invades Nino's home to stop his torment. Yet what appears to be a break from simulation merely marks the transition to a different set of cinematic or media allusions. In a sequence reminiscent of the burglars' invasion in *Home Alone* (1990), Bruno crawls through the pet door, where, stuck, he is attacked by Nino's mother's cat. He shoves the cat in the refrigerator's freezer. The mother dies of shock – she falls over backwards like a cartoon character – when she discovers her frozen pet. Subsequently, Nino extracts his revenge – plays tricks and pummels – on Bruno for his mother's death during the filming of a television show. Afterward the narrative splits and alternates yet again, to include the tale of stardom from the point of view first of Nino, then Bruno.

One of the difficult moments for the viewer to follow is the transition from the sequence of maximum estrangement, which occurs at the same time as Tejero's coup attempt, to Nino's interpretation of events. Until we see Bruno's version later in the subsequent scene, we take Nino's story as the only or 'true' one. In Nino's version, Nino is an international pop singing star and Bruno a drug-addicted cripple. In Bruno's version, Bruno recasts the act with a dog-faced sad-sack called Tino, and Nino lives on the streets obsessed with his next meal because Bruno has framed him in an airport drug bust.

It is worth addressing these sequences, and the transition, in detail, since such moments need to be understood as privileged moments in the film's interpretation. Moreover, topically speaking, in *Muertos de risa* they clearly represent critical moments in the production of recent Spanish history. Tejero's coup attempt, in Spain popularly called 'F-23' since it occurred on 23 February 1981, challenged Spain's status as a democracy. *Muertos de la risa* stresses that the interruption occurred in virtual reality, just like the Gulf War, or O. J. Simpson's highway chase interrupting President Clinton's State of the Union address, did. The nation unfolds from within TVE, the national television station. How do national and global interests play out in this conflict? With these terms in mind, let us consider the sequence 'Golpe de estado' ('Military Coup').

In the previous sequence Nino and Bruno are filming a comedy routine based on a magic act, a staple of 1970s television, and a talking animal. Remember Ed the talking horse? The *mise-en-scène* is absolutely 1970s television – vaudeville variety in front of a purple shimmery curtain, done on a sound stage. Bruno is supposed to be interviewing Nino to see if he can manage the part of a rabbit in the magic act. What shifts the dynamic to allow the long-suffering Nino to finally take revenge on Bruno, who has always hit him, is the 1990s media subtext. From the perspective of the 1990s, the rabbit is coded as the Energizer Bunny. This campaign was well distributed throughout Europe and had a major impact. In Spain, Felipe González, the Spanish Socialist president, was caricatured on the cover of a major news magazine as the Energizer Bunny for his durability in office despite the scandals emerging over his handling of a covert war against the Basque ETA militia.

What is most interesting about this sequence, which intercuts real TVE footage of the coup, is the depiction of the commanding officer and his troops as everyday Joes, doing forced military service, looking for a beer or a cognac, and definitely more interested in cultural icons, in what is on entertainment television, than in political upheaval. The exchange between the television workers and the military more closely resembles a common stick-up. Moreover, as important as what *Muertos de risa* shows of the event of the coup on television, is what it does not show. History books praise King Juan Carlos for addressing the nation via television, thus aborting the coup and affirming the constitution. In *The Spectacle of Democracy*, the most complete account to date of the relationship between Spanish political and media history, Richard Maxwell explains:

> After midnight, and after many helpless hours, Spaniards watched as the king of Spain appeared on TVE. No one knew for sure until then that he refused to join the coup or that he had not been killed; it had been a very long while before he appeared. It was not clear that TVE had been recaptured by troops loyal to the government, and the king was the first to report that there was going to be no uprising and no end to democracy. He calmed fears and, as if speaking directly to them, commanded the insurgents to follow. Later it was revealed that the king had rallied all but two divisions to the defense of Spanish democracy. … That night, many believers in democracy became monarchists, if only for a brief time.[27]

61

De la Iglesia does not 'centre' the film on the monarch's calming discourse. Instead we have the television executives and workers witnessing the spectacle of an idiotic colonel who thinks the television station is shut off by literally pulling a plug out of the wall and who takes most pleasure in the high-jinks found on Saturday morning cartoons. Some Spaniards have long speculated that the King in fact was only a reluctant defender of the constitution, and was also aware of the coup before it began. They further speculate that his own more liberal father made him speak to the nation against it. Hence the ellipsis in *Muertos de risa* directs attention to a contested moment in the historical record as well.

The anticipated image of King Juan Carlos on television does appear in the second half of this same sequence, long after the coup has been defused and archived. It foreshadows the next sequence, called 'El Reencuentro' ('The Reunion'), or Nino's version of triumph, because we think it can only be a dream of self-promotion. As viewers, we lose our critical edge to interpret narrative when we enjoy the humour of recognition evoked by a nationalist media spectacle. Nino is inserted into historical events, specifically the 1992 Barcelona Summer Olympics opening ceremony, in a technique recalling Woody Allen's *Zelig* (1983). First Nino is catching up to the official Spanish delegation in the opening parade of athletes, then he is shown as the famous archer who lit the torch, and finally he appears in place of the tenor José Carreras singing the incredibly saccharine Olympic song, 'Amigos para siempre' ('Friends Forever'). The whole royal family, the Prince, a weeping Princess Elena, Queen Sofía and King Juan Carlos, melodramatically perform the bonding of the nation through spectacle. The film cuts immediately to 'El Reencuentro', the manager's attempt to reunite the comedy team. Because this idea is such a standard promotional tool we do not catch that this tale of success is according to Nino. Also, Santiago Segura, as Nino, steps out of a limo fastidiously coifed and dressed in a white suit to resemble the pudgy Spanish singer Raphael Martos, simply known as Raphael, the epitome of a melodramatic crooner of Spanish pop ballads. Raphael is known for his world tours and is often the object of gay, camp performances. Again, the viewers are put in the position of celebrating the media spectacle first, and of seeing it as overtly secondary to national concerns. Here, in particular, I would see a move to emphasise globalisation and critique the commodification of culture.

## A FINAL LOOK AT STAGE AND SCREEN: FROM POLITICAL ICONOGRAPHY TO GUILTY PLEASURES

*Muertos de risa* parodies Raphael, Spain's pure showman of melodramatic ballads, who has been going at it – Energizer Bunny-like – for well over 25 years, with 56 albums and 9 feature films, including a documentary on his life that he had pulled from the market due to its unflattering portrayal of 'la fragilidad del mito' ('the fragility of the myth'). A Spanish audience would be well aware that Raphael has long been seen as a darling of the political right. Esteve Rimbau, in *Diccionario de cine español*, makes it acerbically clear how closely Raphael was associated with not only the 1970s, but with a particular political line then:

That very same year, 1975, the singer appeared in the television series *The World of Raphael* and, although he has continued to lavish forth musical performances on diverse national and international stages, his star has not come back to shine with the same intensity as during the Francoist years.[28]

Raphael's own official website today continues to proclaim that he has performed for audiences across the political spectrum. This apolitical disclaimer only makes the rightist association more pronounced.[29]

Within the context of the film the character Bruno plays at being an anarchist, going to a rally to hang out with an attractive girl whom both of them are wooing. Nino and Bruno have their first falling out over an extended gag that Nino plays on Bruno. Secret police, 'acting' for Nino, falsely arrest Bruno for printing seditious pamphlets. As in the case of Nino/Raphael, for a Spanish audience the film here is re-enacting the politics of the media performance artist known as 'El Gran Wyoming' who is playing Bruno. El Gran Wyoming is a well-known leftist. In the 1990s he accused the socialist Prime Minister Felipe González of selling out, bringing to the surface again González's 1970s ultimatum to the PSOE, 'Marx or me'.[30] El Gran Wyoming was instrumental in forming the new party/alliance Izquierda Unida (United Left). Embedded in *Muertos de risa* is a coherent iconography of national politics, yet the film overall does not operate only on that terrain. In particular, the final joint self-destruction of Nino and Bruno is less strongly marked by political caricature than any other part of the film.

*Muertos de risa* never puts us in the position of a studio audience. In this the camera's point of view is absolutely the opposite of *Día de la bestia*, where we became part of the television programme's invited audience for Professor Cavan's show on exorcism. The film comes full circle to its beginning as Nino and Bruno march onto the stage to shoot each other. We are them, not the innocent studio audience. I would suggest that this positioning of the camera on the stage behind Nino and Bruno, and then in an overhead crane shot to view the bodies – both what I would call 'subject positions' – shocks us into seeing our complicity, our guilty pleasure at the staging of violence through humour. The overall effect of this critique, however, is gently diffused in the film's bemused 'happy ending'. As in a cartoon or video game, excessive violence does not necessarily mean death. The coda posits a fantasy of this kind of closed system and returns us to our pleasures as viewers of spectacle. Both comedians are revived to survive on life-support. Technology and the screen, in their heart monitors, again define their lives. In intensive care Bruno keeps Nino alive by slapping him to start his heart, a graveside wry gesture of hitting the mark as a saving grace.

## CONCLUSION

Alex de la Iglesia is an important case study for the directions of recent Spanish cinema. We have seen how the expectation of technology is a key element in the definition of this market, nationally and globally, and likewise in the interpretation of those films. Through the close analysis of *Muertos de risa*, with particular attention to the way that F-23 is inserted in the film, we have seen how the narrative works against the leveling effect of pastiche to produce a sense of historical consciousness. *Muertos de risa* calls the viewer to rethink the links between the history of Spanish democracy and its media history. It also actively positions the viewer within that process.

# CHAPTER 5
# ALTERNATIVE BELGIAN CINEMA AND CULTURAL IDENTITY: S. AND THE AFFAIRE DUTROUX

Ernest Mathijs

## INTRODUCTION: 'NOBODY IS INNOCENT'

'Nobody is innocent' is the subtitle of *S.* (1998), Belgian director Guido Henderickx's most recent film, his fourth in almost 25 years. The phrase not only reflects the motivations behind most of the actions of the film's main character (a young woman called S.), but also the intentions of the makers. Henderickx has more than once referred to *S.* as a film he was forced to make, as a reaction against a degenerated Belgian society of the mid- to late 1990s, and the infamous Affaire Dutroux in particular. As such, *S.* stands among several other artistic attempts representing and criticising the underlying assumptions of contemporary Belgian cultural identity.

But, unlike many of these other attempts, *S.* not only comments upon several of the excesses of that culture; it also *is* excessive. Its story literally shows what it wants to refute, and its formal organisation constantly shifts between conscious artistry and exploitative trash.

This chapter attempts to show how *S.* achieves this complex position both on a textual level and within the cultural discourse of the late 1990s. First, I will frame *S.* in the context of Belgian (film-) culture at the end of the twentieth century. As many commentators have pointed out, this is a time when the legitimacy of Belgian culture, both internally and internationally, was in much doubt. By offering a brief overview of the cultural discourse of the time, I intend to demonstrate how cultural representations reacted to this crisis. Next, I will emphasise how the contrast between intention and reception, and the inability of Belgian film culture (critics, producers) to develop a frame of reference to discuss *S.*, mark the film as a failure, commercially, aesthetically and culturally. Finally, I will explore the implications of one particular element of the film, namely its radical portrayal of the human (female) body in crisis, to show how it sets itself up as both a reflection on cultural abjection, and as culturally abject itself. The notion of bodily abjection, as embodied by both the female protagonist and her actions, not only provides an explanation for the film's reputation but, metaphorically, also allows for a new perspective on the *fin-de-siècle* crisis of Belgian cultural identity.

## THE AFFAIRE DUTROUX AND BELGIAN CULTURAL IDENTITY

The internationally most recognisable key words describing Belgian culture of the twentieth century are peaceful anarchism, surrealism, heritage and (documentary) realism. Linked to such ideological and stereotypical notions as hedonism ('the good life'), social solidarity and consociational 'shrugged consensus'-politics, and a lack of belief in grand narratives (particularism), this set of words has become emblematic for cultural representations from Belgium. By the mid-1990s this frame of reference of cultural specificity even became fashionable on an international level. But the Affaire Dutroux, with its dramatic rescue of two kidnapped girls and the subsequent arrest, in August 1996, of their kidnapper Marc Dutroux (who had previously served prison terms for rape and deception and had been released early for good behaviour) brought this new renaissance to an abrupt end. With the later discovery of the bodies of four more kidnapped girls (aged 6 to 19), and the blatant incompetence of police and justice departments in preventing and following up the affaire, the events seemed tailormade exploitation/horror film material.

Philip Mosley describes the Affaire as 'a major political and constitutional crisis', which

shook Belgian morale to the core, forced another painful reassessment of national identity, and once again endangered the precarious unity of the state. In October 1996 the White March, the largest single demonstration in Belgian history, brought three hundred thousand people into Brussels to protest the official handling of the case.[1]

Gradually, in the years following 1996, the Affaire Dutroux became paradigmatic for what in preceding years had already been labelled as the 'Belgian disease'. This term related to an alienation of the political and judicial establishment (often accused of mismanagement and corruption) from the people. Mosley lists the Agusta-scandal of the late 1990s (kickbacks over defence contracts made to the governing Socialist party), which led to the resignation of the Belgian Secretary-General of NATO, as an example.

To Mosley's example several other instances of the Belgian disease can be added. These included the long-lasting and still-unsolved case of the Bende Van Nijvel/Tueurs du Brabant ('The Killers of Brabant', a series of violently brutal hold-ups and robberies by one single gang – including ex-police officers – in the 1980s). Added to this were numerous rumours about call-girls and paedophile networks serving high placed politicians (the 'Pink Ballets' and 'X-1' cases), as well as the kidnapping of former prime minister Paul Vanden Boeynants. As a result, writers such as Marc Elchardus have indicated that the Affaire and its context revealed a growing sense of crisis of legitimacy of Belgian cultural identity.[2] Equally, many of the facts in the Affaire (physical violence, sexual abuse) also enabled the 'Belgian disease' to be connected with larger cultural discourses on permissiveness and moral laxity being exploited by the political right. It placed issues of sexual identity (and practice) and its social implications firmly on the country's agenda, leading to a paranoid sensitivity of social and sexual 'Otherness'.

It took a while for Belgian cultural representations to relate to this new situation. In fact, there was some indignation that it took major producers of cultural representations a couple of years to include the recent events in their work. But gradually works started to appear that, directly or indirectly, addressed the Affaire and its contexts. Flemish literature saw the publication of a number of experimental and popular books, which either used the events in their narrative (Pieter Aspe's *Het Dreyse incident/The Dreyish Incident* and *Kinderen van Chronos/Children of Chronos*, and Tom Lanoye's *Het goddelijke monster/The Divine Monster* and *Zwarte tranen/Black Tears*) or made metaphorical use of them (Jeroen Olyslaeghers' *Open gelijk een mond/Open like a Mouth*). Theatre productions like the Shakespeare adaptation *Ten Oorlog/To War* or several plays by Alain Platel and Arne Sierens, and television drama productions like *Stille Waters/Quiet Waters* also referred extensively to the Affaire.

Evidently the Affaire also had a powerful resonance in Belgian film culture. By 1999, the otherwise not-so-prolific Belgian film industry had churned out five films that had taken their inspiration from the Affaire or from related issues (Agusta-scandal, Killers of Brabant). These titles included *Bal Masqué* (*The Masked Ball*, Julian Vrebos, 1998), *Pure Fiction* (Marian Handwerker, 1998), *Film 1* (Willem Wallyn, 1999), *Blue Belgium* (Ron Van Eyk, 1999) and *S*. Similar themes were also running through the anarchist films of Jan Bucquoy (*Fermeture des usines Renault/Closing of the Renault Factory*, 1998; *La vie politique des Belges/The Political Life of the Belgians*, 2002). The Belgian disease similarly informed the narrative of prize-winning films like *Rosetta* (Dardenne Brothers, 1999), which won the Palme d'Or in Cannes, and Dominique Deruddere's *Iedereen Beroemd* (*Everybody Famous*, 2000), which earned an Oscar nomination. Given the size of Belgian film culture this represents significant attention.

But, unlike many other cultural representations, Belgian cinema had already been dealing with such issues long before the outburst of the Affaire. As I have argued elsewhere, Belgian cinema has a long reputation in portraying sexuality (*Daughters of Darkness* (Harry Hümel, 1971) and 1970s permissive cinema) and (anti-) political pamphlets (the documentaries of Henri Storck, Frans Buyens and Fugitive Cinema).[3] The 1992 realist horror film *C'est arrivé près de chez vous* (*Man Bites Dog*, Rémy Belvaux, André Bonzel and Benôit Poelvoorde), had also dealt with and portrayed child killings, kidnappings and rape. The Dutroux case triggered a retrospective reconsideration of these films, leading to the canonisation of *Man Bites Dog* as a 'prophecy' for the Affaire.

Other films, like *La vie sexuelle des Belges* (*The Sexual Life of the Belgians*, Jan Bucquoy, 1994), *Hombres complicados* (Dominique Deruddere, 1997) and the documentary on terrorism, *D.I.A.L. History* (XXX John Grimonprez, 1997), with their appeal to a kind of 'guerrilla cinema', helped to create an awareness of physical violence and sexual identity in Belgian film culture with which post-Affaire films easily connected. In doing so, the Dutroux-theme became almost paradigmatic for Belgian film culture, putting many of the already established characteristics in a new perspective. Depictions of physical sex and violence, which had never caused too much controversy, now became pressing issues, loaded with political and cultural significance.

## S. AND THE AFFAIRE DUTROUX: INTENTION AND RECEPTION

Of all films dealing with the Affaire, *S.* is probably the most radical and alternative. The film tells the story of a young Belgian woman, S., whose dreams of having a normal life are destroyed through a history of criminality, corruption, sexual and physical abuse (she is raped and beaten). After finding out that her boyfriend cheats on her (she films him having sex) she kills him. S. attempts to escape from her past by returning from New York to Belgium. In Belgium, she tries to come to terms with her actions by mapping her past in a different way, but the people who are supposed to help her do this (her mother, grandmother, friend) all want to distance themselves from S.'s inquiries.

When her relationship with her girlfriend, Marie, breaks down, S. becomes an angel of vengeance, acting out her frustrations towards everyone who exploits her. She kills a guy who tries to seduce her, physically humiliates, and then kills, a priest who makes a pass at her, and shoots her pimp after he beats her. But as her video diaries become more intimate and therapeutic, she sinks into an angst-ridden spiral of madness, meaningless sex and violence. She finally returns to New York to another former girlfriend, Angie, only to find that she is no longer welcome. Back in Belgium she finally hears the truth about how she was abused as a child, and she visits Marie in a peepshow performance, losing herself in a dream of perfect love, but unable to reach a catharsis.

*S.*'s style is as radical as the narrative. It is filmed in true 'guerrilla style', referencing a rough and ready punk attitude. Here, the excessively self-referential is indicated via the use of jump cuts, wipes (resembling peepshow shutters), video-cam inserts, and the suggestion of snuff movies (a video one of her boyfriends makes her watch shows the baseball bat killing of an innocent woman). The film contains not one single outdoor shot, creating a claustrophobic atmosphere of cheap apartments and cafes, peepshows, confession boots and car interiors. New York is portrayed as hot and sweaty and Brussels as rainy, and throughout the film fluids of all kinds (snow, tears, slime, blood, urine, melting butter, water and sperm) abound. With this gruesome, cut-up, radical look, *S.* places itself in the tradition of alternative films like *Ms. 45* (Abel Ferrara, 1981), *Liquid Dreams* (Mark Manos, 1992), *Bad Lieutenant* (Abel Ferrara, 1993), *Crash* (David Cronenberg, 1996), and exploitation films of the 1970s and 1980s. It is also reminiscent of American Gen-X literature (most notably that of Brett Easton Ellis and Douglas Coupland).

It is not difficult to see how the story and style of *S.* connect to the Affaire Dutroux and its contexts. Sexual abuse, violence, murder, corruption, distrust in official institutions and moral decay are central to the narrative, and the aggressive and radical look of the film seem to suggest a certain

**FIGURE 8** The 'guerilla style' look of *S.*

position by the filmmakers on the themes. In several interviews Henderickx explicitly addresses this connection. When critics ask him if it was really necessary to use such explicit imagery, Henderickx makes a reference to the Affaire by stating that, 'Yes, because that's what happens in real life.'[4] He additionally expresses his attitude towards it by saying that 'unless you're a moron, you can't walk through life pretending nothing's wrong'. Apart from describing the film as 'a search of young people for happiness', Henderickx further identifies *S.* as 'a comment on our voyeuristic society', thus including the self-referentiality of the film in the critique it forms of the Dutroux context.[5]

However, it is strange to find no reference to the Affaire in the press kit or any other release materials surrounding the film. Instead of politicising it, the degree of sex and violence in the film is put in an exploitative framework, with Belgian director Marc Didden identifying the film in the press notes as an 'erotic road-movie'.[6] The national reception of the film, too, tried to avoid making the connection with the Affaire as much as possible. The opening of the film (including a gala screening at the Gaumont cinema in Antwerp) generated a lot of media attention, and *S.* was widely publicised on national television, even in political talk shows. However, the interest quickly disappeared after the release. Eventually, *S.* played in national cinemas for only two to three weeks, drawing no more than 20,000 viewers.

The video release by Polygram a year later drew even less attention, although more than 1,000 copies of the film were circulated. Similarly, the prevalent position among national film critics was one of disregard. In most cases, reviews referred to the film as having laudable intentions, being radical and raw in its look (with some implying that this was the result of its lack of budget). Some reviews went as far as to suggest that these features did not necessarily make a good film, or even refusing to pass any judgement on it. The most recurrent key words were 'brutal', 'rough', 'reckless', 'distasteful' and 'violent', without too much explanation.[7] According to several critics, the continuous and explicit emphasis on abuse, humiliation and resistance of and by S. was too dominant to allow any psychological motivations and/or social contexts to be addressed. Henderickx was apparently unable (perhaps too eager) to explain the relevance of his approach in interviews, and the interviewers refused to use his comments in interpreting S. as a critique of the 'Belgian disease'. Instead, they adopted a traditional critical approach, looking for connections between the film and the nation's film legacy (failing to find many), and focusing on trivial stories around the film. It is symptomatic that one such ancillary story, on how the debuting lead actress, Natali Broods, had been expelled from acting school by her then teacher Dora van der Groen, who plays her grandmother in the film, gained more press coverage and prominence than the cultural implications of the narrative.

It is by no means exceptional that a film's reception fails to address some of its cultural implications. And within the context of Belgian film discourses, it is even part of a well-established tradition. Belgian film critics have always tried to exclude social commentary from their interpretations, focusing instead on *film as film*, and trying to draw aesthetic comparisons instead of cultural ones, even if this implies a retreat from a position as public intellectual. It is an attitude typically occurring at moments when criticism fails to find a suitable frame of reference to place a cultural representation in. In this case, it is indicative of the fact that many critics, at the time, were not able (or willing) to see the cultural frame of the Affaire which S. was addressing.

This inability is all the more striking when the international reception of S. is taken into account. Although S. did not do well internationally, and was only screened at festivals, and although international critics have more difficulty tapping into Belgian cultural frameworks (which have hardly any relevance for their local readership), the connection was more visible than in its national reception. As a case in point, Dennis Harvey's review in *Variety* mentions Henderickx's intention to make 'a sombre social statement about apathy and collapsed morals, inspired by recent Belgian paedophile crimes'.[8] Similarly, the brief mention of S. on the Hollywood.com website cites 'a Belgium reeling from the discovery of a paedophile murderer'[9] as essential background of the story. Finally, screenings of S. at specialist Gay and Lesbian festivals (San Francisco Lesbian and Gay Film Festival, Inside Out in Toronto) also imply a cultural framing of the film. The near-explicit mentioning of the Affaire in the international reception, and the willingness to put S. in a cultural frame of reference distinguishes the international critics' reception from their Belgian counterparts (who have ready access to the context but decline to make the connection).

## THE DUALITY OF BELGIAN FILM CULTURE

Strangely, the duality between S.'s intentions and its reception makes it symptomatic for Belgian film culture. Like many controversial films before it, S. positions itself on the threshold between two dominant frames of reference of Belgian cinema: an auteurist framework of state-supported, aesthetically accomplished cultural heritage cinema, and an alternative framework of commercial, experimental and exploitation films (whether porn, genre efforts, avant-garde or controversial cinema). In official discourses on Belgian cinema, the former has always been pushed forward as the only desirable goal, whereas the latter has been denied all cultural relevance.

In general, this privileged framework has functioned well in reflecting topical issues of Belgian cultural identity. Several of the above-mentioned key words of Belgian culture are frequently represented, in particular realism (in the form of documentary), surrealism (in the form of magic realism), and social solidarity and particularism (culminating in the struggle of the individual to escape his smalltown surroundings). But since the Affaire, Belgian culture has changed so dramatically that this framework no longer captures cultural reality. It refers to a past that, in retrospect, was disguising some of the more pressing issues that the Affaire placed on Belgium's cultural agenda.

At the very least, then, the Affaire should have led to a willingness to revise the dominant framework. It should have allowed some attention to elements of the alternative frame of reference, especially since many of the films around the Affaire and its contexts are characterised by a sense of immediacy and rawness that is more easily associated with the exploitative and experimental framework. They deal with terrorism, homosexuality, the different faces of explicit violence, and they reflect an anarchist attitude towards contemporary culture, desperately (perhaps naively) trying to understand a culture that is caught up in intense turmoil. But, as the case of *S.* shows, not many participants in Belgian cinema culture are willing to make that opening.

As with most of the other films reflecting on the Affaire, it received bad reviews, was prevented from making a commercial impact (no funding, no opportunities to run in big theatres), and there was a general tendency to dismiss it as excessive; to forget it as soon as possible. It leads to the interesting observation that Belgian critics, and most of the official Belgian film discourse (selection committees, television executives, producers, festival organisers, fellow filmmakers) seem to be unwilling to stay in touch with a significant part of their own subject.

In the remainder of this chapter I will discuss one particular reason for the film's curious exclusion, which relates to its ability to not only address certain cultural issues, but also to play a wider role in supporting and creating attitudes that form part of that culture. In the case of *S.* this means that it not only comments *on* the Affaire (the auteurist framework), but that it is also an example *of* the 'Belgian disease', exploiting it (the exploitative framework). It explains the particular distinctions between the intention and reception of *S.*, and it demonstrates the unease of Belgian cinema with the cultural implications of its subject. In what follows I will focus on one such implication, in order to introduce a new perspective on the film's meaning and relevance.

## S. AND THE HUMAN BODY IN CRISIS

It is not difficult to make an interpretation of *S.* On an obvious level the film shows, pretty explicitly, the actions of a desperate young woman trying to survive (and avenge) the horrible humiliations she suffers by resorting to the same kind of violence as used against her. This urge for destructiveness is the ultimate form of resistance – it also almost kills S. Instead of committing suicide, however, S. finds comfort with Marie, the only person who has not tried to deceive and/or abuse her. The environment in which S. tries to survive is depressing: filled with dysfunctional families, unrequited love, crime, prostitution, sexual violence and abuse, governed by the seductive power of the sex economy. All this

**FIGURE 9** Unrequited love and crime in *S.*

of course recalls the Affaire Dutroux, the organised abduction and abuse of children, with the failure of justice by any other means than through outright anger and violence itself, reflecting popular opinion in Belgium at the time of the Affaire's eruption. The claustrophobic atmosphere of *S.* also calls into mind the situation in many metropolitan areas, with a continuous climate of fear and insecurity, governed by organised crime.

More importantly is that, through its suggestion of the intimate connection between sex, violence and power, *S.* puts the human body at the centre of social conflict and cultural crises. The true meaning of *S.* lies in the link between the Affaire and the human body of the protagonist, both victim and perpetrator. First of all, there is the issue of the film's story world. Strictly speaking, the film shows a reality that is politically, socially and psychologically undefined, and which does not readily represent a known real-world fabula. But even though *S.* may be fictitious, the way in which it is shown (explicit, blasphemous and raw) makes it all too real. This is largely the result of the emphasis on the physical aspects of the story world.

Because they take up so much screen time, the viewer is forced to watch the intimate and gory details of the humiliating, horrible and, literally, dirty situations in which S. finds herself. The film abounds with blood, sweat, tears, run-down make-up, rain running from faces, spit, organs, wounds, tattoos, intestines, urine, sperm, and other fluids and marks associated with the human body (soap, vaseline, hair gel…). The frequent use of close-ups zooming in on these details allows no escape for the viewer. There are hardly any establishing shots, backgrounds are mostly underlit, and we are not even granted a short glimpse of the outside world (not even through a window). Significantly, the moves from New York to Belgium and vice versa are suggested through miniatures in glass bowls, safely sealed off from the outside world, and all shots of S. driving her car are set against a moonless black night. This way the film pushes the viewer onto, even *into*, S.'s body, making that body the story world.

Second, the emphasis on the human body also extends to the film's narrative structure. Technically, *S.* has a beginning, a middle and an end that adhere to traditions of storytelling, including a plot construction and a catharsis, but they are a long way from what is conventional. Information on time and space, for instance, are kept to a minimum, preventing a clear setting. Many storylines are abruptly opened and shut. A Dutch boyfriend suddenly appears and disappears. We do not even know where Angie, one of S.'s closest friends, comes from, nor do we know how Marie and Angie meet up (and break up). It even remains unclear if S.'s father has already been executed or if he is still waiting on death row. *S.* is hence unarticulated, immature, unpolished and sometimes unattractive, much like the film's main character's body.

And even within its story world and narrative *S.* shows an imperfect, undesirable world, broken to pieces, kept together only by S.'s awareness and use of her own body. From what we can judge, the social order ruling our society no longer exists in *S.*; neither do the symbols we usually attach to that order retain their function. Church, law, state, morality and common decency are either absent or stripped of their aura. A Catholic priest, peeping at S. from his confession booth, sees his fantasy come true (she seduces him) only to be humiliated and killed. Even the ultimate symbolic means through which social order is pressed, our arsenal of punishments for crimes, is trivialised. Through his video diary, S.'s father, sentenced to death, plays an ultimate power game with her, revealing how he molested her as a child, hurting her from beyond the grave.

With this lack of structure and boundaries S. can only fall back on herself. As a subject, she is traumatised and threatened in her further existence, making her retreat onto herself the only possible means of gaining any kind of survival. Unconventionally, but true to herself, she captures on video what she values most in her life, herself. And in her retreat she concentrates on what remains the only reliable point of reference, her own body. Using her body as a tool in coming to terms with the chaos around her, S. exploits it to the limit. She dances in a peepshow, parades her body in the subway, films herself, lets her body be touched by others. In a telling scene, she asks her boyfriend to make love to her 'so that she doesn't need to see him, just feel him'.

Whenever the limits of her own body are reached, through rape, physical violence, abuse or otherwise, murder is the only way out. Through the act of murder, literally destroying the body of the attacker through violent penetration, S. manages to protect her body from continuous invasions from outside. The periphery of S.'s body, her skin and bodily fluids, play an important role in that protection. Throughout the film, S. uses them as tools to fend off attacks or to express her emotions. She urinates on the priest she kills; she closely examines the blood that runs freely from her nose while she kills her pimp; she caresses her own body and that of Marie with ice cubes, and she 'asks' for butter

**FIGURE 10** S. finds comfort with Marie

when her former boyfriend has anal sex with another woman. It is no coincidence that S. films her home videos in the bathroom and on the toilet, cultural places dedicated to the transfer between the inside and outside of human bodies.

There is only one occasion when S. is not entirely on her own in the film, when she trusts another person/body, and that is when she falls in love with another woman. With her own body, S. also explores that of her girlfriend, Marie, with whom she has a short but intense love affair. S.'s reunification with Marie, at the very end of the story, is by far the only bright spot (literally) in the film. Similarly, S. longs for the love of another woman, Angie, throughout the film, only to find that love unrequited. In a remarkable comment on this lesbian motive, Henderickx claims that S. is not lesbian by choice, she *has* to become one.[10] Only in the body of another woman can S. find comfort, physically and culturally – only through another female body can S. become a culturally acceptable (and accepted) subject herself. Together the three female bodies form the last stronghold against complete disintegration. Fundamentally then, S.'s cultural identity, even her chances for survival, almost entirely depend on how she deals with her changing body and its physical and cultural limits.

## S., ABJECTION AND DUTROUX

Through its positioning of the body at the centre of attention and action, *S.* becomes an almost perfect illustration of the specific concept of abjection in representations commenting on the loss of social order and its symbols. In *Powers of Horror* Julia Kristeva, building on work by René Girard and Mary Douglas, pointed to the possibility to see the link between the emphasis on the bodily characteristics of the human subject, and the ugly, indecent and immoral aspects of human bodies, as a critique of social order.[11] Literally, abjection means degradation, a low or downcast state, but the term also references disgust and subordination, even up to the point of wilful humiliation.

For Kristeva, abjection is a synonym for the activity of the self-effacing body, submissive to a system, model or order that presents itself as perfect. Emphasising the less desirable elements of that body then becomes an act of criticism against that order. In this meaning, abjection has been used by filmmakers and critics as the concept that links the subversion of the mostly male-dominated modern world to the resisting feminised body.

Critics like Laura Mulvey put it pretty simply: the current social order, on which a capital-intensive creative industry like film is highly dependent, is patriarchal and is represented by the active, mature, robust, ascetic, male body.[12] That order is threatened by the female body, which is reduced to a passive object in most films, as well as by any imperfect body (children, freaks, clowns, cyborgs, visible wounds) and bodies out of control (maniacs, orgasms, rages, hysteria). But at the same time, according to Mulvey, female bodies constitute a source of viewing pleasure, voyeuristic and appealing to instinctive reactions. They are harmless as long as they can be contained. Likewise, abject bodies in general have always been sites for the reinforcement of cultural order (in circuses, road shows, in the media) – as long as they did not become a real threat. Since Mulvey and Kristeva, it has become a tradition in film studies to try to identify such moments of threat.

In Belgian cinema culture, the first time such a threat became remotely visible was when the link between social order and the human body deviating from the norm became a pressing issue with the release of *Man Bites Dog*. The rape scene that dramatically changes the mood in the film (and the viewer) from innocent social satire to a registration of a diseased cultural identity was widely praised as relevant and impressive. As writers such as Frank Lafond have argued, in this moment, *Man Bites Dog* became a sign of the times, symptomatic for the decay of Belgian society.[13] In *Man Bites Dog*, the threat is ultimately contained by an external explanation: it is the media that are to blame for the overexposure of abject bodies. The style of the film, with its mimicking of *cinema vérité* patterns, explicitly refers to reality television. The inclusion of such media in the narrative, suggested that it was not so much Belgian culture, but rather the symbolic representation of that society through media, that was being criticised. So, while making an important statement on the mass-mediated means of representing reality, *Man Bites Dog*, and its critics, ignored its address of abjection.

Despite this critical invisibility, *S.* resolutely addresses abjection. Humiliation, degradation, disgust and the revolt of the female body against a social order which it sees as threatening and chaotic are central to the narrative and style, and are put much more directly than in *Man Bites Dog*. Moreover, the film does not look for an external explanation for its presentation of abject bodies; the rest of the world is simply ignored. The mass media from *Man Bites Dog* are replaced by home video equipment. In *S.* the media are not identified as the scapegoat for the destruction of social order, *S.*'s tapes are merely registering her resistance to it. In fact, *S.* does not attempt to give any explanation outside the direct confrontation of *S.*'s body with specific aspects of a cultural order in crisis. It forces viewers to acknowledge the issue of abjection, both as a threat to order *and* as a resistance to the excesses of that order.

**FIGURE 11** The voyeuristic look at the female body in *S.*

In a clever way, this turns the film into a critique of a society that has tried to ignore its connection to abject bodies. *S.* explains that when the social order, to which every deviant body is subordinate, becomes corrupt, everyone's particular identity, and the identity of a culture in general, are in danger, unless the abject body revolts. *S.* explains how the cultural acknowledgement of the imperfect body, stressing differences instead of similarities, becomes a way out of the impasse Belgian society found itself in after the Affaire Dutroux.

The Affaire had placed imperfect bodies, children's bodies, violated and abused bodies, bodies of maniacs (many newspapers focused on the physical features of Marc Dutroux) and bodies in distress at the forefront of Belgian culture. By addressing the ability of such bodies to resist and revolt against a corrupt social order, *S.* offered a much better way of coping with the aftermath of the Affaire than any other explanation. The battered body of *S.* then becomes a metaphor for the shock Belgian culture went through after the Affaire. In order to play that metaphorical role, the cultural context of *S.* is essential. The film was consciously developed in an era in which Belgian society saw its own order crumble, and it capitalises on a then omnipresent sensitivity for the human body in crisis. Around the Affaire dozens of smaller stories and news facts circulated around the concept of the abject, degraded and violated body. These included features on sects with bizarre rituals, sexual harassment at the workplace, paedophile practices of Catholic priests and Jesuit teachers at boarding schools, judges caught up in sadomasochistic activities, and so on. Stories like these have always appeared in press reports, but had never threatened the social order of Belgian culture. Now, with the impact of the Affaire shedding a new perspective on the human body in crisis, these stories suddenly became symptoms of a society in decay. Just as S.'s body becomes a threat to its attackers when its limits are reached, so the Affaire turned these stories from innocent *fait-divers* into guilty pleasures. By serving its viewers a voyeuristic look at the abject, female body being tested, and forcing them to face the consequences when the limits of violation are reached, *S.* is a paradigmatic example of how Belgian culture was offered the chance to see how its pleasures were never innocent.

## CONCLUSION

Almost a decade after the Affaire, Belgian films still show a striking interest in the topic. Recently, the 'militant edge' of the prison film *Une part du ciel* (*A Piece of Sky*, Bénédicte Liénard, 2002), using real-life prisoners to create a sense of urgency and authenticity, brings the Affaire to mind. Similarly, the Dardenne Brothers' *Le fils* (*The Son*, 2002) demonstrates a particular interest in the human body as the final refuge in case of social conflict. The latter tells the story of a carpenter who trains a young man released from a juvenile detention centre; the trainee having killed the carpenter's son. Here, the Dardennes used a new lightweight camera to foreground the body of the main character/actor to ensure the prominent place of the human body in the film. According to the pair, *The Son* is about 'a human being in a situation of extreme pain', something they inextricably link to a social and cultural context. 'One's whole life is expressed in the body,' they add.[14]

*S.* predates these concerns. On several levels it offers a view on the relationship between culture and the human body. On a first level it shows what happens to a woman's body in extreme situations, not dissimilar to those particular to the Affaire Dutroux. On another level *S.*, according to the intentions of the director, is a representation of the 'Belgian disease' of which the Affaire is the culmination. As a representation it puts the context of the Affaire in a new light by addressing its connection to issues involving the cultural function of the human body in crisis. On yet another, conceptual level *S.* links the concept of abjection to the cultural presence of the human body and its place in (Belgian) culture. Through the concept of abjection even the most radical and extreme actions in the film can be seen as both victimisation and rebellion of the body in a cultural framework. The resistance of S. against anyone who exploits her calls for respect of the human body as the last refuge in times of cultural crisis, making it possible to see it as a solution for a situation in which it has become a pivotal social issue. For S., her body is the only solution.

Given the situation in Belgium at the end of the 1990s, there is a possibility that this gives the film an all too real connotation. To what extent this has been understood by critics and audiences remains unclear. It is at least remarkable that literally no one picks up on it. Could it be that the sensitivity for abjection and its relation to social order was too uncomfortable an issue (even in a metaphorical or conceptual way) to address at the time? Perhaps ironically, the absence of references to abjection in the discourse around *S.* seems to reinforce the suggestion that it is of crucial importance in making sense of Belgian cultural identity of the time.

# CHAPTER 6
# VIOLENT JUSTICE: ITALIAN CRIME/COP FILMS OF THE 1970s

Christopher Barry

## INTRODUCTION

The rogue cop's appeal in popular/trash cinema is not hard to understand when considering it as a reflection of the demands governing the male psyche. As film theorists have long argued, most men can find an outlet for their social and sexual fantasies watching genre films, and cop thrillers/crime melodramas are no exception. There is no doubt that male audiences can relate to the notion of a 'half embittered detective and half Superman'.[1] Rogue cops and their larger-than-life qualities speak volumes about male fantasy life explored while safely perched in a darkened theatre. The individualist cop, the macho law enforcer silent while withstanding pain, only spurs his 'appetite for the dirtiest, most demanding police work'.[2] Ultimately, these films become a medium not for reflecting truth but for reflecting desire.

The fantasy, *or desire*, for the common man is to face insurmountable challenges with a collected cool, with an appetite for demanding and, one hopes, dirty work. The reality, however, is based in that most undesirable affliction – the mundane nine-to-five existence, which leads to an embittered outlook at this thing called life. At the other end of the spectrum, audience members may relate to the victims of crime and so desire a Superman to swoop down and eradicate the problem.

The crimes committed in these films are so extreme that a knee-jerk response by the audience is required for them to justify and, thereby, accept the brutal lengths these cops will go to bring down dangerous drug kingpins or psycho killers. The crimes in these films feed on the paranoia audiences already feel – paranoia that is spoon fed to them by the media regurgitating crime statistics, murder in the streets and endless threats of terrorism.

## AMERICAN ENFORCERS

But if audience members stopped and closely analysed the personalities of American cinematic law enforcers like Jimmy 'Popeye' Doyle, Frank Bullitt or Harry Callahan, they may actually (and rightfully) be shocked at these cops' borderline psychotic behaviour. In fact, these cops are remarkably close in spirit to Paul Schrader/Robert De Niro's Travis Bickle in *Taxi Driver* (Martin Scorsese, 1976). Each of them – the cops, Bickle – 'God's lonely man' unhappily embroiled within the 'system', personifying a 'real rain' ready, and more than willing, to 'wash the scum off the streets'. However, cops can pop a bullet in a brain in the name of the law, while Bickle remains on the periphery of edict.

But maybe rogue cops in American cinema during the early 1970s were not really psychotic as much as they were right-wing vigilantes – particularly Harry Callahan in *Dirty Harry* (Don Siegel, 1971). As Peter Lev has noted:

[Harry's] agenda is, in an American context, right-wing, conservative, law and order. In the second half of [*Dirty Harry*], Harry disobeys a series of orders and solves the Scorpio threat using his own values and methods. He becomes a police vigilante. Does the nightmare of Scorpio justify a cop unrestrained by law or government?[3]

Because messages in films like *Dirty Harry* require visceral reactions to crimes so unbelievably heinous, the answer is a populist yes.

Ironically, during the early 1970s, these conservative cops were as easy to relate to by the liberal left – that is the hippie movement in America, which advocated individualism, 'doing your own thing' and bucking the 'system'.

Conservatively, from a male audience perspective, the nightmare of a psycho killer or a drug dealer infecting the streets is enough to justify vigilantism – especially under the umbrella of the law. A film like *The French Connection* (William Friedkin, 1971) almost seems to favour giving individual cops such as Jimmy 'Popeye' Doyle (and his partner Sonny Russo) autonomous power to exercise the casual violence needed to get the job done efficiently. Society accepts this type of behaviour in exchange for social order.

In terms of modern American images of the rogue cop, Peter Yates' film *Bullitt* (1969) can be seen as one of the first cop films made specifically for male fantasy. Here, Steve McQueen portrayed

Detective Frank Bullitt with a controlled no-nonsense attitude. And, where day-to-day existence relies upon taking a certain amount of crap, most men would like to think they have the cool control of Frank Bullitt even when real life says differently. In the later film *The French Connection*, Gene Hackman played detective Jimmy 'Popeye' Doyle with a volatile realism in direct opposition to Bullitt's collected cool. In fact, it is Doyle – not Bullitt – who exemplifies the archetypal outlaw cop that is now providing a basis for cinematic law enforcers all the way up to Joe Carnahan's *Narc* (2002) and Ron Shelton's *Dark Blue* (2003).

Based on a real New York City detective, Hackman's portrayal of cop as angry everyman was simply easier to relate to than Bullitt – Doyle was paunchy, foul-mouthed, dishevelled and mercilessly under the thumb of his superiors. Within the system, Doyle was a loose cannon, breaking as many rules as necessary to get the job done. Doyle's mission was not based on busting law-breakers because they were breaking the law – his mission was based on vendetta. Doyle took his work personally. Watching Doyle's explosive personality is a cathartic experience – a caustic release of anger rather than an internalisation of daily frustrations.

However, the most influential and iconic cop who refused to play by anybody's rules but his own actually burst onto the scene before *The French Connection*. Don Siegel's *Dirty Harry* – a film that portrays loner cop as combustible human being and saint – set the standard for cop films not only in the USA but around the world. And it is easy to see why. Harry Callahan's mission is based on one thing alone – justice.

In her 1971 review of *Dirty Harry*, *New Yorker* film critic Pauline Kael stated as much:

> Harry Callahan is not a Popeye – porkpie-hatted, and lewd and boorish. He's soft-spoken Clint Eastwood – six feet four of lean, tough saint, blue-eyed and shaggy-haired, with a rugged creased, careworn face that occasionally breaks into a mischief-filled Shirley MacLaine grin. He's the best there is – a Camelot cop, courageous and incorruptible, and the protector of women and children. Or at least he would be, if the law allowed him to be. But the law coddles criminals; it gives them legal rights that cripple the police. And so the only way that Dirty Harry – the dedicated trouble-shooter who gets the dirtiest assignments – can protect the women and children is to disobey orders.[4]

*Dirty Harry* struck a chord so deeply that the film spawned four sequels – *Magnum Force* (1973), *The Enforcer* (1976), *Sudden Impact* (1983) and *The Dead Pool* (1988).

It was *Magnum Force* that transformed the rogue cop's modus operandi into a fetishist worship of Callahan's weapon: the .44 Magnum. This in turn became a symbol for impotent man's rage against the impenetrable 'system'. Whether the system is of the law or of the workplace or home. No doubt, the .44 Magnum was Callahan's signature in *Dirty Harry*, but in *Magnum Force*, the gun was laboured on, doted upon, lovingly shot from all angles to almost pornographic excess, as if Callahan was proud of this John Holmesian appendage. Even though 'a man's got to know his limitations', Callahan was all too happy explaining that his .44 Magnum 'is the most powerful handgun in the world and can blow your head clean off', thereby alleviating said limitations. Also Callahan's hatred of the 'system' is something he has to stick with 'until something better comes along'.

## POLICE – ITALIAN STYLE

As noted above, cinematic studies have identified the ideological and social pressures that inform American images of the 'rogue cop' (and the desires they gratify within their audience). However, very little critical work has been undertaken on comparable European images of law enforcement, even considering the enormous influx of crime/cop films produced in Italy from 1971–79.

One of the first Italian crime/cop films to get noticed was Stefano Vanzina's *La Polizia ringrazia* (1971) and was, subsequently, given its own classification – the *poliziotteschi* (or police) film. Vanzina (also known as Steno) brought a frenetic, almost comic sensibility to this new genre. The filmmaker directed the *Piedone* ('flatfoot') series ranging from *Piedone lo sbirro* (1973) to *Piedone d'Egitto* (1979). These slapstick cop films starred Bud Spencer, (who played 'Bambino' in the spaghetti western *Trinity* series with Terence Hill). The *Trinity* series was outrageously popular in America during the early 1970s, unlike the *Piedone* films, which never caught on in the US. Though Vanzina basically started a new genre in Italian film, he went back to directing comedy/slapstick movies.

Director Enzo Castellari, who started his career directing westerns (*Vado ... l'ammazzo e torno* (1967)) moved easily into poliziotteschi with *La Poliza incrimina la legge assolve* (1973). Castellari was able to assimilate the cinematic aesthetics (and excesses) of Sam Peckinpah into the cop genre with a balletic blaze of gunfire and car chases.

Consequently, these directors paved the way for other notable Italian filmmakers to enter the genre. These included Umberto Lenzi – a director who is probably known more for his horror film excesses (specifically 'cannibalsploitation' films like *Mangiati vivi* (1980), *Cannibal Ferox* (1981) and 'zombiesploitation' flicks such as *Incubo sulla citta contaminata* (1980)) than poliziotteschi. Arguably, his most accomplished films are cop thrillers such as *Roma a mano armata* (1976), *Il Trucido e lo sbirro* (1976), *Napoli violenta* (1976) and, before going the way of the cannibal, *Da Corleone a Brooklyn* (1978). Lenzi not only borrowed from American directors such as Peckinpah and William Friedkin, he understood the nuances of Francis Ford Coppola by incorporating – in even the hardest cops – the pathos of loyalty and friendship.

It is easy to misinterpret Italian crime/cop films from the early 1970s as brazen *Dirty Harry* knock-offs because, more often than not, these films incorporated a lone cop fighting the 'system' – using brute force to bring the 'bad guys' down, much the same way Callahan did in his work. However, Italian crime/cop films were a reflex reaction to the explosive political environment found in cities like Rome, Naples and Milan during the 1970s. Like Callahan, the 'lone wolf' in Italian crime films was, many times, a cop on the force who had no choice but to fight violent behaviour with even more brutal violence.

In fact, many Italian crime/cop films had titles that reflected the incendiary atmosphere of the city where they took place – for example, *Roma violenta* (1975, aka *Violent Rome*) or *Napoli violenta* (aka *Violent Naples*). Yet audiences – particularly American audiences, who saw these films at inner-city grindhouses, drive-in theatres or on late-night television – saw them presented with reworked titles based on the *Dirty Harry* theme. With titles like *Una Magnum Special per Tony Saitta* (1976, aka *Blazing Magnum*) and *Napoli si ribella* (1977, aka *A Man Called Magnum*), it is easy to see why viewers regard these Italian films as forgettable rip-offs. But in actuality, Italian crime/cop films used

**FIGURE 12** Fighting back against an explosive social situation: *Revolver* (1973)

the American movies as a springboard with the directors diving into their own violent culture to flesh out brutal but no less heroic tales of subversive crime fighters.

## GOVERNMENT-SPONSORED TERRORISM

Even a surface look at the churning Italian political scene during the late 1960s and into the early 1980s brings about a deeper understanding of these films, which were steeped in brutality, sex, drugs and other Western trappings. The majority of these films were produced with a blatant anti-government agenda. Italian crime/cop films not only stood against the police force but they blazed away at the government as a whole, which is always represented as crumbling into despair and fully corrupt. The best films of the cycle (*Milan Trema – la polizia vuole giustizia* (1973), *Revolver* (1973), *Napoli Violenta, Una Magnum Special per Tony Saitta*) portray a weakened police force liberally accepting a bloody terrorist reign and fascist syndicates spearheaded by government officials.

Italy was battling to become a more capitalist (therefore, more democratic) society, trying, in part, to embrace Western values. But, as the struggle became more intense, there was an overwhelming movement of repression toward the country's citizens. There was a repression by employers lording over workers in the factories and repression by the police (which also represented repression by the government) toward society in general mixed with a contradictory liberal 'let it be' view of crime and criminals. It was not long before government resistance by Italy's citizens began to take hold. The most infamous (and violent) resistance group being the Communist-based faction 'The Red Brigade'.

In actuality, many of these resistant groups were terrorists taking advantage of the wave of anti-government resistance, demonstrated by ordinary citizens. Terrorist rampages were replete with bombings at demonstrations and public meetings as well as the bombing of trains and railway stations. The police, meanwhile, were rendered helpless and, many times, rolled over for these violent terrorist groups that may have been, ironically, headed up by government officials – hence the idiom 'violent professionals'.

Italian-produced crime/cop films gave oppressed citizens an opportunity to see on the screen what newspapers at that time did not dare show – that corruption was rampant and the police accepted it as part of the system. However, even if the police system was under the thumb of politicians and/or terrorists, there was bound to be a maverick cop on the force willing to provide citizens with two things sorely missing: law and order. And, ironically, law and order depended on the rogue's use of extreme violence to get the job done.

## VIOLENT PROFESSIONALS – TERRORISTS, COPS OR BOTH?

On its surface, Sergio Martino's film *Milan Trema – la polizia vuole giustizia* (1973, aka *The Violent Professionals*) can be seen as a cop-bent-on-vengeance flick because, on its simplest terms, it is. French actor Luc Merenda plays police Commander Giorgio Caneparo in much the same way Eastwood played Harry Callahan – a man of few words, with action speaking louder than bombs. And *Milan Trema* is literally bumper-to-bumper with furious car chases *à la The French Connection*. And like 'Popeye' Doyle, Caneparo is a character waiting to explode. Caneparo himself sums up his volatile

**FIGURES 13 & 14** Although dominated by gun fights and car chases, Italian cop films display cultural anxieties of the 1970s: *The Violent Professionals* (1973)

personality as follows: 'Give Giorgio a free hand and he'd kick the hell out of half of humanity. And put a slug in the rest.' After all, in Caneparo's world, humanity is filled with thieves, anarchists, prostitutes and corrupt cops under the screws of even more corrupt politicians.

In the film, Milan police chief Johnny Borelli (Rosario Borelli) chastises Caneparo for his use of extreme violence after taking out a couple of murderous escaped prisoners. The character's criticism that Caneparo is teetering on a tightrope and Borelli wants to curb the young cop's bloodlust even though it tends to get the job done is not new (indeed, it is particular to almost every American cop film produced during this era). Caneparo justifies his actions, but Borelli sees it differently. He is part of a new police order – a new 'kinder, gentler' approach toward criminals and their behaviour. He believes that even known murderers must be brought to justice via the court system and not by the revolver of a revenge-fuelled cop. Caneparo calls Borelli a saint, which of course is akin to the kiss of death. Naturally, it is not long before the police chief is assassinated in the middle of a crowded street (director Martino could not resist placing Guido and Maurizio De Angelis' upbeat pop music in the background during Borelli's savage murder – if not for the sake of twisted irony). And, shortly after Borelli's funeral, Caneparo is suspended from the force. This leads to Caneparo's vow to Borelli's wife that he will avenge the police chief's death.

From this point, director Martino leads us into an abyss. He weaves a labyrinth of conspiracy alluding to Milan's deadwood police force whose hands were tied in the wake of an actual 1969 bombing by possible government-sponsored terrorists attempting to quash anti-state demonstrations and public meetings that were erupting all over the city at that time. In *Milan Trema – la polizia vuole giustizia*, Martino emphasises the dismal performance of the police by showing how the assassination of Borelli is eventually buried by newspapers that quickly give the event short shrift with smaller, more insignificant headlines nonchalantly stating the police have no leads. Caneparo knows instinctively that Borelli's assassination was not the work of a random thug and he openly vocalises that this event will be made insignificant by the media. Caneparo's suspension propels the cop toward his own investigation, which quickly points to the incompetence prevalent within the police force. But the incompetence may actually be part of a larger network of conspiracy at work.

In fact, *Milan Trema* (as with other films of this nature) foreshadows the real-life shoddy police work that occurred immediately after the infamous Aldo Moro murder case of 1978. (This case was itself ripe for conspiracy theorists around the world.) Such theories in the Moro case involved not only the Italian government, but also the CIA, Henry Kissinger, Mossad, the KGB and other entities and individuals either singly or in diverse combinations.[5] Indeed, it has even been suggested that Moro's belief that the Communist Party should be represented in Italy's ruling coalition may have lead him to being sacrificed on the altar of Cold War politics.[6]

In fact, reactionaries on both sides of the Atlantic welcomed Moro's kidnapping (and subsequent murder) and, by refusing to negotiate for his release and failing to mount an effective police search, sent him to his doom.[7] One of the biggest contributors toward the making of this particular conspiracy was, indeed, based on incompetent police work:

> The dismal performance of the Italian police in their search for Moro has given conspiracy theorists plenty of ammunition. The police forgot to follow up important leads, they lost evidence and they did not think to keep obvious suspects under surveillance. To produce a record as egregious as this, conspiracy theorists argue, would require a conscious effort. By the law of averages, the police should have gotten something right at least, but failure crowned every one of their efforts for 55 straight days. By and large the Italian people have refused to believe that so much police power could have been employed over such a long period to achieve no crime-fighting purpose whatsoever unless by conspiratorial design.[8]

Because the police work in *Milan Trema* is similarly incompetent by design, it is up to Caneparo to find Borelli's killers – by any means necessary. But Caneparo does not actually realise the conspiracy around him until, during his investigation, he hooks up with a politically savvy prostitute, whose mission is actually to set the suspended cop straight. As a hooker with underworld connections, Maria (Martine Brochard) is eager to embrace Western values predominant during the early 1970s – open drug use (she artlessly smokes marijuana) and free love with a feminist's control. But she talks a communist game with obvious anti-capitalist disdain.

When Caneparo picks her up in a stolen Rolls Royce, she refers to it as a 'monster', a 'monolith', and a 'water buffalo'. But she happily jumps inside because, after all, it is stolen goods. Stealing the Rolls is a slap in the face of excessive consumerism, which is so obviously anti-capitalist. This is also reflected by the mansion where Maria flops – a mansion filled with hippies engaging in open sex and copious drug use.

Maria confuses her freedom of choice with intellectual pursuit and spouts her pseudo-intellectualism to Caneparo, telling him of how she dropped out of high school because her philosophy professor was always trying to 'feel her up'. Her next, most logical step, was to become a model for a 'nudie rag', which led her to gaining a 'social conscious' because in that business, 'you feel like a slave, like you're being taken'. Maria's social awakening reflects Italy's oppressed minions but she justifies her 'modelling' career because she's making good money – at least enough to live on. 'Hey, dummy', she thinks out loud, 'what's there to fight when you're making 35,000 per session? Look, if you don't like it pack your ass. Go to Russia where you have to show it for free to the "Party".' Then she purposely misquotes – 'All the world's a toilet, as Shakespeare says.'

Ultimately, Maria knows that her stage (life) is in the toilet but Caneparo is able to gain insight and empathy for one of Italy's citizens held down by government repression. 'Well', Caneparo says, 'if you can't find heaven at the Kremlin, there's always Mao.' Maria states that she is way ahead of that 'Mao crap' and that the only way to topple a corrupt government is through protest. Violent protest. Caneparo then refers to her as Maria X in wry allusion to Malcolm X, which Maria does not quite catch. So Caneparo shrugs it off saying, 'Maria X. You don't like it? You got a short memory. X that. X this.'

It is significant to note that Caneparo's statement is lost in the film's translation to English – Martino was trying to throw as much political allusion into the pot as he possibly could. But that was Martino's impression of Italy's political make-up during the 1970s – a hodgepodge of conflicting ideologies that saw a drive to find individualism among a morally corrupt government, a need for empowerment and acceptance of the self within the ruin of oppression. Ultimately, Caneparo is led to a powerful publishing magnate named Salisario (Richard Conte) who controls the media while engaging a gang in terrorist activities to 'shake up' the system with violence – a concept embraced by Maria X. The violence, according to Maria, creates chaos to 'build this country all over again'.

Because Caneparo is conservative by nature (he is offended when Maria X brings him to her mansion where there's a sex-and-drugs orgy going on), he believes radical groups have to be stopped even with a measure of reaction verging on fascist violence. In a sense, Caneparo's approach is as radical as Salisario's. But, Caneparo justifies his actions in the name of the law – even though he has been suspended and his mission is based on vengeance. In Caneparo's eyes, the law should represent what's needed most – justice.

85

**FIGURES 15 & 16** One man against a corrupt system: *The Violent Professionals* (1973)

*Milan Trema* reiterates the theme of police corruption when Caneparo discovers that police commissioner Vitiani (Silvano Tranquilli) is actually the head of Salisario's terrorist group. Following this revelation, Caneparo's impressions of the law are completely splintered. After crashing his car into Vitiani's and pushing it off of a cliff, Caneparo drops his gun to the ground in disgust (the scene being comparable to Harry Callahan throwing his badge into a dirty reservoir after taking out the psycho Scorpio in *Dirty Harry*). *Milan Trema – la polizia vuole giustizia* ends with a statement common to most films and literature – 'Any similarities to persons living or dead is a coincidence.' But, considering the political backdrop in Italy – especially in cities like Milan – during the 1970s, this final statement should actually be considered with tongue planted firmly in cheek. And, in a way, it is as powerful a political statement as that found in Costa Gravas' politically charged potboiler *Z* (1969) – 'Any similarity to actual persons or events is deliberate.' Although director Sergio Martino was trying to cover himself with his 'coincidence' statement, *Milan Trema* provides accurate coverage of the whole of Italian political mayhem during the early 1970s.

## BLOOD IN THE STREETS

Beyond its depiction of contemporary social turmoil, another important and driving motif in Italian crime/cop films is that of pain. Specifically, inflicting and receiving physical pain is central to this cycle as a whole. Nobody is immune: not bystanders milling about on sidewalks or drivers just trying to get their vehicles from one point to another. Even children and other 'innocents' are subject to intense pain and random violence. These are films that depict Milan, Rome and Naples as ticking time bombs, where every alley has a waiting thug with a blackjack in his pants and a stiletto in his boot. Any café can become a bomber's target. Just getting into your car can be dangerous because the backseat is likely to be occupied by a couple of psychotic kidnappers armed with pistols.

Whereas American cop films during the early 1970s addressed violence in the abstract, Italian crime/cop films exploited different levels of violent behaviour whether enacted by a terrorist group or the individual – and they raised the violence bar tenfold. In this sense, these films were more like Sam Peckinpah's 1969 film *The Wild Bunch* (complete with spurting blood and the expression of pain) than American images of the rogue cop from the 1970s. Indeed, even Dirty Harry's .44 rarely spilled as much blood as was on display in the Italian cop films produced during the era.

This is because life in Italy's major cities during the 1970s was under the oppressive pall of random acts of violence (be they by underworld gunfire or terrorist bombings at public establishments). Terrorist violence found in Italy during the 1970s can be divided into two sections – left-wing violence and Mafia violence. As Alison Jamieson has noted:

> Left-wing violence derives from Marxist-Leninist revolutionary theory, is altruistic, symbolic and has long-term aims; its targets are the representatives of a power system to be overthrown in favour of a dictatorship of the proletariat. Mafia violence, by contrast, is immediate and pragmatic, aimed solely at the pursuit of profit and the conservation of power and influence for the clan. Rather than overthrow institutional authority, the Mafia prefers to erode and suborn it; hence its essentially conservative nature.[9]

In that Italian crime/cop films echo these duel forms of violence, they also contain the necessary presence of a third force of violence: the rogue cop resolutely beating his fists against the 'system' – a system, which, for the most part, is exemplified by a passive police force. And, in these films, it was actor Maurizio Merli who spearheaded the rogue cop persona in a more intense, furious and enraged fashion than Hackman's 'Popeye' Doyle or Eastwood's Harry Callahan (although the American actors and their characters were obvious influences on Merli).

Though stereotyped as brutal cop throughout his career, Merli had all the right tools to play the part – dirty mop of blond hair, thick bushy moustache, unruly mutton-chop side-burns, rose-lensed aviator shades, chipped teeth, clenched fists and a wardrobe straight out of *Shaft* (Gordon Parks, 1970). Merli played a hard-bitten cop in at least twelve films from 1975–79. And according to director Stelvio Massi, who worked with Merli in eight of those films (including *Poliziotto sprint* (1977) and *Poliziotto senza paura* (1977)), the actor may have enjoyed his role too much – actually smacking down stuntmen during fight sequences.

Merli's pivotal cop role was that of Commissario Berti (some sources spell his name Betti) – a fist-driven character first introduced in Marino Girolami's *Roma violenta* (1975). Berti returns in Umberto Lenzi's *Napoli violenta* and comes back for a third round in Girolami's *Italia a mano armata* (1976). Whenever Berti was in town, he was there to serve justice – not necessarily to serve the law and, most definitely, not to serve his superiors.[10] It is *Napoli violenta* that really flows with blood – in fact, the violence on display is stunning. For instance, a thug's head is smashed in with a bowling ball in extreme close-up; a woman's head is bashed by a moving train; and a crook is impaled under his chin on a fence while trying to escape from marauding cops. Here, Lenzi's direction is also intended to beat the viewer into submission with whiplash camera spins, close-ups of relentless spine-smashing and merciless head-butting. Lenzi's Naples is overrun by a different type of terrorism than the politically, government-sponsored terrorist violence of *Milan Trema*.

In *Napoli violenta* the emphasis is on Mafia-style violence and oppression. Mafioso protection rackets hold small business owners hostage by demanding cash to keep their businesses running. If they do not pay, pockets of thugs ride through the cobblestone streets on motorcycles wielding chains and throwing rocks through plate glass windows. If you really want to 'buck the system', these unholy rollers will burn your place of business to the ground with you and your family inside. Berti is sent to Naples from Rome for one reason – to pummel the mob. Says Berti, when he arrives in Naples, 'They send me where they want because they know I'm hung up on the job.'

As soon as Berti steps off the train, he runs down a car thief, grabs him by the collar, smashes him in the face then slams the hood of a car down on the thief's head half a dozen times. He then slaps the crook's face and kicks him in the groin, dropping him over the car's trunk. For his first day on the job in Naples, Berti brings the thief to the Nucleo Polizia Criminale station as a 'present' – a specimen that comes cheap in Naples. From these actions, it becomes obvious that Berti has little regard for the law – even though this is a sticking point for the chief of police (Guido Alberti), who has resigned himself to Berti's tactics. 'I know just how you operate to bug your suspects', the police chief says to Berti, 'I admit your system works. Though I don't admire police brutality. I suppose the results are your excuse for using them.'

The police chief's statement, which incorporates tension between Berti and his superior, reflects what was happening in some police sectors in Italy during the mid-1970s. Some elements within Italy – specifically in cities that were overrun by terrorist or Mafioso groups – responded with sanctioned and exceptional police brutality and an instrumental approach to extreme right-wing violence. As Donald Reid has noted:

> Italy promulgated a series of laws that bolstered police powers at the expense of individual rights and gave a special place to informers; increased the time an individual could be held in preventive detention; and made individuals of the same group liable for the same sentence despite differences in individuals' actions.[11]

These authoritarian measures are replicated by the Italian cop films of the 1970s. In the case of *Napoli violenta*, the police chief's comments reveal that he was covering himself and the force by showing disgust at Berti's approach while, at the same time, acknowledging Berti's effectiveness by sanctioning the cop's practices. Berti's contempt for this official police policy is indicated in the film by his statement that 'Cops like me are fine for combating violence with violence and brutality. But the minute they get in the way, they become scapegoats for politicians.'

## CITIZEN'S ARREST

In Sergio Sollima's complex film *Revolver*, enforcing the law is not left exclusively to law enforcement officials and, though they will not directly admit it, they sanction brutality in much the same way the police chief does in *Napoli violenta*. But in *Revolver*, raising a fist against corruption is left to one man – a working stiff who is, in a sense, on the fringes of law enforcement. Vito Cipriani (Oliver Reed) is a prison warden and is confronted with a moral dilemma – he must allow a prisoner to escape from jail to be traded for his own kidnapped wife, Anna. The prisoner, Milo Ruiz (Fabio Testi), is being set up by a tangled band of terrorists run by a capitalist named Armand Collas who wants Ruiz dead. If the trade is not made, Collas will have Cipriani's wife killed.

**FIGURES 17 & 18** Abandoned by the legal system, Oliver Reed takes his own revenge in *Revolver* (1973)

Cipriani and Ruiz run over the Italian border to France where the trade will occur. But Cipriani starts to like Ruiz and is having a difficult time turning him over even though he has no doubt about saving his wife. The only thing Cipriani can do is go to the police for help – which is a mistake. The police tell Cipriani to consult a lawyer for advice. When he does so, the lawyer admits the futility of exclusive law enforcement by the police pitted against organised crime or corruption. And, in a sense, he is right. In *Revolver* the struggle against organised crime and corruption cannot be left exclusively to law enforcement and regulatory systems and to the professional guardians of society.[12]

In effect, the lawyer strongly suggests that Cipriani should murder Collas because, after all, Collas kidnapped his wife – not to mention that he is in need of some 'bureaucratic adjustment'. And the only way for Cipriani to get to Collas is by murdering Ruiz. Only then will Cipriani's wife be free and justice for taking down two criminals – Collas and Ruiz – will be served. As the lawyer explains to Cipriani: 'Armand Collas was a great oil magnate. But he refused to respect the interests of his industry. He was under the illusion that he could alter the balance of or break up the established order.' But the 'law' cannot come to grips with murdering Collas, so finding an unwilling assassin – even if he is a law abiding citizen – is key. And Cipriani is expendable enough to be used.

Of course, this attitude by the law toward one of Italy's law-abiding citizens is appalling but that is director Sollima's intent. The film makes a joke out of how, the regulatory/law enforcement system has to protect those who acquire and disseminate knowledge about crime and public corruption. There are few conditions more frightening than the fear that police or [law] officials will retaliate against whistle blowers through fear and psychological intimidation. This fear can even stimulate further corruption.[13]

Law enforcement in *Revolver* breaks Cipriani down psychologically by making him think that by going to the lawyer for advice, his moral dilemma – save Ruiz or save his wife – will be solved.

As the film indicates, the law justifies using a citizen for its dirty work to assassinate Collas, a capitalist whose political line went against the interests of the government. Toying psychologically with an innocent man, the police essentially force Cipriani to take Collas – 'a traitor to the people he worked for, to appease his own self interests' – out. This 'bureaucratic adjustment' is easily justified by the lawyer: 'Is [eliminating] the elements that create a disturbance against the interests and welfare of the community anything more than a bureaucratic operation?' Ultimately, the only way Cipriani can save his wife is through death, through violence and by way of the gun. 'Society has many ways of defending itself – with red tape, prison bars and … the revolver,' explains the lawyer as he places a gun in Cipriani's hand.

## CONCLUSION

*Bullitt*, *The French Connection*, *Dirty Harry* and its sequels may have answered domestic American audience frustrations but, between 1971–79, Italian filmmakers liberally borrowed the American rogue-cop icon and made it their own. They provided psychological twists and sociological turns with even higher stakes alluding to and incorporating real political events occurring in Italy at the time. These films also questioned the idea of law enforcement as capable protectors of the country's citizens – where justice was only efficiently shelled out by the angry hand of one individual against a corrupt system.

89

**FIGURES 19 & 20** The private citizen as Italian enforcer: *Revolver* (1973)

But, confronted by worldwide uncertainty, cops like Giorgio Caneparo and Commissario Berti and even private citizens like Vito Cipriani, who is forced into corruption, provide a sort of comfort – as cold as it may be. These men provide a strong arm to protect us from something they grappled with everyday – government corruption and politically-sponsored terrorism.

## CHAPTER 7
## MISE-EN-SCÈNES OF THE IMPOSSIBLE: SOVIET AND RUSSIAN HORROR FILMS

Christina Stojanova

This is not life but shadow of life and this is not movement but the soundless shadow of movement.
    – A. M. Gorky[1]

Every drive is virtually a death drive.
    – Jacques Lacan[2]

### INTRODUCTION

When discussing 'Russian' Horror Cinema, we are looking at almost a hundred years of filmmaking, the larger part of which (1917–91) encompasses the Soviet period, flanked by two relatively short and very different traditions: the Russian Imperial Cinema (1907–17) and the New Russian Cinema

(1991–2004). There exists a general consensus, summarised eloquently by Josephine Woll, that the Soviet period should be excluded from the discussion as 'the genre of horror films and the formulas that constitute its essence contradict almost every major tenet of Marxist historical materialism, of Soviet doctrine, and of Socialist Realist dogma'. This is because,

> the fears and anxieties underpinning horror films – of the uncanny or supernatural, of chaos, of the irrational – contravene a materialist philosophy that holds as self-evident the primacy of man as a social and rational being, who acts primarily out of motives of material interest, and whose alienation stems from specific economic and social conditions.[3]

This chapter is a diachronic discussion of major motifs of supernatural mysticism, physical and psychological horror in Russian and Soviet cinema and their transmutations over years and genres. It is divided into four parts, concentrating on recent works, but also referring to films from all three periods, thus allowing for a broader perspective on the idiosyncrasies of Russian and Soviet cinematic mysticism and horror. The specificity of the Russian and Soviet perception of horror in general and of its cinematic representation in particular prompts the need to view its cultural, political and aesthetic aspects in a larger philosophical framework. As Sergei Dobrotvorsky has put it, 'the mythology of Soviet cinema operates on a social and collective level, manipulating collective instincts, and ignoring or repressing the individual-physiological ones that constitute the usual target of [traditional, Western] screen horror'.[4] Philosopher Nikolai Berdyaev's concept of 'the Russian Idea', interpreted by Oleg Kovalov, provides the framework for discussion of the 'mythology of Soviet' and post-Soviet cinematic horror.[5]

## THE RUSSIAN IDEA, PSYCHOANALYSIS AND CINEMA

Nikolai Berdyaev (1874–1948) understood the Russian community in terms of what he called 'the Russian Idea', or the mission of the nation in a context of strenuous co-existence of socio-psychological and ethical extremes:

> despotism, hypertrophied role of the state and anarchism, frivolity; cruelty, violence and gentle kindness; ritualistic conservatism and restless truth-seeking; individualism, heightened sense of personal responsibility and faceless collectivism; nationalism, arrogant self-promotion and human solidarity and universalism; eschatological-messianic religiosity and phony piety; God-searching and belligerent atheism; humility and arrogance; slavery and rebellion.[6]

Following the tradition of nineteenth-century Russian philosophy, Berdyaev sees these extremes in the light of his concept of the '*noumenal* world-in-itself which is spirit, personality, freedom and creativity', and the '*phenomenal* world, which is alienated from personality and imposes general laws and material objects as limitations of human freedom'. The 'dualism of these two worlds', he claims, 'is the source of universal tragedy'.[7] Calling himself a 'religious existentialist', Berdyaev defines the Russian Idea as mystical, expressing 'the thought of the Creator about Russia', and also as a socio-religious one, proclaiming 'devotion to a common good rooted in Christianity'.[8] Therefore he sees the only salvation from the perils of the phenomenal world in *creativity*: following God, one should 'create oneself' and one's noumenal world 'from *nothingness*'.[9]

Berdyaev's Russian Idea, Freud's death drive and cinema all curiously meet in the myth of the fantastic (or phantasmic) city of Kitezh (Kitezh-grad). The legend of Kitezh is amongst the few ancient Slavic myths that has survived to this day. It dates back to the times of the Tartar-Mongolian invasions of the thirteenth/fourteenth centuries and corresponds to other world myths about the Great Time (*illud tempus*) of 'the beginnings'; as such it thus relates to the Judeo-Christian eschatological belief in the Golden Age that awaits the righteous at the 'end of times'. The myth tells the story of how beautiful Kitezh-grad, pillaged and destroyed, went under the waters of lake Svetloyar and became invisible for non-believers until the 'second coming of Christ'. And only the muffled ringing of its church bells, coming from the depths of the lake, reminded pilgrims of its mystical existence. There is a less popular, demonic side to the myth of this Russian Atlantis: long before the Tartar-Mongol invasion the lake Svetloyar was sacralised as one of the 'entrances' to Kupala, the nether kingdom of the dead.[10] From the nineteenth century on, Kitezh-grad crossed over into the secular domain and became a favourite mystical symbol of modernity, a national myth of sorts, popularised by the Silver Age poetry and symbolist paintings.

Berdyaev emphasises the role of Kitezh-grad as the grand national myth of escapism: 'Russian thinkers, artists and politicians kept ignoring the agonies of their bleak historical present' and turned instead to the *illo tempore* – the mythical past or future – where the glories of 'the true kingdom of the Lord, Kitezh-grad' lay hidden under the lake.[11] In other words, the national myth 'provided a representation of, and a solution to major enigmas'.[12] From a psychoanalytical point of view, the Kitezh myth is a frankly pessimistic *eschaton* (a myth about the end of the world), being an invitation to collective suicide. The numerous devastating attempts, known from Russian history, at annihilating the historical reality in the name of a mirage, buried under its horrors can be interpreted as 'compulsion to repeat' a collective death wish. Following Jean Laplanche and Jean-Bertrand Pontalis, then, the films under discussion in this essay can therefore be viewed as '*mise-en-scènes* of the [impossible collective] desire', where the 'unconscious implications' of the Russian Idea 'are organised' into the 'fantasies or imaginary scenarios' of the national myth 'to which the [collective] instinct becomes fixated'.[13]

## IDEOLOGICAL BOUNDARIES OF THE SUPERNATURAL: SOCIALIST REALIST ESCAPISM AND DISSIDENT MYSTICISM

Kovalov points out that 'while unequivocally detrimental for state, individual and the world at large', the extremes of the Russian Idea proved 'beneficial for the nineteenth and early twentieth-century art'. In its painstaking mediation, along with its pursuit of the evasive spiritual salvation, it provided the much needed cathartic effect of enlightenment and salvation on the individual and social level. Russian Imperial cinema, on the other hand, 'remained foreign to the role of spiritual mediator because its … poetics … was stuck in the concreteness of matter'. Most notable films from that period – the school of Yevgeni Bauer – had 'more in common with the cosmopolitan tradition of *art nouveau* or *modèrn* (as it is known in Russian), with their universal *fin-de-siècle* obsession with Gothic mysticism and death' than with the indigenous myths and 'the cosmogony of the Russian Idea'.[14]

The Golden Age of mediating the Russian Idea on screen, Kovalov argues, came in the 1920s when the young medium and its avant-garde began churning out aesthetically astounding projects for shaping Russian society in the image of Kitezh-grad. As an example Kovalov singles out Sergei Eisenstein's *Staroe I Novoe* (*Old and New*, 1929). Formally dedicated to the benefits of village co-operatives, the film furnishes a superb *mise-en-scène* of collective desire, in which millions of subjects/dreamers were the protagonists. In real life, 'Marfa Lapkina's village is dark and destitute', hell on earth. The 'utopian commune', however, 'enjoys bright modern buildings, well-fed herds and gushing streams of milk'. According to the indigenous folklore and the Orthodox tradition, it 'does take a miracle (or rivers of blood, for that matter) for a national dream to come true'. And while Eisenstein parodies the 'trance of the peasant procession praying for a miracle against the draught [he] equally ironically features … Marfa's milk separator … not as a 'new' and rational response to the 'old' unenlightened ways, but as a magical source of affluence, an Aladdin's lamp of sorts'.[15]

Historical and economic changes remain ineffective before the powerful drive of the collective unconscious to 'fixate its instinct' to the national myth of the miraculously attainable Paradise on Earth, thus transferring its awe-inspiring numinosity from the domain of the Orthodox Christianity to that of the New Life.

In the early 1930s, the Socialist Realist canon purged the intellectual and formal ambiguity of the avant-garde. The privilege to formulate the *eschaton* scientifically went to new theoretical disciplines like 'dialectical materialism' and 'scientific communism', which could not endorse magic separators due to obvious reasons. The supernatural component moved to the fairytale and to popular genres like the musical and the historical epic, where the 'perfectly legitimate stylistic mode of the … fairytale-like structure … elevated the subject matter into the realm of a 'dream' … enabling the spectator to "rise above" reality and regard it in a more sublime manner'.[16]

A key figure here is Alexander Ptushko. He owes his place in Soviet film history to his talent to harness Slavic legends and put them in service of the Communist state. From *Novi Gulliver* (*The New Gulliver*, 1935), one of the first full-length animation films, to his last release, *Ruslan I Ludmila* (*Ruslan and Ludmilla*, 1973), a set-designer's *tour-de-force* packed with special effects of his own making, Ptushko kept selectively popularising the Norse Slavic tradition of enchantment and the fabulous, carefully avoiding its horror and death-related mysticism. He was allowed a relative artistic autonomy and lavish budgets for the intricate settings of his phantasmic world. Nourishing the imagination of generations of Soviet children was unquestionably a noble task; sustaining the belief that the good life is attainable only through a miracle was a strategic one, as it helped the official mythology maintain its grip on the collective unconscious.

In 1967 Ptushko designed the special effects of *Vyi* (*The Spirit of Evil*), revealing another, repressed and archaic, side of Slavic folklore. The film follows the story from Nikolai Gogol's famous *Evenings* collection, with its eight narratives about peasants and boisterous lads, about devils, witches, abounding in genuine folk flavor, including Ukrainian words and phrases. Directed by Georgi Kropachyov and Konstantin Yershov, the film introduces some of the most popular female symbols of repressed sexual desire known from the Ukrainian and South Slavic demonic tradition.

The film is about a drunken seminarian (Leonid Kuravlyov), who falls asleep in a barn but is stalked by a broom-flying hag, an exact replica of Baba Yaga, one of the scariest personages of Slavic folklore. When he refuses to make love to her, she jumps on his back, forcing him to run until the first cockerel song at dawn revokes her evil powers. In a fit of revenge the seminarian whips her savagely, but is scared witless when she turns into a beautiful princess. Later in the day her father's servants drag him to a remote village, where he finds out that she has been dead for a day. His pathetic prayers fail to relieve her soul of her naughty designs and, after terrorising the poor lad to death, the vampire princess turns again into a hag. The film ends without giving sufficient clues whether the whole story is conjured up by the almost permanently intoxicated seminarian, or did indeed happen. Ptushko's work on *Vyi* is remarkable for the three church sequences, culminating in a scary parade of evil creatures – flying coffins and harpies, rattling skeletons and midget gargoyles. After so many years *Vyi* remains one of the best Gogolian movies, complete with Kuravlyov's tongue-in-cheek anticlerical innuendos and the ironic commentary of Khachaturian's original score, underlying its sublimity.

Alexander Rou's *Vechera na khutore bliz Dikanki* (*A Night Before Christmas*, 1961), and Yuri Ilyenko's *Vecher nakanune Ivana Kupala* aka *Nich pid Ivana Kupala* (*The Eve of Ivan Kupalo*, 1968) were also inspired by Gogol's *Evenings*. While the former went unnoticed by Soviet film historians as yet another fairytale (Rou was also a writer of fairytales), extrapolating fabulous motifs from the Russian classics, the latter is an undeservingly forgotten masterpiece. And four years earlier, Ilyenko had photographed Sergei Paradjanov's much acclaimed *Tini zabutykh predkiv* (*Shadows of Forgotten Ancestors*, 1964). These films saw the light of day as a result of a larger, centrifugal drive towards a revival of indigenous traditions of the Soviet republics, encouraged by the relative ideological 'thaw' in the 1960s. Ukrainian mystical, semi-Christian beliefs quietly endorsed the Ukrainian language and culture on screen, challenging the official Russification policy. In addition, Paradjanov and Ilyenko defied the positivist romanticism of Socialist Realism with their obsession with the 'terrifying mystery' of death and afterlife, 'not simply unknowable but linked with desires better kept unknown'.[17]

According to Socialist Realism, the 'traditional way of life was to be portrayed as uncanny'.[18] Or, in light of Tzvetan Todorov's discussion of the fantastic, 'the supernatural is explained, leaving no doubt that superstition and backwardness were the only explanations for the persistence of demonic and "semi-Christian" beliefs'.[19] On the other hand, 'representations of the supernatural in traditional/folkloric discourse could be defined as marvellous by definition', where the 'supernatural remains unexplained'.[20] Paradjanov and Ilyenko tell archetypal stories about the marvels of love in an exalted mythological (and native) context, 'signaling a rupture in the natural order, one, unlike the miraculous, not necessarily divine in origin and a challenge to rational causality'.[21]

*Shadows of Forgotten Ancestors* is a mystical story about Ivan (Ivan Mikolajchuk) who falls in love with Marichka (Larissa Kadochnikova), the daughter of his father's killer. They grow even closer after she drowns, suggesting that the true kingdom of God (and love) lies beneath the waters and beyond death. When Ivan remarries, her ghost keeps visiting him. In her jealous desperation Ivan's wife seeks help in divinations and evil spirits, and finally entices her lover, a sorcerer, to humiliate and kill him. Ivan's tragedy is seen in poetic harmony with nature and the perennial rhythm of the lively and colourful village life, of its work and holidays, changing with the seasons.

In tune with Gogol's original, *The Eve of Ivan Kupalo* plunges into the sinister side of the Kitezh myth. The story takes place on the eve of Ivan Kupalo, the magical all saints' night of the summer solstice, when the spirits of the dead are roaming and all wishes come true. A celebration of the ancient Slavic God and ruler of Kupala, it is also a tribute to the Christian saint John the Baptist (whose name literally translates as Ivan Kupalo).[22] Pyotr (Boris Khmelnitsky), a peasant lad in desperate need of money to marry his great love (Larissa Kadochnikova), strikes a deal with a demon, who promises a fortune if Pyotr would bring him the magic fire flower that blooms only on that night. Pyotr brings the flower only to find out that the stakes have gone up. And, while the village girls are sending candles afloat down the river to honour the underwater entrance to the land of the dead, and while his peers are jumping over bonfires to ensure the fertility of land and cattle, he kills a child for the loot. He can now marry his girl, but has lost the desire to do so along with his soul.

Ilyenko's experimental visuals reveal giddy spaces and flying camera angles from falling tree tops, from the point of view of a drowning woman, a dying man, a child, innocently unaware of the approaching peril. The nightmarish perspectives assault our senses, luring us into the forbidden domain of the divine and the demonic. The surreal atmosphere, enhanced by the contrasting effects of black-and-white, red and blue elevates these simple stories to the level of mythical narratives about the enchanted *illo tempore* when man and nature, the mundane and the magic were inseparable.

*Shadows of Forgotten Ancestors* and *The Eve of Ivan Kupalo* transcend the fossilising tendencies of the official ideology and 'render the supernatural sublimity [of the folklore] more efficient for the deeper life of the psyche'.[23] Their achievements remain isolated and, apart from the static and didactic science fictions from the 1980s, thriving on the waning Soviet technological might – based mostly on Kir Bulychyov's novels and a couple of classical literary science fiction works – the supernatural all but disappeared from the Soviet screen in the 1970s and 1980s. One major exception is Andrei Tarkovsky's metaphorical forays into space — cosmic and psychic. A God-seeker and 'religious existentialist' himself, he vehemently rejected the 'phenomenal world' to become a demiurge of a rich spiritual and moral universe of his own making, created out of the 'nothingness' of Brezhnev's stagnation. In *Solaris* (1972) he links the gothic horror motif of the creator and his monstrous creation with that of the 'double',[24] initially associated by Freud with the 'immortal' soul, the first 'double' of the body, which gradually lost its numinous aspect to become 'an uncanny harbinger of death'.[25] The supernatural beings terrorising the inhabitants of a spaceship are therefore 'phenomenal objectifications'[26] of the spacemen's long ignored noumenal worlds, their monstrous creations so to speak. After struggling with the uncanny apparition of his beloved dead wife, the protagonist (Donatas Banionis) comes to the realisation that the 'tragedy of creation' could be transcended only through faith and love. The final image, one of the most eloquent representations of *mysterium tremendum*[27] on screen, shows him kneeling in awe before his 'father' at the doorstep of a solitary 'home', lost in space.

In *Stalker* (1979), conversely, a couple of seasoned sceptics, a burnt-out writer and an uninspired scientist, led by an experienced Stalker or Follower who has lost his faith, set out on an uncanny trip into the forbidden 'Zone' to find the place where one's secret desires come true. Instead of finding the awesome mystery of life, they come face to face with 'nothingness' – a dreary, polluted landscape and an empty room with a ringing phone. The key to this mystical text is the Follower's daughter, a handicapped child with supernatural powers, his most cherished creation and a spiritual 'double', but the question about the divine or demonic nature of this 'double' still remains unanswered.

When in the mid-1980s Gorbachev's policies of *glasnost* and *perestroika* admitted officially to the obvious failure of the myth of the unassailable Good, Soviet filmmakers eagerly embarked on violating the taboos its representation entailed. Oleg Teptsov's 1989 film *Gospodin Oformitel* (*Mr. Decorator*) rehabilitates urban mystical motifs. Designed every bit as a Western horror film, it elegantly employs the cultural symbols of pre-revolutionary St. Petersburg – symbolist paintings, *art nouveau* architecture, cemeteries and special light effects. The main character, a famous set-designer and a Faust-like figure (Viktor Avilov), causes the death of one of his models – a poor girl (Anna Demyanenko), suffering from tuberculosis – by egoistically 'stealing her soul' for one of his famous mannequins, made in her likeness. The Decorator falls in love with the mannequin and its mysterious disappearance triggers his breakdown. Years later he is jolted out of an alcoholic stupor by a mysterious offer to decorate the haunted villa of a rich merchant (Mikhail Kozakov) whose childlike wife Maria looks exactly like the mannequin (and the deceased model). The ensuing strange events lead to the Decorator's tragic death.

It is not difficult to identify in this brief outline a number of mystical and surreal symbols, populating turn-of-the-century art – 'high' as well as 'low'. The Frankenstein motif of the creator whose creation goes awry is certainly central, followed by that of the double (a tribute to Bauer), of death and afterlife. *Mr. Decorator*'s butler is a Mephistophelean figure who dominates him, while the sinister-looking Merchant is definitely an offspring of Pushkin's murderous Gambler from *The Queen of Spades*. Unfortunately, such a rich constellation of mystical symbolism remains ineffective outside the messianic context of the melodramatic culture once sustaining it. Therefore any uncanny experience the film evokes only stems from the return of repressed extra-diegetic memories of the (red) terror the pre-Revolutionary culture was wiped with. Thus the film gets stuck in-between cosmopolitan mysticism and post-*perestroika* social and historical criticism, with the latter eventually prevailing, diluting the numinousity of the narrative. *Mr. Decorator* ultimately reads as a modernist *auteur* film with formal subjective allowance for the idiosyncrasies of the hero's artistic vision and internal psychic reality.

## BETWEEN MYTH AND REALITY: POLITICAL CHANGE AND BODY HORROR

Elem Klimov's *Idi I smotri* (*Come and See* or *Go and See*, 1985), reflects the intense spirit of *perestroika* times. It is about a sixteen-year-old boy, Florya (Alexey Kravchenko), who joins the Resistance to fight the German invaders, becomes a reluctant witness and victim of abject atrocities; he survives miraculously but his psyche remains damaged for life. Arguably the first film ever made on Russian soil to introduce uncensored torture scenes, it also brought to light the strictly prohibited topic of the collaboration of anti-Soviet Ukrainians and Belo-Russians with the Nazis.

Following Freud's discussion of the uncanny, which attributes terror to the collapsing of the psychic boundaries of self and other, life and death, reality and unreality, the disturbing representation of Nazi terror in occupied Belo-Russian villages can be explicated with reference to the collapse of boundaries between the national myth and reality. The excess of graphic mutilations, culminating in

**FIGURE 21** Florya from *Come and See* (1985): a reluctant witness and victim of abject Nazi atrocities

burning women and children alive in a church, goes far beyond the needs of a typical World War Two Soviet film. The depiction of gore and horror is linked to the fundamental shift in the 'unconscious implications' of the Russian Idea, identified so far exclusively with the myth of the unassailable Good. The radical aesthetic and thematic change of settings is of special interest here as it suggested a need to relieve the collective unconscious of its long-repressed negative contents and restore the balance in the representation of the Russian Idea.

Oleg Kovalov's compilation documentary, *Ostrov Myortvykh* (*Island of the Dead*, 1992), is devoted to 'Vera Kholodnaya, the Queen of the Russian Screen'. Kholodnaya was discovered by Yevgeni Bauer, the most original director of Silent Russian cinema. He gave her the breakthrough role in Turgenev's *Pesn torzhestvuyushchei liubvi* (*Song of Triumphant Love*, 1915).[28] Unfortunately, all that is left from her substantial creative record are a handful of films, which Kovalov inter-cuts with excerpts from amateur documentaries, newsreels, animation films like Wladyslaw Starewicz's pioneer *The Cameraman's Revenge* (1912), and from fiction films like Yakov Protazanov's *Aelita* (1924) and Sergei Eisenstein's *Battleship Potemkin* (1925).

Albeit structured as a philosophical essay about the tragedy of the Silver Age generation, *Island of the Dead* reads as a postmodern thriller with explicit instances of bodily horror. The unfolding atrocities, least we forget, were executed with the best intentions and in the name of the forthcoming Paradise on Earth. Kovalov foregrounds the unique role of arts and culture in the attempts at redesigning the collective unconscious in accord with the pressing needs of the national myth to justify the atrocities. His film highlights the peculiar impersonal nature of Soviet and Russian horror and its inherent relation to the tragic history of the nation. The exposure of pure evil, hidden behind the banners of freedom, is illuminated by Kovalov's masterful deconstruction of the national myth through classical works of early Russian and Soviet cinema.

The collage aesthetics of images and sounds relies on the postmodern interplay of alienation and identification, creating a cathartic effect of releasing memories – both uncanny and beguiling – from beneath the waters of the collective unconscious. As the film progresses, the ghost of 'the city on the marshes' and its celebrities is conjured up, but the serenity of scenes, featuring pastoral walks and afternoon teas, recreational army exercises, casual snapshots of the Emperor's family, and school parties of cute girls and boys, is undermined by a growing sense of foreboding, emphasised by gathering clouds. Combined in seamless sequences in the tradition of the Soviet montage, these images clash with the mounting chaos in the streets, on the front, in the villages. The expressive soundtrack, featuring nostalgic period *chansons*, dramatic opera and symphonic pieces as well as arrogantly ironic musical burlesques, triggers yet another level of associations, leaving the imagination to act on a few hints from the inter-titles.

The close-ups on Kholodnaya's melancholic face ('My eyes are my bread!') and the fleeting images of her fellow-artists convey the rising terror of entrapment. In the context of pending disaster, epitomised by images of Protazanov's Aelita, the scenes featuring Kholodnaya, the poet Mayakovsky and his muse, Lilly Brick, theatre director Meyerhold, prima-ballerina Anna Pavlova lose their original melodramatic vaunt and acquire the numinosity of fables about martyrs. 'The difference between Terror and Horror,' we are told, 'is the difference between awful apprehension and sickening realisation: between the smell of death and stumbling against a corpse.'[29] Thus the Martian princess Aelita, in her pompous *art nouveau* attire, is a belligerent symbol of the revolutionary, albeit doomed 'art of the future'. She also emerges as a formidable Goddess of Terror, conveying the 'awful apprehension' of war and the two ensuing revolutions.

The terror spills into horror with a close-up on Aelita solemnly clutching her fist, followed by a zoom-in on a flag, silently waving its *Long Live the Red Terror* inscription, inter-cut with scenes of the infamous Battleship Aurora sailors making merry on a fairground (*Battleship Potemkin*). The climactic sequence, a 'cruder presentation of the macabre by an exact portrayal of the physically horrible and revolting'[30] quickens its pace, resembling a truly diabolical St. Vitus' dance. Pieced together from virtually unknown documentary footage, the narrative literally 'stumbles against corpses'. A scene of a cheering mob chasing a 'class enemy' to strip him of his clothes in a manner most humiliating is followed by a shot of a woman stupefied with horror, sitting among scattered corpses of children and adults, and instinctively pulling on her torn dress to cover the evidence of a recent assault. Images of a crowd wildly singing and dancing are juxtaposed with a panoramic shot of grief-stricken refugees, crammed on board a ship, steaming away in haste. The last we see of them is a man trying to jump overboard at the sight of the vanishing shores. The sequence closes with the haunting image of a little girl with surreally big eyes sticking out amongst a bunch of horribly famished children.

The montage rhythm is slowed down by scenes from rarely seen newsreels of Kholodnaya's funeral. Her untimely death from the Spanish influenza in February 1919 at the age of 26 triggered a mass outpouring of grief in Odessa. Kovalov constructs this sequence as a nostalgic lament for the fragile normalcy of life. The final montage episode infers the perpetuation of Russian intelligentsia's compulsion to repeat its messianic and self-destructive delusions, and features 'comrades' Malevich, Rodchenko and Tatlin, the soon-to-be also wiped out masters of the 1920s avant-garde art.

It is easy to identify the principles of Eisenstein's 'montage of attractions' in the clash of charged visuals, symbolising the confrontations of old and new, high and low art, art and life, rich and poor, but also the binary oppositions of the Russian Idea. On the one hand, the fragile aesthetic universe epitomised by Kholodnaya's decadent beauty and Malevich's portentous Black Square is part of the 'noumenal world, which is creativity'. The egalitarian ethics of the rebellious masses of workers and peasants, on the other hand, are manifestation of the 'phenomenal world, which imposes material objects as limitations of human freedom'.[31] Thus Kovalov illustrates Berdyaev's tenet that in Russia (and in the Soviet Union) it is religion (or ideology) and philosophy, and not economics and politics that determine the history of society.

It is no coincidence that Tepzov and Kovalov's films are produced by the St. Petersburg's film studios, take place in St. Petersburg and its vicinities and are directed by local directors. *Lenfilm* has traditionally enjoyed the reputation of being ideologically the more open studio, and St. Petersburg is the home of the so-called first, or *perestroika*, avant-garde (1984–89). Its most notorious and radical trend was *necrorealism*, founded by Evgeni Jufit, the uncontested leader of Leningrad's underground. In 1985 he made *Hospital Attendants-Werewolves*, considered a manifesto of the *necrorealist* naturalistic-nihilistic aesthetics. In 1991 he made his first feature film, *Papa, umer ded Moroz* (*Daddy, Father Christmas Is Dead*) – a sadomasochistic tale of psychological perversion and physical mutation. In spite of their suggestive titles and subject matter, these works are not horror films *per se* but rather satirical social metaphors featuring 'the official "zombies" of the Brezhnev era … the "necrophiliacs and corpses" of post-Soviet life, a "world of walking dead". These are cult movies, seen by very few people'.[32]

This trend was taken further by two other St. Petersburg films: *Upyir* (*Vampire*, Sergei Vinokurov, 1997) and *Okraina* (*Outskirts*, Pyotr Lutsik, 1998). Both are postmodern pastiches of popular (Western) horror themes, employing bodily horror. The former was scripted by Dobrotvorsky himself in his efforts to facilitate the emergence of '[the] indigenous horror genre [responding] to the current fast re-orientation from the collective towards the personal encounter with existential problems'.[33] The film is about a post-Soviet provincial town, most of whose citizens have turned into vampires (i.e. New Russians) and a handsome vampire-destroyer – a latterday hero (Alexei Serebryakov) – is sent for to cleanse it. Unfortunately, in spite of the long Slavic vampire tradition and the original music by the famous group *Tequilajazz*, the film is too brainy to be scary and too straightforward to become an elaborate metaphor of the post-Communist individuation. According to one of the sternest critics of the film 'the individual has … not yet succeeded in separating himself from the social mass', which is the *conditio sine qua non* for the emergence of real heroes and traditional genre cinema.[34] In other words, good and evil, the self and the other, the rational and the irrational still remain nebulous collective entities without an articulated cinematic iconography.

In a manner reminiscent of Kovalov's, the late Pyotr Lutsik identifies as powerful sources of horror the collapsing boundaries between the collective and the individual, capitalism and socialism, the old and the new. In a paradoxical reversal of post-Communist loyalties, the source of the uncanny

99

in *Outskirts* is the tension between the 'new' Russian way of life and the 'old' Soviet one. Structured as a postmodern pastiche, the film mobilises the early Socialist Realism aesthetics, signified by the borrowed title of Boris Barnett's 1933 classic and by the black-and-white visuals. The characters, an unruly bunch of peasants from the Russian hinterland, are ironic replicas of famous cinematic prototypes from the period, and so is their textbook opposition to capitalism. They take their explicitly sadistic tactics against de-collectivisation of their village all the way to Moscow, where hell breaks loose. Lutsik's 'perfect sense of pastiche' allows him to 'lean heavily on [the] source material and yet manage to maintain [the film's] own stature [in this] attack on capitalism which even Soviet cinema in its heyday could not rise to'.[35]

Maverick director Artur Aristakisjan joins Lutsik in this unprecedented 'attack on capitalism'. His two docudramas *Ladoni* (*Palms*, 1994) and *Mesto na zemle* (*Place on Earth*, 2001) feature close observations of the abject lifestyle of urban outcasts whom Aristakisjan spent quite a long time getting to know. His films deliberately pursue the cutaneous sensation of humiliation and physical trauma, culminating in the self-mutilation scene in *Place on Earth*, where the hippie leader cuts off his penis in a symbolic protest against people leaving the commune, and in the particularly sadistic episode where a desperate mother tortures her child out of fear that it would be taken away from her. And although the director prefers to describe these shocking images as expressions of the raw romanticism of

**FIGURE 22** The new hyper-realist face of the horror genre: *Place on Earth* (2001)

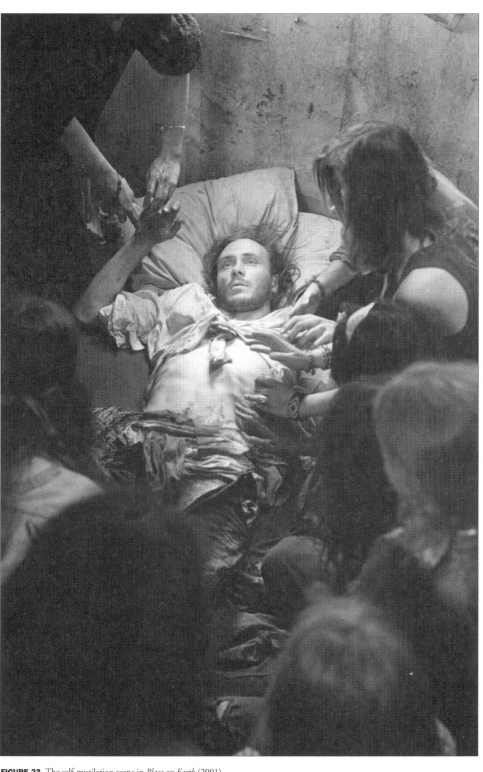

**FIGURE 23** The self-mutilation scene in *Place on Earth* (2001)

absolute freedom,[36] they constitute a new hyper-realistic development of the horror genre. Predicated on exploitation of the 'new' Russian poor – hippies, drug addicts, beggars, alcoholics – it reverses the noumenal obsession of Russian literature with the 'lower depths', prompted by its sense of guilt and compassion, into its diabolical double: intense psychological fear of destitution, born out of purely phenomenal – and neo-capitalist – preoccupation with physical and social well-being

## OF FREAKS AND MEN: PSYCHOLOGICAL HORROR FROM THE MODERN INTO THE POSTMODERN

After the collapse of the Soviet Union, society was gripped by profound disappointment and scepticism, threatening to wipe out not only the myth of Paradise on Earth but also the very notion of good. This bleak mood is best reflected in Alexei Balabanov's *Pro urodov I ljudei* (*Of Freaks and Men*, 1998) as it ventures into the little discussed pornographic industry, identifying sex with waste of creativity, with nothingness, the major cause for the 'universal tragedy of the dualism of the phenomenal and noumenal worlds'. Like *Island of the Dead*, *Of Freaks and Men* is a meta-linguistic pastiche about the formative years of Russian cinema. Both films recognise the ambiguous role of the new medium in the 'universal tragedy' but Kovalov believes in cinema's mediating power to break the compulsory cycle of repetitions and exorcise the collective unconscious from its death wish before it is too late.

Conversely, Balabanov sees cinema as an accessory to this death wish, worse – its instrument. The allure of death in Russian arts has traditionally defied the magnetism of sex. The presence of death – whether related to Christian Orthodox mysticism or violations of its powerful taboos or by imports of the Gothic – is strongly felt in the Russian arts from the turn of the nineteenth century. Indeed, what many leading *literarati* saw in the new medium was its death-like quality, linked to temporality and material decay. Maxim Gorky's feeling of cinema as 'The Kingdom of Shadows',

> was shared by many … Russian writers [who] treated cinema as a minor literary cliché … a convenient metaphor for death. … For Zinaida Gippius … the colorless figures of the screen evoked the legendary 'White Nights' of Russia's northern capital and … the phantoms they were believed to conjure up. … The 'symbolism' that [her hero] perceived in the cinema … was a part of a larger cultural pattern, the so-called 'myth of St. Petersburg' … a favorite point of reference for Russian Symbolist writers, to whom the ending of the world and the swamp-like instability of seemingly solid reality were of special interest as literary motifs.[37]

Lacan's argument that the death drive is by far the strongest one,[38] overpowering even the sexual, is very relevant to the discussion of Balabanov's film, arguably the first one featuring intense psychological horror to come out of contemporary Russia. The film is structured around characters, introduced in three episodes, made in the style of the first silent shorts. Their theme is announced in inter-titles: 'Johann passes through immigration control and enters the town', 'Doctor Stasov adopts the Siamese twins' and 'Engineer Radlov and his wife photograph their daughter Liza'. The ensuing events take place a few years later and feature the same characters, their families and maids,

**FIGURE 24** Sex as a form of mundane horror: *Of Freaks and Men* (1998)

entangled in a complicated relationship, based on shared dirty secrets and passions. It turns out that creepy Johann (Sergei Makovetsky) produces nude flagellation scenes in a cellar, helped by Putilov, an upstart and somewhat mawkish photographer-cameraman. Johann is the brother of Grunia, engineer Radlov's maid and, after his wife's death, his mistress, while Putilov is Liza's suitor. The plot thickens when Victor Ivanovich (Viktor Sukhorukov), Johann's right hand and a porn peddler whose clients include Liza (Dinara Drukarova) and Stasovs' maid Daria, develops an unhealthy 'artistic' interest in the angelic-voiced Siamese twins, Kolya and Tolya and, as a side effect, enters into a sadomasochistic relationship with their adoptive mother, Ekaterina Kirilovna (Anzhelika Nevolina). In the meantime engineer Radlov dies of a heart attack after Grunia informs him of his virginal daughter's secret passions. Johann kills Dr Stasov who comes to rescue his kidnapped sons, photographed in the nude in Johann's underground studio. After the death of their *pater familias*, the two respectable upper-class families are left to the mercy of the nightmarish duo. The 'freak show' expands to include Putilov's 'cinematographic' shorts and live cabaret performances, where the teenaged twins sing, while their mother and Liza are spanked by either Johann's senile nanny or Daria. When the nanny dies, Johann falls into a psychotic fit; the twins kill Victor Ivanovich and flee East, while Liza chooses the West. At the end Tolya dies of alcohol somewhere in the East, Liza gets her spanking from a professional leather boy in the West, where, thanks to his smut flicks, Putilov ascends to international fame, while the psychopath Johann literally drifts into oblivion down the Neva River.

Shot in dull sepia, emphasising its temporality and material decay, the film is a sublime trip through the 'lower depths' of society and the repressed bourgeois psyche, 'revealing Petersburg's most grandiose buildings as hiding murky subterranean secrets'.[39] The city has a deserted, graveyard look to it, hinting of perversity and psychological abuse. Yet there are no victims and victimisers; everyone seems to be confined to the uncanny sex-related torment of his or her own choice. Satsov's nightmarish run to Johann's den is a 'near imitation of Gothic flight, where branching corridors and circular passages transform forward movement into endless repetition'[40] while Liza's 'accidental walk into a bordello district of a foreign [Western] town' could be coming straight from Freud's infamous autobiographical description of the uncanny experience. To quote Berdyaev again, a 'contemporary man is free to choose between the religion of Satan and the religion of God, but cannot help being religious'.[41]

The avalanche of melodramatic coincidences and doublings (Johann and Viktor Ivanovich, the twins, the maids, and so forth) of urban myths (mostly about 'innocence unprotected'), and exotic perversities (a blind woman, Siamese twins and a virgin) is left deliberately ambivalent and, dependant on the viewer's predisposition, could be read either as ironically alienating or voyeuristically engaging. Balabanov 'exhaustively drags the high canon of Russian cultural values down to cinema level, enlisting the music of Prokofiev and Musorgsky, and the scrupulous reconstruction of decadent symbolism and necrophiliac melodramatism. The ominous contrast between divine music and corrupt reality creates titillation mixed with a sense of terror and guilt at the uncanny recognition of forbidden pleasures, 'familiar and old-established in the mind' yet 'alienated … through the process of repression', imposed by the long years of Tsarist-Orthodox and then Soviet censorship.

In psychoanalytic terms, the obsession with sex and death, with sex as death and cinema as death, is an expression, to quote Dobrotvorsky, of the 're-orientation from the collective towards the personal encounter with existential problems' by ignoring the collective instincts and releasing the repressed individual-physiological ones.[42] This explains the numerous staging of primal voyeuristic scenarios (the libidinal tensions between Liza and her father, resulting in his death; the twins watching their mother spanked; numerous peeping scenes, etc.). The attempt at restoration of the psychic boundaries between the collective and the individual, the public and the private, comes through every bit as tortuously uncanny as their collapse and sex emerges from the postmodern ambiguity as a form of mundane horror, 'vertiginous and plunging – not a soaring – sublime, which takes us deep within rather than far beyond the human sphere'.[43]

## CONCLUSION

Balabanov's, and recent Russian Cinema's, unequivocal ethical standing becomes explicit in the light of his other two major works, *Brat* (*Brother*, 1996) and *Vojna* (*War*, 2002), where he openly challenges the ongoing liberalisation and Westernisation of Russia as the source of lawlessness and ethnic wars. His is not a new sentiment – it has been around since the times of Peter the Great and intensified in the late nineteenth and early twentieth century, but its traditionalist Slavophile, anti-modernist impetus that has inspired Berdyaev's 'The Russian Idea' has never really been tackled by cinema. The Russian Imperial cinema and the Soviet avant-garde, as stated above, were powerful channels of Western modernisation, while the Soviet cinema mobilised anti-Western feelings for its own brand of anti-traditionalism, epitomised by the national myth of the Socialist Paradise on Earth.

The tragic clash between tradition and modernity that has engendered the Gothic novel and drama, and has historically nurtured horror cinema, is played out with a vengeance in *Of Freaks and Men*. It could be seen as a textbook rendition of Berdyaev's 'religious existentialist' tenet that the 'history of society is determined not by economics and politics but by religion and philosophy'. And, one is tempted to add, by cinema.

# CHAPTER 8
# MASOCHISTIC CINESEXUALITY: THE MANY DEATHS OF GIOVANNI LOMBARDO RADICE

Patricia MacCormack

Giovanni Lombardo Radice is an Italian actor who appeared in many low-budget Italian horror films from 1980 to the early 1990s. To English-speaking audiences he is more familiar as 'John Morghen'. Far from being typecast as villain or victim, Radice's characters in these films ranged from the imbecilic to the ecclesiastic. He began his film career in Ruggero Deodato's *La Casa Sperduta nel Parco* (*The House at the Edge of the Park*, 1980), playing a mildly retarded outsider assisting David Hess' brutal Alex in tormenting and torturing Italian bourgeois youths. He appears in the films of many Italian horror greats – as the coke-snorting sadistic Mike in Umberto Lenzi's *Cannibal Ferox* (1980) and the crazed but sympathetic cannibal Vietnam vet Charles Bukowski (!) in Antonio Margheriti's *Apocalypse Domani* (*Cannibal Apocalypse*, 1980). He is a village idiot scapegoat in Sergio Martino's *Il Mistero Degli Etruschi* (*Murders in the Etruscan Cemetery*, 1982). Radice appears in the first three of Michele Soavi's films; as gay ballet dancer Brett in *Deliria* (1986), as a priest in *La Chiesa* (*The Church*, 1988) and a suicidal cult member in *La Setta* (*The Sect*, 1990). He is what can only be described as a 'horsey type' – patrician, gay and hedonistic – in Lamberto Bava's *Body Puzzle* (1991) and most famously he appears as naïve, neurotic pervert Bob in Lucio Fulci's *Paura nel Citta dei Morti Viventi* (*City of the Living Dead*, 1980).

This chapter is an experiment utilising the many varied deaths of Giovanni Lombardo Radice to suggest viewing Italian horror film as a corporeal, non-dialectic experience – horrific but pleasurable nonetheless. I have chosen Radice because his gender resists the arguments that need to be addressed in thinking the aesthetics of violence when viewing women as victims, hence subverting the conventional positioning of the gaze as heterosexual and male. But his deaths are visually engaging in a way that goes beyond the gender of the viewer, thus the practice of viewing itself, beyond character identification is what solicits desire, launching the viewer upon a line of flight through the intensity of the film. This pleasure beyond the gender and sexuality of the viewer, the pleasure of cinema for cinema's sake, is a mode of sexuality purely of and for cinematic images. I have termed this *cinesexuality*.

## A RESUME OF DISGUST

Between 1980 and 1992 Radice appears in ten horror films and is violently killed in seven. He is wounded seriously, mocked and beaten in one other. In *Cannibal Ferox* Radice gets his hand chopped off, his penis and testicles cut away and eaten and the top of his skull sliced open and his brains eaten. In *Cannibal Apocalypse* he gets a hole blown through his abdomen through which the camera frames the action behind. He is burned alive in *Murders in the Etruscan Cemetery*, stabbed, beaten, taunted and humiliated in *The House at the Edge of the Park*. In *Deliria* he is kidnapped, bound, gagged and dismembered, he 'disappears' viscerally in *The Church* and in *The Sect* he shoots himself fatally in the mouth.

Radice's most famous extreme death occurs in *City of the Living Dead*, where he is the victim of a long, delirious death scene. As the town scapegoat Radice's character Bob is laid against an impossibly enormous drill by the town's paternal figure Mr Ross (Venantino Venantini). The camera oscillates between closing-up on Radice's terrified face and the oncoming drill for a painfully extended period of time. Against all expectation the camera does not turn away at the point where it is expected to. Instead, we see in loving close-up the drill bit enter, traverse and exit Radice's head, followed by a frame of his head pierced with the still rotating drill. This image achieves its intensity through the force of the action, the tension of temple against rotating tip, the polyphony of screeching drill and cries, the glisten of rolling eye and the merging of audience conviction that the drill will not (*cannot*) go in with the drill's actual penetration. The reorientation of function of this image away from the plateau of screen (what the image means within the narrative) toward the viewer (what the image does to us) extends and exceeds the immediate signification of a 'drill through the head'. Horror fans are, in Jean François Lyotard's words, the 'disciples of its affect'.[1]

## CINEMASEXUALITY: FROM STEELE TO RADICE

In this particular representation of horror, the traditional proclivity to a sadistic gaze is renegotiated. As a result, cinesexual viewers transform into cinemasochists – those who watch for the particular pleasure of the 'pain' of viewing baroque Italian horror images, defined by their defiance of reality for the affective potentials of the flesh and its possible contortions.

Throughout books, journals and fanzines on Italian cinema two stills prevail as the most frequently reproduced. One is the spike-punctured face of Barbara Steele in Mario Bava's *The Mask of Satan* (*La Maschera del Demonio*, 1960) and the other is Radice, with head parenthesised by the drill. What is the possible function of desire elicited through viewing his suffering? The scenes have no third-order signification or iconographic quality to the destruction of this body. Although this is the site of contention which many theorists claim reduces horror to low art, they fail to address that the power of horror is that it is about flesh, quality, volume and affect that connects image to viewer. Radice's presence in a film often heralds elongated torture and visceral death. Any follower of horror film accepts the signifier 'Giovanni Lombardo Radice' not as indicative of a certain role, style or quality of acting but a certain possible affect due to the probability of a visceral death. The spectatorial investment in differently gendered bodies performing similarly is evinced in *Deep Red* 5, in which Chas Balun reviews Ricardo Freda's *L'Orrible Segreto del Dr. Hichcock* (*The Horrible Dr Hichcock*, 1963) and *Lo Spettro* (*The Ghost*, 1962). He premises the reviews with 'Let's talk Barbara Steele … That face. Those eyes. Those lips. That body.'[2]

It is interesting that the same issue of *Deep Red* has a pioneering article on Radice by John Martin, but the focus shifts entirely to a heterosexual and traditional gender stance. Radice is said to 'head-butt drills, splitting *his* guts in sewers and *donating* brains to hungry natives'.[3] Grammatically Martin describes Radice's body as volitional rather than passive and any sense of the actor in a victimised or masochistic sense (and any seduction this could insinuate) is avoided. Although these semantics alter during the 1990s, he is yet to receive the attention of Steele or any of a number of other Italian and French female horror film stars. The fetishisation of the male and pleasure at his suffering simultaneous with his potential capacity to make others suffer constitutes somewhat of a blind spot in the celebrations and analyses of European horror. Carol Jenks' extensive analysis of Steele primarily points to the failure of psychoanalysis to fully explore the nuances of what is importantly and particularly a European version of the actress. She points out that 'supposedly only a woman can constitute a fetish object'.[4] The fetish, the part that stands in for the whole, and repudiates maternal castration, acts primarily as catharsis to the trauma of female lack.

But precisely why the deep ambiguity of Steele, what Jenks calls her 'ambiguous ecstasies',[5] her threat which exists simultaneous with her deliria inducing beauty, conforms to fetishism, traditionally aligned with the purely cruel woman, remains unclear. Ambiguity in its simplest definition offers a conflation and diffusion of a binary. With Steele we have pleasure and pain but also, in these psychoanalytic interpretations, the binary positioning of the (male) viewer and female fetish object. Thus spectatorship and gender invest for their meaning in their opposition. Because she is ambiguous Steele, like Radice, offers a primary site of binary diffusion. The casualty of this ambiguity is the viewer's capacity to comprehend or orient desire psychoanalytically through opposition.

If Steele opposes herself as both cruel and frail or beautiful and hideous the viewer takes a third position. Risking the charge of fetishising European film I would claim the European (and, especially because of its gore) Italian, horror film frequently depends on this ambiguity to sustain its affective purpose – that of a beautiful or pleasurable horror. We often see the elicitation of a protracted look in Italian horror so that our pleasure in the film is not through catharsis but a reflection upon what is considered desirable. Italian horror is a pleasure to look at but not through traditional paradigms of what is considered pleasurable – Steele in *The Mask of Satan* as beautiful 'victim' with holes in her face of whom *we* are frightened. Viscous coils of viscera, stitched flesh or even the saturation of colour seduce in the later Italian gore films. These images offer pleasure without shock (I think here specifically of films such as *Il Mostro e in Tavola* (*Flesh for Frankenstein*, Paul Morrissey/Antonio Margheriti, 1974) which are shot beautifully, populated by beautiful people but are nonetheless extremely gory). If the catharsis no longer prevails then we must ask, is psychoanalysis still the most effective or interesting way to think of these films?

Thus the definition of 'fetish' as a cathartic repudiation may need to be refigured to address the ambiguity of so-called 'fetish' figures such as Steele. A turn to French post-structuralism, in this chapter to Lyotard, may help think this different form of fetishism and its reformulation of the viewer and her/his pleasure. The choice of Radice will enhance the ambiguity in the suitability of choosing a male through which to rethink fetishism while pragmatically offering an analysis of an ambiguous male horror figure. I also wish to trouble the trace of psychoanalytic primacy of the male viewer by offering a male who demands to be looked at (by both sexes).

Radice presents traumatised flesh that momentarily escapes the need to speak the problems of gender in horror. Italian horror is frequently cited as misogynistic, yet ironically repetitive and rudimentary representations of women are more frequently found in Hollywood horror, where female characters resonate around a few stock types – sexualised victim, virginal last girl and empowered (but masculinised) heroine. These versions of femininity necessarily oppose feminist ethics to the pleasures of watching bodies in distress, because many horror films relish the deaths of women because they are women. More so, the structuring of women as volitional and complex into 'types' fulfils certain expectations of femininity as both predictable and resolvable and hence their fate performs a social catharsis akin to a modern morality play. Neither these representations nor my unsatisfactorily simple reflection upon them addresses the pleasures of viewing extremes of the body beyond a form of aggression. Taking a male actor's suffering can afford a masochistic rather than a sadistic form of cinesexual pleasure if traditional gaze theory that anchors the act of looking around a male viewer is employed. The focus on female death as either misogynistic or aesthetic is an astonishing specularisation of women over that of male characters. Dario Argento's films are cited repetitively as performing female aestheticisation of violence, yet his films include as many male deaths that could be equally analysed as aesthetic. Additionally most of Argento's murderers are female characters, which would lend his films to a lesbian analysis of the pleasures of violence, yet this analysis is yet to appear. It seems, then, that this is a blind spot not within the films but rather the theoretical field.

## THE MASOCHISTIC BODY: RETHINKING THE FLESH OF ITALIAN HORROR

The reason Italian horror becomes scapegoated is perhaps due to its sacrifice of character and plot for a celebration of the intensity of the flesh in various dishevelled and persecuted states. Extremity of gore and flesh confounds the very meaning of the body beyond gender to infer bodies defined through the ways in which they open, reanimate, terrify and nauseate. Radice's cornucopia of embodied suffering is about the ecstatic display of extremities of flesh more than narrative cohesion, more expressionism than realism. His deaths are moments of pure cinema, desired, experienced and given meaning by the viewer. His characters are not distilled into a single stereotype. Radice dies as an aggressive, racist cocaine addict (*Cannibal Ferox*), a sexually frustrated neurotic (*City of the Living Dead*), a mentally challenged but essentially harmless youth (*The House at the Edge of the Park*), a Vietnam vet (*Cannibal Apocalypse*), a cult member (*The Sect*). But if we are tempted to say all his characters are dysfunctional he is also killed playing a priest (*The Church*) and a ballet dancer (*Deliria*).

Essentially, Radice's characters are less important than his deaths, because although some may deserve the extremity of their demise, most of the characters die in films where almost *all* the characters die. However, Radice's deaths (with the exception of *The Church*) stand out as spectacular. These deaths are fascinating to both genders, and it is the extreme conditions of his flesh that the viewer libidinalises, not his character or his potential as object of desire. Because this is pure cinema of the body-in-pain, both his and our pleasure is masochistic. His because he heralds and signifies the experiencing of pain in most films in which he appears. Ours because the pleasure of viewing him is not so much sadistic (a rudimentary and unnecessarily binarised positioning of the pleasures of viewing gore films) as masochistic – hard to watch, harrowing, deliriously beautiful, thus evoking conflicting and perverse definitions of pleasure in the act of viewing.

Because I aim to pervert the persistent use of psychoanalysis in analysing Italian horror film, I choose Lyotardian masochism over Lacanian desire (as satisfying lack) as the model through which to tease out my argument. Masochism is a perversion in psychoanalysis beyond heterosexual desiring dialectics; masochism is a particularly male pathology, evinced even to renegotiations such as Gilles Deleuze's rereading in *Coldness and Cruelty*; masochism in Lyotard is a jumping off point to entirely other ways of thinking desire. Lyotard concludes that the point of masochism as being simply an openness points to the possibilities of what he terms 'use me'. An occlusion of space between viewer and viewed results from the opening up of the embodied desiring self as infinite void. Radice's suffering is not about gender reversal or a master/slave dialectic but corporeal excess in the activity of viewing. The cinesexual masochist begs '*Use Me*' outside of any 'reality'. Neither the image nor the pleasure it evokes is transcribable to reality but is an event of pure cinema. Bravely against and outside of the master/slave insinuation, Lyotard is adamant:

> The question of 'passivity' is not the question of slavery, the question of dependency not the plea to be dominated. There is no dialectic of the slave, neither Hegel's nor the dialectic of the hysteric according to Lacan, both presupposing the *permutation of roles on the inside of a space of domination*. This is all macho bullshit … The passion of passivity of this offer is not *one single* force, a resource of force in a battle, it is force [*puissance*] itself, liquidating all stases which here and there block the passages of intensity.[6]

Passivity is openness to opening, to non-thought and to possible libidinal banding with a certain strangeness. In essence the viewer submits to the submissive Radice. This redoubled submission suggests the turning back of a term on itself as not representative of negation or absence but a twist toward a new becoming. Redoubled submission is infinite openness rather than the eternal return to prior self-masochism demands. Its result folds the two – viewer and viewed – into one continual band(ing) of affect. When the viewer desires an image, the opposition of viewer and object of desire is exchanged for durational folding of material image and imaged body. Because desire sets itself within a system of opposition, Lyotard uses the word 'libidinal' to express the folding, working through or theatrical 'band' that twists the 'inevitable confusion'[7] of oppositions. Libido is an openness to the excesses of the everyday by refusing to lose the intensities and affects of all experience blocked by signification. Such an engagement allows for the possibility of the breaks and flows implicit in the relationship between discourse, matter, affects and chance to express force (*puissance*) and hence differing, multiple futures.

Lyotard names his conception of this plane of intensity 'the great ephemeral skin'. This skin also includes (but because it is figural does not oppose) image, the viewed, the flesh of others and the opened body flattened out toward infinity. The skin is not 'one's' skin, or 'my' skin, it does not enclose or integrate, it continually extends and opens. Radice's flesh in pain is not material in that we can reach out and take his body as real, but it is material in that we enter into an affected and actual intensification and libidinal 'turning' with, and inextricable from, the images.

If critics of European horror claim these films and scenes make no sense, what is the sense of pleasure found within them? A drill through the head, the top of the head sliced off, dismemberment, a shot to the mouth make perfect sense if it is the sensorial we are after. But our pleasure makes no sense either. It is not realisable in the 'real', yet it is realised in the viewing flesh. The tension of seeing Radice enter only to await his inevitable and spectacular 'exit' plays an important role in the situation in which we view. 'How' and 'when' become important expectations for Radice's fans. His death is extended in *Cannibal Ferox* into a triptych death of castration, dismemberment and decapitation. It is doubled in *City of the Living Dead* as he returns from the dead. In *Murders in the Etruscan Cemetery* he creates a postmodern referent to his own persona when he replays the character of Bob from *City of the Living Dead*, which immediately sets him up for a visceral fall. Michele Soavi cleverly foxes expectation in *The Sect* when Radice shoots himself within the first ten minutes of the film, almost getting his death out of the way so that the audience will concentrate on the plot and not await Radice's demise. Radice's screaming face and tortured body contort with our wide-eyed shocked pleasure, and, as Soavi clearly acknowledges, overwrites character, plot or narrative.

The redoubled submission of opening to Radice's body-in-pain evinces passivity as not within a binary economy space of domination limited to which gender holds which role, but of passivity as a sexual *and* political openness to (becoming) force itself. Force insinuates change, temporal (not temporary) differentiation. Differentiation is different to absolute difference, which carries the possibility of negation because it always only refers to different to one. Differentiation is constant multiplication, proliferation of intensities and possibilities. It may result in the same but only as a possibility among many rather than either different to or not.[8] The horror of watching his deaths liquidates our gendered desiring gaze and our understanding of what is pleasurable and what is traumatic. The viewer reflects his screams and groans and yet ours are elicited simultaneously and beyond the binary of agony and ecstasy.

**FIGURE 25** Masochistic suffering in the jungle: Radice in *Cannibal Ferox* (1980)

When we see our first Radice film there may exist a traditional dialectic of sadistic gaze and victim, but by the time we reach our third or fourth Radice film there is a sense that *this guy is* (as are we) *enjoying it!* Like masochism, his suffering is repeated over and over, presenting an eternal return that is both the same and different every time. Interestingly in Italian horror the male body in pain is frequently 'enjoyed' by the camera. As well as Radice, most *gialli* include a relatively balanced series of male and female deaths (especially in Argento's mid-career films). Gore films also fetishise men in pain. For instance, this is seen emphatically in the deaths of Udo Kier in *Flesh for Frankenstein*, where his hand is cut off and he receives a barge pole through his gall bladder. It is also seen in *Dracula Cerca Sangue dei Vergine e Mori di Sete* (*Blood for Dracula*, Paul Morrissey/Antonio Margheriti, 1974), where his arms and legs are cut off and he is staked, but only after he has vomited his way through two women and a pool of hymen blood.

It would reduce the impact of these scenes to relegate Kier's and Radice's deaths to the binary option of feminisation, despite the symbolic suggestion of appendage removal and penetration of the body or head. If this were so the male viewer would desire the feminised bodies and hence the gaze would become homoerotic, therefore through the homosexual turn the viewer's identification would also be masochist. Here scenes both trouble and *exceed* binaries, not simply of desire and pleasure and pain but of the positioning of content and form, legibility and affect.

What do we desire in these images? What they signify does not seem to encompass the pleasure they afford. Traditional signification – the sign of a screaming body or the metonym of a drill through the head – does not begin to explore what it is about these moments that the viewer delights in. Radice's body is the literal incarnation of the materiality Lyotard suggests in the shattered partial objects. He as a 'character' and we as gendered 'viewer' are shattered into plateaus of expectation, intensity and pleasure. Lyotard states: '…frontier or fissure? No it is rather the region of transmutation from one skin onto a different skin.'[9] The screen is neither frontier nor fissure but the region where the image of one skin directly affects our viewing flesh. We do not see in Radice *a* face with a mouth and eyes that appeal to us, or even a head drilled though.

Our pleasure in Radice's films (and more importantly his deaths) is the elicitation of ecstatic excess beyond our demand for narrative or comprehensible pleasure. We no longer desire some*thing* (character, meaning, resonance with reality, obvious beauty), but take pleasure in everything we cannot vindicate or explain. Deleuze claims:

> Our lived relationship with the brain becomes increasingly fragile … and goes through little cerebral deaths. The brain becomes our problem or our illness, our passion rather than our mastery, our solution or decision. The brain cuts or puts to flight all internal associations, it summons an outside beyond any external world.[10]

Watching horror points to the fragility of the dialectic relationship because narrative is subjugated to effect and empirical succession shows incomprehensible series' of reanimation after death, drills in the head, living after dismemberment and castration. Watching a film with Radice in it opens the brain to a certain force that may rely on incommensurable signifiers as creating ideas that redirect our lines of flight.

## CORPOREAL PERFORMANCES

In a film like *City of the Living Dead* the image of Radice's drill-penetrated skull can affect in any number of ways. The surface of skin and metal inflects into a new configuration and it is all incomprehensibly *too* much but not enough to *mean* anything – not a sign but force. Ironically this scene, unlike many others, does not show us any secret layers of the flesh. There is no profane plateau of the flesh exposed in the drill scene, the site of Radice's death.

Yet, later in the film, Radice's flesh does peel away to expose nondescript flaps of skin and flesh, but the excavation of his flesh also heralds the overturning of his death. Radice has returned to the living, albeit the living dead. His body has returned *differently* as his life has differentiated itself from his character to a form of autonomania. He looks different and the audience looks at him differently. Transformation punctuates any investment the audience risks by investing in a Radice character.

In *Cannibal Apocalypse* he scares us as an unhinged Vietnam vet but not as much as when we realise he has transferred his sexuality to consumption when his 'seduction' of a woman in a movie theatre expresses itself as cannibalism (see interview, following chapter). Pleasure, sex, repulsion and horror return in *Cannibal Ferox*. Radice's character, despicable to a pantomime level, affords enormous pleasure to us, not when we see him naked in his sex scenes but semi-naked when he is castrated. Although a rudimentary reading of this scene could see it as 'just desserts' there is something tersely and curiously erotic about seeing a male rather than a female being punished in a clearly and traditionally masochistic performance. Here, he is tied to a tree and corporeally described through a direct connection of genitality to suffering rather than sexuality. Even though *Cannibal Ferox* is the seediest of Radice's films – racist, misogynistic and unethical in its real-life killing of animals – Radice's death is anchored entirely on the perversion (rather than reversion) of traditional power binaries. By comparison, the infamous scene of a male sucking a woman's brains directly from her head through a straw in *Bloodsucking Freaks* (Joel M. Reed, 1976) is repulsive not because of its extreme gore but its simplistic and repetitive re-establishment of traditional power relations.

In essence, the above example it is not very different to the idea of a vampire sucking the neck of a victim. However, usually in vampire cinema the female victim is willingly seduced, while in *Bloodsucking Freaks* the meanness of the scene comes from the forceful, childish expression of male power borne of nothing more complex than masculine anxiety. In *Cannibal Ferox* Radice's Mike is established as another of these hyper-masculine figures, but his seat of masculinity – his penis – is removed. Traditional symbols of technological advance and logic are graphically destroyed as his hand is lopped off and his skull sliced open so the brains can be eaten by Amazonian natives. Unfortunately Radice's death is the only one that renegotiates power relations. (The death of Pat (Zora Kerowa) is predictably oriented around her being sexualised – she is pierced through the breasts 'man-called-horse' sun-dance style.) Reading this death through its symbolic referents, however, reduces the scenes to simplistic catharsis. Describing Radice's death purely through symbols and racial signs brings theorising the power of the scenes to an equivalently predictable 'male' (logocentric, Lacanian) level. The risk is not in reading the images but confessing their power goes beyond their immediate meaning. Watching Radice's body in a state of extremity, folding with our viewing body into modulations of viewing enjoyment, suffering and ex-stasis produces material changes and temporal becomings. Cinesexuality

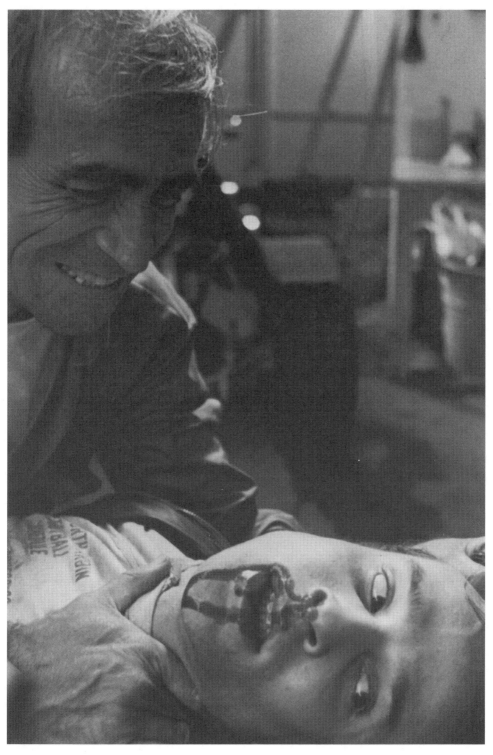

**FIGURE 26** Character cruelty and spectator pleasure – Radice's most famous death: *City of the Living Dead* (1980)

is perverse seduction because, like true masochists, we are the – not willing, but demanding – victims. We want to watch because watching extreme and impossible images is the true encounter of film – becoming open to worlds, textures, sounds, colours and intensities unable to be encountered in the 'real' world. The sadistic gaze becomes the masochistic demand of the viewer upon the suffering body of the victim on-screen thus perverting the order of signs in film language and systems of images.

Radice's body becomes a form of the body-without-organs, de-stratified and re-signified through protean transformations facilitated by everything from extreme but possible violence to becoming-zombie. We are continually reminded he is less a male than a series of fleshly fabulations. Even though he is castrated in *Cannibal Ferox*, invaginated in *Cannibal Apocalypse*, penetrated in *City of the Living Dead*, dismembered in *Deliria*, stabbed (another invagination) in *The House at the Edge of the Park* and fellates a gun in *The Sect* his body is less feminised than functionally renegotiated altogether. His masculinity is broken down but this does not necessarily mean his femininity is built up. Resisting binaries places the emphasis on our capacity to break down our role as master of the meaning of the images and allow ourselves to be used by Radice's flesh. He is a body in a visceral but not subjective sense. Representations of the internal plateaus of his flesh and the possible plateaus of his pain are the layers of the body with which we can identify over character. Any discursive practice located around the body cannot contain its excesses, just as any claim to excess corporeality, through practices from perversion through body modification and becoming cannot exist without a discursive system, as a referent, a residue or a memory.

## CONCLUSION

Whether stabbed, drilled or cannibalised, Radice's visual texture in these films is a line of flight toward an openness to the excesses of signification to do with gender, sexuality and pleasure. This deliberately rudimentary experiment in thinking European horror as renegotiating traditional paradigms of desire resonates with post-structuralism's project of utilising the unbound potential of desire to trouble traditional notions of subjectivity. The increasing popularity of non-canonical European cinema, particularly horror, simultaneous with its burgeoning popularity in academia, clearly highlights cinema as being pleasurable and available along different paradigms to those familiar to us as 'Hollywood cinema'. This chapter has attempted to offer both an addition to the increasingly complex academic interest in these films, and also a discussion of the ways in which, through ambiguity, gore and beauty, Italian horror can assist in thinking the viewer, desire and pleasure differently. Radice as an Italian actor in Italian films offers a rare glimpse, against the Hollywood obsession with masculinity in crisis, of masculinity in crisis and *enjoying* it. Jenks points out that Steele is horrific primarily because she is 'not the site of lack but too much body'.[11] Radice is male and flesh and living and dead and thus no longer reliable as a guarantee of traditional gender or viewing or even human positions. What psychoanalysis and post-structuralism has always known is that desire and pleasure are unreliable, something to be controlled to express our gender, rather than let loose. Italian horror is brave in (literally) letting loose the flesh, leaving the viewer in an abyss of cinematic pleasure with few binary markers intact to orient this pleasure. Perhaps this is why they have been maligned and banned. But it may explain why they have also become such ripe territory for philosophical analysis.

## CHAPTER 09
## MALE MASOCHISM, MALE MONSTERS: AN INTERVIEW WITH GIOVANNI LOMBARDO RADICE

Interview by Patricia MacCormack

Giovanni Lombardo Radice is an extraordinary figure in the Italian horror canon. Because of his repetitive, elaborate suffering in many of the films in which he appeared, he is something of a pariah within the horror tradition. This is because his work contradicts many of the dominant norms of the genre, where the camera often fixates around images of female suffering. Radice is tortured across many films, and thus he is recognisable as much for his gruesome ends as for his acting and unusual look. Far from his neurotic, skinny and often lithe image of the early 1980s, Radice is an imposing figure, far taller than he appears in the films and now bald, like an Italian Foucault without the glasses! His extensive experience as a theatre actor and director is evident in his cultured, learned demeanour.

Radice's walls are lined with books and original art. He is a great mimic and performs other people during the interview with a hilarious clarity. His humour invades each response and he is altogether precisely opposite to creepy Bob of *City of the Living Dead* or crazed, racist, sexist and generally unpleasant Mike in *Cannibal Ferox*. This may explain why he is not happy about being remembered purely for his horror career. The marked juxtaposition of Radice the horror star and the person may testify to his acting ability in the films. However he is a very genial person who does not refuse his horror career even though he does not like it, and I thank him for allowing me once again into his home to conduct this interview.

*Patricia MacCormack: You have said in interviews that you don't like all these horror films you have appeared in – why did you do them?*

Giovanni Lombardo Radice: It's very simple, because of the money. It just happened by chance. In a moment when I was very young, 24 or 25, and I was passing a major economic crisis, and my first movie was offered to me, and I didn't really care what it was. I said yes of course and as a matter of fact it was not a horror because *House at the Edge of the Park* is not a horror, it was more a thriller, but it could have been whatever, I would have done it. So then after that first one I was very happy, I learned a lot and I always like acting. If instead it would have been musicals or romantic stories it would have been the same to me.

*What were you doing when Ruggero Deodato's mother-in-law discovered you?*

She started everything. Ruggero was married to an actress, Silvia Dionisio [Pearla in Antonio Margheriti's *Dracula Cerca Sangue*], and that lady was Silvia's mother, she was working as an agent. I had done a theatre production in the famous Spoleto festival. I was working in a little theatre which had just reopened, measuring the stage to see if the production could fit there. There were a few people there and this lady watched me from the seats…

*She watched you measure?*

Yes she watched me measure, not acting. I was there in a pair of blue jeans, just saying '8 metres by 9…'

*So it was just the way you looked?*

Yes, because in Italy acting didn't used to be considered a profession. She knew I was an actor, she asked, 'have you ever been in a movie?' I said, 'Lady for some money I would walk on my hands with a red nose on, so sure why not.' Surely, she saw what she thought was a classic 'movie face', strong cheek bones and blue eyes. In addition I didn't look Italian, I spoke good English and had stage experience. I don't think she saw something special connected to the horror genre, she was just casting for Deodato and suggested me. Ruggero was casting and she proposed me for a role that had already been cast, and Michele Soavi was cast to do it. Michele was an actor, he had a great face and was a good actor. Then Ruggero changed his mind.

*Was that the beginning of your relationship with the actor-turned-director Michele Soavi?*

Yes, Michele, poor guy, we became great friends, but I stole a role twice. But we didn't know each other then. I stole Ricky and I stole Bob from *Paura* (*City of the Living Dead*). Michele had been cast for Bob. But Michele wasn't really interested in acting, he knew he wanted to direct. He was acting in that little role in *Paura* as the guy in the car with a girl, and he was also volunteering as assistant director. He is not credited but he was. So acting was a pastime and a way to be in the movies. So the first time we met during *Paura* he made a joke, he said 'Fuck, you just stole two roles from me.' And then we became great friends.

*It is well known that you are not that keen on your horror roles.*

I have to say that I don't really like that kind of movie. That's why when people ask me if I think Deodato's *House at the Edge of the Park* was based on the Wes Craven movie [*Last House on the Left*], I say, 'I don't think anything because I didn't see it.'

*Have you seen your movies?*

Not all of them.

*Has your family seen your movies?*

My mother died when I was very young. My poor father, who has now died, back in the early 1980s he said, 'I want to see your movie, the first one', and I said 'no daddy please, you have a bad heart and they are really shit – don't go! Its not worthwhile', but he did and he said, 'look, I am so sorry but after a while I walked out', and he didn't like the fact that I was in these movies because he knew theatre was my great passion.

*How do the differing mediums of film and theatre affect your performance technique?*

With film, you have to know and understand what's going on with the camera. In theatre it's the whole body, I trained as a dancer and use the animal technique, zoomorphia, studying animals to work in characters. You are face body hands legs, in the space. In film you have to have a relationship with the camera, you need to know if it's a close-up or long-shot. And the director is everything. On stage you are in control. In movies you read the screenplay but it is the director who retains control.

*What about the relationship with the audience – in film you have a very immanent relationship with the audience?*

Some directors shoot very still, with others the camera moves with the actors. With that kind of director stage experience is very important. It's a dance you do with the camera.

*The extraordinary things about your role in this genre is the masochistic positioning of your body and what happens to it in almost every film. Although masochism is clinically a male neurosis, I still think it is a rare spectacle to see repetitive male suffering in horror film that isn't simply a punishment for moral indiscretion. Also the audience are seduced into suffering with you and pleasurably so. Is there something about you that made directors say, 'it is delicious to watch Giovanni suffer'?*

You shouldn't forget that all the horror movies I was in were not written with me in mind. This means that the hurt and the sufferings dedicated to a male body pre-existed in the mind of directors or screenwriters. There can be many reasons for these fantasies, but from a psychological point of view I can say that most probably they are a vehicle for some hidden homosexual longing and this leads, in a way, to one of the reasons I might be cast for those roles. I never hid the fact that I was (and am) bisexual and I have to say that constantly in my life I received the attentions of straight men. Without being effeminate, I had (much more than now) something very frail and delicate that inspired both protection and sadistic instincts.

*That's fascinating. So one could claim it is actually the director with sadistic intent that makes both you and the audience suffer against their will, but in a way where we obviously enjoy it! Why didn't Michele kill you off in such graphic on-screen ways? Although you die in all three films, we don't see you suffer in any except at your own hand in The Sect.*

A reason could be that Michele loved (and loves) me very much and didn't want to dismember me, but I don't think that's the point. Basically Michele is much better than the other directors and had better taste, which finally made him switch from horror to other stuff.

*Ha! That says a lot about my taste and what I have chosen to write about...*

It seems a bit strange to me that such a refined analysis should be dedicated to a bunch of B-movies, but by now I learned not to question anymore the reasons for them not to be forgotten!

*In the horror films especially, when you are very objectified by the camera, you are very still when terrible things happen to you. You have to act the impossible. How do you prepare for a drill to go through your head as in City of the Living Dead?*

That is in your eyes and face. There is nothing to do but be very careful – in such instances the leading actor is the special effects guy.

*Did [special effects artist] De Rossi create these particular effects with you in mind – knowing you would be in the film? Did he try to make the deaths elaborately violent and graphic?*

My relationship with De Rossi was nothing special. I suffered terribly during the creation of my fake head that was needed for the drill scene in *Paura* and made clear to him that it was better if he carefully store the result, because I wasn't going through that ordeal once more. He was a very good professional, that's for sure. In *Cannibal Apocalypse*, as a matter of fact, I remember [special effects assistant] Bombardone (Big Bomb) more than De Rossi, but maybe that's just because Bombardone was crazy and I was pretty scared to be in his hands. I don't think these scenes imply a great deal of acting, although Fulci was very impressed in the way I moved my body as Bob, but I refused to wear the fake hunchback. I did study a way to move my body, for Ricky and for Bob. When I was preparing Ricky I studied a kind of John Travolta way of walking.

*You look very fragile and light in that movie.*

He wants to be tough but isn't. As an actor it is always very interesting to study for movies. Even now I would do horror movies. I like most everything. Of course I prefer Dostoevsky to Fulci!

*These films had good people in them, they did the best they could on the budgets available.*

The only one I saw over and over was *Cannibal Ferox* and I can testify I am horrible in that!

*My favourite roles you have done are those you have called the neurotic, weak, frail characters – Bob [City of the Living Dead], Ricky [The House on the Edge of the Park], the characters in Murder in the Etruscan Cemetery and Deliria. I get uncomfortable that many of your male fans usually like Cannibal Ferox most but rarely point out the rarity of suffering male bodies in horror, usually focusing on the extreme images of female mutilation in the film.*

I read some commentaries from fans on the internet about how they love *Cannibal Ferox* so I wrote something public and published it in the newspaper. I knew it was shit from the beginning. Lenzi offered me a minor role but I said I wanted the main role.

*Compared to some of the other movies in which you have appeared, it's quite a mean film.*

At that time I was used to the fact that these movies generally appeared in Rome and Milan for ten days in September, the lowest point of the season. Videocassettes had been invented but in Italy nobody had one. I thought it was a Kleenex movie and if I had known that after twenty years the movie would be for sale and people would still be watching it I wouldn't have done it.

*Is it just that film?*

Just that film. The only one, because the others were bearable. Also because it is not rooted in fantasy. The most stupid and tasteless thing if it is rooted in fantasy is okay. Like the Margheriti film

[*Cannibal Apocalypse*] which is funny – the idea that if I bite you and you become a cannibal yourself, that it is a disease like AIDS. I don't like violence. Even with Japanese cartoons I don't like [it] and with my son I tried to not let him watch them. Even fairytales are very violent. In Cinderella the stepsisters have their eyes pecked out by birds. It's very scary and bloody! I think it is immoral when it pretends to be rooted in reality.

*Although it has its moments, Cannibal Ferox has some very offensive ethnographic issues and issues to do with animal ethics...*

This comes from the Jacoppetti movies [mondo movies, beginning with *Mondo Cane* in 1962] that were censored in this country. There were actually trials because of this, and Jacopetti was a known fascist, in the first line of the fascist party. But it's something the directors like and for some reason the audience like them to.

*But you see horror as certainly having a different function.*

Yes, but many times in the horrors I did there was always some sex and tits.

*But there is no sex or tits in City of the Living Dead and none in Cannibal Apocalypse.*

Are you sure?

*Oh yes, there is that scene where you bite the girl's breast.*

That breast scene was done with a prostitute. The scene was shot in Madrid and the girl was a minor and so we couldn't do the close-up of me biting her tit. So after they called me for figatelli, meaning little entrails, the post-production scenes missing in the movie. So they asked me to come over and I got into a cab and there was a lot of traffic so I was late. The producer opened the door to the huge studio with one chair in the middle and there was a big fat lady with dyed blonde hair and just a big coat sitting there. She looked at me and said in that strong Roman dialect [affects hilarious voice] 'You made it, now let's bite, fuck!' With this, she opened her coat and I said 'Good morning … aaahhhh!' because she was naked under the coat and was prepared with the special effects.

*Is there anything you are proud of about these films – they are an important part of the horror canon?*

Proud is a big word. In them I am doing my job and I am not doing it badly. But I am not the kind of person who says that easily. I am very critical toward myself. I am proud of some of the roles I had in theatre. Comic stuff, I am a very good comic actor. I brought the work of Alan Maitland to Italy. I think he is great, the modern Chekhov. I translated and directed his plays in Italy. But also in theatre you can never watch yourself. It was fun making *Cannibal Ferox* but not because of the quality of the film.

*It is a shame you don't know about the place of these films within horror. Films like City of the Living Dead and the Margheriti and Soavi films, they offer something different, something baroque, perhaps particularly Italian, that does not resonate with the repetition of many modern American horror films.*

I am not familiar with the originals. I do like thrillers but the problem is that I really do get scared. I remember in *City of the Living Dead* when I saw it I put my hand on my face in my own scenes because what scares me most is when something happens all of a sudden. I don't remember, maybe it was the scene with the hanged man, but I do remember putting my hand over my face. I do like thrillers like *Se7en* and *Silence of the Lambs* and *The Usual Suspects*, but when there is an idea or thought behind their images. My son is 13 and has grown out of Disney, unfortunately, because I do adore Disney. Often I try to find some kid or other who I can take to see Disney.

*What actors inspire you?*

As an actor I am like a sponge. When I was little I used to go to the movies a lot with my mother and my two brothers, who were much older than me. So we would go to the opera or to the movies which she loved so much. So from the point when I was little, I was feeling like the leading actors, identifying with them: man, woman, boy, girl, whatever. I felt like Samson and Scarlet O'Hara! So I was inspired by everything. I love the actors of the past. I loved Jeremy Irons in *Dead Ringers.* He was so fantastic.

*When he won the Best Actor Oscar for Reversal of Fortune the person he thanked was David Cronenberg for his influence on Irons as an actor.*

*Dead Ringers* was amazing. Irons was able to portray twins without changing his look. Generally, if you do twins one has a moustache or another different look, but you knew which twin it was without anything. It is something sexual when I see such a good job as an actor. I am not very fond of star quality. I do love Leonardo DiCaprio not because he is a star [but] because he is a good actor. I went to see the movie about Verlaine and Rimbaud because I was interested in the story. After 5 minutes of watching DiCaprio I asked 'who is this guy?' He was amazing. And he is Romeo! He is a great actor in spite of his looks. Extremely good looks are something that prevents good acting. If a person, a man or a woman, is so beautiful it is difficult to go through that beauty to see the acting. There are perfect beauties and beauties which are expressive.

*Horror fans rarely talk about Barbara Steele's acting or characters, they mainly focus on her extraordinary, expressive face. Alain Delon is also a good example.*

Yes, Alain Delon was so beautiful that it was sometimes difficult to pass through his beauty. So there's a lot of actors I love from the past. I had a passion for Vivian Leigh but that was more for her looks and because my mother looked like her. And nowadays there are so many good actors, Jeremy Irons, Daniel Day Lewis, Kevin Spacey. So I do like actors that act.

*Are there any directors you would particularly like to work with?*

Maybe I didn't have a great relationship with all the directors but I had a great relationship with Roger Young in *Saint Paul* when I played Herod. I do like directors who know what they want and know what to say to actors. Basically, I think a director should be an actor, or have trained as one, to be interesting directors for actors. At least they must understand actors.

*Do you think certain directors let their own fantasy of their artistic importance cloud their ability to work with actors?*

No. A lot of them really don't know what to say to actors. I think one of the reasons I was popular in the horror movies was the word spread that I was a director in the theatre. If a director comes to me and says 'I want this and this' I try to do it but if he says nothing I have my idea of the character. I don't stand there waiting for him to come in and direct.

*Is that how you direct?*

I don't care about scenery, costume, lighting – only the actors. My idea of the perfect show is an empty stage with just actors. I had a very good relationship with Roger Young, he is a very closed man, but he complimented me in a way that I was really happy with. He said 'I thank you, you are like an instrument and a director can play you.' With Fabrizio Costa I got along very well. With Michele of course, maybe because we were such friends and he was an actor and always was accepting, in a friendly way because he asked me I always revised Michele's scripts, even the last one which was on *St Francis*. Whenever he writes something he always wants me to read it. On *Deliria* I also worked on the dialogue, 80 per cent of my dialogue I wrote.

*Are there any directors from your 'horror days' that you particularly enjoyed working with?*

Yes, some directors I was very fond of, Antonio Margheriti for instance. Not because he was a great director, not because he says things that made him a genius or because I could say he changed my life or my way of acting, just because he was a gentleman.

*And he made some wonderful films, particularly his 1960s films like La Virgine dei Nuremberg.*

He is an interesting figure: clever, funny and ironic. He is always laughing about what he is doing. He wants the money, he knows he is not working on a masterpiece, he knows that he is doing these films to get his bread and butter. So he is always laughing about this and that is why it was wonderful working with him.

*I suppose Cannibal Apocalypse is quite a joyously ironic film.*

Yes, so many times I had problems trying not to laugh when making this film. There is a scene in which I laugh all the way through, it is a long-shot so probably you cannot see. Because I hadn't realised, it wasn't in the script. This is the scene when we have just escaped from the hospital and we stop by a gas station, and we kill the owner, okay that was in the script. After that we resume escaping and Margheriti said, 'Okay you run this way and you run that way and John is first and Giovanni is second and whatever… Okay, ready ready', and then at the very last moment the prop man gave me a plastic bag with something inside and blood dripping from it. Margheriti says, 'ready ready, okay camera…' and I say 'what's this?' and Margheriti says, 'it is a bit of the gas station owner, and you are taking it just for something to eat. Action!' You know, it was take-away for the cannibals' breakfast the next morning! We didn't have time to eat the poor guy entirely so we just brought something for a snack. So I was laughing all the time!

*By way of closing, I thought it would be interesting to see what you are hoping to do next?*

First of all I am hoping to work, in whatever! It is a very bad moment in Italy for actors in TV and movies, there is a big economic crisis. What I really would like to do is to be out of Italy. My dream would be to go to L.A. for six months and see what happens. Many people told me over and over, and now I know they were right, 'you don't have an Italian face'. In Italy you are always confined to some roles and so they said I should go elsewhere. And I think they're right and I would like to try. Also in respect to being continuously interviewed and people remembering these horror films. So I say, 'Okay if I really have fans which is a funny idea to me. In America especially there are people who would like to see me on screen, why not go to America and see what happens?' Right now I was thinking of finding an agent in L.A. There are some Italian actors who live in L.A.

*Well I know your fans will wish you luck. Thank you, Giovanni for your time and hospitality.*

Interview conducted in Rome, 5 November 2002.

# CHAPTER 10
# BARRED NUNS: ITALIAN NUNSPLOITATION FILMS

Tamao Nakahara

## INTRODUCTION

Images and narratives of sexual or sexualised nuns have appeared sporadically over many centuries. They feature in the real-life stories of Héloïse and the nun of Monza; in literature such as Giovanni Boccaccio's *Il Decameron* (*The Decameron,* 1351), Pietro Aretino's *Ragionamenti* (*Dialogues,* 1600) and Denis Diderot's *La religieuse* (*The Nun,* 1762); as well as in films such as Benjamin Christensen's *Häxan* (1922), Michael Powell and Emeric Pressburger's *Black Narcissus* (1947) and X-rated nun porn to name but a few examples.[1] What stands out from this intermittent attention given to the lives of nuns and, in particular, to that of transgressive nuns, is a brief period in the 1970s in which three to four Italian exploitation films per year were devoted to the narratives of naughty nuns. These 'nun exploitation' films were produced around the globe in countries as varied as the US, UK, Spain, Australia, the Philippines and Japan; however, the highest concentration of production came from

Italy in the early to mid-1970s.[2] The first part of this chapter will explore the cultural, economic and cinematic influences that led to such a uniquely high production of nun exploitation films in 1970s Italy.[3]

'Nun exploitation', as the term appears today on video jackets, fan sites and in a few academic essays, includes any exploitation film that takes as its main content nuns and, more often than not, naughty nuns. Referred to as 'convent-sexy' in Italy since their appearance in the 1970s, these exploitation films soon received the label 'nunsploitation' in Anglophone countries that were giving birth to the expressions 'sexploitation' and 'blaxploitation' at that time. Most recently, the title, 'Nasty Nun Sinema', has been used in Steve Fentone's exhaustive encyclopaedia of the nasty nun visual culture to cover films that deal with mild to pornographic transgressive sisterly behaviour. To be more specific, I propose that nun films be defined along a spectrum from those that are 'nun-connoted' (their narratives are not concentrated on the lives of nuns but do, nonetheless, exploit the fantasies and representations of naughty nuns) to those that are fully 'nun exploitation' or 'nunsploitation' (films that devote most or all of their screen time to unveiling the forbidden interior of convents and of repeating the various exploitation tropes of scandalous behaviour). This chapter will begin by exploring the cultural, economic and cinematic influences that led to such a uniquely high proportion of nun exploitation films in 1970s Italy, and conclude by discussing the nunsploitation tropes and how their role in the films' ideological and cinematic structures contributes to the fan viewer's pleasure and keeps nunsploitation an enduring cult genre.

## CULTURAL, ECONOMIC AND CINEMATIC INFLUENCES OF NUNSPLOITATION

Culturally, the 1960s were a time of great change in which mores on sex and sexual discourse were being questioned and altered. 'Sexual revolutions' were put in motion in places such as San Francisco, Paris and Rome, and many students were moved to actively and publicly challenge traditional views on gender, sexuality and sexual behaviour. Cinema was an area in which these changes were realised both on screen and behind the scenes. Films with nudity and strong sexual subject matter such as *I, A Woman* (1965) and *I Am Curious (Yellow)* (1967) were coming out of Scandinavia, piquing the curiosity of viewers in Europe and the US and mobilising censors against them.[4] In 1968, the president of the Motion Picture Association of America, Jack Valenti, abolished the Production Code and opened the possibility of releasing rated but uncensored films in the US. The following year, John Schlesinger's *Midnight Cowboy* made history as the only X-rated film to win an Academy Award and, by 1972, Bernardo Bertolucci's *Last Tango in Paris* and Gerard Damiano's *Deep Throat* were pushing the boundaries and ultimately defining the limits of what could reach mainstream screens on both continents.

Even the Church went through a modernisation process in which Pope Paul VI and the meeting of the Second Vatican Council (1962–65) altered or abolished many prohibitions that had existed for centuries. Among the changes that the Second Vatican made on everything from choice of language during sermons to new designs for clerical attire, those on freedom of expression had an effect on films that toyed with religious subject matter.[5] Although scandalous films continued to be heavily censored or confiscated in Italy, filmmakers and writers could criticise the censors more openly during the 1960s. By the 1970s, although government censorship was still in place, the Church could rarely muster the influence to interfere with film releases (beyond its usual public denouncements) and could not stop the majority of religiously themed films such as Pasolini's *Il Decameron* (*The Decameron*, 1971) and nunsploitation films.

It would be erroneous, however, to picture the situation as a type of cinematic explosion out of a period of Church repression. Arguably, the economics of the film industry had a greater influence on the record production of nunsploitation films in Italy than changes in clerical regulation. By the time any cultural shifts were finding visual realisation on screens around the world, the Italian film industry already had a well-established popular and 'trash' film wing that was happy to benefit from showing nudity and adult situations. With the rise of television and other competing entertainments, Italian movie ticket sales had been steadily on the decline since the mid-1950s and film studios struggled to create products that would guarantee high or even mediocre profits.[6] Thus, from the early 1960s, film production and distribution began to split between the few well-financed and widely distributed 'quality' films and the low-budget and regionally distributed exploitation 'quickies'.[7] If a given film proved successfully entertaining or titillating, a series (or, in Italian, '*filone*') of copycat 'quickies' were hurriedly cranked out and distributed to take advantage of the short-lived trend. This was the case for so many Italian popular and cult *filoni* of the period such as the 'Mondo' films, peplums, spaghetti westerns, sex comedies and *gialli*. Nunsploitation, like these other genres, was to find its moment in the spotlight, and its time was to come around 1971.

Thus, though it is possible to see the proliferation of nun films as something particularly Italian for its Catholic culture, it is extremely important not to lose sight of the central role that the – also particularly Italian – *filone* industry played in the rise of Italian nunsploitation. Italy produced more nunsploitation films than any other nation for the same reason that it produced more peplums, spaghetti westerns and sex comedies than any other nation. Its *filone* industry was based on the over-production of films and the over-saturation of the market of any trend that would get people in the theatres as soon and as often as possible.

For producers to succeed at making money or breaking even with the quickies, they needed *filone* themes that would attract a large enough audience and movies that were not expensive to throw together. As Christopher Wagstaff has argued, *filone* films such as spaghetti westerns appealed to 'a typical Italian audience member' of the late 1960s and early 1970s by providing 'either one or a combination of three pay-offs: laughter, thrill, titillation'.[8] In the same way that the *poliziesco* crime films combined thrills and titillation, and sex comedies provided laughter and titillation, the nunsploitation *filone* was amenable to any combination of the three as it shifted between sex comedy, soft porn and even horror during its short lifetime. Nudity and sexual subject matter helped increase the appeal of nunsploitation to its male viewers.

Making nunsploitation films also appealed to producers because, as with peplums and westerns, it was possible to recycle sets and costumes and therefore lower production costs. In fact, it offered the advantage that nun habits were simpler and easier to acquire than cowboy or gladiator outfits, and one rarely had to worry about variety of costume from film to film. Also, since even cheaply made spaghetti westerns and *gialli* demanded a certain budget for outdoor location scenes, they often suffered from claustrophobically from stilted shots that could not pan or zoom out because doing so would capture telephone poles or other unwanted images.[9] This problem did not exist with nun films that naturally had to occur within the secretive walls of the convent and whose very nature was 'cloister-phobic' to begin with. A remarkable example of the economies of making nunsploitation is Bruno Mattei's and Claudio Fragasso's ability to make both *L'altro inferno* (*The Other Hell*, 1980) and *La vera storia della monaca di Monza* (*The True Story of the Nun of Monza*, 1980) simultaneously by using the same habits, actors and building for both films.[10] Fragasso shot *The Other Hell* downstairs, while Mattei shot the Monza film upstairs, and they would trade places if a particular area of expertise was required, resulting in about 70 per cent Fragasso/30 per cent Mattei credit for the two films. The 'convent-sexy''s affordability made it a *filone* worth investing in and one to extend for as long as the trend would last.

Cinematically, there were several trends that triggered the beginning of nunsploitation in 1971. Two key influences were the Medieval sex comedies and Ken Russell's film, *The Devils*, and a third, less direct, influence was the story of the nun of Monza. The first influence comes from the development of the Italian sex comedy and in particular the Medieval/Renaissance sex comedy strain, the nun-filled Decameron-erotico, or 'Decam-erotico'. Triggered by the successes of Mario Monicelli's popular Medieval costume comedies, *L'armata Brancaleone* (*The Brancaleone Armada*, 1966) and *Brancaleone alle crociate* (*Brancaleone at the Crusades,* 1970), and Pasolini's 'art film' trilogy (*Il Decameron*, *I racconti di Canterbury* (*Canterbury Tales,* 1972) and *Fiore delle mille e una notte* (*A Thousand and One Nights,* 1974)), a flurry of Decamerotico films were produced from 1971–76. These playful sex comedies took advantage of the changing times, the increase in overt exploitational sexual content in films, as well as the literary inspirations for these films that were perhaps the only existing texts that defended the naturalness of sexual desire and embraced sex playfully and non-judgmentally.

The importance of the Decamerotico as a nunsploitation influence is that it provides one visual progression from nun 'shorts' to nun feature-length films. These films, like Boccaccio's original *The Decameron*, usually consisted of a number of short stories with comic and sexual plotlines. The appearance of nun-filled vignettes in these sex comedies was quite a natural one, for the literary source for the stories already included several comic tales of monks and nuns who sought and found sexual gratification. Of the book's one hundred tales, one of the most famous – the Masetto story of Day 3 Novel 1 – recounts the story of a group of nuns who take advantage of and share their young, handsome gardener. The earliest cinematic examples of Decamerotico shorts follow the literary short-story structure and make their homage clear with titles such as *Fratello homo, sorella bona – nel Boccaccio superproibito* (*Get Thee to a Nunnery,* 1973). Another literary short story with erotic nuns comes from Renaissance writer Pietro Aretino, who devoted a third of his highly pornographic *Dialogues* to all sorts of decadent and orgiastic convent activities. A Decamerotico film that follows the same rules of vignette structure and title homage is *Le notti peccaminose di Pietro l'Aretino* (*The Sinful Nights of Pietro Aretino*, 1972). In one of its vignettes, a monk is called to a convent to heal a nun who has been struck by the devil's work. The monk's healing consists of his and the nun's playful sexual intercourse and a promise for later meetings. Soon all of the other nuns beg to be healed of the same ailment and the monk must exhaustedly offer his services to each of the members of the convent. Finally, a non-vignette Decamerotico film from the same year, *La bella Antonia prima monica e poi dimonia* (*Naughty Nun*, 1972) by Mariano Laurenti, helped to introduce longer segments on convent life that would lead to feature-length nunsploitation films. In the film, Edwige Fenech decides to become a nun when she is prohibited from marrying her lover and subsequently carries on her romantic affairs once in the nunnery. Within the Decamerotico vein, this film was the middle step between the nun vignettes and full-length nun exploitation films that were beginning production at that time.

A second lineage to nunsploitation comes from Russell's *The Devils*, which shook viewers around the world in 1971, the same year as the release of the first Decamerotico film, *La betia,* and Pasolini's *The Decameron*.[11] Though *The Devils* was based on an earlier work, Aldous Huxley's 1952 novel, *The Devils of Loudon*, Russell's film was what gave the story public attention and notoriety. In it, Oliver Reed plays Father Grandier, a powerful and progressive priest in the town of Loudon whom many of the men envy and most of the women love. There, the Mother Superior, played by Vanessa Redgrave, shows an obsession with the priest that increases to the point of sexual hallucinations, masturbation and finally hysteria. While the Decamerotico films followed a gradual movement from nunsploitation shorts to features, *The Devils* provided a worldwide and explosive reaction to and interest in films that exploited nun transgressions; and while the Decamerotico films embraced playful and liberating nun sexuality, Russell's film set a new standard for 'the forbidden' and the punishments of a patriarchal society. Although the film made profound statements about human desire, possession, mass hysteria and witch hunts, much of its impact was first lost in its high degrees of distracting sex and violence. *The Devils* caused uproar and sparked protests in various parts of the world for its attack on the Catholic Church and its institutions. Italy also contributed to the mixed reactions of interest and disgust: the film was often confiscated and, when shown, it was heavily censored. Among the scenes taken out, the most unsurprising were those with sex (the nuns' collective hysteria, masturbation and lesbianism) and violence (the graphic Inquisition torture). In fact, the film caused such a scandal in Italy that both Vanessa Redgrave and Oliver Reed were accused of public defamation of the national religion of Italy and were prohibited from entering the country for three years.[12] In spite of – or because of – Russell's scenes that were rich with shock value, the filmic trend of nunsploitation was set in motion among some circles of filmmakers and filmgoers.

Finally, a third and perhaps lesser nunsploitation tradition comes from the well-known seventeenth-century scandal of the nun of Monza. It is a narrative that remains in the Italian imagination and which reappears in one of the most important novels of Italian literature, Alessandro Manzoni's *I promessi sposi* (*The Betrothed*, 1840), and sporadically in some post-war Italian films, such as Raffaello Pacini's *La Monaca di Monza* (*The Nun of Monza*, 1947). Forced into the convent by her aristocratic family, Virginia de Leyva (or the nun of Monza) first snuck in her lover then practically continued the life of a married woman by having and raising two children with him. After the two were discovered, they used threats and even murder to avoid persecution. Virginia, after a long and recorded Inquisition trial, was sentenced to live the rest of her life (thirteen years) cemented inside a small and isolated cell. Although by today's standards Manzoni's representation of the nun seems quite innocuous, at the time it caused such a scandal that the archive that had lent the author the Inquisition documents closed its doors around 1836. The reopening of the archive to scholars after keeping the documents in the dark for over 120 years and the subsequent publication of studies on the nun in 1961 and 1964 by Mario Mazzucchelli helped renew the interest in cinematically depicting the Monza scandal in greater detail.[13] It is worth listing some of these films in order to indicate just how much of an influence the story was. Earlier or satirical films include Carmine Gallone, *La Monaca di Monza* (*The Nun of Monza*, 1962); Sergio Corbucci, *Il Monaco di Monza* (*The Monk of Monza*, 1963); and Giovanni Grimaldi, *Puro siccome un angelo papà mi fece monaco … di Monza* (*Pure as an angel, father made a monk … of Monza*, 1969). The exploitation Monza films include Eriprando Visconti, *La monaca di Monza* (*The Awful Story of the Nun of Monza*, 1969); Bruno Mattei, *La vera storia della monaca di Monza* (*The True Story of the Nun of Monza*, 1980); and Luciano Odorisio, *La monaca di Monza* (*Devils of Monza*, 1986).

## NUNSPLOITATION TROPES AND IDEOLOGICAL STRUCTURES

The sexual, hysterical and murderous nuns that appeared in the above cultural predecessors to Italian nunsploitation contributed to the numerous images and scenarios that 1970s nun films would repeatedly exploit to the point of cliché. Here, I will briefly list the tropes and discuss the structures that govern them. A common scenario in nunsploitation films (as opposed to nun-connoted films) is that the opening briefly narrates how the protagonist is forced to become a nun. Often she is raped (*La monaca del peccato* (*The Convent of Sinners*, 1986)) or has a lover (*Storia di una monaca di clausura* (*Story of a Cloistered Nun*, 1973)) and is sent off by her parents to preserve the family name. In the nunnery, she finds other girls like her who are there against their will. To release their pent-up sexual tension, they often masturbate (*Interno di un convento* (*Behind Convent Walls*, 1977)), become lovers (*Immagini di un convento* (*Images in the Convent*, 1979)), sneak in male lovers (*Le scomunicate di San Valentino* (*Sinful Nuns of St. Valentine*, 1973)) or have hysterical bouts of religious/sexual ecstasy (*Behind Convent Walls* and *Flavia, la monaca musulmana* (*Flavia the Heretic*, 1974)). In some cases, the girls put out their frustrations in rivalries over who will become the next Mother Superior (*Le monache di Sant'Arcangelo* (*The Nuns of Saint Archangel*, 1973)) or who will be her lover (*The Convent of Sinners*). Some nuns will stop at nothing to gain power in the convent hierarchy and will resort to witchcraft (*The Other Hell*) or murder (*Suor Omicidi* (*Killer Nun*, 1978)) to get what they want. To maintain order in the convent, aberrant nuns are usually punished with eroticised bare-breasted whipping (*Story of a Cloistered Nun*, *Images in the Convent* and *Sinful Nuns of St. Valentine*). Finally, a common ending to nunsploitation films occurs when the word gets out that the convent has become a veritable brothel, madhouse or house of Satan. When this happens, the male authorities of the Church swoop down to lay down the law and end the mayhem (*Sinful Nuns of St. Valentine*, *The Convent of Sinners* and Monza films).

When looking at these tropes, it is important to recognise the structure within which they appear; that is, the films are organised around the promise that they will provide the viewer with the 'truth' about convent life and, once the camera has entered the forbidden space, that the revealed truths will be shocking and titillating. Once allowed inside, we are to play the role of shocked viewer. 'Gasp! Nuns masturbating?! Nuns sleeping with other nuns?! Black magic nuns with knives who bear satanic babies and set priests on fire?!' As the many titles suggest, the films invite us to see the sexually explicit *Images of a Convent* and what really goes on *Behind Convent Walls*. Films such as *Story of a Cloistered Nun* or *Killer Nun* also open or close with a written statement – playfully in the style of the historical or gothic novel (or the more recent 'ethnographic' Mondo films) – that testify to the

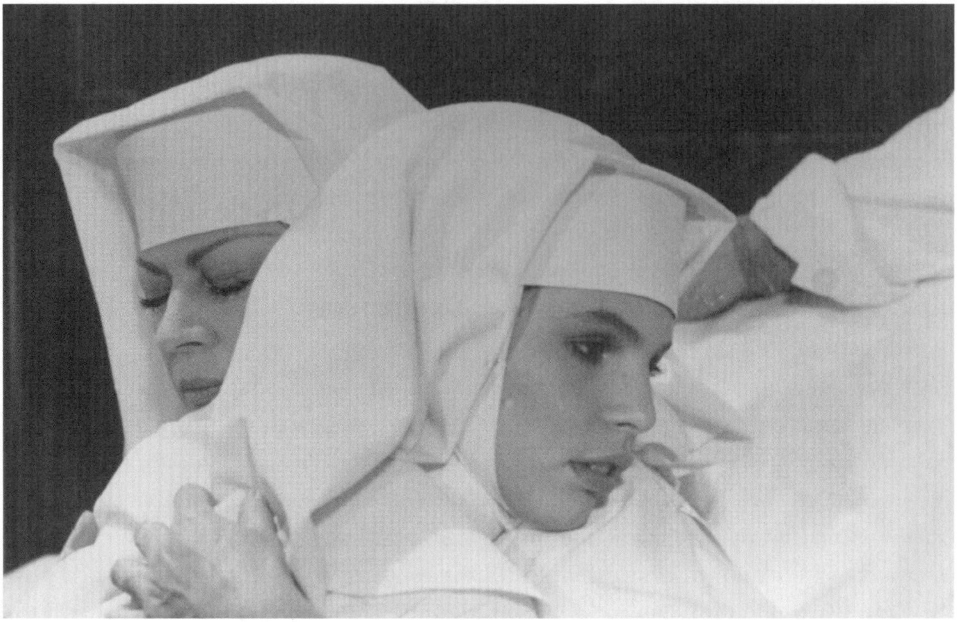

**FIGURE 27** Promising the titillating and shocking truth about convent life: *Killer Nun* (1978)

veracity of the events depicted. These titles and statements act as frontispieces to the overall structure of nunsploitation films and their promise to document and show us 'what really happens' of a world that usually remains hidden from view.

The way in which truth is revealed in nunsploitation films is through various modes of bodily and verbal confession. Besides the obvious use of nuns going to confession as part of their religious regimen, the films exploit the fantasy of voyeuristically entering the forbidden cloister with the camera and of cinematically framing the women's bodily confessions; that is, of catching the girls in naughty acts. Mary Russo writes in *The Female Grotesque: Risk, Excess and Modernity* that being 'caught in the act' is more often than not a feminine danger. A nun, as a woman on the convent stage, is set up to be caught in various compromising positions and at risk of 'making a spectacle out of herself'. In this moment of being exposed, she has transgressed 'proper' behaviour – moving from quiet to laughing too loudly, from old to dressing too young, and as Russo states, from being the 'cloistered St. Clare' to becoming 'the lewd, exuberantly parodistic Mae West'.[14] Nunsploitation films are about repeating this moment of revelation and of frenzied bodily confession, in which the virginal nun is caught showing her Mae West underside. Although verbal confession is an obvious part of Catholic iconography and narrative, here I would like to focus on the bodily confessions that occur at the junction between convent imagery, exploitation fantasy and the medium of film.

In *The History of Sexuality*, Michel Foucault argues that Western sexuality has been governed by a *scientia sexualis* – a cultural power-knowledge matrix that is forever in search of the 'truth' about sexuality and sexual pleasure.[15] He finds that our various social and scientific institutions are so structured within this matrix that we have engineered spaces in which we can control and attain those truths – spaces that encapsulate bodies and that make them confess their truths. In *Hard Core:*

*Power, Pleasure and the 'Frenzy of the Visible',* Linda Williams contributes to this argument by defining cinematic pornography's role in this culture of *scientia sexualis.*[16] From the beginning of the moving photograph, the leading belief has been that the mechanically-produced image provides a more truthful account of the world especially when it comes to the study of bodily movement. From this basis, the moving picture has maintained its ethos of showing what the naked eye fails to capture, of making the filmed bodies confess truths that were not previously apparent without the mechanical apparatus. Williams argues that hard-core pornography develops from within the framework of *scientia sexualis* and contributes to the culture of cinematic sexual confessionals.

From this point of view, nun exploitation is one logical conclusion to the quest for confessed sexual truths on the cinema screen. At several points in his study, Foucault returns to the role that Catholic confession played in the formation of the *scientia sexualis.* He writes that the current practice of 'transforming sex into discourse', which has become secularised and compartmentalised into various institutions such as psychiatry and pedagogy, originated in monastic life and in Counter-Reformation enforcement of confession. Moreover, 'by making sex into that which, above all else, had to be confessed', Foucault argues, the Christian pastoral contributed to the core motivation of *scientia sexualis,* that of 'speaking of (sex) *ad infinitum,* while exploiting it as *the* secret'.[17] Nunsploitation films, by adhering to the Catholic context and frequently narrating from the historically repressive Inquisition period, return the secularised and scattered manifestations of the *scientia sexualis* to their religious and historical origins. This movement gives the films other levels of truth in which to divulge: 'real' historical nuns, 'real' historical moments of overt and visual oppression, and 'real' sexual secrets kept within the convent walls. As a result, the secret of sex no longer becomes one component of the films' 'cinematic discourse', but becomes the actual structure and driving force for the narratives in which the convent itself becomes a type of safe, the keeper of *the* secret that we desire to know. The only apparatus that holds the key to this safe is the voyeuristic camera.

One world-famous Italian filmic tradition that specialised in using this type of prying and 'ethnographic' camera was that of the early 1960s Mondo films, which were themselves a spin-off of the earlier 'sexy by night' films from the late 1950s. Films such as Alessandro Blasetti's *Europa di notte* (*European Nights*, 1959) and Gualtiero Jacopetti's *Mondo cane* (*A Dog's Life,* 1962) were intended to be pseudo-ethnographic documentaries of the harsh realities of cosmopolitan nightlife and the uncivilized within our seemingly civilised society. They instead sparked *filoni* of their own as producers sought to exploit the films' freak show and financial potential.[18] Soon the 'by night' and 'Mondo' coverage of alienated cosmopolitan life and Asian dog-eaters began to increasingly focus on strip clubs, prostitution and nude tribeswomen, providing the viewer with a first-hand account of what goes on in these closed-off or far-off spaces. Considered the 'reality TV' of their times, these films also smacked of 'the prohibited' and were perhaps the earliest Italian films to exploit the notion of capturing 'real' sinful behaviour on camera.[19]

Like these Mondo films, nunsploitation – with its claims to veracity and its 'ethnographic' camera that documents the secret lives of nuns – promises to capture 'real' images of girls committing sins. For one, the films stage and are founded on the same principles by which Foucault explains why it is 'so gratifying for us to define the relationship between sex and power in terms of repression. ... If sex is repressed, that is, condemned to prohibition, non-existence and silence, then the mere fact that one is speaking about it has the appearance of a deliberate transgression.'[20] These exploitation films, therefore, repeatedly set up a system of repressive and silencing forces to extract confessions from the nuns' bodies in the form of transgressive sexual acts or irrational outbursts. By establishing the familial and monastic institutions that control the girls' sexuality and, in a Foucauldian way, establish that the nuns are neither in the social position or location to merit sexual expression, the films play out the fantasy of showing frustrated girls who then masturbate, sleep with each other, sneak in lovers, or confuse sexual ecstasy with orgasm. By setting the Church as an institution with traditionally strict rules and Inquisition punishments, the films use those rules and punishments as an excuse to show nude whippings and torture that are necessarily eroticised. By presenting the convent as a prison with internal strife (playing off girl prison films), the films show the girls use murder and witchcraft as an alternative means to power. Although a couple of the Decamerotico-influenced nun films represent a world that Foucault has looked back to – a pre-Victorian, pre-repressive era when bodies openly 'made a display of themselves' and were not *put on display* as examples of aberrant behaviour – it is significant that the overwhelming majority of nun films take place during or after the 1600s, the exact period that Foucault marks as 'the advent of the age of repression … after hundreds of years of open spaces and free expression'.[21] By setting the narratives in a past governed by the patriarchal Inquisition, ruled by institutionalised sexual repression, and regulated by penalties of unlimited torture, nunsploitation films lay the groundwork for women to willingly or even mistakenly transgress the rules and be caught in the act.

Nunsploitation films, however, do not elicit a response from the viewer simply because they show girls breaking the rules; they are pleasurable because they set up the repression/transgression structure and the voyeuristic 'ethnographic' lens around a stage on which anything that appears is constructed to horrify and excite us, and to excite us because it horrifies us. We are to play the role of shocked viewer, for the mixture of transgression and spectacle is the very basis for nunsploitation's continued success as cinematic peepshow and freak show. Thus, it is not just that the girls are not supposed to be sexual, it is that they are not supposed to exhibit sexual speech in a space that is not designated for such expression. In Foucault's discussion of institutionally and socially regulated places of speech and silence regarding sex, one of the spaces that he claims is designated 'for illegitimate sexualities' is the brothel, a place where those sexualities 'could be reintegrated, if not in the circuits of production, at least in those of profit'. As he explains, at the brothel 'words and gestures, quietly authorised, could be exchanged there at the going rate. Only in those places would untrammelled sex have a right to (safely insularised) forms of reality, and only to clandestine, circumscribed and coded types of discourse. Everywhere else, modern puritanism imposed its triple edict of taboo, non-existence and silence.'[22] In the 'real world', a nunnery is not supposed to take on similar qualities as the brothel or to become a safe haven for untrammelled sex. At most, the meditative space of the cloister must remain insulated from sinful desires that can only be released within the controlled box of the confessional. But in the fantasy world of nunsploitation films, the most virginally pure sanctuary takes on the role of container of uncontrolled sex, conflating the spaces of the convent and brothel and transforming the convent as a whole into a cinematic confessional in which sex is put on display. When this happens, the films set up a necessary conflict and confusion of where sexual expression should or should not be contained.

## CONCLUSION

It is precisely the confusion and instability of institutionalised containment of expression that allows the 'images of a convent' to be read as simultaneously horrifying and exciting. When the brothel can no longer be the Foucauldian space that is 'quietly authorised' and safely tucked away from public view, and when the convent can no longer be the guaranteed and architectural protector of virginity, the world of exploitation fantasy must contend with the scenario in which each institution starts to spill into the other. The result, and the source of the horror, is that the very structures of civilisation that are meant to protect 'modern puritanism' from the 'other Victorians' seem to give way to the irrational and 'primitive' forces of the women who are allowed to rule themselves without male supervision. With the fantastical ethnographic touch borrowed from Mondo films of the uncivilised within our civilised world, nunsploitation films display the nuns as the primitive within our modern culture. They are represented as caged tribeswomen who follow their own rules, power structures, and rituals that are not always comprehensible to 'logical Western man'. Once the camera enters the forbidden space of the cloister, it presents a freak show in which the unruly girls behave like primitives, expose their breasts, battle over convent hierarchy and partake in bizarre ritual whippings, all under the roof of the Church-sanctioned nunnery.

Nun exploitation films, by combining their ethnographic camera that unveils the truth of cloistered life and their freak-show spectacles on the convent stage, re-enact the conditions that Mary Russo has described with sideshow freaks. On one hand, the women are the 'performers of ... objective bodily "truth",' a throwback to nineteenth- and twentieth-century medical discoveries and exhibitions, and on the other, they are the caged spectacles in the sideshow whose exotic lives are narrated by a barker.[23] The films shout, 'Masturbating nuns! Lesbian nuns! Black magic nuns with knives who bear satanic babies and set priests on fire!' It's time to buy your tickets for the Mondo Monaca.

133

## CHAPTER 11
## EMMANUELLE ENTERPRISES

Garrett Chaffin-Quiray

### INTRODUCING EMMANUELLE

It is virtually impossible to satisfy the thirst for *Emmanuelle*, and no single essay can ever do justice
to the complexities of the character or the series. Like the character herself implies, a voyeuristic
description is the next best thing to the real experience. From the distance of decades, director Just
Jaeckin's *Emmanuelle* (1974) sits atop a number of historical debates that position the film as a
grandmother of modern pornography. Produced as a response to Hollywood's conventions, and as
redress for older cinematic practices in France, it also offers a snapshot of changing aesthetic priorities
in European movies of the early 1970s.

The point is never so striking as in the difference between the uniformly negative critical reactions
and the number of paid admissions, which made it the biggest ever box-office draw in France during
1974.[1] Some critics dismissed the film as 'pretentious twaddle',[2] while being 'fussy, overdecorated,

and tricked out with a silly plot about a young woman's discovery of the ultimate turn-on'.[3] Others derided it as 'a provocatively boring film with no characters, just mannikins; no acting, just gesturing; no sensitivity just gloss'.[4] These reviews were similarly critical of the film's 'philosophising about personal relationships and liberated approaches to marriage – probably ooh-ha back in 1957 and still pretty racy in France – is not only stale stuff but pretentiously banal as well'.[5]

When considering its original gross totaling some $4 million[6] on a budget of £220,000–$600,000,[7] the film's popularity nevertheless outweighs the objections of its critics. In this way the film exhibits a by now familiar binary between a high culture standard, determined as well-produced art serving a fundamentally moral purpose, and a mass entertainment result, viewed as a disposable commodity providing visceral, amoral thrills.

To then assert *Emmanuelle* was a successful product is precisely the point. With its exploitative tendencies foremost in our thinking, we can turn to examine its wider influence. Such context positions it as a nodal point in French filmmaking history both instrumental to, and symptomatic of, a more generalised commercialisation of erotic images.

Down this road exist grindhouse raincoaters, art-house patrons, curiosity seekers and everyday people craving entertainment from the most readily available sources. Into this diverse spectatorship is the novel, film and enterprise, *Emmanuelle*. As one title among several to permanently re-direct French, and perhaps global, film culture, the behind-the-scenes view argues for the film's inclusion in the recognised canon despite its critical marginalisation in film history.

This chapter accounts for *Emmanuelle* from not only a European, but also a specifically American, viewpoint in order to trace its unusual history through to the present. Thus, the question is how do we explain the film's status as a cult classic to certain aesthetes, a fetid backwater detracting from French film culture to others and, to those interested few, a point of contention concerning all these constituents? By first concentrating on the literary source, the answer is to be found in the resulting back-story detailing the film's production circumstances and the overlapping participation of its notable star, Sylvia Kristel. Lastly I shall consider *Emmanuelle*'s influence on not only numerous erotic movies and television programmes, but also on the debates around certain types of European low/trash culture impulses that become recast in high culture publications.

135

## THE CASE FOR A NOVEL

Marayat Bibidh was born in Bangkok, Thailand in 1932 of mixed Thai and French descent. Little is known of her early life and sifting through the few available biographical details to form a complete portrait offers three complicating twists of fate.

First, Ms Bibidh was married to a member of the French delegation to the United Nations Educational, Scientific and Cultural Organisation (UNESCO) and thus assumed the name Marayat Rollet-Andriane. Second, she began a hobbyist's career writing novels, for which she adopted the pen name Emmanuelle Arsan. Third, she became an actress and used the name Marayat Andriane for such work as Maily, the Chinese prostitute, in *The Sand Pebbles* (Robert Wise, 1966), and Tiree, the Tahitian bondwoman, in episode 2.26, 'Turn of a Card', of the American television show *The Big Valley* (Virgil W. Vogel, 20 March 1967). Together these name changes and career paths mean the woman at the heart of the puzzle is difficult to pin down, all the more so when considering the reception of her first novel, *Emmanuelle*, beginning in 1957.

Focused on the young, libidinous wife of a French diplomat stationed in Bangkok, the eponymous heroine enjoys never-ending recreation in her adopted country. She embraces her pansexual tendencies, debates philosophy anchored to the limits of personal eroticism and is rewarded with plenty of sex play. First published in France by Eric Losfield, the book brought the wrath of no less a personage than Prime Minister Charles DeGaulle, who condemned it as an outrange and suppressed its further publication. Consistent with vilified cultural expressions striking a responsive cord, however, suppression led the book into the world of underground sales where it enjoyed tremendous popularity.

Meanwhile, Losfield was convicted of offending public morality for publishing the novel and was kept from earning any royalties. Into this gap stepped another publisher in 1967, after which *Emmanuelle* was sold in the mainstream marketplace on the way to being read by millions.[8] Still Ms Arsan remained a public mystery, no doubt to encourage wide interest in her presumably autobiographical heroine. Moreover, her anonymity was likely necessary for protecting Mrs Rollet-Andriane as the spouse of a politician, not to mention her career as a struggling actress and upstart author of erotic novels.

*Emmanuelle II: L'Anti-Vierge* (*Emmanuelle II: Against Virginity*), the debut's sequel, was published in 1968 and ably contributed to the popularity of its predecessor. This novel was itself followed a year later by *Nouvelles de l'Erosphère* (*News from the Erosphere*), by which time Arsan's niche was well established. Indeed, by the time that the New York-based publishing house Grove Press began translating her work with the English-language version of *Emmanuelle* in 1971, she was already preparing her fourth title, *L'Hypothese d'Eros* (*The Hypothesis of Eros*), eventually published in 1974.

A highly marketable property from the first, *Emmanuelle* is, at base, an expression of changing cultural mores. Begun with an aphorism from Antonin Artaud, it offers erotica, travelogue and hints at strains of critical theory. 'We are not yet in the world / There is not yet a world / Things are not yet made / The reason for being is not found.'[9] So reads Artaud's remark after which Emmanuelle boards a jet to rejoin her husband, Jean, in Bangkok, although she is first initiated into the 'mile-high club' by two nameless men before landing.

Afterwards she is reticent to confide in the other French diplomats' wives with whom she associates. One of them, Ariane, is particularly friendly and through her Emmanuelle learns the promiscuous lifestyle, including a session of mutual masturbation with Marie-Anne, a knowledgeable and beautiful teenager. What ensues is her formal education. Which is to say she enjoys a tryst with a masseuse, makes love with Ariane and meets an American student named Bee. Soon crushed by the failure of her love affair with Bee, however, she is introduced to the cultured aesthete, Mario, with whom she debates the basis of freedom, art and eroticism. Putting word into action they venture to an opium den and discover a phallus-worshipping sect of virile men. Finally returning to his home, they invite their driver in for a threesome before Emmanuelle's climax ends her adventures, crying out, 'I'm in love! I'm in love! I'm in love!'[10]

Sketched in this way, *Emmanuelle* is reducible to three movements of experimentation, reflection and conquest. In the first, our heroine intimately encounters Ariane:

Her fingers were as deft, skilled and efficient as her tongue. They grazed Emmanuelle's clitoris, then both hands, held together, plunged resolutely into the depths of her flesh, stretching the walls of her vagina and massaging the resistant protuberance of her womb with admirable animation and discernment. She let herself be drawn into orgasm without resistance, gather her strength to make her pleasure as intense as possible, opening herself and thrusting against the hand that was probing her.[11]

Such is the tone of erotic passages throughout the novel, thick with euphemism and simile.

The book's second movement concerns Emmanuelle's realisation of purpose from Mario's direction when he explains, 'the only art that's not futile is the story of your body'.[12] Eventually suggesting she embrace the unusual, asymmetric, numerous, situational and the abnormal, his is a method of evolution. As he comments in the novel: 'Eroticism is not a handbook of recipes for amusing yourself [sic]. It's a concept of human destiny, a gauge, a canon, a code, a ceremony, an art, a school. It's also a science.'[13] Moreover, he believes that 'the art of erotic pleasure is what matters and that we must constantly offer ourselves, give ourselves, unite our bodies with more and more bodies, and count all time spent out of their arms as wasted'.[14]

Acting on his thesis, Emmanuelle reaches the natural conclusion of her empowerment in the arms of two simultaneous lovers:

The *sam-lo*'s hands pressed Emmanuelle's breasts and she sobbed with pleasure, arching her back to let him enter her more deeply, panting that she was happier than she could stand and begging him to tear her, not to spare her, to come in her. Mario sensed that the *sam-lo*'s endurance was inexhaustible, but he himself could hold back no longer. He sank his fingernails into his partner's flesh, as though giving him a signal. The two men ejaculated simultaneously, the *sam-lo* into the depths of Emmanuelle's body, feeling himself invaded at the same time by another outpouring.[15]

Given such heroic sex play, *Emmanuelle* is a complicated palimpsest of cheap thrills and lofty ambitions. Firstly concerned with carnal pleasure, it turns into a lengthy treatise on bourgeois morality before exploding that morality through drug use, paedophilia and sexual orgy.

*Emmanuelle*'s phenomenal success also meant it was a naturally pedigreed source for aspirant filmmakers. If nothing more than a well-written 'stroke book', it pays lip service to feminism's concerns over sexual identity and the subversion of patriarchy. At the same time, its representations were designed so as not to alienate conservative readers primarily interested in erections, vaginas, bosoms and body fluids.

After movie producer Yves Rousset-Rouard optioned the novel, it entered a cinematic context emptied by the breakdown of Hollywood's global hegemony before the blockbuster renewal of the mid-1970s. Space was therefore available in theatres and it was filled with works from many national contexts produced by opportunists, speculators and filmmakers capable of working against the conventional view in an industrial circumstance ready to receive them.

## ADAPTATION, SUCCESS AND SUPERSTARDOM

Nouvelle Vague, or New Wave, refers to the group of French filmmakers who rose to prominence in the late 1950s and includes personalities like François Truffaut and Jean-Luc Godard. They were born under the shadow of rising Nazism and come-of-age in the spoils of World War Two but were disturbed by a post-war rural exodus and the vast suburban construction programmes splintering villages, families and a sense of personal identity.

Often anti-authoritarian, they loosely organised around the Cinémathèque Française run by Henri Langlois. There they found meaning over the course of days spent watching movies from local and international sources, sometimes multiple titles a day for days on end. They also refined their sensitivities and wrote extensively for André Bazin's magazine, *Cahiers du Cinéma*, wherein art and entertainment broadly reflected the circumstances of their age.

Coincident was an influx of Hollywood titles held in abeyance due to wartime restrictions. Following VE-Day, when much of Europe reconnected with the West, but especially with the United States, French movie houses were literally flooded with Hollywood product, to the extent that their native industry was hurt by the foreign invasion.

Simultaneously the separation between French society's old guard and the younger generation widened. The *Cahiers du Cinéma* critics reacted with praise for older filmmakers like Jean Renoir and his masterwork *La Règle du Jeu* (*The Rules of the Game*, 1939) while ignoring more contemporary figures. They also learned to value aesthetic cues discovered in the Italian Neorealists exemplified by Vittorio De Sica's *Ladri di biciclette* (*The Bicycle Thieves*, 1948). In so doing they longed for a new kind of cinema to remake the world. Not to be overlooked, certain Hollywood figures also rose in their estimation, such as Howard Hawks, who was largely restricted to genre ghettos in pictures like *The Big Sleep* (1946).

Unfurling a call-to-arms, Truffaut wrote his influential essay, 'A Certain Tendency in the French Cinema', in 1954. Opposite the traditional attitude towards moviemaking as an anonymous exercise of collaboration, the *Cahiers* group, in line with Truffaut, believed films were an extremely personal medium. Simultaneously a number of technological improvements affirmed their purpose, including lightweight cameras, faster film stock and portable sound equipment and lighting kits, along with the continuing collapse of the French studio system.

With Jean-Pierre Melville's *Bob le flâmbeur* (*Bob the Gambler*, 1955) as a model of experimental narrative style and inexpensive production craft, the *Cahiers* group equally valorised sensational story lines pursued by the likes of Roger Vadim in *Et Dieu … créa la femme* (*…And God Created Woman*, 1956). Using government subsidies from DeGaulle, they then became moviemakers, first doing shorts but later producing feature-length motion pictures.

Available light and ambient sound was preferred. Street scenes were commonplace and camera work was mobile, editing obvious. Long takes were the rule containing real-time narrative events where randomness and a general lack of resolution punctuated performances by actors encouraged to improvise dialogue. At the Cannes Film Festival of 1959 Truffaut's *Les Quatre Cent Coups* (*The 400 Blows*) won the festival's Best Director award and Godard's *A Bout de Souffle* (*Breathless*) became a European box-office smash. Importantly, the New Wave was thereafter prolific and consistently experimental with narrative form and genre. By the mid-1960s, however, these once revolutionary tendencies were widely co-opted by mainstream filmmakers. Enter Rousset-Rouard and Jaeckin with Arsan's novel, a bestseller and franchise of literary sequels ready for movie-friendly audiences, additionally positioned to capitalise on newly relaxed standards friendlier than ever to sensual imagery on-screen.

*Emmanuelle*, along with Bertrand Blier's *Les Valseuses* (*Going Places*, 1974) and Walerian Borowczyk's *Contes immoraux* (*Immoral Tales*, 1974), formed France's 'l'epoque erotique'[16] wherein cinematic sexuality was encouraged rather than suppressed. Though French filmmakers had once been known for extending the limits of permissible subjects in the cinema, they had been systematically herded in a more conservative direction during the post-war years.

While American critics and viewers paid admission to, and then puzzled over, Jaeckin's film and its out of sync imagery (as they also did with the current spate of carnal cinema stateside), France entered a far more prurient phase. Characterising the times, A. H. Weiler wrote in the *New York Times*, '*Emmanuelle* is a fluffy consignment of romantic, slick, softcore, sexual simulations that is largely uninspired and hardly a revelation to enthusiasts long exposed to the genre.'[17] Missing from his remarks, however, is the incredible sense of difference in Jaeckin's film since the French were not supportive of erotic films in quite the same way as their American cousins.

Nowhere as detailed or licentious as any scene from Arsan's book, Jean-Louis Richard's adapted screenplay is, nonetheless, lush with exterior shots of Thailand and liberal use of Sylvia Kristel's body in acts of simulated intimacy. Jaeckin's further application of fashion lighting, pop music and suggestive sexual coupling, even tripling, was a brilliant flash of provocation. When added to the reputation of the source novel, little else was needed to make the film a success, although certain key additions were made, arguably to the picture's detriment.

Opening with Emmanuelle (Kristel) dressed in a scant robe, she quickly boards a jet, all innocence and wonder. As in the novel, she takes two different male lovers en route to Bangkok before landing in the arms of her husband, Jean (Daniel Sarky). Overcome by the awesome poverty and physical beauty of her new home she is nearly undone by a crowd of beggars. To calm her, the reunited pair make love as two household servants look on with an echoing frenzy.

In Jean's subsequent absence tending unknown responsibilities, Emmanuelle visits the local club frequented by diplomats' wives. There she meets Ariane (Jeanne Colletin), a pretty and notably older cynic, along with Marie-Ange (Christine Boisson), a lovely teenager she invites home for easy companionship. At a party she then meets Mario (Alain Cuny), though she considers him far too old, and instead falls for Bee (Marika Green), an archaeologist.

The Sapphic pair then vanish on one of Bee's digs to explore the sights and sounds of the Thai wilderness, ostensibly to mine historical ruins, though they actually have sex before breaking up. In his wife's absence Jean visits a strip bar, gets drunk and rapes Ariane in a pique of anger recuperated as the stuff of violent fantasy, another uncomfortable departure from Arsan. Returning home, then, lovelorn and confused, Jean welcomes Emmanuelle and suggests she pursue a relationship with Mario to distract her troubles. So begins our heroine's roundabout as Mario meets her for dinner before taking her to a cocaine den where she is raped at his insistence. Afterwards they watch a boxing match where he offers her as the prize for the winner and their evening ends in a threesome just as in the novel's erotically overwrought finale.

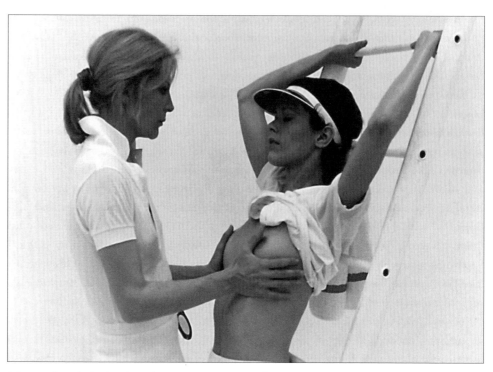

**FIGURE 28** Emancipation through sexual experimentation in *Emmanuelle* (1974)

All key departures from page to screen rest on the ease of translating Arsan's erotic passages versus excising her philosophical wormholes. In the first half of the film we are introduced to Kristel's Emmanuelle, along with the Thai countryside, preening Euro-harlots and numerous sexual encounters. Masturbation holds centre court. Nearby is prominent lesbian activity and just off in the distance is a high-gloss presentation of the female nude, everywhere an object of lust and beauty, identification and wonder.

Professional lighting and recorded, or dubbed, sound is standard. Outdoor scenes and controlled backgrounds are commonplace and camerawork is static, editing seamless. Long takes are the rule with performances punctuated by awkward dialogue. In short, *Emmanuelle* is the obverse of the New Wave style and its return to a traditional production standard is what causes the film to sputter.

While intended to fulfil our heroine's sense of bliss, the penultimate three-way demonstrates the point because of its brevity and uneven result. The real failure is Jaeckin's softcore simulation when remembering Arsan's hardcore source that, no matter the newly liberal permissiveness of French film culture, remains unrealisable without more explicit means. As Pierre Schneider noted:

Judging by Just Jaeckin's film, the difference between eroticism and pornography is art. *Emmanuelle* is a glossy sex travelogue [sic]. One is reminded of the exotic backgrounds chosen by fashion magazines to present the new couture collections. Indeed, Mr Jaeckin's astuteness has been to realise that these magazines are the rightful heirs to the publications specialising in artistic nudes, popular and even acceptable in France around the turn of the century [sic]. It takes money to achieve this kind of artistic quality in a movie. One definition of the difference between pornography and eroticism might therefore be: the size of the budget.[18]

Despite this financially pragmatic point of view, much of what makes *Emmanuelle* shine is Ms Kristel's star persona.

## STAR PERSONAS: SYLVIA KRISTEL

Born on 28 September 1952 in Utrecht, Netherlands, Sylvia Kristel was reared in a convent. Entering early adulthood she worked various jobs before finally stumbling onto what appears to have been her calling as a model. Then voted Miss TV Europe, she was signed to several Dutch features, including *Frank en Eva* (*Living Apart Together*, Pim de la Parra, 1973), though her wave clearly crested when *Emmanuelle* catapulted her to fame.

Neither well trained nor especially gifted in theatre craft, her great physical beauty, her 'moist-mouthed mixture of exoticism and sensuality',[19] meant her blank affect and questionable talent made her a perfect cipher for Jaeckin. Namely, she became a fantasy object through terrific images that helped transform her from mere flesh into an icon of the times.

For Kristel, *Emmanuelle* was 'an experience in photography',[20] and, as such, she appeared reticent to reprise the role in a sequel, not seeing the point.[21] History, of course, reveals her shortsightedness, although Kristel's subsequent career, with highlights including *The Concorde: Airport '79* (David Lowell Rich, 1979), *Lady Chatterley's Lover* (Jaeckin, 1981) and the infamous *Private Lessons* (Alan Myerson, 1981), generally rests on her exhibitionism bordering on sexual self-exploitation.

Given her pale skin, auburn hair, long limbs and large, round eyes, she bore the stamp of a certain female archetype. Her willingness to pose nude for filmmakers, photographers and journalists on both sides of the Atlantic further added to her allure. One need only consider the evidence of her filmography involving a number of sequels to her most famous role. These included *Emmanuelle 2* (*Emmanuelle: The Joys of a Woman*, Francis Giacobetti and Francis Leroi, 1975), *Emmanuelle 3* (aka *Goodbye Emmanuelle*, Francois Leterrier, 1977), *Emmanuelle 4* (Leroi and Iris Letans, 1984) and Francis Leroi's six-part confection, *Emmanuelle's Revenge* (1992), *Emmanuelle's Perfume* (1992), *Emmanuelle's Magic* (1992), *Emmanuelle au 7ème ciel* (*Emmanuelle 7*, 1993), *Emmanuelle's Love* (1993) and *Emmanuelle pour toujours* (*Emmanuelle Forever*, 1993).

Nonetheless, the value of Jaeckin's picture, in light of its transformation from novel to film, is its ability to succeed in both media based on a female character in a decade often noted for hyper-masculine heroes. More to the point, Kristel's persona encouraged viewers to join her in various softcore adventures as a fantasy ideal, always eschewing the unpleasant aspects of hardcore entertainment and ignoring modern crises like crumbling nuclear families and AIDS.

## WAVES OF LUST AND WAVES OF INFLUENCE

Distributed under the wire of relaxed censorship standards, *Emmanuelle* was instrumental in modernising French cinema insofar as it openly embraced simulated sex play. That it avoided 'harder'

**FIGURE 29** Sexual sequels: Sylvia Kristel (middle) and friends discover the erotic Orient in *Emmanuelle 2* (1975)

sexual imagery equally set a standard for future productions. So too was its appeal to audiences of all social strata, but especially women.

Columbia Pictures president David Begelman expressed his interest in distributing the studio's first-ever X-rated film in *Emmanuelle*, according to apocryphal research done on a Parisian sidewalk. 'The line outside the theatre was made up of about 75 to 80 per cent women. We would have had no interest in the film if its appeal was totally to men. Then it could be taken as pornographic.'[22] Shrewd to the last, Begelman pioneered the American movie markets for more adult titles just as he was lambasted for diminishing 'good taste' in favour of lower moral standards.[23] As *Variety* noted at the time:

> with the combination of 'class' generally associated with European product imported for U.S. consumption and the kind of softcore that shocked the U.S. perhaps 15 years ago – but which is still torrid going in many European countries – *Emmanuelle* producer Yves Rousset-Rouard came up with the right picture at just the right time.[24]

Foremost in Begelman's consideration was the key difference between softer and hardcore entertainment. That is, the differences between simulation and realisation, representation and presentation, professional distance and amateur proximity. Always a capital market, the movie industry of 1974 was in a state of recovery. Focusing just on the United States where box office has long been carefully studied, 1974 was the first time box-office grosses improved on the national record of $1.7 billion set in 1946.[25] Earning some $1.9 billion with over a million viewers paying an average of $1.88 a ticket,[26] movie distributors and exhibitors began to see the impact of a generation weaned on daily television spectatorship. Of necessity, this class was marketed with subjects of obvious appeal like overt sexuality and graphic violence.

Given the 156 titles and 32 reissues distributed in 1974 by the major American studios United Artists/MGM, Columbia, Twentieth Century Fox, Paramount, Warner Bros., Avco Embassy, Universal and Allied Artists, the overall number declined from previous years.[27] Still, the Motion Picture Association of America rated 522 movies indicating a massive influx of independent and foreign titles.[28] Among this wider canvas were X-rated, 'adult only'-oriented movies and a greater number of G-rated titles appealing to the widest possible audience.

At the time of Begelman's decision to pick-up *Emmanuelle*, Columbia was reeling over the big budget failure of its G-rated release *Lost Horizon* (Charles Jarrott, 1973). This meant the major studios, but especially Begelman at Columbia, were eager to recapture the financial security of the mid-1940s so an X-rated foreign title was undertaken to right a sinking ship.

Directly competing with the American-born 'raincoater' ideal advanced by the likes of *Deep Throat* (Gerard Damiano, 1972), *Emmanuelle* was a viable alternative for on-screen sensuality. As Arthur Winsten commented: 'What's not included is the hardcore views that have repelled some delicate segments of the American porno audience. Thus this picture can be legitimately classed as aphrodisiac in effect, not embarrassing for mixed company, and an inspiration to those who might, for whatever reason, be inhibited.'[29] Significantly, these characteristic softcore traits made the title, and others following in its wake with a preference for story development, however slight, and character development, however two-dimensional, more easily adaptable to the introduction of home video technology and cable television.

Where few dispute the popularity of hardcore sexual imagery in selective audiences and isolated conditions, the more spectator-friendly *Emmanuelle* was all but invited home for late night movie television channels and videocassette time shifting. This general welcome also meant Arsan's heroine was adaptable to still other media, in variously many national contexts.

Surveying the viral growth stemming from Jaeckin's film, Mick Brown wrote on the phenomenon in the relatively conservative *Sunday Times Magazine* as early as 1980:

Even without [Sylvia Kristel], Emmanuelle has continued to thrive. In the flood of films that have been released to capitalise on the name, she has popped up in Denmark, America and Japan, met wife-swappers, white-slave traders and cannibals, had a daughter and become a nun. There have been Black, Yellow, even Pink Emanuelles [sic]. Any resemblance between the original Emmanuelle and her successors is usually purely accidental – the single 'm' or 'l' in the Emanuelle of most titles avoids any breach of copyright. The majority of films are made in France, Germany and Italy, often under a title which has nothing to do with anybody called Emmanuelle whatsoever.[30]

Continuing his point, Brown specifies the motive for so many filmmakers to involve themselves with Arsan's heroine: 'Commercial success is almost guaranteed; no matter what race, creed or colour she may assume, the very name Emmanuelle seems to have become a hallmark for a certain sort of satisfaction, if not quality, among connoisseurs of softcore porn.'[31] *Emmanuelle*'s influence also established various formulae for eroticism on-screen. Considering it is long list of sequels, leaving aside the uncountable rip-offs, look-alikes, homage and copies, Jaeckin's now decades-old film is something more than a popular phenomenon. It is a demonstration of shrewd notions about expressive freedom and the exploitation of cast and setting to turn *Emmanuelle* into a brand carefully prepared for an increasingly global culture trading on visible entertainment.

Notably, its cinematic practices and cultural values were quickly absorbed across the world, but especially in Hollywood by the mid-1970s. In the intervening decades adult entertainment has splintered along a range from prostitution through personal ads, with academic programmes, pornographic movies, fashion magazines and phone sex ads in between. Focusing just on pornographic movies, the splintering forks into softcore, non-penetrative, narrative-oriented entertainments and more hardcore, penetrative, non-narrative-oriented stimulants.

## CONCLUSION

Since its release in France on 26 June 1974, *Emmanuelle* has become a seminal text for contemporary adult entertainment. To many viewers its success is astounding due to the consensus of negative opinion about the film, roughly echoing one anonymous *Variety* writer:

> Based on a bestselling book about the sexual liberation of a young woman, and with some production dress and the exotic locale of Bangkok, this is still softcore in its lack of deeper resonance of its characters, simulation, and a sort of coy 1940s-type under-the-counter affair in contrast to today's outspoken hardcore pix Stateside. Also lacking a sense of humor, [the] film is a series of glossy images and appears more a come-on for the civil service than for femme lib.[32]

Heedless of such criticism, the film was a hit and, in the case of its debut at the Parafrance Champs-Elysees Theater, Paramount City, it ran for 552 consecutive weeks, served 3,268,875 spectators and earned its producers their investment from just one screen.[33]

No matter detractors and supporters, an undeniable effect of *Emmanuelle* is its definitive model for a new kind of on-screen erotica. Because it was produced using the high production values of fashion photography, it appealed to cinephiles longing for new, more explicit content in movies but who were still interested in well-made films. Within the French context it also reaped the benefits of experiments in film content begun by the New Wave, although its emphasis was purposefully on conventional formal elements than on any alienating innovations. *Emmanuelle* was also a trend-setter and the beneficiary of relaxed standards of permissible imagery resulting from wide social upheaval in the 1960s. One result, aside from a movement away from imagined sensuality and towards its detail in the mass media, was a permanent, paradigmatic shift in the way French movies approached sex play.

Among the first films to capitalise on this new condition, *Emmanuelle* was a runaway hit, first on booksellers' shelves and then in movie theatres. As noted above, *Emmanuelle* is a disorderly phenomenon outside the prevailing standards of genre, national sensibility, or even what constitutes superlative work in the medium. Having concentrated on the film's literary source with its own colourful history, Jaeckin's film becomes both a product and expression of the long struggle surrounding Marayat Rollet-Andriane's most famous heroine. Recognising the fantastic appeal of Sylvia Kristel in the role adds fuel to the contention that not only is *Emmanuelle* a successful novel, film and video series and cultural key note (in short an enterprise unto itself), she is the friendly grandmother of contemporary adult entertainment.

Put in context opposite the hardcore American films of the early 1970s, Jay Cocks wrote in his 1975 *Time* review, 'it should be kept in mind, of course, that the well-lathered extremes of American porn are banned in France. Without knowledge of *Deep Throat*, *Emmanuelle* might seem like pretty hot stuff. This gives the film rather too much credit, however. *Emmanuelle* would have to go up against something like *The Greatest Story Ever Told* before it could begin to look titillating.'[34]

Its fundamentally different standard for on-screen erotica also means Jaeckin's picture was suitable for a more mainstream audience. Yet both films, *Emmanuelle* and *Deep Throat*, did fantastic box office for a modest investment, thereby supporting an obvious dichotomy. For hardcore enthusiasts the point is made in wholly base, direct and relatively unproduced forms, distanced from any kind of thoughtful spectatorship. Indeed, interactivity rather than contemplation is encouraged as a sexual aid to some, as substitute fantasy for others and as a scandal in miniature for exploiting the body's appetites for general consumption. Hardcore therefore equates to excess without reliance on storytelling or aesthetic consideration, hence beauty and transcendence is not the point when disposable experience is key.

For softcore the purpose is less severe. Suggestion is preferred to overwhelming sensations or a one-dimensional, visceral tug. Within this softer method, sensuality is a curious condition along the margins of mainstream narrative entertainment that benefits from the dominant technical tools and storytelling structures, all to the point of capturing truth through sensual subjects instead of simply discarding them as empty fantasia.

Where *Emmanuelle* remains pre-eminent is in the fact of its global popularity and celebration of softcore experience. It earned a lot of money on both sides of the Atlantic and along the Pacific Rim, and was seen by a lot of people making it a symbol of the early 1970s.

Arguing over the relative importance of any picture when compared to Jaeckin's is useful, but does not take on board issues of artistic excellence. Such discussion is moot since *Emmanuelle* withers under rigorous criticism without regard to context or its enterprising influence beyond the pages of a single novel or feature film. More, its model of serialisation, first based on Arsan's work and later metastasised across multiple sequels and the work of copycat filmmakers, has meant a long afterlife for Emmanuelle, the wife of a French diplomat looking for good times in Bangkok.

## CHAPTER 12
## BLACK SEX, BAD SEX: MONSTROUS ETHNICITY IN THE BLACK EMANUELLE FILMS

Xavier Mendik

### INTRODUCTION

For centuries, the uncertain continents – Africa, the Americas, Asia – were figured in European lore as libidinously eroticised. Travellers' tales abounded with visions of the monstrous sexuality of far-off lands, where, as legend had it, men sported gigantic penises and women consorted with apes, feminised men's breasts flowed with milk and militarised women lopped off theirs.[1]

According to Anne McClintock, the principles of oppression that underpinned European expansion and colonisation into non-Western lands until the late nineteenth century were often coded as an erotic and yet monstrous journey into the unknown. Part of the appeal of foreign exploration was the idea that European 'adventurers' would come into contact with exotic and unusual forms of sexuality.

Western impressions of these locales as sites of physical excess reflect the levels of sexual repression and morality that dominated Europe at the time.

Although McClintock's account deals primarily with the social and sexual tensions that affected images of race during earlier historical periods, they can also be applied to more recent cinematic representations drawn from the European experience and imagination. Specifically, I wish to use such theoretical advances to consider the 1970s *Black Emanuelle* films created by the Italian exploitation director Joe D'Amato (real name Aristide Massaccesi). In a career that spanned the genres of horror, pornography, post-apocalypse science fiction and mythical adventure, the late D'Amato pioneered a series of bizarre and trashy genre-hybrid movies designed to tap into the 'sex and death' tastes of European grindhouse audiences. At its most extreme, this controversial cross-generic overload produced films such as *Le Notti Erotiche del Morte Vivante* (*Erotic Nights of the Living Dead*, 1979) and *Holocausto Porno* (*Porno Holocaust*, 1980), which used third-world locations as a 'primitive' backdrop to juxtapose explicit sex scenes with extreme acts of violence. (The most outrageous example of this cross-over horror/porn strategy remains a scene from *Porno Holocaust* in which a European woman is forced to have anal sex with a black zombie.)

Beyond these infamous productions, it was a preoccupation with the monstrous nature of ethnic sexuality that also dominated the *Black Emanuelle* series with which D'Amato became associated in the 1970s. The cycle featured the Indonesian actress Laura Gemser as a photo-journalist who scoured the globe exposing not only herself, but also acts of violence and injustice perpetrated against women. In true exploitation fashion, the series had been 'hijacked' by Italian filmmakers from the earlier and more polished French template of Just Jaeckin's *Emmanuelle* (1974). While liberally drawing from Jaeckin's original source material (Emmanuelle Arsan's novel of the same name), Italian producers even reduced the spelling of their heroine's name from two 'm's to one, to avoid any legal wrangles. While Joe D'Amato was not the only director who deployed the talents of Laura Gemser as a vehicle to exploit the success of Jaeckin's film (other notable directors included Alderberto Albertini, discussed below), he became synonymous with the cycle for two reasons.

Firstly, the *Black Emanuelle* series initiated his longstanding working relationship with Laura Gemser, who went on to appear in more than twenty films for D'Amato as well as providing costume design for many of the movies distributed through the director's *Filmirage* production house. Indeed, it can be argued that the only coherence provided to the cycle emerged from the repeated participation of Gemser who played *Black Emanuelle* in sixteen films (three produced back to back in 1976 alone). Alongside the cycle, she also worked for D'Amato in a series of related erotic dramas such as *Eva Nera* (*Black Cobra*, 1976) which were subsequently re-titled as 'Emanuelle' adventures for sale in foreign territories. Secondly, Joe D'Amato's entries in the *Black Emanuelle* series can be distinguished from other Italian emulations in the field because of the macabre fashion by which they situated the heroine in repeatedly ghoulish, violent and grisly situations. By pitching his heroine against rapists, cannibals and snuff movie directors as well as slave traders and manipulating mystics, D'Amato constructed a series of narratives more befitting a horror 'Scream Queen' than a porn diva. As Gemser's deathly status was often conflated with her blackness, D'Amato's films provide a way into understanding the very specific European fears and contradictions around black sexuality and savagery underpinning this cycle of 'exploitation' cinema.

**FIGURE 30** Laura Gemser became closely associated with the Italian *Black Emanuelle* films of the 1970s

## TRAVELOGUES OF DESIRE

If the *Black Emanuelle* series did demonstrate a set of longstanding European concerns around the presumed monstrous nature of black sexuality, then these tensions were reproduced by the narrative structure and organisation of the films within this cycle. In particular, by depicting Laura Gemser as a photo-journalist who tours the world seeking out scandal with the assistance of hidden photographic equipment, the series immediately introduced an element of 'image'-based power and concealment into its examination of aberrant, non-Western sexuality. In this respect, it can be argued that the series reproduces what post-colonial theorists have referred to as the traits of 'ethnographic' cinema: narratives that existed across fiction and documentary forms and aimed to provide a near scientific exposition of non-European cultures. According to McClintock's analysis of the colonial imagination, it can be argued that this style of cinema reproduces the Western drive towards exploration and travel. Implicit in these advances was the exposition of an 'exotic' environment from a (privileged) European perspective.

For film, such ethnographic fascination was not new. From the end of the nineteenth century, cinema had come to play a crucial place in processes of colonial domination, with the development of silent 'panorama' films that allowed the viewer access to exciting and 'unusual' areas of the world. In her book *The Third Eye*, Fatimah Tobing Rony argues that the 'ethnographic' film has continued to serve a number of functions within twentieth-century society including colonial propaganda, pseudo-scientific exploration of other cultures, travelogue loops and even 'jungle' adventure films. As she notes, in its documentary format, ethnographic cinema frequently presents its viewer with 'an array of subsistence activities, kinship, religion, myths, ceremonial ritual, music and dance, and – in what may be taken as the genre's defining trope – some form of animal sacrifice'.[2]

Even when ethnographic cinema merged with fiction film, it retained a scrutinising gaze at ethnic difference as its central motif. For instance, the *Black Emanuelle* series can be classified as a variant of the 'Mondo' tradition of ethnographic film popular in Italy during the 1960s and 1970s. This format (as popularised by titles such as *Mondo Cane* (1962), *Africa Adido* (1966) and *Africa Segreta* aka *Secret Africa* (1969)) utilised different documentary loops from across the world and often embedded these short excerpts within a fictional or 'staged' format that were then marketed on their factual information and 'educational' content. However, the Mondo film's obsession with documenting images of primitive black sexuality and its associated links with 'savagery' demonstrates the extent to which the cycle's pseudo-intellectual aims concealed a salacious drive consistent with 'exploitation' cinema.

Central to the appeal of the Mondo film was not merely an exploration of racial Otherness, but also 'an aestheticisation' of difference within its 'natural' domain. Typically, this meant the reduction of the non-European landscape to a form of picturesque display, to be surveyed by Western travellers. Thus, it seems appropriate that when Rony refers to 'travelogue cinema' as a branch of ethnographic film, she is in fact referring to a type of production that represents 'travel as penetration and discovery'.[3] The central features of the format of the travelogue genre (as defined by their peak period of production between 1898–1922) included a narrative structure that was short in duration, beginning and ending with a panoramic view of the landscape. This type of production also provided a guiding narrational device in the figure of the white tourist/narrator. Equally, Rony notes that unlike narrative fiction the travelogue production made little effort to conceal its basis in documentary, with people openly addressing the gaze of the camera (and that of the white explorer behind it).

The format of travelogue cinema, with its emphasis on a tightly constrained duration as well as its spurious fusion of fact and fictional orientated titillation, is directly reproduced in many of the projects that Laura Gemser undertook during the 1970s. These included the series of 'sexy' documentaries such as *Le Notti Porno Nel Mondo* (1977) and *Emanuelle E Le Porno Notti Nel Mondo 2* (released in Britain as *Mondo Erotico*, 1978) which she completed for Italian exploitation directors such as D'Amato. These works cast Gemser as on-screen host/narrator who oversees the 'documentary' inserts from swingers' clubs, massage parlours and racy discos dotted around the world. As well as disclosing (and unclothing) between the excerpts, these films also saw Gemser dispatching a rather curious brand of puritanical morality upon selections of film footage that had clearly been collated for jaded European audiences. Although these sexy documentaries were essentially light in tone, they retained travelogue cinema's obsession with replaying colonial myths surrounding the savagery associated with black sexuality (albeit in comical form). For instance, the opening excerpt from *Emanuelle E Le Porno Notti Nel Mondo 2* finds Gemser narrating a night-club scene where a white maiden prepared for tribal sacrifice endures intercourse with a primitive 'monkey man' in order to secure her freedom.

Although the *Black Emanuelle* series that Laura Gemser completed alongside these documentaries retained the elongated type of duration normally associated with feature-length fiction productions, this does not invalidate considering them as a branch of travelogue cinema, using the criteria that

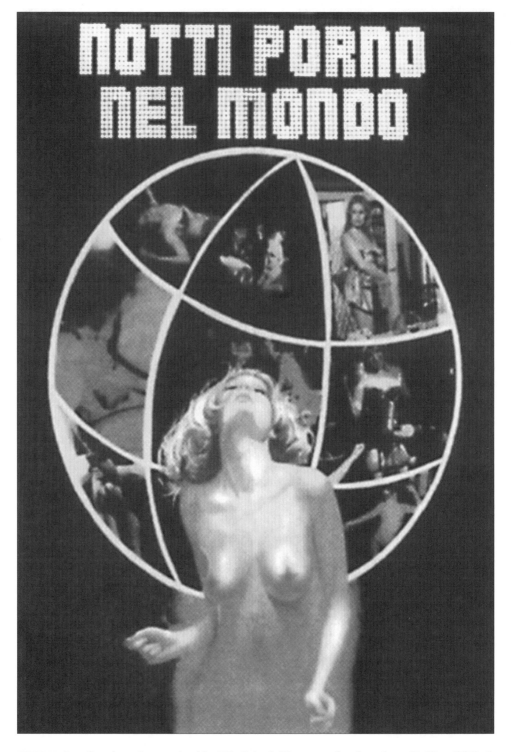

**FIGURE 31**  Laura Gemser's sexy documentaries of the 1970s display the Western gaze of travelogue cinema: *Notti Porno Nel Mondo* (1977)

authors such as Tobing Rony have outlined. Indeed, the duration of these films are dramatically reduced if one considers them as actually embedding two types of narratives together: extended scenes of fictional action with shorter documentary scenes around the 'exotic'. The significance of these shorter, more constrained, factual elements are underscored by the fact that they actually work against the progression of the text's fictional dynamics.

An example of these 'embedded' travelogue traditions can be seen in Joe D'Amato's 1977 film *La Via Della Prostituzione* (*Emanuelle and the White Slave Trade*). Here, the narrative oscillates between a fictional focus on the heroine's attempts to expose an intercontinental sex trade in women and a documentary exposition of the 'colourful' cultures she witnesses during this journey. The tension between these two cinematic modes is indicated in the credit sequence of the film. Here, fictional shots of Laura Gemser and her white companion Susan Powell driving around Kenya are intercut with documentary footage of tribal activity and scenes of wild antelope roaming across the African planes. These scenes, along with shots of Emanuelle buying 'traditional' jewellery and trinkets from local traders, are all photographed by the heroine, thus fixing the local landscape within a primitive (and visually decodable) past. Via these features, the sequence performs a similar ideological procedure to both the ethnographic and travelogue traditions that Rony has explored. Namely, by diluting other cultures to a picturesque (and desirably photographic) status it reduces its inhabitants to a 'people without history, without writing, without civilisation, without technology, without archives'.[4]

Rather than functioning in isolation, these initial documentary depictions of the exotic form a pattern that dominates D'Amato's film, and the cycle as a whole. Indeed, Rony's comment that travelogue cinema often begins and ends with trains/ships either entering or leaving an exotic location is replaced in the cycle by an overemphasis on plane travel as a European mechanism of discovery. It seems hardly a coincidence that from Gemser's first appearance in the role of Emanuelle, plane travel either features prominently in the credit scenes of these productions, or else airports are used as locations where important narrative information is divulged. For instance, in the case of *Emanuelle and the White Slave Trade*, it is while waiting at an airport that Gemser first discovers evidence of the illegal trade in white female prostitutes between European and African gangsters that motivates her subsequent quest. In the course of this investigation, the film even goes so far as to disguise the heroine as an air hostess, as seen in a sequence where Emanuelle and Susan try to entice information about local racketeers from an Eastern prince who has just arrived at Nairobi airport.

Although the film eschews plane travel in favour of a motor vehicle in its opening scenes, the use of a Land Rover (with its overtones of safari travel and Western exploration) maintains these established travelogue connotations. The trait of air travel is, however, included in a later scene in the film, when Emanuelle and Susan are treated to a ride in a hot air balloon, during which the heroine photographs both the landscape and its inhabitants below. In this respect, her role provides parity with Rony's figure of the narrator/tourist: someone allowed to survey, both the environment and the body of the Other from a privileged, voyeuristic position. As such, Emanuelle's dual status as traveller and photographer underscores the fact that racial power and identity is 'signified by whom gazes at whom. Performers do not look at the camera, but the gaze of the scientist is often acknowledged'.[5]

## DESIRE, DISGUST AND DOUBLE FEATURES

While the *Black Emanuelle* films clearly display some of the features of ethnographic cinema, to write off D'Amato's films (or indeed the cycle as a whole) as *merely* ideologically laden on a colonial level provides only a simplistic analysis of the tensions inherent in the series. The position of these works is arguably complicated by the format in which they appeared: that of exploitation cinema. As Barry Keith Grant has argued, cult and exploitation movies frequently oscillate between definitions of the conservative and the transgressive because of the way in which they give access to otherwise marginalised sexual and ethnic voices in the figure of the 'Other'. Importantly, Grant acknowledges the essentially contradictory nature of the Other in the cult film, noting its frequent associations with constructions of the monstrous. As he notes in his essay, 'Second Thoughts on Double Features', while such works

> commonly seem to offer some form of transgression, many of them also share an ability to be at once transgressive and recuperative. These are films which reclaim what they seem to violate. … They tend to achieve this ideological manipulation through a particular inflection of the figure of the Other. This figure which, while of course present in and fundamental to several genres, becomes in the cult film a prominent caricature that makes what it represents far less threatening to the viewer.[6]

What complicates ideological readings of the *Black Emanuelle* films is the fact that its contradictory attraction to and repulsion from the black body are mediated through a heroine who is herself defined as racially Other. It was a shift from replicating the white European body of the original *Emmanuelle*, Sylvia Kristel, to the black body of Gemser, which goes some way to explaining the different narrative trajectories that the two cycles took. As Linda Ruth Williams has argued, Just Jaeckin's original *Emmanuelle* displayed a pseudo-philosophical edge to its depiction of desire through a quest to 'unite the cerebral with the animal'.[7] As Williams indicates, Jaeckin's movie sought to popularise an aestheticisation and acceptability of porn that paid as much attention to chic interiors, abstract art and cheese plants as it did to any act of fornication.

However, the *Black Emanuelle* cycle that emerged from this 'feel-good' template replaced any drive towards emancipation with a disturbing focus on death, decay and the macabre. This was achieved by adding outrageous overdoses of horror and mutilation to an already eroticised text. Through these deviations, the *Black Emanuelle* films maximised an appeal to differing grindhouse audiences. Simultaneously they also alienated and outraged those critics searching for a radical message in 1970s 'porno chic'. It is undeniable that such economically motivated cross-generic overload reveals the series as disparate and hastily assembled. Yet I would argue that the *Black Emanuelle* films retain a cultural significance relating to their focus on a black female protagonist whose erotic and implausible investigations embroiled her in archaic and monstrous situations. If, as Grant has argued, the cult film works through a contradictory double feature, whereby the Other's position is both elaborated, and then coded as monstrous and transgressive, then it seems appropriate to consider the way in which Gemser's construction and activities isolated her from the original, white Emmanuelle. The central differences that separated the black Gemser from Sylvia Kristel's white character were mapped out in *Emanuelle Nera* (*Black Emanuelle*, 1975). This film, directed by Adalberto Albertini, featured Gemser in her first appearance as the heroine. During the narrative, she travels to Kenya to provide a photographic record of the European business and beatnik classes that reside there.

With its subsequent emphasis on the heroine's endless and emotionless encounters, Albertini's *Black Emanuelle* clearly emulates the Arsan/Jaeckin model. For instance, it mimics the opening section of the novel. Here, the plane-bound Emanuelle expands the concept of in-flight entertainment by indulging in a number of sexual encounters with staff and fellow passengers. However, the opening of Albertini's film also uses the musical score to signal its departure from the Jaeckin template. Sylvia Kristel was introduced as the original Emmanuelle via a perky, up-beat piece of Euro pop sung in both French and English by Pierre Bachelet. By comparision, the theme that accompanies *Black Emanuelle* is far heavier in tone, combining a set of screeching soul sisters and a tribal beat over a tune arranged by Nico Fidenco.

From the very opening then, the film alludes to the ethnicity of the star as a central feature separating the two cycles. It seems pertinent that Gemser's blackness is frequently commented upon by her fictional white lovers, usually in violent or aggressive terms. For instance in Albertini's film, the heroine's lover, Gianni, informs his colleague that one could never fully love or trust a black woman like Emanuelle in case 'she might devour you'. This threat was itself literalised in the theme tune that Fidenco later constructed for D'Amato's *Emanuelle and the White Slave Trade*. Here, the by now familiar tribal tune about the heroine is accompanied by lyrics referring to her as a cheetah whose breath her lover's feel down their backs before realising their 'clothes are in rags'.

**153**

## FROM WHITE EMMANUELLE TO BLACK EMANUELLE: FROM DESIRE TO DISTRESS

The contradictory construction of black female sexuality as a source of both desire and threat is partly traceable to longstanding constructions of Otherness that Italian popular fiction draws upon. For instance, in her work on *Faccetta Nera* (or Italian Blackface), Karen Pinkus has discussed the ways in which the black body connotes a monstrous excess of sexual attraction *and* repulsion in Italian culture. Although this dual fascination and fear of the Other has its roots in the nation's colonial past, she notes that 'even today … blackness always elicits a gaze; a black body is black before it is anything else'.[8] In terms of the *Black Emanuelle* series, Gemser's blackness is used as a way of anchoring the non-Western regions depicted.

Unlike Sylvia Kristel, whose European status guaranteed her an inoculating distance from the landscapes under review, Gemser's blackness condemned her to being slotted into any exotic culture. Indeed, it is significant that Kristal's tropical explorations involve a detailed examination of usually only one foreign landscape at a time. For instance, the title sequence for the 1977 film *Emmanuelle 3* (aka *Goodbye Emmanuelle*) features a panoramic bird's-eye view of the Seychelles. The camera gradually closes in on the location in the same way as its fictional European protagonists. In contrast to this colonial centredness, *Black Emanuelle* literally spans the world in the course of a 90-minute production. This transnational quest was often made explicit by the poster campaigns that accompanied the series. These frequently depicted the heroine against historic and culturally definable backdrops (as in *Emanuelle Nera: Orient Reportage* aka *Black Emanuelle Goes East* (1976), *Emanuelle in America* (1976) and *Emanuelle: Perche' Violenza Alle Donne?* aka *Emanuelle Around the World* (1977)), or else juxtaposed her against representations of the globe itself (as in the case of *Le Notti Porno Nel Mondo*). It was the heroine's ability to shift from one culture to another, seemingly without any problems of assimilation, which led Richard Combs to argue that the series demonstrated 'an orgy of globe-trotting [which] quite overshadowed the sexual activity'.[9]

Throughout the cycle the black heroine was depicted as a variety of nationalities from Arabic, African and Indian, to Chinese and Japanese. For Italian journalist Manlio Gomorasca, regardless of Gemser's fictional nationality, 'she was made to reincarnate all the temptations of the earth, thanks to that little bit of exoticism that the colour of her skin guaranteed'.[10] If the series equated the heroine's exoticism with a sense of racial ambiguity, then this seems confirmed by the frequency with which Westerners mistake her for 'native'. An example of this is indicated in the credit sequence of *Black Emanuelle*. Here, a hippie missionary attempts to flirt with the heroine by talking seductively to her in Swahili. When Emanuelle replies that she does not understand his language, the missionary responds in English stating that he naturally took her for an African. This interaction sets up a pattern by which Gemser is increasingly absorbed into the landscape, much to the disgust of her white travelling companions.

The reason for their widespread European unease relates to the way in which the African landscape and its inhabitants evoke not only desire (by virtue of an exotic sexuality), but also death (via a repeated connection with contagion and decay). From the missionary's revelation that he works with natives whose minds are 'clean and uncontaminated' to Gianni's definition of Africa as seductive like 'an incurable disease', the fear of infection can be seen as lurking behind this film, the rest of the cycle, and, indeed the Italian cultural and psychic machinery that has produced it. As Karen Pinkus has noted, since the 1930s a mythology of corporeal and hygienic deformation had been as a central part of the Italian perception of the black body. As a result, non-European lands were re-configured as a site of sexual and primitive chaos focused on acts such as 'masturbation, incest, polygamy and excessive sexuality'.[11]

Importantly, such Eurocentric notions concerning the unclean, non-Western body are also central to Arsan's novel *Emmanuelle*. For instance, it details a near-paranoid obsession with the 'unknowable' nature of the Thai landscape. Here, the locale is divided into a series of 'picturesque' scenes; sites and restaurants,[12] while the frequent nakedness of its inhabitants are referred to as 'the Orient you see in films'.[13] However, behind these definitions lies a far more threatening and unstable environment that the narration gradually exposes. For instance, chapter four of the novel centres on Emmanuelle's exploration of the city while waiting for her lesbian lover, Bee. Here, she stumbles across the horrific sights which remain concealed from the self-styled 'palace' she refers to as her 'observation post'.[14] For instance, the narration remarks that she

> was frozen in horrified contemplation of a leper sitting on the sidewalk. He was moving backward, supporting himself on his decomposing wrists and dragging the stumps of his thighs along the soiled ground. She was so shaken by the sight that she was unable to start the engine of her car. She sat there paralysed, having forgotten where she wanted to go and the movements she had to make, with her undecayed feet, her healthy, fragile hands…[15]

Following this traumatic encounter, it is a reluctant Emmanuelle who explores the more uncivilised regions of the city in the final chapter of the novel. The heroine completes her sexual training under the guidance of Mario, an ageing playboy who promises to show her something 'out of the ordinary'. The narration codes this journey within a vocabulary of disgust: terms such as unclean, mouldy, stench, smell and plague dominate the narration. Equally, the heroine's disdain at the sight of a man urinating in a river reiterates the exposure of both protagonist and reader to a different set of body fluids than have been in evidence so far.

Emmanuelle's expedition includes visits to a number of sex dens where she is forced to lie on filthy bedding and masturbate with wooden dildos described as 'revolting', 'rough' and 'dirty'.[16] The heroine's ordeal culminates with Mario's coercing her into intercourse with a young native. This encounter is further coded in terms of the heroine's distress. Thus, when Mario commands Emmanuelle to suck and drink from the native's penis, her response is 'to struggle against nausea' during the act.[17] The narration then goes on to describe the differences between the native and European body which provoke Emmanuelle's unease:

It was not that she felt that it was degrading, in itself, to perform that act of love with an unknown boy. The same game would have pleased her greatly if Mario had imposed it on her with a blonde, elegant boy who smelled of *eau de cologne* in the bourgeois drawing room of a Parisian friend … but with this [boy]. It was not the same. He did not excite her at all. On the contrary he frightened her. Furthermore, she had at first been repelled by the thought that he might not be clean…[18]

Arguably, the *Black Emanuelle* cycle that followed Arsan's novel shares many of the contradictions surrounding the monstrous nature of non-Western sexuality. As with Arsan's novel, there is evidence of the glamorous and profoundly de-historicised exotic displays performed for the white explorers: 'Africa reduced to colourful ribbons or vaguely tribal jewellery … assimilated into the vocabulary of the West',[19] as Pinkus would term it. Beyond these pleasant parameters, there is also a more dangerous environment that conceals chaos, violence and the monstrous.

However, what crucially separates the two cycles is the ease with which the black heroine becomes associated with such filth and degradation. Indeed, in Albertini's *Black Emanuelle*, Gemser is asked by a young African boy 'why are we the colour we are', to which the heroine replies 'let's tell people that we never wash'. In contrast to Arsan's Emmanuelle, physical revulsion is replaced in Gemser by physical possession as her body literally becomes invaded by the primitive forces surrounding her. This process of physiological contamination is indicated in Albertini's film through a disorientating dream occurring to the heroine. Here, Emanuelle imagines that she is involved in intercourse with a tribal chief (who manages to maintain full ceremonial headgear during the sex act). This encounter results in a delirious and de-subjectified dream scene where the heroine imagines looking at herself and Gianni making love. (The camera alternates between the actual act of intercourse and shots of Gemser looking in on the scene and masturbating.)

Crucially, it is not merely the attitude to the black physiology and sexuality that separate white from black Emanuelle. Rather, it is the fact that as the *Black Emanuelle* cycle progressed under Joe

155

D'Amato's direction, he literally rendered his heroine as 'monstrous' via Gemser's increased exposure to horror, savagery and death. This direction of the cycle can be inferred by a brief consideration of other key titles in the series, such as *Emanuelle E Gli Ultimi Cannibali* aka *Emanuelle and the Last Cannibals* (1977). In this episode, the heroine investigates the existence of cannibals in the Amazon jungle, after discovering ancient tribal markings on the vaginal lips of a white female mental patient. (This intercontinental theme of savagery once again links the emergence of a European 'symptom' to an underlying ethnic problem.) In many respects, *Emanuelle and the Last Cannibals* takes its travelogue roots to an extreme in the scene where Gemser and her anthropologist lover Mark Lester watch Mondo-style footage of a ritualistic execution. The sequence, which conflates colonial fears around sexuality and death (via the punishment of a couple's illicit relationship), features the graphic castration and consumption of a man's penis.

These acts, as well as the savage butchering of a European couple that Emanuelle photographs during the climax of the film once more confirm Tobing Rony's claim that anthropological cinema represented 'a science strewn with corpses, one obsessed with origins, death and degeneration'.[20] However, as with the other films in the cycle Gemser's own blackness provides a position from which to not merely judge and survey, but also to be assimilated to the Other. This is seen in the finale of the film where Emanuelle disguises herself as a water goddess in order to rescue her white lover Isabel from the cannibal lair. As she explains to Lester, 'As I look very much like them, they will believe their water god has come to receive their sacrifice.'

**FIGURE 32** Notions of primitive sexuality and ethnicity are conflated: *Emanuelle and the Last Cannibals* (1977)

LAURA GEMSER
EN
"*Emanuelle y los ultim...*
*Canibales*"
GABRIELE TINTI · SUSAN SCOT
DONALD O'BRIEN

**FIGURE 33** Attentive and deadly: Gemser in *Emanuelle and the Last Cannibals* (1977)

Under D'Amato's direction, even the more innocently titled films from the series continued the tradition of immersing the heroine in death and decay. For instance, *Emanuelle in America* finds the reporter investigating a trans-continental snuff-movie ring, where women are raped and tortured on-screen. This film, with its frequent and unmotivated oscillation between sexual pleasure and death not only reiterates the heroine's connection to the monstrous, but also provides an interesting overview of the way in which the series manipulated the motifs of eroticism. Although one of the more extreme examples from the series, a witnessed act of intercourse combining eroticism with either humiliation, violence or implied threat remains central to the series as a whole.

## DEADLIER THAN THE MALE: BLACK MAGIC, BLACK BODIES, BLACK COBRA

The tensions around monstrous sex that the cycle displays are also present in *Black Cobra* (D'Amato, 1976). Although not strictly an example of the *Black Emanuelle* series, the film clearly draws on Gemser's established (and increasingly monstrous) 'black' persona. She is cast as Eva, a woman who performs an erotic routine with snakes at a Bangkok nightclub. The film details Gemser's ill-fated relationship with the wealthy Judas and his treacherous brother Julius. This bizarre love triangle ends with the heroine plotting a deadly revenge against the latter after he murders her white lesbian lover Gerry.

While this plot overview indicates that Gemser becomes once again associated with death and the macabre, *Black Cobra* also demonstrates the elements of ambiguity surrounding racial and sexual identity that the heroine experienced in key examples of the *Black Emanuelle* cycle. For instance, from the outset of the film, Eva is depicted as a character whose origins and relationship with the East remain unstable. The opening sequence (staged once again at an airport), finds a surprised Julius discovering that Eva is not a native as he had presumed, but rather that she is very much a tourist determined to discover the Hong Kong 'we don't know about'.

As with the *Black Emanuelle* films upon which the narrative heavily draws, this initial uncertainty over the heroine's racial origins allows the narrative to gradually incorporate her into the exotic regions under review. (These locations are depicted in a series of Mondo-style documentary sequences set in temples, exotic restaurants, massage parlours and lesbian discotheques.) Indeed, after discovering that Julius is responsible for releasing the snake that kills Gerry, it is marked that Eva plans her revenge by taking him to the island where she was born. However, other than describing her village as a region 'not yet discovered by tourists', the film does not reveal the specific name of the location or indeed its geographical relationship with the other Eastern regions the film depicts.

Not only does *Black Cobra* continue the ambivalent construction of its heroine's ethnicity (seen in previous Laura Gemser roles), it also ties Eva's ambiguity not only to the exotic, but also to the primitive and deadly (via her affiliation with snakes). This archaic set of associations is first intimated in an erotically charged dream that occurs to the heroine soon after the depiction of her first nightclub routine. Eva lies on her bed and looks off-screen left at images of herself performing with the snake. This fantasy provokes an act of autoeroticism, to which the heroine responds by initiating masturbation. The imaginary act is then accompanied by another separate vision in which Gemser begins to make love to a Chinese girl. In both cases, these illusory flashes of the female self-gesture looks back to the bed-bound Eva, indicating a split in her identity.

Thus, while the *Black Emanuelle* films frequently used dream scenes to double images of the heroine's (as if to underscore her identity as fissured), with *Black Cobra*, D'Amato triples this sense of self in a truly disorientating manner. This loss of subjectivity also comes to the fore in the climax of the film when Gemser leads an unwitting Julius to his death on the unidentified tropical island. Here, the heroine becomes fully incorporated into sexually aggressive notions of the primitive that haunt the narrative. As a Western observer to this transformation, Julius responds with an appropriate degree of disgust. For instance, he makes clear his unease at Eva's insistence that she be allowed to sleep on the filthy floor of a fisherman's hut just as 'she had to do as a child'. This alteration in behaviour locates Eva as a site of excess sexual desire (taunting Julius by indulging in group sex with the local natives), primitive and magical acts (by performing a black magic ceremony before killing Julius), as well as also savage brutality (by killing him with a snake that burrows its way out of a victim's body).

Although *Black Cobra* reveals how the heroine's association with snakes is mirrored by Judas' obsession with reptiles, the film is careful to split this duel interest along racial lines. For instance, during their first meeting, Jules informs Eva that the routine she enacts has 'ancient origins', which 'most people cannot perform'. This statement (along with Eva's own admission that the male character caresses her as if she were a snake), strategically distances Judas' own reptilian obsessions, which take the form of the classical colonial collector. (He informs the heroine that his 'prized' specimens include examples from Africa, the Sahara and South America.) Once more, these processes indicate the way in which Laura Gemser's casting in the film extends the connotations of sexuality and ethnicity established in her role as *Black Emanuelle*. Equally, it also confirms the status of both this character and Eva as sites of sexuality *and* death. This is confirmed in the finale of *Black Cobra*. Here, Eva is killed by Judas' prized snake after she returns to tell him how she engineered Julius' demise.

## CONCLUSION

Eva's death in many respects represents the logical conclusion to the monstrous status Gemser demonstrated as Emanuelle. In terms of Grant's analysis of the tensions contained within the cult and exploitation text, the film recuperates 'that which has initially posed a threat to dominant ideology'.[21] This is a figure that by virtue of her sexual and racial difference both attracts and repels, a figure whose contradictory status is first elaborated and then expelled. In this respect the fate of Eva and the many other Emanuelles before her highlight the monstrous constructions of female sexuality and ethnicity haunting this cycle of European exploitation cinema.

On a somewhat more general level it also shows to what extent the figure of Black Emanuelle is a site both of confirmation of European fears, and of a desire to sexually exploit those fears. The *Black Emanuelle* cycle can be seen as addressing long-standing colonial traditions which seek to depict the black body as an erotic and disturbing spectacle. At the same time, its generic self-consciousness questions the gratuitous display of sexually ambiguous attractions of the exotic and monstrous 'Other' for European cultures. This makes Black Emanuelle a transgressive icon indeed, continuously sliding back and forth, culturally in *and* out of place.

## CHAPTER 13
# JEAN ROLLIN: LE SANG D'UN POÈTE DU CINEMA

Colin Odell and Michelle Le Blanc

> All you need to make a film is a girl and a gun.
> – Jean-Luc Godard

## INTRODUCTION

All you need to make a Jean Rollin film is two girls and a gun. Rejected by critics and ignored by mainstream audiences, the cinema of Jean Rollin is one of stark contradiction, the blurring of art and artifice. His films portray a visual richness that is more akin to painting, with narratives and editing that are closer to poetry. His plots derive from the world of the pulp novel and sado-masochistic literature. Although he has ventured into other genres, including a number of zombie films, and worked extensively in the porn industry (using pseudonyms and generally taking the job for the pay cheque attached), Rollin is best known for his cycle of vampire films. As a filmmaker Rollin's style may seem audacious, but his use of subject matter and imagery is basically highly personal. He is not a horror director. The supernatural themes that he adopts may be associated with the horror genre, but they do not conform with its narrative or stylistic conventions.

Similarly, his works contain erotic elements and plentiful nudity, but cannot be classified as pornographic. His influences too are less cinematic and more painterly or poetic. If he does reflect a cinematic tradition, it looks far earlier than most of his contemporaries. His debut fantasy *Le viol du vampire* (1968), released in the heady days of the Paris riots in May 1968, may have caused a scandal, but only because the revolting students and critics did not understand it or its use of cinematic language.

The vampires portrayed in the film were unconventional and far removed from the accepted representation – the Bela Lugosi/Christopher Lee or Max Schreck models, resolutely evil and anti-Christian. Instead, an Amazonian-style vampire queen dominated the screen, four vampire girls were treated mainly as victims in the narrative (rather than aggressors) and one explanation for vampirism (there are many) pointed to drug-enhanced hypnosis as opposed to any form of devilry. In many debut films, art often derives from accident and *Le viol du vampire*'s cast and crew not only had a minimal budget, but were also very inexperienced. Many scenes were improvised. It was originally made as a short but at the suggestion of his producer, Rollin filmed additional footage to release the film as a feature, and boldly resurrected the cast members he had killed off at the end of Part One (another aspect that infuriated contemporary audiences). In other hands this would be a cheat, but Rollin imbues it with the logic of the penny-dreadful, of Sax Rohmer and of the Saturday morning serial.

In this respect the black-and-white cinematography helps bridge the connection to Saturday serials, although in subsequent films Rollin finds his feet as a master of lurid colour compositions. At times he also resorts to fashionable film language (jump cuts, deliberate violation of the 180-degree rule, irregular spatial continuity, and so on). In later films he would retain some instances of these elements but reject others. There is, for example, a well-constructed car chase sequence that looks back to Godard's *A Bout de Souffle* (1959) but Rollin's techniques would later show little reliance on other filmmakers and more on painters or perhaps cine-poets, such as Sergei Paradjanov or Jean Cocteau. *Le viol du vampire* provides a template for much of his subsequent work.

## PULP FOUNDATIONS

Mystery is there because the poetic image has a reality of its own[1]
– René Magritte

The pulp nature of Rollin's debut would feed not only into his narratives but also into many of the visual aspects of his work. The opening shot from *Requiem pour un vampire* (1972) features two girls and a gun blazing from the back of a stolen car. It perfectly illustrates the basic thrusts in Rollin's work – two girls, pulp plot, exquisite composition and dynamism. That the first half of the film is almost entirely without dialogue also provides a link to the silent serial director Louis Feulliade. The second half deals with quite lengthy and contrived plot explanations and this shows the leanings towards the popular narratives of the 1920s and 1930s, especially the work of Sax Rohmer. Indeed Rohmer's combination of contrivances and sado-masochism are given an outlet in many of Rollin's more outré works. *La vampire nue*'s (1969) story is either unbearably complex or paradoxically simplistic. The plot (perhaps) for this film follows a young man who resolves to discover the secrets of a bourgeois and exclusive society which appears, upon first inspection, to be a bizarre suicide cult. A mysterious young girl is involved, but is she victim or protégé? And then there is the laboratory and scientific experiments. Rollin's narrative ensures that the mystery surrounding the cult and the girl unpeels like the layers of an onion and that no information given to the audience is extraneous. When all the layers have been revealed, the audience is still left with mystery.

Much of Rollin's style harks back to Feuillade in his 'cinema of attractions' approach to story-telling. Here:

> the spectator is external to the story space, an effect created by tableau staging, long takes and the essential autonomy of each shot. The overall strategy is one of showing: the displaying of events, tricks and scenes rather than the telling of, or immersion in, a story.[2]

Although he does not necessarily shun classical Hollywood narrative devices, Rollin often creates a tableau for each scene through which he allows the audience to immerse themselves. Continuity editing in these sequences is absent and he rarely employs shot/counter-shot in establishing character relationships. His narratives are generally linear and flashback devices or other temporal shifts are rare. If they are employed (the childhood memories of both *Lèvres de Sang* (1976) and *La morte vivante* (1983)), they are used to enhance the audience's emotional understanding of a situation rather than provide an explanation of events.

Rollin's use of the static shot and long-shot puts him at odds with the over-reliance on fast editing that plagues much of modern cinema. Audiences nowadays are bombarded with images to intensify a film's pace. They are not given the chance to sit back and soak up a scene. In Rollin's oeuvre the camera often lingers on a single framed shot through which the characters move and the action takes place. It allows the viewer to absorb the details (including the incidentals in the background) rather than be shown exactly what is 'significant' in any given shot. This brings attention to the links with painting and poetry (where similarly words are to be savoured longer because of their basic brevity) as well as re-emphasising Rollin's intention to provide mystery. He often selects settings of natural beauty or unusual locations.

## LANDSCAPE AND LOCATIONS

In many of Rollin's films the action takes place at a chateau in the rolling French countryside, which is filmed as lovingly as any of the characters and is complementary to his use of framing and the long take. Similarly, Rollin has a favourite beach, near Dieppe, where many of his vampire films conclude. In *Le viol du vampire* it is the place where new lovers run to their untimely but ultimately short-lived deaths. The beach is their death but also their resurrection through blood – their executioner is killed and, as the camera tracks perpendicular to the beach breakers, their naked bodies stir, revived by the freshly flowing blood on the rocks. The beach also provides a setting for the resolution of plot threads

**FIGURE 34** Untamed exterior landscapes frequently dominate Rollin's vampire films: *Les frisson des vampires* (1970)

and ideas. It is the place where the water meets the land, the journey between one life and the next. It represents change, finality and otherworldliness. The beach is a happy destination in *La vampire nue*, and *Lèvres de sang*, but it can also be a setting for the cruelty, the unfairness, torture and chaos of the world(s). Commenting on the repeated use of this iconography in his films, Rollin has stated:

> I have seen many beautiful beaches in my life, but this one, I don't know why, for me represents mystery itself. It's a surrealistic beach. Three elements: the falaise [cliffs], the sea and the mouettes [seagulls].[3]

Although it does not technically fall into his vampire canon (arguments could be made for the mentor of the two girls imbuing them with power through a form of vampirism) *Les démoniaques* (1974) is quintessentially Rollin, both thematically and structurally. The wreckers who are the film's central villains lure ships to their doom in order to plunder their cargoes. This leads to much of the action taking place on a rocky beach – the uncertainty of the waves clashing chaotically on the coastline. It is on this beach that much of the narrative thrust is derived. The sea's chaotic nature accentuates the narrative turns in many of Rollin's films – the waves here mark the turning points: the rape of two girls and their subsequent doomed attempts at vengeance.

Rollin's use of *mise-en-scène* is similarly intriguing for interior locations. He is just as focused on filming the environment as he is his actors – for him the decor is a character in itself (a trait he shares with Walerian Borowczyk and Jan Švankmajer). His chateaux are filled to the brim with candles, bizarre decorations, stuffed animals, even a flaming skull in a fishbowl. Spiral staircases obtain a life of their own under Rollin's camerawork and composition. Through his use of props he balances the pulp aesthetic and the art aesthetic with striking results. There is very little in the way of foreshadowing in Rollin's work (his films have a languid stream-of-consciousness feel to them that would make any such foreshadowing thematically incongruous) and thus attention to objects is a matter for thematic or emotional coherence and not narrative coherence. The answers lie not in the use of an object but the meaning of the object – the attachment with its environment and its relationship to the characters, or simply its aesthetic appeal. Vampires are ancient and so are their artefacts, their religions and rituals. Rollin's interest in filming rituals also links in with underground fetish writing and comics where the ritual itself is given as much (if not more) significance than the sexual act. Ritual becomes sex.

Rollin also desecrates the Christian ethos with his treatment of marriage in *Le frisson des vampires* (1970). Here the conceit of period pornography provides the springboard for the film's narrative – in this case an unconsummated wedding. It gives Rollin the opportunity to fetishise bridal attire as he depicts the disintegration of a marriage, in the sense that there is one as the bride Isa is drawn into an older vampiric tradition, the pull of a natural urge that is connected to her through breeding. The scenes where Isa is approached by the Vampire Errant, Isolde, provide the film with some of its most arresting imagery as she emerges from a grandfather clock at the stroke of midnight or suddenly reveals herself in all her naked splendour at the head of Isa's bed. These work like an eroticised version of Max Shreck's emergence from the coffin in *Nosferatu: eine Symphonie des Grauens* (1922).

**FIGURE 35** Objects and cluttered *mise en-scene* indicate the archaic world of the Rollin vampire: *Le frisson des vampires* (1970)

Rollin often employs the use of a stage within his narratives, reflecting the theatrical quality of his work. The nature of the theatre is such that each scene is played out in one static location and Rollin's actors move through his film space in the same manner as they would on a stage. Most of the vampire rituals that take place are staged for diegetically dramatic effect – the Great Blood Wedding of *Le viol du vampire*, for example. Linked to this is the idea that things cannot be taken at face value, and are not necessarily as they appear. Part of the fetishistic allure of Rollin's work is his emphasis on masking, of things beneath the surface being contradictory to our expectations. This also serves to emphasise the artifice in his films and distances the viewer from emotional attachment (with the possible exception of *La morte vivante*). Masks have numerous uses – either to disguise identity, as part of ceremony, to intimidate or to represent change. In *Requiem pour un vampire* the first shot comprises Marie and Michèle firing guns from the back of a car window in order to escape their pursuers. Both are dressed as clowns (we later find out that they were responsible for killing a man at a fancy dress party). When they remove their make-up in a river (causing the water to burst in blooms of red and white) and change into their normal clothes they return to their innocence. By detaching the viewer through essentially non-narrative form and denying our expectations through his use of visual representation, Rollin allows us the privilege to view his works on an objective (inasmuch as it can be) Kantian aesthetic level. The use of masks, theatre and artificiality bring home the unreality of the events and allow us to view them without preconceptions.

The opening of *Fascination* (1979) enforces the literary and artistic precedents of the visual aspects of Rollin's work – a painting in the background, candles flickering as a hand caresses the pages of a book like a lover. Rollin employs static symmetrical tableaux at key points in the film. The shots are composed like a static painting; full-length and held for several seconds, allowing the viewer to revel in the richness of it all. In *Fascination* the first major tableau shot occurs at the abattoir. Eva and Elisabeth stand with half-raised glasses of ox blood, seemingly oblivious to the offal and gore-drenched floor. At once we can see their aristocratic aspirations, their quite literal *sang-froid*, their close relationship and an indication of the film's time frame, in this case 1905. In terms of their attire, they reflect Magritte's *La grande guerre* (1964) although one is dressed in white, the other black. This covers the two girls up but acts like a fetish – Rollin enjoys the idea of playing around with decadence in a time perhaps more associated with moral fortitude.

Like Magritte's *La grande guerre* the effect is both anachronistic and erotic. Plot-wise the film has familiar associations with the pulp novel – a thief with a chest of gold on the run from his gang, seeks sanctuary in the house of two apparently aristocratic women. As it is pointed out in the film 'it's all very melodramatic' but the actual tone and situation is that of the Victorian underground S&M book. Rollin depicts many familiar vignettes but subverts them as the film follows the flirtatious but menacing games played between bandit Mark and an ever-increasing group of girls. Mark wins dominatrix Helene in a game of blind man's bluff and forces her to strip but she is clearly in control of the situation. He is an outsider to the group's world not because of his gender but because of his sexual persuasions. The scene plays under the watchful eye of a painting hanging over the fireplace. The 'painting as voyeur' is a visual motif that is used in the film a number of times during sexual

**FIGURE 36** Startling compositions permeate the tableaux shots of *Le frisson des vampires* (1970)

couplings – both when Eva and Elisabeth make love and when Eva and Mark do. Both of these scenes are filmed in an arresting and intimate handheld style that at once implicates the audience as a voyeur and contrasts with the tableaux shots used elsewhere. These scenes act as rhythm in Rollin's cinematic poem. He often repeats themes in a similar way.

At the film's opening Elisabeth smears ox blood seductively over her lips. This is shown in extreme close-up so that there can be no doubt of its sexual symbolism; make-up is sex and blood is her make-up. When she kills the bandit's wife on the bridge the shot is briefly reprised beneath the shadow of her deadly scythe. The meaning of the opening scene is now confirmed, her sexuality is death (the scythe of course being death's chosen weapon), a point emphasised by the film's climactic revelations. The film ends with the blood on Elisabeth's lips – it has come full circle visually and thematically from the opening. As one of her companions points out: 'You're beautiful like that, with his blood on your mouth.'

## COMIC BOOK CONSTRUCTIONS

Tableaux shots can also be used to represent comic-book imagery and much of Rollin's visual style derives from the comic-book ethos of unusually-angled composition or use of symmetry. Indeed Rollin was heavily involved with comics in the mid-1960s, creating *Saga of Xam* in 1967. The opening credits of *Fascination* depicting two girls dancing on a pier to the sound of a wind-up gramophone is composed diagonally across the screen, splitting it in two. This motif is repeated later with the lips and scythe shots. Similarly much of the composition involves symmetry or semi-symmetry, where the composition is symmetrical (either strict or rotationally) but the depicted objects are opposite – black and white or yin and yang. Eva is blonde, Elisabeth is brunette, one wears white, the other black, and they often share opposing sides of the screen's symmetrical space.

Similarly in *Lèvres de sang*, angular compositions play an important part in proceedings. As Frederic sits at the cinema watching Rollin's very own *Le frisson des vampires* (1970) (although the cinema's art deco poster is advertising *La vampire nue*), Rollin composes the shot of the mystery girl beckoning Frederic to follow her up the stairs. This complements and contrasts with the on-screen shot of Isa and Anthony climbing the steps to the chateau. Both staircases point towards the same physical direction and lead to the same thematic direction. *Le frisson des vampires* excels with its astonishing use of colour gels to create a comic-book sense of garishness. The opening cemetery shot features light streaming through the gravestones towards the camera to give a sense of motion in an otherwise static frame. Locations are clearly defined by their colour divisions. Inside the blue walls of the chateau the servant twins climb a red spiral staircase leading to a room, inside which lurks a staked vampire.

*Les démoniaques* (1973) pushes Rollin's comic-book derived pulp visual style even further. Despite the sordid nature of the narrative, the visual stylisation places the film entirely in a melodramatic context. The opening is a case in point. Rollin introduces us to the wreckers in a manner familiar to readers of European comics or Victorian penny-dreadful covers – the *dramatis personae* are illustrated in oval silhouette-style frames against a backdrop that forms the setting to the story. The colours are saturated and the impression of the piece is akin to Fritz Lang's 1955 film *Moonfleet* (complete with skeletons, lurid lighting, decay and coast-bound skullduggery) – although the story's concern with the attempted vengeance of two violated innocents falls firmly into penny-dreadful territory.

167

Rollin's style is not limited purely to static tableaux shots. He is not afraid to move the camera or adopt unusual editing techniques, although these are still employed to enhance the compositional (the use of space) rather than dynamic effect. On occasion his characters or objects are 'introduced' to the audience in one single extended pan-around. The constantly revolving camera is a common feature of his style and is used extensively in *Le frisson des vampires*. When Anthony and Isa learn from the servant 'twins' that her cousins are not dead as expected, the camera pans to each actor's face, they speak their line of dialogue and the camera moves on to the next character. This plays with the space the group inhabit and also causally defines the elements of the dialogue as each speaks in turn. Similarly,when Isa's cousins reveal their origins to an incapacitated Anthony, the camera pans around the whole room with dizzying effect.

In *Requiem pour un vampire* a spiral staircase is given animated life by the camera's rotational movement, though again the dynamic effect of the movement is employed more for compositional reasons. In *Le viol du vampire* the two lovers bend towards each other to kiss, but as their lips touch Rollin cuts to a disorienting upside-down shot of the very same embrace. The finale of *Le frisson des vampires* is a riot of imaginative camerawork as Anthony 'rescues' Isa from her initiation. As he flees along a railway track, the shot is completely symmetrical as he runs towards the camera. When he has passed the camera's view, Rollin cuts to an upside-down shot of Anthony receding into the distance. The action moves abruptly to the beach where Anthony finally loses Isa to the call of her id and her vampire cousins. Rollin achieves this by simply having the vampires disappear on the beach, in one shot, without the pretence of fading or other more overt cinematic trickery. This is an audacious move akin to earlier works by Cocteau and is successful precisely because it is so jarring and obvious – it has not dated because it was a trick that was already seventy years out of date in the first place!

## FATAL FEMALES: ROLLIN'S DEPICTIONS OF GENDER

> I've seen how pure-hearted they are. How innocent they are.
> – *Les démoniaques*

In her book *Vampires and Violets: Lesbians in the Cinema*, Andrea Weiss dismisses Rollin's work:

> Rollin's iconography features leather and metal chains, spikes protruding from women's breasts, scenes of gang rape, and vampires reduced to drinking from their own veins.[4]

This assertion denies the variety and richness of Rollin's female characters and reduces his work to cheap exploitation or pornography, which is just not the case. His female characters are unashamed of their sexuality even if, like Rollin's male characters, they are identifiable by their role. The dominatrix features heavily in Rollin's narratives – the Vampire Errant, Isolde, in *Le frisson des vampires*, the vampire Queen in *Le viol du vampire* and Helene from *Fascination*.

More distinctive, though, is Rollin's use of non-identical (and occasionally identical) twins. They are innocents, in the sense that they are creatures of nature and not nurture, to be violated by a cruel world. They are amoral Alices, wandering through Wonderland, oblivious of the consequences of their actions – they derive power but also, paradoxically, vulnerability. They are sexually alluring precisely because of their flirtatious innocence – Eva and Elisabeth from *Fascination*, Marie and Michèle from *Requiem pour un Vampire*, the servant girls from any number of films. Such characters are frequently depicted lying like tame panthers at their masters' feet or clad in alluring but impractical dresses of Perspex disks on metal hoops, or wandering through a chateau carrying candelabras. These depictions shows a sense of symmetry that would not be out of place in a Peter Greenaway film or *L'année dernière à Marienbad* (1961).

Rollin cites artist Clovis Trouille as an influence and nowhere is this more apparent than in his portrayal of the two girls.[5] Trouille's paintings have a similar erotic charm in his depictions of embracing women entwined. Much of Trouille's use of colour is also reflected in the costumes these twins wear. An example of Rollin's same-but-different fixation occurs in *Requiem pour un vampire* when one of the two girls seeks vampirism and the other (by deliberately losing her virginity) cannot. Marie and Michèle are aware of their power over men but view sexual flirtation as gameplay and not inherently dangerous. They are mischievous but not malicious in their seductions – indeed they both begin the film as virgins with Sapphic tendencies. Rollin's penchant for twins reaches its zenith in *Les deux orphelines vampires* (1997); even the title is a dead giveaway. In keeping with the twins' assertion that they can only see blue (and only at night), the colour palette reflects this for much of the time, creating a sense of *frisson* to the film and diminishing some of the emotional attachment. The two girls

**FIGURE 37** Rollin's sexual imagery has frequently produced controversy: *Le frisson des vampires* (1970)

tap their white sticks rhythmically during the daytime, one in the left hand, the other in the right. In most Rollin films the twins undergo a series of Trouille-inspired costume changes and *Les deux orphelines vampires* sees this reach its obvious conclusion.

## SURREALIST TENDENCIES

What you have seen and what you will see are only partly reality.

– *La vampire nue*

Time and again Rollin refers to the peripheries of the surrealist movement (including those whose work reflects surrealist sensibilities) and his shots often contain such elements in their composition and structure. Belgian artist Paul Delvaux appears to be an influence. His tableau of sensual women in *Sleeping Venus* (1944), some clothed, some naked and some skeletal(!), reflects Rollin's penchant for the surreal within his *mise-en-scène*. In *Requiem pour un vampire* wannabe vampire Erica performs an organ solo to a group of robed skeletons. By having the luxury of time within his medium though, Rollin can extend the principles of the surrealist painters' compositions. Magritte's oft-painted sea-scapes are a case in point. Rollin would often film at the beach near Dieppe in a manner reflecting Magritte's paintings of the sea (*La naissance de l'idole* (1926), *La traversée difficile* (1926), *inter alia*). Rollin also has his characters move from interior locations directly to the beach in a manner that is causally unlikely. The spatial jump to the sea can also be seen as a reference to the similarly startling edit that closes Buñuel/Dalí's *Un Chien Andalou* (1928). This is mirrored in the closing sequences of both *Le frisson des vampires* and *La vampire nue*. The sea offers the sound of gulls and waves, which sometimes invade areas apparently far removed from the sea. In *Le frisson des vampires* the soundtrack often comprises animal noises that reflect the characters and indicate their association with primordial or natural impulses. When Isa devours a dove these animalistic noises represent her return to primitive desires, but visually the scene harks back to Magritte's *La plaisir* (1927). Her *plaisir* lies in her freedom to return to the id but this is contradicted by her disgust at her bloodlust. This creates both a visual and aural bond with the beach scenes – even far from the shore it still invades the cinematic space.

In *Les démoniaques*, when the mystery demon makes love to the young rape victims, thereby imbuing them with his power, as the girls climax their excited sighs transmute into the cry of seagulls. Visually striking, *Lèvres de sang* also adopts surrealist-inspired literal visual wordplay. At the film's opening, two corpses, enshrouded, are interned in a castle crypt. The bodies are clearly breathing. Despite only seeing cloth we know straight away that these are literally the living dead – *les mortes vivantes*. This relation is further emphasised by the film's audacious close, which sees the naked couple enter a coffin and drift away on the ocean waves. Again the sea and beach represent the journey between life and death: the couple are both living and dead. These contradictions play in all of Rollin's films; the living dead and the blind that see. In *Les deux orphelines vampires* the titular characters are blind during the day but can see in their natural nocturnal habitat. There are also blind characters in *Lèvres de sang* and *Le viol du vampire*.

## IMAGE, SOUND AND EXPERIMENTATION

The integration of sound and dialogue within Rollin's work is normally employed in a symbolic or (apparently) non-diegetic way. In terms of exposition, he tends to use monologues to explain the plot, but the effect is usually that of extending the mysteries within the narrative. The mystery lies in the lack of explanation, and the meaning within the lack of meaning. In *La vampire nue* a lengthy monologue explains the actions of animal-masked men intimidating a girl, but do these revelations go any way to enhancing the viewer's previous experience of these events? Ultimately by the time everything has been explained, its relevance has passed. We know we are watching a poetic film rather than a conventional narrative. Rollin's sleight of hand in these dialogue scenes occurs not so much to explain earlier mysteries but to provide a bridge to later events. In *Requiem pour un vampire* the explanation as to the last vampire's predicament may 'account for' what has happened to the girls and why they are menaced by cultists, but its real purpose is to set up and justify the ending and its meaning.

Like much of Rollin's dialogue this is steeped in the pulp tradition – the arch nemesis reeling off the full deviousness of his or her diabolical plans. In *Requiem pour un vampire* the dialogue revolves around the sole true vampire. For the first half of the film there is virtually no dialogue of merit (dialogue as incidental/diegetic sound) and later on most of the non-vampire dialogue is abrupt or re-iterative ('Why won't you tell them?'). This again points to Rollin's affinity with the visual medium and early – silent – cinema. This is not to say that sound is irrelevant (any more than it would be to say that sound is irrelevant in 'silent' cinema) but it plays a different role to that which the modern audience is accustomed. It can be representational but also symbolic or relational to the character's emotional or spiritual state. In particular the use of music in some of Rollin's films approaches modern interpretation of silent screen music. In *Le frisson des vampires* the intense musical soundtrack is freeform, all engulfing and representative of the music associated with (sound) re-issues of German expressionist or surrealist silent films – rhythmic but avant-garde. In contrast the music to *Requiem pour un vampire* is more in tune with what people 'expect' from a silent soundtrack – the music either reflects the themes (ominous graveyard at night = organ music) or uses leitmotifs to represent characterisation. A good example of this strategy lies in the scene where Michèle and Marie try to escape from the vampire's gang. Both the pursuers and the pursued have quite strikingly different pieces of music to represent them – the girls' music plays as we see them run but as soon as the vampire gang come into shot it alters to their theme. This helps mirror the events on-screen to create a sense of urgency but it also draws attention to itself as a stylistic decision that heightens the pulp nature of the proceedings. Similarly the scenes of Michèle and Marie romping around with randy passers-by is accompanied by a more jovial tune, to emphasise the seaside (there it is again!) postcard nature of the goings on.

## CONCLUSION

After over thirty years bringing audiences his unique vision, Rollin is still making films, and more importantly still making vampire films (at the time of writing his most recent film is *La fiancée de Dracula* (1999)). Although attitudes and censorship have changed constantly over this time, his driving visual thrust has remained remarkably consistent. His (vampire) films are no more pornography than a painting by Delvaux, although the opportunity to extend the more risqué elements of his work has always been available to him. This is not to say that he has not altered his manner of showing us his artistic endeavours. Since *Le viol du vampire* there has been a definite path that takes him further into the realms of narrative film and coherent plotting. While this makes his films more accessible (*Fascination* and *La morte vivante,* for example) they also lose some of their enigmatic veneer. Although visually resplendent, *Les deux orphelines vampires* appears to be a far more conventional film than his earlier, more experimental, work. The balance between mystery and understanding is what defines his films, the scales being tipped towards understanding the further into his career one looks. That said, his body of work is still far removed from the mainstream of cinema and remains one that will continue to exert delicious fascination upon anyone who falls for its dreamy, erotic and surreal charms.

## CHAPTER 14
## BOILING OIL AND BABY OIL: BLOODY PIT OF HORROR

Leon Hunt

Mankind is made up of inferior creatures, spiritually and physically deformed, who would have corrupted the harmony of my perfect body.
> – Travis Anderson (Mickey Hargitay), *Bloody Pit of Horror*

One of the ways boys get interested in other boys is by building up their own bodies … Inevitably … they compare their bodies with those of other boys, and they both admire and envy those with better bodies than their own. This admiration can take the form of being sexually aroused by the others, and out of this comes the desire to have sex with the body of another person.
> – Wardell B. Pomeroy[1]

## QUALITY VS 'SLEAZE': DICHOTOMIES OF ITALIAN HORROR

Insofar as *Il Boia Scarlatto* (*Bloody Pit of Horror*, Massimo Pupillo, Italy/US, 1965) has a 'reputation', it is largely confined to the ambivalent psychotronic gaze of trash aesthetes. It is seen as both a 'sick piece of sixties schlock' and a 'masterpiece',[2] 'a great sleaze-trash classic',[3] 'the apex of the seamy streak that ran parallel with the greatest achievements of Italian horror',[4] 'a breathtaking blend of cheesecake, pop art, and Sadean excess'.[5] The film fares less well in those accounts that attempt to measure its cinematic achievements. Cathal Tohill and Pete Tombs clearly like it, but find it 'too daft to be described as bona fide sadism',[6] while the *Aurum Film Encyclopedia* condemns it to being 'only of interest as a case study to illustrate a theory of cinema-as-fantasy in psychoanalytical terms'.[7] Tim Lucas constructs a two-level hierarchy within 1960s Italian Horror; a 'quality' tradition of auteurs like Mario Bava and Riccardo Freda, and 'sleaze-mongers … mining torrid trash from the same raw materials that their colleagues polished with individuality and pride'.[8] It is not difficult to guess which category *Bloody Pit of Horror* fits into.

One of the film's perceived absences, as Lucas' comment suggests, is an auteur figure, a mark of distinction as significant in cult as canonical film discourses. *Bloody Pit of Horror* lacks either a distinctive stylist like Mario Bava or even an efficient, and periodically inspired, journeyman like Antonio Margheriti (aka 'Anthony M. Dawson'). Director Massimo Pupillo also directed the Barbara Steele vehicle *Cinque Tombe per un Medium* (*Terror Creatures from Beyond the Grave*, Italy/US, 1965). It is of limited significance that Pupillo used a pseudonym for both films, 'borrowing' producer Ralph Zucker's name for *Terror Creatures from Beyond the Grave* and becoming 'Max Hunter' for *Bloody Pit of Horror*; some of Bava's, Freda's and most of Margheriti's best films used pseudonymous director credits. Commenting on his directorial credit (or lack thereof) on two 'cult classics', Pupillo observed, 'I didn't give a fuck.'[9] More importantly, there is no sign of the stylistic consistency craved by auteurists in Pupillo's two best-known films. *Terror Creatures from Beyond the Grave* conforms to the atmospheric Gothic of other, more celebrated, Barbara Steele vehicles directed by Bava, Freda and Margheriti; the *Aurum Film Encyclopedia* suggests that its stylishness might be attributed to cameraman Carlo di Palma.[10] *Terror Creatures from Beyond the Grave* and *Bloody Pit of Horror* also share the same writers, Roberto Natale and Romano Migliorini, who also wrote Bava's extraordinary *Operazione Paura* (*Kill, Baby, Kill!*, Italy, 1966). *Bloody Pit of Horror* is still the odd one out of the three, though, perhaps because it is more of a hybrid than the full-on Gothic of the other two.

## QUEER GOTHIC

Both *Bloody Pit of Horror*'s detractors and fans seem agreed on two things. Firstly, if the film seems to lack an 'auteur', its aesthetic centre can be found instead in the extraordinary, barnstorming performance of former Mr Universe (and Hercules) Mickey Hargitay as the eponymous *Boia Scarlatto* of the Italian title. Secondly, there seems to be something very queer going on in this particular Bloody Pit. As Harry M. Benshoff argues, Gothic horror was 'tinged with a queer presence from its inception', populated by Gothic villains whose sexuality in some way 'deviates from the standard heterosexualized drive'.[11] The *Aurum Film Encyclopedia*'s review discerns in *Bloody Pit of Horror* 'a classic example of repressed homosexuality transformed into sadistic aggression towards women',[12] but it does not really take a crash course in psychoanalysis to notice 'the prominence accorded to [Hargitay's] well-oiled, hairless torso'.[13] One of Amazon.com's customer reviews wonders whether 'Mickey running around half-naked throughout in his red tights' meant that 'they [were] also going for a gay audience', while Frank Heinenlotter describes Hargitay as looking 'like a gay icon gone berserk and babbling narcissistic, Nietzschean rants'.[14] One perhaps has to ask whether 'The Most Perfectly Built Man in the World' could be anything *but* camp – this is, after all, the man who shared Jayne Mansfield's 'Pink Palace' and compared chests with her in *Gli Amori Di Ercole* (*The Loves of Hercules*, Carlo Ludovico Bragaglia, Italy, 1960). But it is worth pondering the relationship between bodybuilding, sadistic spectacle and male narcissism. To do so, however, we need to put trash aesthetics on one side for a moment and think about cultural and generic context. Put simply, however deliriously out-of-this-world trash 'classics' may seem, they *do* come from somewhere.

A scroll unravels, revealing a 'quote' from Sade, or rather the 'Sade' of pop culture ('the evil, depraved Marquis de Sade' as the trailer describes him) – 'My vengeance needs blood!' – a line later uttered by Travis as he is 'possessed' by the Crimson Executioner. This is not necessarily the Sade who wrote *Justine* and *120 Days of Sodom*, not even the libertine Sade of *Marat/Sade* or the mischievous roue of the more recent *Quills*. If anything, he is closer to the Sade whose skull menaces Peter Cushing in *The Skull* (Freddie Francis, UK, 1965), the Sade who stands in for all manner of evils, but who, above all, promises depravity and perversion, ingenious tortures visited on female flesh. The film opens in 1648 as the Crimson Executioner is dispatched in his own Iron Maiden and then sealed within it as punishment for sadistic tortures motivated by 'hatred and self-gratification'.

Three centuries later his castle is occupied by Travis Anderson, a former actor who 'used to be a muscleman in costume pictures'. Travis has withdrawn from the world and, significantly, from his engagement to Edith (Luisa Baratto). He now lives alone but for his muscular henchmen, clad in tight T-shirts and chinos. Travis has two all-consuming obsessions; the Crimson Executioner, 'a man of extraordinary physical strength, obsessed by an ideal of perfection', and his own 'perfect body', the latter modelled on the ideal of the former. His isolation is rudely interrupted by a group of photographers and models in search of a suitable locale for horror/*giallo* book covers. The group includes horror writer Rick (Walter Brandi in his customary comatose state) and, more importantly, Edith, now dowdied down as a wardrobe girl. Travis is initially inhospitable until he sees Edith, whereupon he invites them to stay. The bodycount soon begins, and the film dispatches its male victims as quickly as possible. One has his neck broken, another falls victim to a spiked pendulum when a rope is mysteriously severed during a photo shoot, a would-be-escape car performs circles as its driver's neck is pierced by a crossbow arrow, a greedy publisher is burned alive. The 'Cover Girls', on the other hand, as in most *gialli*, receive rather more lascivious treatment. Suzy (Barbara Nelli) ends up in the Iron Maiden. In the film's most bizarre sequence, Kinujo (Moa-Tahi) is tied to a gigantic spider web as a grotesque (mechanical?), poisonous spider closes in. Nancy (Rita Klein) and Annie (Femi Benussi) are strapped to a revolving pylon as a column of knives is pushed ever closer by Travis – in a series of close-ups, the knives scrape their cleavages and tear off slivers of black brassiere.

The film is well into its overheated climax by now, so Annie also gets a dose of the rack and Nancy has icy cold water and boiling oil poured onto her naked back. Travis spends most of the first half of the film in the sort of flowery, silk dressing gown Jason King would be envious of, but I do not imagine that anyone is surprised when he turns out to be the muscular, bare-chested figure in mask, hood, medallion and crimson tights. He oils himself up in front of facing, multiply reflecting, mirrors and dresses in the Executioner's outfit. 'Now you'll be punished for your lechery', he promises his victims and the mayhem really kicks in. Travis leers, cackles, cavorts, looks positively dizzy with punitive zeal. Only boring, cardigan-clad Rick and Edith survive, but not before she is stripped down to black knickers and tied to an iron 'bull' with a furnace inside. Fortunately for her, a (necessary) continuity error ensures that the furnace is never burning in establishing shots so she survives until Rick rescues her. At least two reviews see Edith's survival as indicative of her moral superiority over the other (promiscuous, exhibitionist) girls.[15] But Edith's 'repressed' exterior also sets her up for a certain Sadean logic – good girls get punished, too – and the film clearly relishes removing more of her clothes than anyone else's. Travis has a protracted struggle with Rick and is finally impaled on a spiked dummy, the 'Lover of Death'. 'My body, my pure body has been contaminated', he gasps before expiring.

## NATIONAL TRADITIONS AND GENERIC HYBRIDS

*Bloody Pit of Horror* is a hybrid of the Gothic, the *giallo* (named after the yellow book covers that denoted the crime genre in Italy) and the *peplum* (costume or muscleman movies). However, it also anticipates the Italian comic-strip adaptations which were to be based on *fumetti* like *Kriminal* (1967), *Diabolik*, *Satanik* and *Mr. X* (all 1968). In this respect, Travis is a hybrid too, a mixture of Kriminal, Maciste, sadistic Gothic villain and the masked killers who prowl the decadent world of the *giallo*. He most closely resembles Mr. X in appearance – and the American character, The Phantom – but the film also alludes to Kriminal in the figure of 'Skeletrix', a black skeletal bodystocking worn by one of the men for the photo shoot. The *fumetti neri* of the 1960s are an important intermediary between the Gothic and the titillating excesses of the *giallo* – the covers of *Diabolik* categorised the comic as '*Il giallo a fumetti*'.

    *Bloody Pit of Horror* actually seems to invite such reflexivity. Given that its two spectacles are muscular male bodies and scantily-clad female victims, it is appropriate that it should allude to two generic forms that embody these pleasures in an extreme way, the *peplum* and the *giallo*. The 'flat and plain' photography *does* evoke 1960s porn,[16] but equally the world of comic strips and lurid book jackets. Carlo Dumontet notes that the new breed of bodystocking-wearing criminal anti-heroes – Diabolik and Kriminal, in particular – indicated some significant cultural shifts in Italy. The 1950s and 1960s marked a period of economic growth, improved living standards and, consequently, some changes in moral and cultural values.[17] Dumontet implies that this involved a break from dominant Catholic values, but I would suggest that it was more of a renegotiation. The *giallo* is especially symptomatic of such a strategy. It is difficult to think of a more puritanical sub-genre, even if it did display more flesh than Italian cinema had previously been used to. (Pedro Almodovar's *Matador* (Spain, 1986) opens with a character masturbating to a video of *Sei Donne Per L'Assassino* (*Blood and Black Lace*, Mario Bava, Italy/France/West Germany, 1964)).

Equally, Diabolik and, particularly, Kriminal, may have embodied a kind of permissiveness,[18] but they usually punished it, too. The aesthetic result was effectively the same – 'Each issue (of *Kriminal*) abounded in scantily attired young ladies, who frequently ended up as half-naked subjects of brutal homicides'.[19] Often they were the victims of the skeletal Kriminal himself, like the girl in 'Omicidio al rigormatorio' ('Murder at the Reformatory', *Kriminal* 5, 1964), impaled on a spiked fence and positioned for the best view of her knickers, stockings and suspenders. Dumontet's announcement that 'They even looked sexy when dead!' sums up a generic imperative which informs *Bloody Pit of Horror* (substituting 'screaming in agony' for 'dead'), but also *Blood and Black Lace* and countless other *gialli*. The cinematic *giallo* is usually traced back to *La Ragazza che Sapeva Troppo* (*Evil Eye*, Mario Bava, Italy/US, 1962). However, it is *Blood and Black Lace* that established the formula of titillation, elaborately aestheticised murders and masked and/or gloved killers that has become the enduring image of the *giallo*, an image cemented by the later films of Dario Argento. The women in *Bloody Pit of Horror* conform to the iconography of the *giallo*, but could just as easily have been drawn by *Kriminal's* artist, Magnus (Roberto Raviola) – curvy, scantily clad, in unspeakable peril if not already dead.

The Crimson Executioner, like Kriminal, simultaneously embodies sexuality (moreover, in a perverse form – 'an egotist obsessed with your sick thoughts' according to Edith) and chastises it. He decries lechery just as his crimson outfit suggests a state of perpetual engorgement. *Kriminal* had first appeared the year before and had pushed the sado-erotic boat further than the already quite racy *Diabolik*. But by 1965, the year of *Bloody Pit of Horror*, a backlash had set in, a campaign against *fumetti neri* not dissimilar to those which took place in America and Britain in the 1950s – debates in parliament, police seizures, concerns about young readers.[20] Travis' descent into dementia is exacerbated by the production of precisely the kind of images that were causing so much concern in 1965 – thus, he is both libidinous and puritanical, both Kriminal and what Heinenlotter calls 'a Censor from Hell'.

## ELECTROCARDIOGRAM THRILLS

There is another way of seeing the Crimson Executioner's quest for 'perfection' and physical purity, but it requires a comparison with Hercules, Ursus and Maciste rather than Diabolik and Kriminal. It also involves looking a little further back into Italy's history. The *peplum* is, in many ways, Italy's first exploitation cycle, the precursor of the Gothics, the *gialli*, the spaghetti westerns, spy and 'sexy' films of the 1960s. In production terms, the genre can be seen partly as a response to Hollywood epics, some of which used Italian technicians and studio space, but the *peplum* was indebted to more indigenous sources, too – silent films like *Quo Vadis* (Enrico Guazzoni, Italy, 1912), the strongman hero Maciste. In distinguishing the *peplum* from its wealthier American rival, Derek Elley notes that the Italian sword'n'sandals 'lacked the sheer weight and portentousness of their American counterparts, possessing a vigour closer to comic-strips or *fumetti*'.[21] Early *pepla* include *Spartaco* (*Spartacus the Gladiator*, Riccardo Freda, Italy, 1953) and *Ulisse* (*Ulysses*, Mario Camerini, Italy, 1954), but it is *Le Fatiche di Ercole* (*Hercules*, Pietro Francisci, Italy, 1958), in particular, that seems to have spurred on the cycle, particularly when it opened up the American market in its dubbed version.

Its former Mr Universe star, Steve Reeves, already suggested a transnational dimension to the film, and other Anglo-American bodybuilders would don loincloths over the next seven or eight years; Reg Park, Gordon Scott (already a hit as Tarzan) and, of course, Mickey Hargitay.

Peter Bondanella calculates that some 170 *peplum* were made between 1957 and 1964, but largely consigns them to the undistinguished detritus of *seconda visione* (second-run) cinemas, films of 'artistically inferior quality and limited cultural significance'.[22] Of all the productive Italian cycles of the 1960s, only selected spaghetti westerns broke into the *prima visione* (first-run) market and established a 'quality' output. But Christopher Wagstaff provides an illuminating picture of the *seconda* and *terza visione* (third-run) market, cinemas attended primarily by working-class audiences. Wagstaff suggests that the mode of viewing elicited by films aimed at the *terza visione* audience was closer to the 'distracted' gaze associated with theories of television spectatorship than the more intensive immersion associated with cinema:

> The viewer (generally he) went to the cinema nearest to his house … after dinner, at around ten o'clock in the evening. The programme changed daily or every other day. He would not bother to find out what was showing, nor would he make any particular effort to arrive at the beginning of the film. He would talk to his friends during the showing whenever he felt like it, except during the bits of the film that grabbed his (or his friends') attention.[23]

These attention-grabbing 'moments' are likened by Wagstaff to peaks on an electrocardiogram, 'supplied by the three "physiological" responses [sex, laughter, thrill/suspense] that were as interchangeable as plot lines'.[24] These 'peaks' appear to be cross-generic – a *peplum* could have 'sexy' and horrific moments – which, along with the need to vary repetitive formulas, would explain an increasing hybridity across Italian exploitation cycles. The *peplum* had already produced Gothic variants such as *Maciste Contro Il Vampiro* (*Goliath Against the Vampires*, Giacomo Gentilimo and Sergio Corbucci, Italy, 1961), *Ercole al Centro Della Terra* (*Hercules in the Haunted World*, Mario Bava, Italy, 1962), guest-starring an undead Christopher Lee, and *Maciste all'Inferno* (*The Witch's Curse*, Riccardo Freda, Italy, 1962).

1965, the year of *Bloody Pit of Horror*'s release, was the year that the peplum cycle began to fizzle out, and the film both references and distances itself from their body-beautiful aesthetics. Richard Dyer sees the *peplum* as a complex coming-to-terms with Fascism. If it seems initially overzealous to find such political subtexts in campy comic strips like the Hercules series (or *Bloody Pit of Horror* for that matter), then Dyer reminds us that it was not until the 1970s that Italian cinema felt able to address the Mussolini era directly.[25] Therefore, is it not likely that such a traumatic memory would impinge, even if only subtextually and unconsciously, during this ostensible twenty to thirty year 'silence'? In any case, all of the 1960s Italian genre directors had lived through, and some (Bava, Freda) worked during, the Fascist era. The *pepla*, Dyer argues, relate ambivalently to Fascism. On the one hand, they offer images of the 'idealised white man, with his spirit-perfected body and capacity to sort out the problems of lesser beings'.[26] Such an aesthetic was prominent both in the Mussolini era and, indeed, in *Il Duce* himself, sometimes referred to as 'the Maciste of Fascist Italy',[27] constantly photographed in 'athletic' poses, often stripped to the waist.

On the other hand, the films' narratives reject Fascism, often embodied in autocratic villains holding forth about 'purity' and 'inferior races' – an example would be the blonde Atlantean Super-Race created in *Ercole alla Conquista di Atlantide* (*Hercules Conquers Atlantis*, Vittorio Cottafavi, Italy, 1961). Dyer observes how Reg Park's toned-to-within-an-inch-of-his-life Hercules embodies the very aesthetic that he is ostensibly fighting against.[28] The *peplum* offered images of strong, white, male bodies at a time when they were being supplanted by technology and industrialisation[29] – at the same time, they conjured up 'a discredited politics of whiteness' which needed to be displaced/disavowed in some way.[30] The casting of Hargitay and the references to musclemen in 'costume pictures' are the most obvious references to the *peplum* in *Bloody Pit of Horror*. Indeed, Gary Johnson sees it as 'a comment on Italy's love of Hercules and other muscle-bound heroes', its 'message' (if that is the word) that '(the) obsession with physical perfection can be mentally destructive'.[31]

Where the film departs from the *peplum*, however, is in embodying fascist aesthetics and fascist politics in the same figure rather than pointedly separating them – it is the Maciste figure who now talks about 'inferior creatures, spiritually and physically deformed'. The Crimson Executioner is, significantly, also a figure from the past, unsuccessfully 'hidden' and forgotten, who returns and regains control over the imagination of the 'disempowered' white male. If industrialisation threatened the working-class male body, the decline of the *peplum* threatened the film careers of musclemen like Hargitay, Reeves, Park and so forth – even Hollywood Tarzan films were on the way out. The bodies of spaghetti western heroes, like James Bond-inspired superspies, were empowered by technology (guns and gadgets) rather than an exaggerated representation of masculine physical labour. Muscular male bodies did not return significantly to cinema screens until Arnold Schwarzenegger and Sylvester Stallone in the 1980s. If Travis is an explicit intertextual reference to the *peplum*'s decline, he now also seems like its return of the repressed. In other words, he is Mussolini in tights, back at the film studio (Cinecitta) built in accordance with his 'vision' but which had subsequently become the site of the cinematic excesses of the 1960s.

Where the film is most knowing of all is in its depiction of male narcissism, although it has become a generic (and homophobic) cliché to equate fascism with homosexuality, not least in more 'serious' Italian films like *Il Conformista* (*The Conformist*, Bernardo Bertolucci, Italy/France/West Germany, 1969). This is where the *Aurum Film Encyclopedia* seems to get the film slightly wrong. According to the unnamed reviewer, the torture scenes function as a 'detour and safety valve', protecting the hetero-sexual male viewer from the homoerotic pleasures represented by Hargitay's naked torso.[32] Granted, male and female flesh do seem to be competing for our attention – it is interesting that Pupillo has claimed that Rita Klein was stuffing her bra and Hargitay his pants to enhance their spectacular appeal.[33] What I would suggest is that the two substitute for one another, but not in the displaced circuit of desire that the *Aurum Film Encyclopedia* offers. Two problems occur to me with that reading. Firstly, the film defuses (or rather, localises) the homosexual 'spectre' by pathologising Travis' narcissism – the women simply are not needed for that task. We are never allowed the same kind of unmediated gaze that the *peplum* facilitates – when Travis is multiply reflected the camera remains at a safe distance and his most extravagant poses are always accompanied by deranged (fascist) ranting. Secondly, does anybody seriously think that the film's main selling point was not something like 'Cover Girls in Torture Chamber', given that such material is not exactly alien to Euro-exploitation? The film is much less 'unconscious' about homoeroticism than it is made to sound, even if it is ultimately homophobic. Travis' sexuality is fairly explicit – 'Don't touch me!' he shrieks at Edith when she attempts to do precisely that, and the bloated, poisonous arachnid menacing Kinujo offers some Freudian clues as to why he fled her in the first place. 'A woman's love would have destroyed me', he tells Edith, and she informs Rick that Travis has 'always been a little strange, even with me – he seemed so cold'. There is clearly a place, however, for other muscular men in his life – Johnson wonders about 'the nature of the relationship between Anderson and his costumed servants'.[34] That is not to say that the film does not display some other anxieties of its own, not least about the very process of male bodybuilding.

## A BODYBUILDER IS BEING BEATEN

According to Mark Simpson in *Male Impersonators* (and what is Travis if not a male impersonator?), bodybuilding typifies the '*flux* of masculinity', the way that 'everytime men try to grasp something consolingly, sturdily, essentially masculine, it all too easily transforms into its opposite'.[35] If bodybuilding ostensibly phallicises the male body, it also feminises it – overuse of steroids can create male 'breasts' or 'bitch tits' and genitals have a way of shrivelling (don't throw away that padding, Mickey!).[36] But already, by the 1960s, there were concerns about all this obsessive interest in male perfection – the image of bodybuilding was of something 'indecent' and 'perverse'.[37] Wardell B. Pomeroy's *Boys and Sex* (1968) spells out exactly the scenario of *Bloody Pit of Horror* – if boys obsess over their own bodies, they're already a short step away from getting interested in other male bodies. Bodybuilding, Simpson suggests, is about becoming one's own object of desire,[38] but *Bloody Pit of Horror* explicitly connects this to 'another' body – Travis' self-love is inextricably linked to his desire for the Crimson Executioner's 'perfect body'.

Where do the 'Cover Girls' fit into all this? The film's original English title, *A Tale of Torture*, gives us a clue, because bodybuilding itself is usually a tale of torture, self-improvement enacted within a matrix of discipline and self-punishment. Simpson calls the gymnasium a 'hi-tech dungeon where the weak flesh is punished by the willing/willful spirit'.[39] It is not such a huge leap from this to seeing Travis' torture chamber as a kind of inverted gym, the women's suffering mirroring his own acquisition of a supposedly perfect, but as it turns out, all too vulnerable body. The rack stands in for weights machines, icy water for cold showers, the knives 'trim' excess flesh; toned, muscular bodies are often referred to as being 'cut'. In addition, these are the scenes where we really see Hargitay's muscles 'working' as he operates his instruments of torture. In 'A Child is Being Beaten', Freud analyses children's fantasies of being beaten both as punishment for incestuous desires for the father and a pleasurable substitute for that desire. As a further disguise/displacement, a third party is often substituted for the subject – it is *someone else* being beaten.[40] We do not need to look very far for the desired 'Father' of *Bloody Pit of Horror*. Travis gazes longingly at the facsimile of the Crimson Executioner – 'created … in his own image', an omnipotent Super Ego – and subsequently is 'possessed' by him. But if Travis substitutes for the Executioner, someone needs to substitute for Travis, which is where the Cover Girls stand in for the Cover Boy.

Stephen Marcus has applied Freud's beating scenario to Victorian flagellation literature, which brings us closer to the disciplinary spectacle of *Bloody Pit of Horror*. 'The sexual identity of the figure being beaten', Marcus suggests, 'is remarkably labile. Sometimes he is represented as a boy, sometimes as a girl, sometimes as a combination of the two – a boy dressed as a girl, or the reverse.'[41] Stories about boys being beaten by women remain within a heterosexual scenario, but gender seems to be more fluid in those stories where girls are beaten by men – the 'girls' are strikingly androgynous (with names like 'Georgy' and 'Willie'), sufficiently so for Marcus to discern an elaborate drag act:

> The heterosexual relation has been abandoned and a homosexual one substituted for it – the little boy has transformed himself into a girl. Yet this transformation is itself both a defense against and a disavowal of the fantasy it is simultaneously expressing. That fantasy is a homosexual one: a little boy is being beaten – that is, loved – by another man.[42]

This substitution is made particularly explicit in *Bloody Pit of Horror* when Travis tries to force Annie into the 'poisonous clutches of the lover of death', the male figure who will embrace – and, indeed, penetrate – him in the final scene. If Travis looks distinctly surprised when he is 'contaminated' (and feminised), he is also, in a sense, getting exactly what he wants, which is to be fucked by the Crimson Executioner.

At one level, this does still leave the male viewer out of the homosexual 'circuit of desire', which is both open and closed by Travis, ultimately another example of what Harry Benshoff calls the 'Monster Queer'.[43] But because the 'beating' phantasy keeps identification and gender in a state of flux, it also does not; Carol J. Clover and Rhona J. Berenstein offer interesting accounts of spectatorial 'drag' in (American) Horror, both suggesting the complexity of gender identification within the genre.[44] In *Bloody Pit of Horror,* the 'Cover Girls' do the exact opposite of what the *Aurum Film Encyclopedia* claims by facilitating another libidinous route into this perverse scenario. Frank Heinenlotter recalls seeing the film for the first time in a cinema on 42nd Street 'where the bloodthirsty crowd wildly cheered Hargitay on, obviously recognising a role model when they saw one'.[45] Quite what such identification involves is by no means straightforward – as Heinenlotter humorously signs off his liner notes to the recent DVD, he promises the viewer, 'now you too will be punished for your lechery!'[46] Maybe the viewer will (silently) cheer that proposition, too.

# CHAPTER 15
# TRANS-EUROPEAN EXCESS: AN INTERVIEW WITH BRIAN YUZNA

Xavier Mendik
Interview transcribed by Adam Rodgers

## INTRODUCTION

While many of the chapters in this volume see European trash and alternative cinema as legitimate reflections of the national cultures from which they have emerged, this often obscures the increasingly trans-national nature that European genre filmmaking is adopting in the face of high-budget Hollywood competition. While this degree of co-operation has always existed *between* European countries, it is also witnessing major fantasy filmmakers relocating to Europe to take advantage of these structures.

One such director is Brian Yuzna, the creator of such American gore classics as *Society* (1989), *Return of the Living Dead III* (1993) and *The Dentist* (1996). In 2000, Yuzna and prolific Spanish producer Julio Fernández formed the Fantastic Factory, with the intention of creating a Barcelona-based outfit able to draw on leading acting and production talents from around the world. As Yuzna is a self-confessed European horror fan, it seemed appropriate that he fully immerse himself in such a filmmaking culture and he has since relocated his family and work activities totally to Spain. The Fantastic Factory have already produced several films with Yuzna in both directorial and production roles. These have included *Faust* (2001) (an updated cult comic-book version of the man who sold his soul to the devil), *Arachnid* (2001) (a scary spider extravaganza directed by Jack Shoulder) and, most recently, the popular sequel *Beyond Re-Animator* (2003).

In the following interview, Brian Yuzna explains his motives behind forming the Fantastic Factory, his dream of remoulding Barcelona as the new horror film centre of Europe, as well as explaining how foreign films influenced his own development as an American filmmaker responsible for a series of gruesome movies that combined blood, humour and cutting social satire. The interview was conducted in March 2001 and includes a closing update of the Fantastic Factory's fantastic progress to that date.

**Xavier Mendik**: *The idea of an American horror director relocating to Europe to begin a new genre production house is an exciting development. Can you tell us a little more about the project?*

**Brian Yuzna**: The production house to which you refer is called the Fantastic Factory and this is a project that I'm developing with Julio Fernández of Filmax International in Barcelona. Filmax is a Spanish distributor and what we aim to do is to create a label of fantastic films from a variety of genres such as sci-fi, horror, science fiction and hard action movies. We intend to create a line of genre films for the international market produced in Spain, but using talent from all over the world. We are going to employ Spanish talents, but we are of course shooting the movies in English, because we want to compete internationally. We are not just interested in being a success in Spain. We want to be a success internationally.

*How did the idea for the Fantastic Factory come about?*

The idea behind the Fantastic Factory began with a conversation I had with Julio Fernández at the Sitges Festival in October 1998. By January 1999 I had moved to Barcelona and I've been living there with my family ever since. That's where we're set – because that's where we make the movies. This is a project that is completely Spanish-financed, with no ownership outside Barcelona. So this will be quite unique in the independent movie world, and I think it's very important for genre movie fans. What we are doing is trying to create something using the inspiration of production houses like Hammer and the American international – those types of early independent genre films. I feel that Hammer was the most successful of all of them, because they had better quality consistently.

*And of course the other thing about Hammer is that it was a factory and as a result there was an internal consistency of its productions.*

Yes. What we are trying to do is make the label meaningful in a similar way. For example, I would go to the video store and pick a Hammer film, even though I didn't recognise it – because I knew how it fitted into their catalogue. Of course at this point we're not comparing ourselves to Hammer. But what we are doing is trying to create a context for these productions. We called it the Fantastic Factory because fantastic is of course a loaded word. On the one hand it's a very positive word – it's 'fantastic'. On the other hand it represents all these genre qualities. We didn't want to call it horror because that was limited, not sci-fi – that's limited, but we felt that with genre cinema I think fantastic fits well.

*I'm thinking that Warhol used the term 'factory' in relation to his work, while the Russian avant-garde filmmakers of the 1920s used the literal factory to make their work. So there's a particularly European currency to this process. And it seems a lot of filmmakers feel the European dimension gives them more control to the whole process. Have you found that?*

I think so. I don't know if it's more control or it's a different attitude. There's an efficiency to the Los Angeles/Hollywood type of movie making while there can be a sort of navel gazing quality to a lot of the European subsidised product. But I think the politics in Europe has changed dramatically in the last five years. These days every country in Europe is willing to try and support the movie industry just as they would support an automobile industry or internet industry. And up until a few years ago this wouldn't have been possible because there was a kind of resistance to the idea that movies were an entertainment product.

Now we all know that even in the most exploitative commercial movie there is a level of artistry involved. This is something we don't focus on and I feel that absence is to the detriment of the public. The idea of the Fantastic Factory is to make movies for the public, but not just the public in Spain, or Europe, but the public in Japan, Asia, North America, Latin America and to that end we have pre-sold the movies all around the world before we have even shot one frame.

*That's very encouraging. You mentioned that Spanish filmmaking will be a totally different concept to L.A.-based productions, do you feel your American background will be a help or a hindrance?*

Well, what I've tried to do in Barcelona is to take what I feel were the strong qualities of movie development and production in Los Angeles and adapt them to a new system utilising the individual character of Spain and Cataluna When I first arrived in Barcelona I found that Filmax didn't really have a structured production system. They did co-productions within Spain, or with Italy or Chile, but they didn't really sell the movies outside of those countries and they did movies more at that time in the traditional Spanish style, in which they waited for directors to come to them with a script and a television sale, with a yes or no if they wanted to pay for it.

So what we're doing isn't really American-style productions, but you can certainly say that we borrowed a lot of American-style techniques. For example, we began a development department to accept scripts, to develop scripts, to look for projects, to find directors, to find interesting creative elements and to develop them. This is something that's not typical in Spain, I think we're the only company that has it, we've got four or five people in this department and that wasn't there when I got here. We started foreign sales; we have a foreign sales company that sells internationally at the markets now, that wasn't there when I got here. We decide how many movies we're going to make and what kind of movies we want and we control them more in the form of a studio. That said, we are certainly not interested in telling a director how to cut his film, or whom he should have to collaborate with. On the other hand we certainly try to give direction to the projects so this is a mix of systems, and the ultimate aim is only to be the best producer of genre films in the world and to make Barcelona the centre of genre filmmaking in the world.

*What about your own influences as a filmmaker; do they cross over from America into Europe?*

Well, I basically I grew up with American movies. But I grew up outside of America – I grew up in Panama and Puerto Rico and Nicaragua. So to a certain degree I was always on the outside looking in, even though I am an American. I always watched movies with subtitles when I was a kid. When I got to high school I was in the States and at that time in the 1960s it was the time of the French New Wave and Europe was where all the great movies were coming from. I think this generation in Europe has forgotten that. I don't think they realise that when they get defensive about movies in Europe, there was a time when movies were way cooler because they were in Italian or French and American movies couldn't be as interesting or as important because they were from the States.

I think this is something that during the 1970s and 1980s Europe forgot and thought 'we can't compete with American movies therefore we must have all these economic rules and defences in place because we are really not good enough to compete'. I think they are ignoring history in that case. I took a lot of influence from the New Wave, like most Americans of my generation. I watched everything from *L'Année Dernière à Marienbad*, (*Last Year at Marionbad*, 1961) and Fellini to Truffaut and Godard. I mean these movies were what were really important during that period.

*Going back to notions of the fantastic, what is so interesting about European cinema is that it transcends the art and commercial divide. You mentioned obvious art movie directors but there's also Spanish directors, Italian directors who were doing stuff that was experimental as well as genre-based.*

Well I think we certainly have to include directors such as Dario Argento, whose work is both fantastical and pretty arty. I also like the work of the Italian horror director Mario Bava. When I look at it, I didn't realise that when I was going crazy for the Roger Corman/Poe movies, I'd never seen movies like *Maschera del Demonio* (*Mask of Satan*, 1960) or *La Casa Dell 'Esorcismo* (*House of Exorcism* aka *Lisa and the Devil*, 1973). Well, I felt a little embarrassed after I saw Bava's films and I realised that Corman was remaking European genre movies in American syntax and that's what I loved. There was a whole period during the 1950s and 1960s when all you had to do was go and look at European movies and come back and make one, because Americans would never go and see them!

And of course if we include Britain in Europe, which normally in America we don't, then I would certainly have to say that the company that recreated the Frankenstein myth and the vampire myth, and Dracula myth, was Hammer. Hammer took the dead Universal series of monsters and they gave it colour, sex and blood – and this was the scariest stuff out in the 1950s. Is that an influence? Is it European? I don't know what you call it. Sometimes I have a hard time putting nationality to a lot of movie influences because sometimes I think they really transcend it. I think in Europe the audiences are more accepting of genre films being movies than in America. In America, this is a cliché, but everything is reduced to money, everything is reduced to a value, quantifiable in dollars. And that's not the case in Europe. That's maybe the most significant cultural difference between the continents.

*It seems to me that the key feature of horror is almost disrespectability. As soon as you make it big budget you make it safe – would you agree?*

Yes. It's a little like comedy. A comedy works better with less production, because there's something about comedy that depends upon timing and indefinable elements, almost improvised elements. With horror it tends to be the same way that sometimes an over-produced horror movie ceases to work.

*What horror does successfully, and your films do in particular, is to draw up certain repressed material, things that society would prefer to ignore. Would you agree?*

Yes, because horror is the 'bad boy' of movies, after you get past pornography – it's just one step up! And what it means is that you can deal with anything! Something that non-horror fans don't realise is that horror films have a very rigid moral structure, more so than normal movies. If you just adhere to the structure, you can do anything you want and this is a kind of a freedom you don't get with other movies. So horror does often deal with things that 'normal' movies would have a hard time touching. There's a fundamental freedom in the horror movie.

*Beyond being the bad boy of cinema, the horror film also deals with themes of incest and sexual perversion, which seem to be repeated features in your own work from Society onwards. Is psychoanalysis something you're interested in?*

Yes, because horror and psychoanalysis both deal with madness. If you communicate an image of madness – then it is in the horror genre. That's what the horror audience thrive on. It's almost like getting an electric shock, and a horror movie is like constantly poking around in an electrical socket! And then at a certain point it just jabs you and you get this feeling in your flesh, your whole flesh crawls from the electrical charge and that's the feeling you get from horror.

For example, *Psycho* (1960) was arguably the original 'slasher' movie and I'm old enough that I saw it when it first came out, when I was a twelve-year-old. The shower scene was physically horrific when we saw it, but the highest horror moment of the whole movie was the very end when we see both the mother and Norman in the same body – this moment is madness, the wobbly knee moment, the skin-crawling feeling. This is horror. It's something that is dreamlike, and something deeply psychological. Ultimately what I do with genre movies is look for the expressionist quality and the surrealist quality to recreate that psychological impact.

*The other feature that unites both psychoanalysis and horror cinema is an interest in the unsettling images and meanings behind dreamscapes.*

Well, one of the scariest movies I know to enter the dream world is Robert Wise's version of *The Haunting* (1963). Wise's version is probably the purest ghost story made into film. It has a poetry of fear that enables you to watch it many times and still get the creeps. And yet this is a movie that only takes you into the madness of Eleanor in the movie. And the big moment is when she is seeing the thing trying to come through the door and she looks at the trim of the paint around the door and suddenly these very innocuous patterns start looking like strange faces mocking. This is the moment you start going crazy, and I think this is very important to horror.

Most horror movies don't work on such a subtle level, but I think though they work on a very crude level they're really in that same continuum. So the head, giving head, in *Re-Animator* (1985) is really on the same level. I mean it seems totally incongruous, but it really is. The idea in *Re-Animator* that a head could talk or breathe just because it was injected is absurd, but there is a more mythical level to this, there's a dreamlike level in which heads can talk and the disembodied intellect is just that, and there's only one way to satisfy a head, sexually. And in this type of stuff there are so many levels of irony that you really are in a dream world of horror. And because it's consistent *Re-Animator* has become a classic. When it's not consistent it just becomes yet another genre movie.

*Just to play Devil's advocate, couldn't you say that the head giving head defines another feature of your films: that they all focus on an excess of immorality?*

I've never thought about these films as immoral, but I do think about them as sexual and I am interested in the ways in which different classes respond to that sexuality. And certainly, I think there is a comparison between *Society* and *The Dentist* in the fact that Billy Warlock's character in *Society* is in the same place as Corbin Bernsen's character in *The Dentist*. They are both just destroyed by the immorality of the sexuality that's around them. I think with Billy Warlock it's an indictment of the upper class, with *The Dentist* it's more of an indictment of the excesses of upper-middle-class consumption. It's a bit like that movie *The Stepfather* (1987), the idea that the guy would rather kill his dirty family than accept them as dirty.

*Horror is often viewed as a male genre, but often underground or independent movies from the genre do privilege the feminine. How do feel about that?*

I think the fact that horror films generally victimise women is probably based on the fact women are generally victimised in society, in some cultures more than others. But women are generally victims of predatory, sexual impulses by males. With a horror movie there is always a sexual component, whether it's buried or explicit. Everything with the flesh has a sexual component. And usually the woman is the victim because she's much prettier, much sexier, she feels much more vulnerable. *Society* is bit of an aberration of that, Billy Warlock is not a girl and *Society* would have a hard time working with a female protagonist. But on the other hand women do tend to be the ones that are chased, whether it's in *Halloween* (1978), or *The Texas Chainsaw Massacre* (1974). But a lot of the times, newer movies have them turn the tables a bit, and give females more power than they otherwise would have in the genre.

The woman I like most in the movies I've made was Mindy Clark in *The Return of the Living Dead III* (1993). The movie was really a reaction to *The Bride of Re-animator* (1990), because we didn't get to see the bride enough! She was interesting but we didn't get to see enough of her. I felt for her – she was like the bride of Frankenstein. I felt the loneliness and the existential horror of her situation. And so with *The Return of the Living Dead III*, I thought just make a zombie the main character and see what happens! And so when you see Mindy Clark – she's the victim and you really feel for her, you never lose sympathy for her, even when she hits that horrible moment and commits a crime by killing the river man, which is when her boyfriend finally turns against her. But to me she is still a modern horror heroine.

*I wanted to finish by returning to the Fantastic Factory. The first movie from this production house is Faust. How does this production fit into where you want to go with the company?*

Well, *Faust* is a funny movie. It is a movie that's based on a very violent, pornographic comic book and really I tried to maintain much of the spirit and images of that comic book. I was very happy that Tim Vigil and David Quinn, the creators of the comic, were happy with the movie. I really didn't want them to be disappointed that it didn't represent their work. The idea of doing *Faust* first was to do something original. This is one caped super-hero that children really shouldn't watch! Also, the film is a mix of genres. It's a movie that has a complicated structure.

We had many challenges to shoot it in Barcelona and part of what I was trying to do was to see what problems we were going to have with the different challenges in Spain – which I had never done before. We were getting Barcelona to double for a North American city, we were shooting action scenes, stunts, all kinds of special effects, we were shooting a comic-book movie – there is

**FIGURE 38**  A modern horror heroine: Mindy Clark in *The Return of the Living Dead III* (1993)

also a great number of Spanish or European actors, and we were still trying to shoot it all in English. And on top of that the film had to be shot with three major genre styles based on the three major characters' points of view of the problem of evil in the world. Detective Margolies' (Jeffrey Combs) view is that bad people do bad things to other people for personal gain – the solution is to put them in jail. So when we see him we tried to shoot his perspective as an action movie, because that's his world. When we get to Jade De Camp (Isabel Brook), her movie is a thriller. For her evil is a disease, the hero is a sexually-disturbed man who is sick and is a predator, and if you could just cure him with medicine, science and compassion then we could solve this problem. These movies always have a lot of shadows so we shot her section as a thriller movie, finding out her back-story – giving her her movie. The third part was shot as a horror movie. John Jasper (Mark Frost) knows evil is the battle between God and the Devil and the soul of every man. It involves the supernatural, miracles, magic and everything in between. You see scenes of him eating a heart which is straight out of a horror movie, something that doesn't belong in the other two characters' movies. But finally all of our characters have to enter the horror movie. And at the end we even have a big monster! So this made the movie very complicated and it made it a danger of losing every audience. We made a lot of choices that limited the audience, like with the music, for which we chose a hardcore heavy metal soundtrack. I thought this is the milieu of this movie – we used them as score and not as transitions for the album.

*Your films are renowned for their flashy, visually interesting film style. Does Faust fit in with this tradition?*

We shot it in a style that is uncomfortable, sexy and violent, which meant we can't have kids. Normally a caped hero has kids – we can't have that. We also cut it in a very aggressive style, which will alienate certain audiences that can't watch that kind of editing. I think it fits the comic book but it certainly doesn't help you expand your audience – which makes it very risky – but you can't ignore it, it's unlike anything else.

*What other projects can we expect from the Fantastic Factory?*

The second movie we made, *Arachnid* (2001), is about a giant spider in the jungle. The film is directed by Jack Shoulder. It's a giant spider movie for your grandmother! You can take your whole family. I think that in the long run, how well *Faust* does is not going to define the Factory – it is certainly going to make people understand we're not going to follow the path anyone else has laid out. That's important for me to say I just don't want to feel we have to play it safe, and this is one way to do it.

*The idea of creating a 'Horror Hollywood' in Spain ultimately seems like a high-risk but creative and ambitious project.*

Yes, you know, it is a high ambition, but I think that's all part of the feeling – there's a spirit in Spain right now that's very ambitious and very open and that's what attracted me. This is because I felt a little of what I loved about L.A. What I love about L.A. is that people go there with incredible ambition and nine out of ten of them crash and burn but they give off a wonderful light as they expire. I feel the same way here in Spain. In Julio Fernández we have a guy who's a visionary, ready to put the money on the line, who has a company that's ready to get behind it and I think we will either have a wonderful success or give off a great, bright light as we expire!

**FIGURE 39** International terror: the monster stalks in *Arachnid* (2001)

## ADDENDUM: 2004

The above interview was conducted in March 2001 at the Brussels International Festival of Fantastic Films when the Fantastic Factory was in its infancy. When I interviewed Brian Yuzna again earlier last year, I was able to assess the progress of his production house to date. Rather than suffering from the potential crash and burn scenario that the director outlined, the Fantastic Factory appears to be going from strength to strength as its personnel adapt to the unique trans-national sets of influences and modes of production that they are operating within. For instance, some commentators complained that early releases such as *Faust* were only partly successful in their integration of American genre motifs with European styles and idiosyncrasies. However, more recent productions such as *Beyond Re-Animator* (2003) indicate that Yuzna's pursuit of a trans-European excess has paid dividends as the Fantastic Factory has evolved.

This sequel to the 1980s horror classic finds the mad scientist Herbert West incarcerated in a prison for his crimes, though he still cannot resist dabbling with body parts and the living dead. With its doses of excessive gore punctuated with moments of very dark humour, *Beyond Re-Animator* maintains the trademark features of Yuzna's American output, while its visual style and casting reflects an increasing European sensibility. Not only did the film make effective use of Spanish locations for its central prison sequences, but the film also featured the self-reflexive casting of local pop culture icons such as Santiago Sagura, who plays a whacked-out convict who fatally shoots up West's re-animating serum. Also featured in the movie is the Spanish pin-up Elsa Pataki, whose clean-cut, domestic image was subverted when Yuzna cast her as a undead dominatrix with a penchant for penis biting. With its fusion of American and European genre-film influences, *Beyond Re-Animator* has proved to be a crowd pleaser that confirms the Fantastic Factory as one of the most exciting projects to evolve in horror filmmaking for quite a while.

I would like to offer my thanks to Dirk Van Extergem, Thibaut Dopchie, Marie-France Dupagne, Christoph Foque, Luc Govers, Dianne Leenders, Freddy Bozzo and all the staff at the Brussels International Festival of Fantastic Film for their assistance in arranging the interviews with Brian Yuzna during the Cult Film Archive's 2001 and 2003 visits.

## CHAPTER 16
## JÖRG BUTTGEREIT'S NEKROMANTIKS: THINGS TO DO IN GERMANY WITH THE DEAD

Linnie Blake

> We are separated from yesterday not by a yawning abyss, but by the same situation.
>
> – Albert Camus

> Everyone bears the guilt for everything, but if everyone knew that, we would have paradise on Earth.
>
> – Fyodor Dostoyevsky

### NEW GERMAN HORRORS

Surprising as it may seem, these two epigraphs, from the opening and closing titles of Alexander Kluge's 1966 work of Young German Cinema, *Yesterday Girl*, provide an entirely apposite introduction to this piece. This is the study of two more recent works of experimental, historically-grounded and hence political German film – Jörg Buttgereit's *Nekromantik* (1987) and *Nekromantik II* (1991). The two titles represent the best known of the Berlin director's highly visceral works of horror cinema. These films (alongside the symphony of suicides that is *Der Todesking* (1990) and the Nazi-inflected serial-killer classic *Schramm* (1993)) have been praised by fans and vilified by critics in fairly equal measure.

In the past, Buttergereit's much-banned necro-porn-horrors have been frequently dismissed as little more than 'disappointingly witless' and 'morbidly titillating' attempts 'to disgust the most jaded conceivable audience'.[1] However, it can be argued that these movies are more thematically complex and technically sophisticated than is popularly supposed. Equally, they share the artistic and ideological concerns more usually associated with the canonic auteurs of the Young German Cinema and the New German Cinema of the turbulent years of the 1960s and 1970s: specifically Volker Schlöndorff and Hans Jürgen Syberberg in the first generation and Werner Herzog and Rainer Werner Fassbinder in the second.

Buttgereit's films dwell on the existential isolation of the desiring German subject and the libidinally ambiguous re-animation of the deeply repressed historical past. As such, they represent highly self-reflexive plays on cinema's capacity for the dissemination and reproduction of regressive ideologies of race and gender. In so doing, Buttgereit delivers not, as has been argued, the 'limp, inane' message that 'it's okay to fuck the dead as long as you don't kill them',[2] but a considered, and often playful, exploration of one of the core subjects of recent German cinema. Through his unruly and repulsive imagery we are offered *Die Unbewaltigte Vergangenheit* – the past that has not been adequately dealt with.

## THE BUTTGEREIT BACKGROUND

Born in 1963, the year following the *Oberhausen Manifesto*'s demands for a 'new German feature film' predicated upon 'new freedoms', liberated from 'the influence of commercial partners' and 'the control of special interest groups',[3] Buttgereit received his first Super-8 camera as a first holy communion present. He made his first film in 1977, as West Germany veered to the political right and various left-wing, feminist, anti-establishment and terrorist groups such as the Red Army Faction and the Baader-Meinhoff group came to the cultural and political fore. In the face of ideological divisions at the heart of West German society, and the evolution of Kluge's Young German Cinema into the distinctively historically engaged New German Cinema, it is notable that Buttgereit's early film career ranged across genres. (These ranged from parodic monster and super-hero shorts to mock-rockumentaries set in the West Berlin punk scene.)[4] However, it is still possible to trace a culturally-engaged thematic continuity across these early works that is of great relevance to German cinema of the period in general, and the *Nekromantik* movies in particular.

In 1981, Buttgereit covertly shot the six-minute short *Mein Papi*, a slice of *cinéma vérité* displaying for ridicule Buttgereit's elderly, overweight and vest-clad father. The film was screened in clubs, mostly as a back-projection to live performances by the experimental noise band *Einsturzende Neubaten*, with Buttgereit being paid for his art in vodka. The real payment, however, as the director remarked in interview with David Kerekes, was the satisfaction of having 'whole audiences laughing at [his] father behind his back'.[5] The New German Cinema's location, in Thomas Elsaesser's words, of 'history in

**FIGURE 40**  The past that refuses to die: Nazi imagery in Jörg Buttgereit's *Der Todesking* (1990)

the home and Fascism in the family unit',[6] was here transmuted into a punkish mockery of the father as legitimate familial embodiment of totalitarian authority and law.

It was a mockery echoed the following year, in *Bloody Excesses in the Leader's Bunker*, a six-minute Super-8 short set in the final days of the Reich. Here, Hitler was depicted by a performer better known for his obscene parodies of the much-loved folk musician Heino, while Buttgereit played his assistant. Whilst the Heino impersonator went down very well with contemporary audiences, it is nonetheless notable that Buttgereit's onetime inclusion of genuine concentration camp footage in the film proved too strong even for the punk denizens of the Berlin music scene. It underscored, however, Buttgereit's own decidedly inventive take on his nation's past, and the connection of that past to the politically divided and culturally confused present – a concern that would, most certainly, feed into the *Nekromantik* films.

In 1985 came *Hot Love*, a self-consciously absurd tale of sexual infidelity, rape, suicide and the slaughter of the transgressive mother by a murderously mutant newborn: the present born of parental sin, the past avenged, the body bloodied and broken, dark humour inescapable. Finally, with the Buttgereit-directed crucifixion sequence in Michael Brynntup's *Jesus – The Film* (1985–86) in which Christ (in vampire teeth) is simultaneously nailed to the cross and staked through the heart, the director's thematic machinery and collection of collaborators was complete. Buttgereit, like Syberberg, evidently recognised that strand of Romantic irrationalism that had lain at the heart of German culture long before the originary unification of the nation in the 1870s. This irrationalism had manifested itself in Goethe's rendering of the Faust legend, Hoffman's tales of the *unheimlich* in prose and later still the horror tales of Weimar cinema – such as Robert Weine's *The Cabinet of Dr Caligari* (1919) or F. W. Murneau's *Nosferatu* (1922).

Like Syberberg before him, Buttgereit also recognised 'the emotional deadness of German society'.[7] This was engendered by the Nazi appropriation of that Romantic tradition and focused in his films on Germany's subsequent repression both of the memory of the Nazi past and the irrationalism that underscored it, leaving Germany 'spiritually disinherited and dispossessed … a country without a homeland, without *Heimat*'.[8] For if Syberberg had the quintessentially irrational Germanic unconscious rise from the grave in the guise of the Fuhrer in *Hitler: A Film From Germany* (1977), then in the *Nekromantik* movies Buttgereit would undertake a considerably more visceral, but no less politically serious, act of resurrection.

## CENSORING THE DEAD

In terms of his productions, Buttgereit operates in a variety of roles and works with a small team, including Manfred Jelinski as producer, Franz Rodenkirchen as co-writer and co-director and actors such as Daktari Lorenz, Mark Reeder and Monika M. amongst many others. Although this group works to insanely unpredictable shooting schedules and on ridiculously low budgets, it seems that Buttgereit had picked up the torch of the *Oberhausen Manifesto's* signatories in his attempt to make something new out of the legacy of the past and the uncertainties of the present. Buttgereit's graphic depictions of sexual encounters with the dead (as well as the mutilation of people and animals), alongside his decidedly idiosyncratic re-animation of the German Romantic tradition (through his disruption of linear temporality, insertion of dream sequences and absurdist parodies of classic films) also resulted in swingeing censorship unheard of in Germany since the days of the Third Reich.

The political climate into which *Nekromantik* was released in West Germany was an extremely conservative one. As in Britain, this impacted directly on contemporary genre cinema. All horror films shown, both on video and in picture houses, were heavily cut, with numerous classics of the genre (such as *The Texas Chainsaw Massacre* (1974) and *Evil Dead* (1982)) being banned outright on video. Refusing to submit *Nekromantik* to the agency responsible for implementing the code of *Freiwillige Selbst Kontrolle*, or 'voluntary self control', under which directors were supposed to work, Buttgereit released the movie directly to cinemas for screening to those over the age of eighteen. And nothing much in the way of reprisals ensued, either from the radical left, known for its attacks on cinemas screening films they considered sexist or pornographic, or from the authorities. Only in 1992, following the scandal surrounding *Nekromantik II*, would sale of the film by mail order be briefly outlawed. The film, it seemed, was too essentially 'arty' for the horror crowd and it passed without a great deal of notice at home, until its enthusiastic reception in America and elsewhere made it something of a *cause celèbre*. *Nekromantik II*, however, released following the fall of the Berlin Wall and the re-unification of Germany, faced a considerably harder time of it, being placed on the list of 'seized videos' whereby it could neither be owned, watched or shown legally in Germany. Orders were thus given, without hearing or trial, for its negatives, production-related and publicity materials to be destroyed. This was a move unprecedented in Germany since 1945 and it was echoed internationally, where the *Nekromantik* movies remain widely banned and largely unavailable.

So, what *is* so dreadful about the *Nekromantik* movies that has driven governments to ban them and critics so consistently to neglect them? Certainly, their heroes and heroines are decidedly unappealing. Rob and Betty of *Nekromantik* are bound together by their shared passion for the dead – Rob working as a 'street cleaner' with the Nazi-encoded *Joe's Sauberungsaktion*, the company logo of which is a skull and crossbones within a pentacle. It is an occupation that allows for the acquisition first of body parts and then of a complete corpse for this oddest of couples' mutual erotic delight. But this is no ordinary body. It is not the product of an automobile accident, as seems to be the case with many of Rob's acquisitions, but was once a young man who was accidentally shot whilst picking apples. The perpetrator of the crime was a beer-guzzling, oompah-listening fat-man, remarkably visually similar to Buttgereit's own father of *Mein Papi*, and extremely reminiscent of the kinds of characters depicted in the *Heimatfilms* of the 1950s – West Germany's most popular post-war genre.⁹ Positioning the murderer in a back-yard deckchair, shooting small birds that fly across the sky, Buttgereit simultaneously evokes and derides not only the *Heimatfilms* as essentially conservative and enormously popular depictions of morally unimpeachable familial and community lives – but also the culture that so enthusiastically consumed them. As Buttgereit makes clear, then, it is neither Rob nor Betty who has transformed the young apple-picker into a corpse. This has been accomplished by an ostensibly morally upstanding member of society who subsequently disappears from view, unpunished for his crimes. Buttgereit's mission, it seems, is to embrace that corpse, and in so doing to raise the question originally posed by Alexander Mitscherlich, Director of the Sigmund Freud Institute in Frankfurt, as to why the collapse of the Third Reich had not provoked the reaction of conscience-stricken remorse one might logically expect; why, in Elsaesser's words, 'instead of confronting this past, Germans preferred to bury it'.[10] The purpose of Buttgereit's *Nekromantik* movies was, like the New German Cinema before it, to dig into the place of burial and engage passionately with the rotting fruits of the past, which we the audience are forced also to embrace visually through the technological mechanisms of cinematic production.

## NATIONAL BOUNDARIES AND BODY MARKERS

Fittingly for a Berliner, and hence one who had grown up in an island city bisected by the Wall and its attendant ideologies, Buttgereit frequently adopts the metaphor of the border, or boundary, as means of articulating the sense of existential isolation, and cultural confusion experienced by his characters. Great emphasis is placed, for example, on the ways in which the most innocuous-looking of apartments, shot from the sanitised safety of the street, can nonetheless house the most grotesque, and historically redolent, realities. Focusing on the interiors of such apartments, Buttgereit not only participates in the New German Cinema's quasi-documentary focus on the real-life spaces inhabited by ordinary people, but points to the essentially *unheimlich* nature of the German home. The apartment inhabited by Rob, and initially Betty, is one such space. Their bed, for example, is swathed in chicken wire, becoming a highly culturally resonant space of physical, emotional and historical entrapment. Here, erotic shenanigans with the bony corpse inescapably evoke the cadaverous figures staring out from behind the concentration camp wire in films such as Alain Resnais' 1955 production *Nuit et Brouillard* (*Night and Fog*). (This image itself being famously quoted as a commentary on the German present by director Margarethe von Trotta in the closing sequence of her 1981 film *Die bleierne Zeit* (*The German Sisters*.) A bed is never a bed in Buttgereit's films, just as a corpse is never simply a corpse. For sexual desire, the world of dreams, the horrors of the past and death itself are all self-consciously entwined in a cinematic spectacle that may shock, but shocks in a way that is intimately involved with the German past and encoded by German representational practices.

Subtly encoded Nazi semiology is apparent, for example, across both movies. Both Rob of *Nekromantik* and Monika of *Nekromantik II* possess a highly distinctive and highly nationally-specific ornament – a miniature version of *The Glass Man*. Originally created by Franz Tschackert of the German Hygiene Museum in Dresden in 1930, this was a life-size model of a male figure whose transparent skin allowed the observer to see the skeleton within, and some of the internal organs. One of Hitler's favourite contemporary artefacts (there are pictures of him posing proudly alongside it), the model was assiduously promoted as an embodiment of Aryan racial perfection, its organs echoing the master race's purity of line and perfection of form, its transparency signalling the eugenic purity of the breed.[11] In possessing such an artefact, in playing with it and re-assembling its body parts with loving care, necrophiliacs like Rob and Monika do seem to be engaging with a particular model of historically-grounded subjectivity that is overtly linked to the discourses of racial supremacism that underscored National Socialism.

But such discourses, Buttgereit again intimates through his *mise-en-scène*, were not the invention of the Nazis, simply appropriated by them. Rob's flat, after all, also contains a large collection of specimen jars holding an eyeball, a foetus, a hand and various unidentifiable organs. These too are highly reminiscent of the discourses of racial supremacy promulgated by Nazi science and explicitly dealt with in films such as Schlöndorff's 1979 film *The Tin Drum*. (Here, the squealing of the boy Oskar shatters the specimen jars of the doctor who seeks to cure him of his refusal to grow up into Fascism.) But such imagery also existed before the rise of the Nazis, specifically in the Expressionist-inflected 'mad-scientist' movies of the early twentieth century. Films such as *Homunculus* (1916), in which a decidedly Faustian scientist pre-empts Hitler's 'final solution' by setting out to overcome the bounds of human knowledge in the creation of a his own Superman, a theme echoed in both *The Golem* (1915) and *The Cabinet of Dr Caligari* (1919).

Beneath the rational consciousness of the street, beneath the present's repressions of the past, Buttgereit seems to argue there is an essential irrationality. It is an irrationality, as for Syberberg, that lies at the heart of the German consciousness and which can be seen in the nightmare world of the ghost train, the crazy logic of dreams, and in the representational strategies of avant-garde or experimental cinema itself. Notably, both *Nekromantik* movies contain lengthy or repeated dream sequences. Examples include Rob's rural visions of a white-clad, long-limbed woman striding across a rural landscape, carrying a severed head in a box before removing it to play a game of catch. This is echoed by Mark's drunken nightmare of burial up to his neck and having his own head placed beneath a box and then stamped upon by a spike-heeled shoe. And there is also Monika's torch song when, accompanied by an androgynous blond pianist on an 'Eterna' piano she sings a love song to death as a giant blood-spattered skull revolves in the background. Surreal visions of death, desire and love coalesce here in a strange dream-logic that self-consciously questions not only the transparency of the cinematic medium but also the certainties of rational discourse, specifically the discourses of history.

197

## DIMENSIONS OF VISUAL PLEASURE

It is notable, in the light of this, that Rob and Betty's erotic desire for the corpse and, hence, their very subjectivity as necrophiles, is predicated upon an act of remembering. That such subjectivity is also tightly bound to the act of looking further implicates us, the audience, in the discourse's scopophilic powers that lie at the heart of Buttgereit's films. Early on in *Nekromantik*, for example, a television psychiatrist talks at length on the ways in which phobic individuals can become de-sensitised to the object of their fear. Such therapy is based on the psychiatrist's observation that teenagers who repeatedly watch video nasties, can become inured to the horrors of what they see. De-sensitisation, the psychiatrist argues, is a product of repeatedly experiencing the horrific – or mass-cultural renderings of the horrific – and experiencing it visually. But as Buttgereit realised early in his movie-making career, there are some things that German eyes, however countercultural, find difficult to look upon. The inclusion of concentration camp footage in *Bloody Excesses in the Leader's Bunker*, for example, was simply too much for audiences to stomach, whatever their punk credentials.

Might it be the case that de-sensitisation to violence is just as likely to happen when we refuse to look, when we turn our head away from reality and look elsewhere – at the world of nature, the rural community, at the falsified present? Nazi cinema, of course, with its promotion of a *volkish* ideology of national community and blood and soil (which entailed the concomitant purgation of all liberal, democratic, progressive or cosmopolitan elements) had effectively instituted a cult of the beautiful as a means of aestheticising the horrific actuality of industrialized genocide. Both the documentary tradition instituted by Leni Riefenstahl's *Triumph of the Will* (1935) and the concertedly anti-Semitic, anti-communist *Hetzfilms* such as *Jud Suss* (1940) or *The Eternal Jew* (1940) had thus counterpoised the essentially wholesome, healthy and beautiful world of National Socialism to the hideously bestialised sexual threat that was the Jew or the communist. And repeated viewing of such materials obviously naturalised the binarism, printed it upon the national unconscious, de-sensitised the audience to the aestheticisation of the political upon which the Final Solution rested. What Buttgereit appears to be proposing, in his insistent looking upon the dead and what may or may not be done with them, is a radical de-aestheticisation of that past. This represents a form of truthful looking that not only cuts through the de-sensitisations of revisionist history and lays the corpse of the past bare, but which points to the strategies of control implicit in all acts of cinematic viewing.

In both *Nekromantik* movies Buttgereit is keen to expose the highly manipulative nature of the medium – specifically in the second film's depiction of heterosexual pornography and the first's re-creation of the slasher horror genre. Mark, the hero of *Nekromantik II,* may see nothing wrong with his job – providing voice-overs for foreign porn movies. But the fact that Buttgereit depicts his employment in ways remarkably visually redolent of the scenes from Michael Powell's *Peeping Tom* (1960) when the sexually dysfunctional hero, also called Mark, repeatedly views the footage he has shot whilst murdering women, would seem to point to a certain matrix of concerns. Specifically, these are the highly fetishistic reduction of the pornographic subject to 'dicks and cunts up close', the encoding of discourses of power at the heart of the gaze and the potentially murderous consequences of such encoding.

In *Nekromantik*'s take on the slasher movie, we find ourselves in classic stalker territory, with audience point-of-view neatly matched to that of the knife-wielding monster. Here, we see his victim's hands above her head, we trace his knife from her shoe, up her stockinged leg into her mouth as she stands, breasts exposed, screaming and moaning in terror and, it seems, ecstasy. The sufficiently de-sensitised audience, which includes Buttgereit in left foreground, are predictably bored by such objectifying shenanigans, kissing, fondling each other, eating, talking – but never actually looking at the misogynistic drive that, for Buttgereit, clearly underscores such images. For as Monika the necrophiliac cries in *Nekromantik II*, it is no more perverse, for Buttgereit, to watch the dismemberment of animals for pleasure than it is to look at heterosexual pornography's reduction of people to their genitalia. It is simply more socially acceptable. The audience has become de-sensitised to the nastiness of such images, even whilst it is unable to look with any degree of clarity or good faith at the genuine horrors of the historic past. At the heart of Buttgereit's oeuvre, it seems, is an awareness of the politically problematic dimensions of visual pleasure, the uses to which that pleasure has been placed in the past and the linkage of that past to the present. There is no easy moralising here, none of the knee-jerk-will-to-censorship of the *Autonome Szene*, contemporary political activists whom Franz Rodenkirchen has deemed practitioners of 'fascism from the left'.[12]

If Buttgereit displays a consistent interest in the relationship between technologies of looking and the perpetuation of oppressive ideologies then, like Roland Barthes, he also appears to associate the act of photographing or filming an object with death itself. Using Super-8, 8mm, 16mm and 32mm film, video, polaroids, stills-photography and television pictures in the construction of his representations

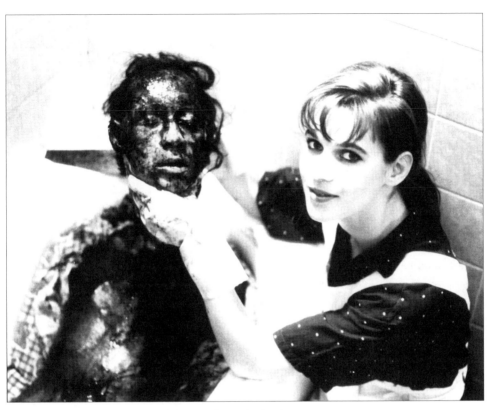

**FIGURE 41** Manipulating the motifs of visual pleasure: *Nekromantik II* (1991)

of the dead and those who love them, Buttgereit thus undertakes a distinctively Barthesian production of what may be termed 'counter-memories'. Examples of this strategy are seen in Monika's photograph album of dead relatives, her hilarious 'family photographs' of herself and her dead lover sitting innocently on the sofa as well as in her newspaper pictures of Rob prior to his suicide. In these instances, we see an attempt not only to record what has been (the living person now dead) but an attempt, in the act of looking at such pictures, to interject the absent dead into the living present. Hereby they become not memories, but counter-memories – a way of remembering otherwise.[13] This is, of course, another aspect of Buttgereit's attempts to revivify the corpse of the past.

By making explicit the linkages between visual representation and memory, by predicating much of his thematic machinery on the will to remember the otherwise absent and forgotten, Buttgereit once more draws our gaze back to that sense of horror that, for New German Cinema, underscored all representations of the past. And he also forces us to look again at that dark irrationality that for Buttgereit, as for Syberberg, lies at the heart of the German subject. His task, akin to that of Claude Lanzmann in *Shoah* (1985), the nine-hour documentary consisting of interviews with survivors of the extermination camps of Auschwitz, Treblinka, Sobibor, Chelmno and Belzec. Namely, this is to bring the past into the present; to indicate through visual representations, that the past is never in actuality over and done with. It is a project, in all its viscerality, that forces the audience to look at that which they would rather avoid, offering a counter-memory to Nazi cinema's elision of its own bloody deeds and a representation of human desire that rejects the power dynamics of heterosexual pornography and slasher-horror alike.

## ALL LIFE ONCE MORE IS DEATH

This, of course, makes Buttgereit a highly self-referential director, one who consistently references, and re-configures, the cinematic medium in his work. Monika and David of *Nekromantik II*, for example, meet at an avant-garde movie, a very funny parody of Louis Malle's *My Dinner with Andre* (1981) entitled *Mon dejeunner avec Vera*. Here, a man and woman feast on hard-boiled eggs whilst sitting naked at a table on the roof of a block of flats. The linkage between the title and any notion of 'truth' remains, of course, opaque. Between the two *Nekromantik* movies, Buttgereit made *Der Tödesking* (1990) in which, ostensibly in the mind of the little girl who introduces the piece, seven characters kill themselves, one for every day of the week. Mulling upon the permeable membrane between lived reality and cinematic representation, *Der Tödesking* repeatedly deploys a Brechtian *Verfremdungseffect*, whereby the constructed nature of the repeated suicide-tableaux is foregrounded through often amusing plays on the medium of film. The entire 'Tuesday' sequence (which includes a man renting a film at a video store and going home to watch it) turns out, for example, to be a horror video, being screened in an empty room in which a body hangs dead in the background. Implicit in German life, as the foetal figure that transmutes into a decomposing corpse intimates, is death. The two are locked in an endlessly repeated cycle, a Nietszchean return, in which the tragedies of German history are endlessly enacted by and repeated in death.

All of this, of course, comes to a head (so to speak) with Rob's suicide in the final moments of *Nekromantik*. Lying on the bed he once shared with Betty, and for a brief interlude with their dead lover also, Rob masturbates his memorably tumescent penis whilst slowly disembowelling himself, coming in an impressively colourful splatter of blood and semen, back-masked sound and chiaroscuro lighting. Far from being gore-for-gore's sake, Rob's suicidal masochism does seem to posit a subjectivity so wracked by sexual dysfunction, existential despair and utter isolation that, as is the case for many of Fassbinder's ill-fated hero-protagonists, suicide is the only option. Populating his films, like Herzog, with characters that exist on the margins of society but, nonetheless 'are not freaks' but 'aspects of ourselves',[14] Buttgereit proposes that a tragic will to self-destruction that manifests itself in failed relationships with the living, and a mordant fetishisation of the dead, lies at the heart of German subjectivity.

It is precisely this paradigm, of course, that is embodied in Monika of *Nekromantik II*, a film whose very credits are interspersed with a grainy, monochrome re-running of Rob's suicide scene (another counter-memory). Disinterring Rob's corpse at the opening of the movie Monika protractedly vacillates between her erotic pleasure in, and visceral disgust at, her sexual encounters with Rob – whose head and (greatly reduced) penis she retains. This cyclical repetition of the love of death, the repression of that love and the visual representation of that death is, of course, echoed in Monika's conscious attraction to the idea of a relationship with the pornographic-voice-over artist Mark, who nonetheless bores her sexually and, as we have seen, finds her liking of animal-dismemberment movies obscene. Echoing the marriage of Maria and Oswald in Fassbinder's *The Marriage of Maria Braun*

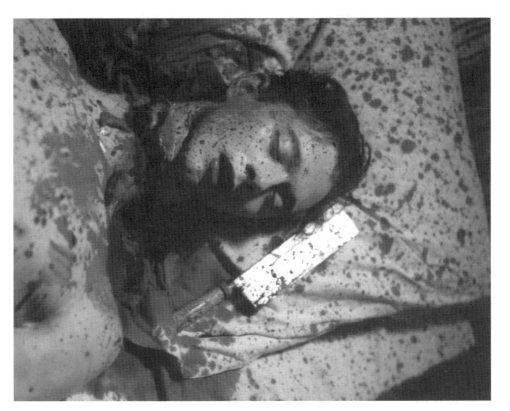

**FIGURE 42**  The love of death in *Nekromantik II*

(1978), and numerous other New German Cinema renderings of the same, theirs is evidently a relationship founded on a shared loneliness, in a world where 'people can't live alone, but they cannot live together either'.[15]

The relationship culminates, of course, with Monika's decapitation of Mark during sex, her placing a tourniquet around his still erect penis and replacing his head with that of the exceedingly rotten Rob. The result of such congress with the living dead is Monika's pregnancy. Although this echoes the unnatural reproduction of *Hot Love*, it does offer some model of authentic subjectivity emerging from her union with the dead. If not, all life once more is death, all becoming is an ending.

Such a cyclical model of life in death and death in life is, of course, built into the very form of Buttgereit's movies. This is most significant in the infamous scene in *Nekromantik*, when prompted by the television psychiatrist's de-sensitisation discourse, Rob appears to recall a distinctively disturbing episode from his past. Here, another unpleasant father figure, in decidedly unattractive blue knitwear, in a distinctively industrial setting, picks up and slits the throat of a fluffy black and white bunny. Said rabbit is subsequently skinned and gutted and hung up by its legs (in a pose most redolent of SM porn), whilst inter-cut footage of an autopsy of a human corpse visually echoes the scene. Thus, the insides of both creatures become their outsides as fur and skin are stripped away and internal organs are removed in wet and gloopy chunks. Once again, Buttgereit is forcing us to look at something we would rather avoid – the industrial scene of slaughter, the protagonist's resemblance to the director's father and the *Heimatfilm* killer of Rob and Betty's beloved corpse being most pronounced.

But there is, perhaps, a further historic reference going on here: the term 'rabbit films' or *Kaninchenfilme* being the collective noun for the twelve films that were banned in East Germany in 1965. These were films that were felt to be too sceptical, nihilistic, relativistic or subjective to conform to statist ideology. As Sabine Hake puts it:

> The directors' failure or unwillingness to develop a dialectical conception of reality, the argument went, had resulted in stories, images and, perhaps most importantly, dispositions and attitudes that were irrelevant, if not detrimental to the self-definition of GDR society. [The move] forced filmmakers to retreat to uncontroversial topics and conventional treatments.[16]

Quite apart from its capacity to shock, what is most extraordinary about the rabbit sequence is the fact that it is replayed, and replayed backwards, in the closing sequence of the film, as Rob ejaculates blood and semen on his bed of death. The rabbit once dismembered is literally put back together again. The trauma that lay deep in Rob's past is exorcised in death: 'what has been destroyed is now restored; old wounds heal and bad things turn good again.'[17] And once more, of course, we are there to look upon the process.

The *Nekromantik* films of Jörg Buttgereit, shocking in subject matter, unflinchingly visceral in their portrayal of sex and death, are evidently important works of recent German cinema. Taking as their premise the horrors of a past prematurely buried, they work to expose the complicity of the film medium in acts of ideological manipulation of the subject and, in turn, point to the ways in which that medium can bring about a re-sensitisation to the horrors of the past. They do so, moreover, with wit that is both suitably mordant and perversely life-affirming. No wonder they have been so widely banned.

## CHAPTER 17
## A VERY GERMAN POST-MORTEM: JÖRG BUTTGEREIT AND CO-WRITER/ASSISTANT DIRECTOR FRANZ RODENKIRCHEN SPEAK

Interviews by Marcelle Perks

Academic books didn't used to run interviews. The old school considered this the province of the popular press or more fitting within the pages of specialist publications. Traditionally, academic papers are published as a *fait accompli*, which the unwitting director might only occasionally encounter retrospectively. Of course, directors like Jörg Buttgereit, who has described his necrophiliac-themed films as 'corpse-fucking art', have only recently been deemed suitable for 'academic' introspection. David Kerekes wrote the interview-based book *Sex Murder Art* (1994) on the Buttgereit phenomena, but Linnie Blake's article in this book is the first to contextualise Buttgereit within the historical framework of German cinema.

Unusually, this interview bridges both populist and academic discourses because Blake allowed me to send her article to Buttgereit and his co-writer/assistant director Franz Rodenkirchen. After an initial interview with Buttgereit, there was a marked change in his approach after he received Blake's article; the next interview was more personal and introspective. Rodenkirchen also generously gave

**FIGURE 43** Jörg Buttgereit

a long interview, speaking candidly about his changing reactions to his own input, as his career has developed from amateur enthusiast to professional script editor.

The questions posed to Buttgereit and Rodenkirchen ranged from intrinsic-to-the-theme convictions, for example, that surely there were subtle sexual codes at work in the use of colour 'red' in the films, to the downright banal: 'Why is sexual failure as a theme so recurrent in your films?' An academic would not normally ask these questions; the interviewees might refuse to comment on such personal topics to journalists. In effect, the result is a collaboration where a kind of intellectual intertexuality is taking place, and some of the honest, blunt answers are not easy to contextualise.

Many of the odd details about the films (why is the opening of *Nekromantik* so dark? Why did Joe's street-cleaning agency not wear gloves?) are simply down to budgetary considerations: 8mm film is hard to shoot at night, using gloves would have added another 100 marks to the over-stretched budget. Many of the clothes and make-up choices were selected by the actors themselves rather than being designed, and so it is difficult to demarcate the consciously constructed images that Buttgereit and Rodenkirchen intended from those that are circumstancial.

Similarly, any attempt to analyse the script of *Nekromantik* proves reductive; Franz Rodenkirchen explains simply, 'The first screenplay was completely ridiculous looking at it from screenplay standards. It was just a file with little ideas brought into a sequence that we immediately dropped when we started shooting.' However, despite many of the pragmatic explanations, certain themes and obsessions seem to be inextricably bound up in the films: an aesthetic preference for the use of the colour red and the depiction of plastic wrapped bodies. Additionally, the themes of cutting/castration and sexual dysfunction seem to be privileged above all others. All of these responses provide fascinating insight into the ways in which 'alternative' European films like those of Buttgereit's transcend the barriers between art-house and exploitation, not only providing an insight into the director's personal concerns, but also a crucial post-mortem on the troubled German imagination.

## JÖRG BUTTGEREIT INTERVIEW I

Initially, Buttgereit does not want to talk about his utilisation of necrophilia as a theme and, in-conveniently, many of his influences prove to be American rather than German. However, he does say that 'Werner Herzog's remake of Nosferatu taught me that it is not impossible to do a horror film in Germany. In his remake I felt the desire I also have: to continue the tradition of horror films that we Germans started in the early twentieth century with *Nosferatu* and *Caligari*.'

**Marcelle Perks**: *Your films are dominated by the figure of the serial killer. What kind of serial killers do you know a lot about?*

**Jörg Buttgereit**: I just did a radio play for a German radio and television station called *Ed Gein Superstar*, so I'm kind of educated in Ed Gein.

*And German serial killers?*

Haarmann of course. I've only read the book by Theodore Lessing. It's quite obvious if you are interested in certain parts it's not very easy to find books, especially in German, about serial killers. Nowadays it is, but ten, fifteen years ago it wasn't.

*What about your main cinema influences?*

My influences came more from underground cinema like the films of John Waters, not so much from horror movies. It wasn't like a plan to do a straight horror movie.

*Were you influenced a lot by the German film scene? A lot of things you've mentioned have been American.*

Yes, the whole approach during that time, when the punk revolution was going on in the early 1980s, was that everyone in Berlin was very open to listen and to watch things you get from an underground scene.

*Nekromantik 1 and 2 are very different – what did you want to do with the second one? I read that you wanted to make a movie for girls!*

The thing was that after *Nekromantik* everyone was expecting something really gross, you know. So the next film we did was *Der Todesking*, which was a totally different thing just to make sure we could get ourselves free from the horror audience a little bit and to get back to art-house roots. But my approach was always to combine this art-house thing with exploitation cinema. I was always fascinated by gross exploitation films like *Faces of Death* (Conan Le Cilaire, 1979). Those mondo films made me think, why am I watching this? You didn't need art-house films to shock youth.

*These two films, although shocking, often don't go in an 'exploitation' direction; they have an arty feel and sometimes I feel the mix doesn't work.*

With exploitation you deal with things in a very open way, when you see the poster for *Nekromantik* the things that happen in your head are more strong than the things you see. The romanticised thing is something that makes it more beautiful and it's not supposed to be beautiful and that's what does the trick. That it's not portrayed in the way it should be.

*Most films about serial killers are shown through the perspectives of their victims, but your films are mainly about the killer/defiler. This is different from the standard in dealing with this subject matter.*

It's the only choice for the audience to stick to this guy because there is no other object. I'm kind of forcing people to deal with them. And I think the fact that I focus on these people is a statement to take them seriously, so they are not like a demon or a monster, but they are real people and then if they are real, then they are true and you believe the stuff they do.

*Sometimes I feel I would like more information on what happened to your characters before they became interested in killing or necrophilia.*

But that's very tricky because then you go to all the clichés you already know. I was so tired of all this because I read so many of these (true crime) biographies.

## JÖRG BUTTGEREIT INTERVIEW II

Buttgereit is so pleased by Linnie Blake's article on his work that he has asked if he can use it for the DVD liner notes for the forthcoming *Nekromantik II* release (although he does not agree with all of its contentions). When asked if there are links between his films and Hans Jürgen Syberberg, he faxes back, 'No, but I might be too much involved to see.' On the question of whether *Nekromantik*'s slaughtered rabbit is a reference to the so-called 'rabbit films' banned in East Germany in 1965, he answers 'I do not know those films.' Buttgeriet goes on to assert that the 'visible man' ornament is not the same as the one in Dresden: 'For Monika, that's foreplay for her final scene with Mark, where she is-rebuilding her lover.' What these comments reveal is that Buttgereit thinks foremost in pragmatic terms. For instance, he explains that Rob's suicide in *Nekromantik* was based on the fact that, 'There are reports of people getting executed and having a hard-on', rather than consciously aligning himself with the German tradition of having a hero who chooses suicide, as in the films of Herzog and Fassbinder.

In a sense though, Buttgereit's inspiration for making these films is clearly his way of coming to terms with death and loss, and the negativity associated with the Nazi past; complex emotions that he would rather not articulate. This is evident in his short film *Mein Papi*, an ambiguous homage to his father, originally filmed secretly to invite mockery, but later edited with photographs and text which place unflattering shots of his rather plump father in a different context. It is also significant that his mother died during the making of *Der Todesking* (1990). As he comments, 'It's funny that my mother wanted to live whilst these people wanted to kill themselves', and that *Schramm* (1993) was made mainly in a flat that belonged to the mother of the producer, Manfred Jelinski, who had recently died before shooting commenced.

The overpowering sense of nostalgia is shown by the importance in the film of a strategically placed painting of Jelinski's aunt and the inclusion of 8mm home footage. (This ironically belonged to the late actor who played the psychiatrist in *Nekromantik* who disliked the film.) The apartment was about to be demolished and Buttgereit adds 'the film is a kind of rememberance. Manfred will always have the home of his mother in that strange film.' The films have an emotional complexity that belies the easy exploitation images suggested by the films' video/DVD sleeves.

**Marcelle Perks**: *You don't have much dialogue in the scripts…*

**Jörg Buttgereit**: If something worked for me on a visual level then I was happy with it, but I didn't find any pictures for it then I wasn't happy. During *Nekromantik* and *Der Todesking* we still rewrote things while we shot the films. But *Nekromantik II* and *Schramm* were more professional. So the script was kind of ready when we were starting shooting. [Rodenkirchen adds to this, 'Jörg thinks very visually, he was often bored when it came to directing a dialogue sequence.']

*As a German, how do you respond to the Nazi period and the concept of Die Unbewaltige Vergangenheit (the unresolved past)?*

You get this information in history at school when you are not ready for it. And later on you still have this articifically implanted guilt and you don't know exactly why, because you don't feel you have done something wrong. And then the punk rock movement came, and when I saw Sid Vicious running around with a swastika T-shirt it was a relief. This punk attitude to Nazism, for example, I used in *Der Todesking*. When I first saw *Ilsa, She Wolf of the SS* (1974), I was totally amazed by the possibilities of doing such an unthinkable thing.

*You are tall and blonde, quite Aryan looking. It seems interesting that all your male leads are short, dark and sexually inadequate…*

We had another actor we considered for the part of Schramm but he was too handsome, it didn't feel right to us.

*The colour red seems to assume a significance in the Nekromantik films. There are lots of red images/*

*objects. Was this conscious?*

Red always has something to do with blood, and it's a film about blood and danger, I think with red it's very easy to obtain certain effects. But if there is a conscious colour scheme for me, then *Nekromantik* is a green movie and *Nekromantik II* is a yellow movie. We had the choice between two materials of film stock when we made the first copy. (The film was done on Super-8 with Kodak film stock and there is no negative.) Kodak stuff is yellow and when we made the first print blow-up we used Fuji 16mm material because it has a green touch to it. We used this to make it look more dirty and grainy.

*Why is the opening of Nekromantik so dark?*

That was made in the backyard of the producer. So we couldn't allow you to see anything because just behind the car is the producer's house.

*Why do you open with a woman urinating?*

Because it is something you normally don't see in films. Body fluids is also one of the themes of *Nekromantik*.

*It's not shot in a very erotic way, though.*

Because it has nothing to do with necrophilia, which is the thing that is sexy in the film. The thing is, but you don't see it because the film stock is not good enough, she's pissing on a dead bird.

*You've also got food and sex scenes juxtaposed, was this conscious?*

Yes, this is one of the things that was actually already in the script. There is the shot from living meat to dead meat. You see the dead meat in the pan and then you see the other dead meat hanging on the wall, which is the corpse.

*There is a scene in the film where Rob is lying in the bath and when he's under the water, it's almost like he's pretending to be dead.*

When he kills the cat and he's sad that Beatrice has left him, I was playing around with the idea that the audience might think that he killed himself. And that should be some kind of hint for the climax already, that he's willing to kill himself.

*When Monika goes to dig up the body in Nekromantik II, she's in full make-up, short skirt, i.e. the clothes that you wouldn't wear if you were going to exhume a corpse.*

But she's going to dig up her lover, so she makes herself nice.

*But when you see the shots, she's not filmed in an erotic way.*

You can see her lips, her legs.

*But these aren't conventional feminine shots, you shoot her hands and feet more erotically…*

They are more like peeks. I think it's erotic, its only foreplay and she is dressed erotically and that should be enough I think. I was afraid to switch over to the exploitation stuff. I wanted Monika as an actress to be taken seriously and not like some piece of meat, so I only took maybe 'safe' close-ups. Also in this film we used 16mm with a not-so-mobile camera, so we couldn't get so close.

*The film shows how much work it is to be a necrophile. She has to undress the body and wash it and so on. You could have shown this in a glamorous way.*

I was going for kind of a documentary style in the movie. It's always this idea of those things that you see on the screen could just happen in the flat next to you and you wouldn't even notice, so I like to shoot very banal and normal things. You only see the result because the characters don't feel the

208

need to justify it every day for themselves. We only give hints like Rob's pet rabbit in *Nekromantik* or with *Schramm* you have this footage from his childhood. I was afraid that if I explained something it would become a cliché.

*The cutting of the flesh in the films is where the characters are the most vital.*

It's a sad moment, because she's cutting up someone she likes and even if he's dead, its kind of a strange situation for her. On one side she wants to be normal again, and wants to have a living normal boyfriend, and on the other hand, she is sad that she is giving up her way of life.

*In her running commentary to the film, Monika M. said that Schramm feels incomplete. The character's amputated leg is never explained.*

I think it's his feeling of not being a real man, not a whole thing, maybe impotence. If his leg falls off he will not be able to run away from himself.

*In the film you have this draw which has lipsticks and a knife with goo attached to it and later the image of a vagina dentata. Why is there so much emphasis on imagery associated with female sexuality in the film?*

That's the stuff he collects from his victims and that's why his bedroom is about all the dead women transformed into that draw into this biting vagina! The lipsticks for me were a very easy way to tell the audience, it didn't work in the end, that he killed a lot of women already. That's why he has all those lipsticks in his drawer. Having a serial-killer plotline would have been an excellent excuse to show shots of women getting killed, but we have only a little bit of killing – this is not important. The lipsticks represent the killing we did not show.

*When Monika is tied up in the house, why didn't you show what happens inside that house?*

Because we had no convincing actors.

*Aren't they like old Nazis? Isn't that the whole point of it? Why does she have to dress up in the Nazi stuff?*

You can assume that these guys are maybe old Nazis or some people who do worse things than Florian can even imagine. It is also a way of feeling Florian is someone who would have the chance to rescue Monika, but because he fell off the ladder he can't do it anymore. Schramm is not only a killer, he can also also be a saviour.

*I can get confused by the characters. On the hand, Schramm seems quite a nice guy when he is with Monika. He doesn't appear to enjoy his sex stuff either, so why does he do it?*

He feels the need to have sex, but normally people don't feel satisfied with the things that they do. In a way it's like the concept of necrophilia. They do something because they can't get the real thing.

*Are there any autobiographical similarities between your father in Mein Papi and the character of Schramm? They both seem to have this problem with their head.*

He looks in his brain, but there's no sickness involved, and I didn't want to have this connection because it makes it seem that these bad things are only done by accident then, and not chosen.

*He's also quite plump and he's got brown hair. He's not unlike your father in Mein Papi?*

But he's younger and he's not that big. I mean my father couldn't kill anybody really because he was too plump I think!

*Are you happy with the Der Todesking?*

Hmmm, I think it's the least successful movie we did. In every scene I could tell you how to do it better.

*In the Wednesday suicide, again a man can't have a normal sexual relationship with his wife, why is sexual failure so important in your films as a theme?*

This fear of sexual failure or this fear of not being complete, or as good as someone else, as good as someone on the movie screen, its approach of being happy as you are doesn't seem to exist for a lot of people.

*Doesn't the Todesking on the poster look a bit like you, aren't you a kind of horror king yourself?*

I wasn't skinny enough (he looks like he's dead) and so it is a projectionist. It was a homage to Joel-Peter Witkin, an American photographer who shoots dead things and if it's still alive it must be crippled or strange. It's interesting that he has to live in Mexico because his work is censored in the US.

Buttgereit asks finally, 'Why do you want to do a piece on my films? Aren't they banned in the UK [apart from *Der Todesking*]? Isn't it worth pointing out that, officially, people still can't see the films?'

## FRANZ RODENKIRCHEN INTERVIEW

Franz Rodenkirchen trained in Media Science and lectured previously on film analysis at Helsinki University. Not surprisingly, he is more receptive to Linnie Blake's work: 'I was quite intrigued by the essay, that it can make such a solid argument and the reasoning is somehow really sound, although I think this is something that happened unconsciously.' He also quotes film references (many of which are from classical texts), which shaped the concepts of the films, and explains how memories of personal dreams and fears were incorporated into the films.

The issue of the unresolved past and Nazi war crimes is particularly poignant for him: 'The points Blake makes are completely convincing now that I look back at it. I know that Jörg has this strong fascination with Nazi imagery and the Nazi period, which I think comes from several aspects coming together. There is of course the punk rock attitude, of the shock value of such things because they were the forbidden, and to bring it out in the open is a sort of provocation. This fascination is denied to Germans, of course, and this is what Jörg is constantly addressing.'

In Germany, Nazi paraphernalia is forbidden, even doing a Heil Hitler salute can land you in jail. UK residents are accustomed to numerous graphic Third Reich documentaries, but in Germany these are not so obviously in public circulation. The representation of Nazi imagery has become primarily utilised and controlled by non-German countries, effectively cutting off many Germans from their emotional past.

The German/French/Greek director Romuald Karmaker is one of the few German-based directors directly confronting this history in films like *Das Himmler Projekt* (2001), although he says his mixed heritage makes this easier. In a separate interview, he commented on how difficult it is for a German to comment on national history: 'We have so many blanks in German history. We don't make films from the perspective of the perpetrators, just the victims.' It is interesting that the Buttgereit films echo this sense of fragmentation. There is no backstory, as if the characters have no history, and often little dialogue, no explanation for why these characters do the things they do. Disturbing issues simply have to be dealt with; thus, dead bodies are sought, washed and prepared.

The relationship between victim and perpetrator is also blurred; Lothar Schramm is both a serial killer and a potential saviour for Marianne (Monika M.) in *Schramm*. People voluntarily choose to commit 'unnatural' acts in *Der Todesking* and the *Nekromantik* films. Necrophilia is, confusingly, a process that involves both mutilation and deification. The killers/defilers are robbed of traditional notions of overriding desire and evil potency; the films abound with castration and sexual dysfunction images; attempts at pleasure are banal and futile. The killers/necrophiles are an antithesis of the perverse power base represented by the SS. Are they symbolic perhaps of Germans confronting their unarticulated past? The films' reliance on visual images also forces the viewer to confront their own desire for wanting to watch such material. Are we, like the female video viewers in *Nekromantik II*, guilty too?

**Marcelle Perks:** *Why do you like to show male counterparts that are inadequate?*

**Franz Rodenkirchen:** Good question, but difficult to answer because we did not really think of them as being inadequate in that sense; they were troubled, peculiar characters, but inadequate in terms of what? Monika M. is so much taller than her leads because we always rooted a lot stronger for the women in the films. It was agreed without even talking about it much that the women were the strong ones in the movies. It just happened the people we approached were mostly friends and the ones we deemed suitable all happened to be that way [short, dark-haired]. Most horror films aren't like that, they have a strong male hero who saves the day, but that was never the idea. This was all about people who are troubled from the start. They were not meant to experience a victorious ending. It was more like them preferring to go down the path thay had chosen or fate took them.

*Lots of details in Nekromantik are unrealistic, most necrophiles don't use a decayed corpse.*

We departed from reality with the first shot basically. There could never be anything like Joe's street-cleaning agency. That's completely fictitious and we knew it. If you enter into a very specific world which is not really the realistic world, but a kind of rendering of an impression of a world, you can start in determining the hows and why of this world. After Joe's street-cleaning agency it was not a problem to have a corpse that was so old. The main reason was that Jörg thought that it looked better and we didn't have to use an actor!

*The endings of Nekromantik 1 and 2 are dependant on shock. With Schramm you start at the end and Der Todesking has a different structure. Was this more complicated to write?*

With *Schramm* we had a role model for that. A movie both Jörg and I really love is the French movie *Les Choses de la vie* (Claude Sautet, 1969). This starts with an automobile accident where the driver basically dies and is lying there in the grass remembering his last weeks and months. So we just adopted that structure and then we felt free to play with it as long as we knew that we have this point to come back to. Actually, what we had to do was compose the short pieces and then think of a structure to connect it.

*Another recurrent theme – bodies wrapped in plastic or wearing yellow gloves or boots.*

Firstly, it is a really household thing which underlines the common aspect of it, we also wanted to approach necrophilia, not as an extreme and rare perversion, but trying to figure it as something that is common to the life of those people. At the same time, the plastic and the gloves detach you. There's always something between you and the object of your desire, which I think is, of course, the simple difference that one is alive and the other is dead.

*The opposite to what a 'normal' serial killer does.*

We once had this idea of necrophilia as something that has been accepted widely. Rob becoming a pioneer, the idea was to rearrange the whole idea of how to handle dead bodies. Instead of burying them they could be collected and given to the needy for their desires.

*Is there any kind of reason why Buttgereit is so attracted to death?*

He is very body conscious. He's done martial arts for 25 years and he's physically very fit, but at the same time he's afraid of decay, fascinated and afraid at the same time.

*Who do the old men in Schramm who tie up Monika represent? I associated them with Nazis because they are very old, and make her dress up in a Hitler youth outfit.*

They are old Germans. The idea, however flimsy it is executed, is that it is more like in the Pasolini picture, *Salo*, where you have the representatives of the state revelling in their very private perversions. The Nazi theme was a little controversial, sometimes I think that Jörg is too much relying on the fact that people are giving him the benefit of the doubt. He is addressing the imagery a little too carelessly, not considering possible reactions.

*In Schramm and Nekromantik II you show how much work it is being a necrophiliac.*

There is a certain kind of necrophilia that is more a necrophilia of the mind in that it is very romanticised. There is also a lot of imagery and stories with beautiful dead women, for example. We wanted our necrophilia to be a more everyday affair, and everyday life isn't that romantic. At the same time, we wanted to portray our chracter as, in a way, ordinary. To approach them in this manner allows them to be taken seriously.

*Do you think the romantic scenes are too long between the live couple in Nekromantik II?*

It's something that Jörg simply wanted to explore more, but I can tell you the whole film team was very infatuated with Monika. I think we simply enjoyed it. It was even longer. Jörg loves the innocence of it.

*They don't act like youths.*

This whole part where they go to the amusement park, it is very much how Jörg may have envisioned being in love, he was a bit old-fashioned then. Once you meet him, you cannot match those two images in your mind (his public personna and his real self). I think that is what he plays on heavily, he knows it, as a good PR person.

*The most erotic shots are of feet and hands, not the traditional ones of breasts and so on.*

Difficult to ask me, this area is one where Jörg and I digress the most. What material is put onto film is completely Jörg's choice. He is a bit prudish, but at the same time he was afraid the female actresses might feel exploited, but I think his eroticism is not so physically orientated. It is not directed towards the usual sexual symbols. Deep inside of him there is a certain really innocent tenderness and it comes out at moments when he is not alert.

*Your thoughts on Nekromantik II?*

I didn't really want to do it that much because I don't really like the idea of sequels and I thought

Jörg was bowing to his core audience because they were so puzzled about *Der Todesking*.

*Schramm – one of the things that confused me was that the amputated leg stuff was never really explained.*

He is imagining the fact that he is losing a leg, it is his sexual defect. We wanted to show that his sexual hangups debilitate him so greatly that he dies because of his strong imagining of the loss of his leg.

*Isn't his dream of having his eye removed confusing, though?*

To me this was the most direct commentary by Jörg himself on how he feels about his movies, because the whole eye thing, the dentist taking out an eye after he has taken out a tooth, was a dream he had. He wanted to incorporate it and I thought we should. In my opinion, the taking out of the eye, like the loss of teeth in dreams, is closely connected psychologically with castration, and this whole fear of castration is running strongly in the movie. I found it a nice in-joke that it was really Jörg's dream. The taking out of the eye to me is a heightening that at the same time, it is a punishment for having looked. He is imagining that his gaze has a kind of life of its own, for which he is punished.

*Who is the woman in the picture above Schramm's bed?*

Do you think it's his mother? That's exactly the illusion we wanted to have, and at the same time not address it. In movies, this is the most common explanation for sexual hangups in men, that they have a problem with their mother. Also to make the audience maybe reflect that they are jumping so willingly to this conclusion is interesting. The 8mm footage is 'found footage' and we decided to use it when we were in the editing stages (it was not in the script). We specifically selected those pieces and had them copied and made longer. To me, the childhood scenes give a very touching lyrical quality to the movie and feel pretty sad.

*The shots of Schramm fondling his own body are odd…*

That's something that Jörg is really fascinated with. We did those shots excessively, actually, where Florian is fondling his own body. For Jörg it must have meant something more than it did for me. For me, it was an odd attempt at the character of Schramm getting in contact with himself.

*The red blood stains on Florian seem oddly marked.*

It's like a stigma in a way. His guilt is placed there. The red marker is really a very intentional thing. It didn't happen by chance.

*It is quite close to Mein Papi.*

It is in a way. *Mein Papi* is the core of Buttgereit actually, in my opinion. It is also the film that a lot of other people feel says something that he normally avoids saying. The completed version when he reworked it suddenly became a process of mourning. It was the first time he actually addressed his anxiety about death in a very personal way and I found it extremely touching.

*Der Todesking seems so negative…*

Does it? I think it's the furthest we ever ventured into a kind of gross-out existentialist angst thing. The negativity is more like an overall perspective on the futility of life which ties in with Jörg's mother having died during the process of shooting, but in the end, there is this odd nice melody and images of the kids playing. It's difficult to say, do the children represent a kind of hope or is it that the children are seen as the next generation to die? We wanted to distance ourselves from the kind of

213

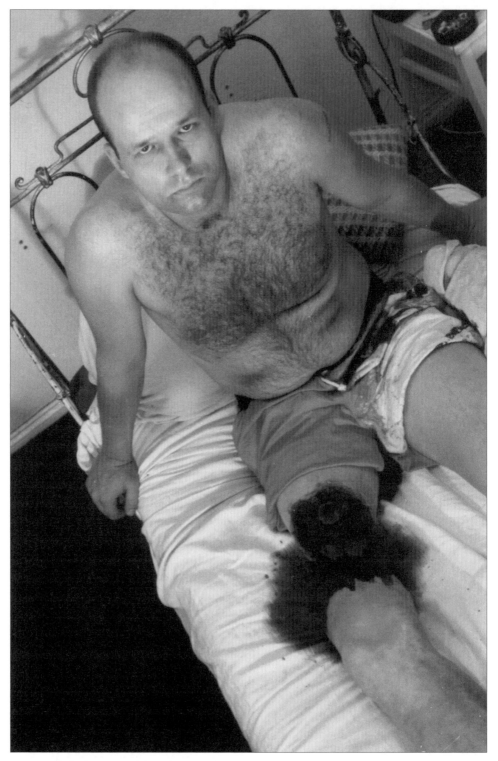

**FIGURE 44** The lost limb as sexual defect: *Schramm* (1993)

suicide as a last straw to draw attention to yourself.

*Of course in Wednesday's suicide you have another man who can't have a normal sexual relationship…*

It was directly inspired from another movie, Abel Fererra's *Ms.45* (1981) where the guy sits on the bench talking about how he killed someone and then Ms.45 draws her gun and shoots him. We took that as a starting point and, of course, invented another dysfunctional character.

*In the David Kerekes book, he said you had a childhood dream about a king and a black and white ball?*

It wasn't a childhood dream, but a little story from a physics class, designed to explain why black objects absorb sunlight faster than white objects and how a condemned men who has to choose a white ball in order to live can do this if he knows something about physics. What I thought I could not convey was the complex motive, the emotional slip-up of, say, the condemned man, who is drawn to the warmth of the black ball because it is warm, while his intellect (his mind) fights to remember that the cold white ball means freedom and the black actually means death. It seems an easy feat: draw out the white, cold ball and go free. But, robbed of his controlling eye, his unconscious wants warmth and emotion – a fatal slip-up occurs. You see, this is difficult to convey without some very inventive visual metaphor. I haven't given it any more thought, but I still think it is difficult to find a short conclusion suitable for the final scene of a short film. I always imagined it in the reduced, kind of archaic style of Pasolini's *Oedipus Rex* (1967).

**215**

My thanks to both Jörg Buttgereit and Franz Rodenkirchen for agreeing to the interviews which appear in this volume.

# CHAPTER 18
# THE BRUSSELS INTERNATIONAL FESTIVAL OF FANTASTIC FILM

Dirk Van Extergem

Tom Goodwin:     Keep behind me. There's no sense in getting killed by a plant.
                                                            – *The Day of the Triffids*, 1962

## INTRODUCTION

There's a thick crowd, packed, waiting in the hallway that leads to the Auditorium of the Passage 44. In the right corner, next to the entrance kneels a small figure, the long black hair covering the face, surrounded by a shrine of more or less religious imagery. She predicts the future: 'The film you're about to see will change your life…'. Two pale-faced, long-legged and sharp-toothed vamps take an innocent bystander by the neck and lead him to the right side of the lobby where for free you can have your face transformed, with the help of gentle strokes of sponges and brushes nonetheless, into that of some creature of the night. Other strange, deformed, latex-like creatures sneak up on non-suspecting spectators, yelling 'boo' or something like that. At a spoken signal the crowd begins to move, bit by bit, body to body … the first literally run up the stairs, paying no attention whatsoever to the giant fresco and other fantastic art objects on display, and rush into the theatre to claim their seat. Soon the theatre begins to fill, nervous laughter, a murmuring that slowly grows into a growl when the lights finally switch off and a graveyard voice announces: Brussels International Festival of Fantasy, Thriller and Science Fiction Film, Welcome…

Shrieks penetrate the theatre, 'Ta ta ta ta taaa', the film rolls, a voice yells: 'Tuer encore!' 'Jamais plus!!' answers a choir of spectators. 'Les cochons de l'espace!' 'Ta geule'…[1] It turns out to be a recurring phenomenon. The ritual, so to speak, is repeated at the beginning of each screening at the major venue. Throughout the film, the audience stays extremely responsive: the spectators applaud the various guests; clap during the credits whenever a name they know appears; playfully warn characters against the potential dangers awaiting them ('Don't go in there!'); and applaud again each time a gory effect fills the screen. Even more, the whole theatre starts howling like a pack of wolves whenever a full moon appears, there's the sound of kissing during romantic scenes, they're crying 'la porte' whenever someone leaves a door to the theatre open…

For more than twenty years now, the Brussels Festival of Fantastic, Thriller and Science Fiction Film (or, the Brussels International Festival of Fantastic Film, BIFFF) has built a firm reputation for being one of the most popular film events in Europe, welcoming approximately 65,000 spectators plus more than a hundred international guests. Above all, the Festival has a reputation for being great fun. Few things are as funny as bad fantasy, horror or science fiction film, and as well as the best, BIFFF has not been afraid to programme some of the worst, particularly late at night, to the great amusement of a boisterous audience. Of course this is not the whole story; the Festival attendants are not to be seen as one unified public but as a bunch of different spectators, bridging the line between age, gender and taste. As a matter of fact, twenty years on, BIFFF still has a lot of its original attendance, but has at the same time always managed to attract young people too, newcomers every year. Some people even take their annual holidays to coincide with the Festival. Others are just there because they happened to be in the neighbourhood and had nothing else to do.

In this chapter I shall try to examine this audience in greater detail, avoiding the trap of a romanticisation of the festival public, but instead relating it to contemporary theories of audience reception where viewing a film becomes an odd combination of distraction and appropriation.[2] Instead of just reading movies, contemporary audiences now adopt movies, create cults around them, tour through them. Applied to this Festival, the audience adopts 'genre', the boundaries of the genre being not that easy to draw, not since the notion of a unified public is considered a reality no more. Watching a film at the Festival is a cult film experience, one of the different viewing positions in a more and more heterogeneous culture.

Therefore the festival public could be described as a cult audience, which is a difficult audience to please. And, as one of the programmers of the Festival, I shall try to explain how we try to nourish this cult, continuously coping with the ever-changing outlook of film in general and genre in particular. A look in the internal kitchen shall lay bare the relations and even tensions between programming and reception, trying to maintain so to speak a well-balanced mix between popularity and quality, cult and kitsch, art house and grindhouse, while constantly being on the look for innovation, averse to any trend.

217

BIFFF 2004
22nd Brussels International
Festival of Fantastic Film
Auditorium 44, Nova & Actor's Studio
12 ‣ 27 March 2004
INFO 02.204.00.13
www.BIFFF.org
CAZA 03

## ONCE UPON A TIME...

| | |
|---|---|
| Colonel Edwards: | This is the most fantastic story I've ever heard. |
| Jeff Trent: | And every word of it's true, too. |
| Colonel Edwards: | That's the fantastic part of it. |

– *Plan 9 From Outer Space*, 1959

Every year, during the month of March, the city of Brussels becomes the Capital of Fantasy. Gathering all the arts that are related to the genre, the Festival presents, alongside an abundant film programme, numerous exhibitions, a make-up and body-painting contest, lots of theatrical interventions, an educational component (workshops, lectures) and the infamous 'Bal des Vampires'. During this 16-day marathon more than 150 films in the fields of the Fantastic, Thriller, Science Fiction, Horror, Cult and Underground are screened, of which there are approximately 80 long features as a first screening, about 30 films in retrospective and some 30 short features. The films are projected in two theatres, two very different places that rather adequately summarise the heterogeneity of Brussels' landscape. At the Passage 44 – the bigger, more comfortable and more technically advanced of the two – the Festival's prestigious guests, the films in competition and the ones intended to please a large audience make their stand. Meanwhile, at Cinema Nova – a theatre that looks both like a bunker and a sex shop – one could see more demanding pictures. The audience for this alternative section grows year after year. Since 1998, the collaboration with the Nova team gives the Festival an additional screen for a more alternative programme. This special section, called 'The 7th Orbit', explores the borders of fantasy and the 'unusual'. The result is an eclectic but nevertheless consistent mixture of more hybrid and radical films; including first screenings, films in retrospective and several events. Finally, the Festival spreads through several other cultural hot spots, such as the Free University of Brussels and the Museum of Comic Strip, to name but a few.

So, laying claim, in large red and black letters, to its macabre vocation, BIFFF has been concerned about upgrading the public image of the supernatural ever since it was first launched. The Festival, which has its roots in the post-punk (hard rock and heavy metal) era, today comes dressed in the most sophisticated magic finery with an increasingly international public, and what in the early days might have passed for a poor cousin of the famous but terminated Avoriaz Festival has since earned its stripes.

The Festival was the brainchild of a non-profit-body, PeyMey Diffusion, set up by a small group of cinema enthusiasts in the late 1970s. They organised a number of different film events and festivals, and in 1982 held a retrospective of fantasy films, organised across the country in different youth centres. It sold, to the organiser's surprise, without much publicity, more than 15,000 tickets. It gave them enough audacity to take their chance in organising the first BIFFF in 1983. The new festival was a huge success, pulling in over 25,000 people. Since then the numbers have more than doubled. Freddy Bozo, one of the founders/organisers of the Festival, long black hair and a beard, appropriately nicknamed Jesus, has this to say about the origins:

It was the public demand for a festival that gave us a boost. We were already active in the circuit of youth houses, where we organised several activities, mostly retrospectives such as 60 years of German film, 60 years of Italian comedy, 60 years of Fantasy films. Already in those days we were adding several activities and exhibitions in the margin of the film happening. Each event drew an audience of about 10,000. These retrospectives created a public demand for a genuine festival. As a matter of fact the public and the film distributors were immediately enchanted by the concept. There were more problems convincing the press and the powers that be (a few small exceptions notwithstanding) of our credibility. Only after it became absolutely clear that our festival was indeed a success, were they 'forced' to change their opinion. But I believe they will always maintain a hint of their initial disapproval.

## GENRE: EVERY ERA PRODUCES THE HORRORS IT DESERVES

Clone:      *C'est moi l'original! C'est moi!*
                                        *– La cité des enfants perdus*, 1995

Fantasy is a house with many rooms: imagination, fairytales, the supernatural, the unconscious, dreams. It is a popular genre that can pride itself on a long and rich tradition, ranging from folk legends, saga's and fairytales (the Grimm brothers, for example) to nineteenth-century Gothic novels like Bram Stoker's *Dracula* and Mary Shelley's *Frankenstein*, but also Goethe's *Faust*, Hoffman's tales, *Baron von Munchhausen*, *Don Quixote* and *Tijl Uylenspiegel*. Furthermore, we could include the paintings of artists like Egon Schiele, Gustav Klimt and Goya, and movements like German expressionism, psychoanalysis and surrealism.

In light of its rich, cultural tradition, it is a crying shame that the genre had to wait so long for recognition and was ignored by the critics and the cultural and political establishment. If there is one genre that is riddled with prejudice, it has to be the fantastic. If already in the 1930s, and up until the 1950s, most of the fantasy movies were labelled by the studios as B-movie products, the 1960s definitely gave voice to a growing protesting choir of concerned parents, priests and politicians, when the genre, especially in America, targeted a new segment of the audience: the lucrative teenage market. The World War Two baby boomers, who were the first to grow up with television and reruns of the horror and fantastic output of the 1930s and 1940s (the Universal horror cycle with classics such as *Dracula* and *Frankenstein*), turned out to be very fond of an entire series of independently and more than often cheaply produced fantastic films by Roger Corman *et al.*, which they went to see en masse in drive-in theatres and second-run theatres.

But this was nothing compared with the ferocious attacks (a final desperate grasp to preserve something like a moral majority?) the genre had to endure in the 1980s, the founding days of this Festival and an era not exactly renowned for its taste. The coming of the VCR, creating a never before seen availability of hard to find extreme viewing material (take, for example, the so-called 'video nasties' phenomenon) and the boom in 'slasher' and 'gore' movies, created an image that did not necessarily fall well with private let alone public sponsoring. The softening of censorship rules and the progress in the domain of special make-up effects allowed for a more graphic depiction of many a gory scene. The formula (innocent teenagers being chased by a psychopath with a knife, axe or other gardening tool) was soon milked to the bone with *Halloween*, *Friday the 13th* and dozens of other spin-offs. Consequently, many people reduced the fantastic to this subcategory of horror films, condemning them for their visceral imagery, as often as not taken out of their fictionalised context. How many, one might wonder, of those who scream blue murder have actually sat through, say, a midnight screening at the Festival, and seen how the public responds and even interacts with the film?

This phenomenon not only stirred up a lot of sensation in the 1980s, it has left its mark and continues to provide ample ammunition for the moral majority and the defenders of 'good taste'. It is perhaps useful to pursue the notion of taste just a little bit further because of the regular recurrence of it in more general (as opposed to specialised) public debates about the depiction of violence in fiction film and horror in peculiar. 'In matters of taste all determination is negation', said French theorist Pierre Bourdieu, speaking about the cultural logic of taste. He makes the statement that class segments define themselves as distinct from one another by virtue of contrasting aesthetic judgements and different attitudes towards art and beauty. In this light, 'tastes are perhaps first and foremost distastes, disgust provoked by horror of visceral intolerance ("sick-making") of the tastes of others'.[3]

Certainly, film studies' theories and canons have been bound up with an economy of taste which influences questions not only of how to approach cinema, but questions of what cinema to approach in the first instance. Dominant notions of cinematic aesthetics have been installed and defended on the basis of the assumed excellence of taste of a relatively few privileged journalists, critics and opinion-makers appealing to canons and principles of art in general.[4] Often, the powers that be adapted those canons, from which they extracted the defining criteria for granting government funding. Needless to say that back in the 1980s a festival which promotes 'blood and gore' had a difficult time getting the necessary money together. Even today, after 22 years of existence, from time to time it still is not obvious or self-evident to convince the relevant ministries and administrations of the cultural role of a fantastic film festival.

So the fantastic, it seems, has always provoked differing, to divergent and opposing, even extreme reactions. If there is one genre that has proven that there is no such thing as one unified public and that there are different, even competing, modes of film consumption, this is the one. Seen in a broader light, part of this is naturally due to the fact that the (industrial, technological and sociological) conditions and terminology of film narrative have shifted their grounds beyond the boundaries that organised film stories for more than fifty years. Take for instance the notion of genre itself.

One way of looking at the profound shift in the notion of genre is explained by Timothy Corrigan. He states that genre has the power to recuperate, ritualise and mythologise cultural history (its forms and representations); it is able to reflect and create rituals of social history and thus to intensify a culture's relation to its social histories. If genre is a way of organising stories and expectations for film audiences and it answers to an implicit demand to produce or to see the same story, the same characters, and the same historical referent again and again, then renewal and naturalisation of the genre depends on the audience's fantasising as natural (that is, historically appropriate) the genre's conventions: those conventions traditionally must be possessed by an audience as adequately representing their own cultural history.[5]

He goes on to argue that within contemporary genre, however, a naturalised public ritual has been replaced by the performance of denaturalised and appropriated generic conventions. Faced with a historical heterogeneity, contemporary genre refuses narrative motivation and naturalisation. In this contemporary audience's relation to its genres, participating in a generic ritual has less to do with socially sharing a public entertainment ritual that integrates a cultural and historical community and more to do with participating in fragmented, narcissistic obsessions with pieces of generic conventions that cannot be naturalised across a large narrative community. For this audience, the sacramental ritualisations of genre become the material props of separate cults trying to return themselves to a place in history.[6]

One of these major shifts in genre appeared in the early 1980s when a profound change in the modes of film consumption moved the film viewing experience massively (more than television did thirty years earlier) from the public to the private sphere. Video, with its incredible innovative ability of repeated viewing, transformed films from collective experiences to privatised commodities which may be used (like any others) in the process of individual identity formation and communication.[7]

Another phenomenon that messed up former viewing practices was the advent of the blockbuster, marked by the unexpected and phenomenal success of *Star Wars* (1977). It scrambled up and ironically reversed the economic and artistic relationships between exploitation film and mainstream cinema. Movie-brat filmmakers such as Steven Spielberg and George Lucas began to take the low-budget adventure movies of their childhoods and recreate them as big-budget, hyper-real spectacular entertainment for large audiences. The Hollywood blockbuster became increasingly dependent for inspiration on the pulp fictions of the cinematic past. Here, the regulating action of narrative has begun to lose its force: together with an attenuation of plot and related breakdown of character motivation, these narratives often seem to undermine their own narrative structures through loosely connected non-narrative events whose excessive display either of the visuals or the music becomes a perpetual or aural format for the audience's own performance.

Far from being a complaint about the loss of good Aristotelian cinema, these two phenomena are symptomatic of a heightened awareness of the differences between audiences and of the importance of specialised constituencies such as fans and cultists. Audiences are no longer envisaged as passive consumers but as active producers of popular culture. As I. Q. Hunter and Heidi Kaye argue, popular culture is increasingly seen as diversified and demanding of its audience's intertextual literacy and interpretative activity. Growing numbers of adaptations of literature, novelisations of films and new media such as DVDs, CD-ROMs and the internet blur the lines between film and fiction, reader and author, spectator and participant as well as between mass (low) and elite (high) culture. The focus is instead on the interactive relationship between heterogeneous, self-reflexive audiences and infinitely reinterpretable texts. Aesthetic judgements, therefore, are not to be taken for granted but should be understood as forms of cultural capital, both exertions of social power and exercises in self-description. Popular culture is engaged in a creative dialogue with its audiences, who choose or adapt texts to suit their outlooks. Texts seem to demand the creation by the audience of yet more texts: fans writing stories for zines, cultists reinventing disregarded films, net surfers trading information on fictional worlds. The interactions within subcultures developed around different cultural forms are located in a variety of contexts, from face-to-face meetings at conventions or conferences, through fanzines and newsletters, to Usenet groups and websites. These different contexts offer a diverse range of 'interpretive communities', positions from which groups and individuals relate to each other and make meaning through texts.[8]

The audience of the Festival of Fantasy Film, apart from the fact that it could be considered as an interpretive community *an sich* (defined by a common interest, fascination even, for the fantastic) houses more groups and rival subcultures than one might assume at first sight. That leaves us no choice as to take a more detailed look at the festival public.

## THE AUDIENCE

Dr Butcher:    The patient's screaming disturbing me, performed removal of vocal chords.

– *Zombi Holocaust*, 1979

Who are those daredevils, those fearless men and women who dare to boldly go in search of places where they have never been before? The figures presented are based on a survey the Festival conducts every year among a representative sample of its audience.

The profile of the public is steady: three quarters are active and those who do not work are almost all students. More than half of those active are employees and the level of education is high (70 per cent higher and university studies). In recent years the Festival seems to have attracted more and more women (based on a comparison between 1986 and 2000). One reason could be an evolution in the films that are programmed: there is definitely less gore and the selection of films is broader than the great amount of horror that was programmed in the 1980s. Being around for 22 years now could also have helped in reducing some tenacious stereotypes about fantastic films. Before, the relation between the sexes was around three males for one female. Now, it is two to one. The fantastic still remains mainly masculine, but the feminine aspect gains ground.

Does the Festival audience get older? Not really, because more than half the audience falls into the category younger than 30. However, due to the loyalty of the public (a good 70 per cent of our audience in 2000 had participated at previous events) which does attend year after year, it is only logical that the number of Festival 'veterans' increases. More than half the visitors (57.5 per cent) make a careful selection of the films (between 1 and 10 films) they want to see. The other 42.5 per cent takes a substantial dose (between 11 and 25 films) or are heavy addicts (more than 25 films and up to 50).

This last category deserves a special mention. For 660 Euro the Festival offers to a limited number of subscribers (178 to be specific) a special pass that gives access to all the screenings. Those passes are in demand, and there is a waiting list for future applicants. All those subscribers are inventoried. The Festival knows by way of surveys that these persons are, outside the Festival period, big consumers of a large number of fiction films on a range of picture mediums. Far from being couch potatoes, they are regular cinemagoers and at home they watch a lot of films on video. It often occurs that they have seen the same film several times. Nearly all display a need to collect, mostly films on tape or DVD, but also comic strips and books. Above all, they appreciate films that 'make them dream', that create an imaginary universe. Gore and on-screen 'fictionalised' violence make them laugh, but many of them have more difficulties putting up with real or realistic violence as in documentaries or news magazines. They become more scared when it becomes more real, so it seems. Nearly all are looking for shivers and thrills, a fear they can control, a 'controllable uncertainty'.

What all of these audiences share, however, is a longing for the satisfaction of appreciating an unusually rewarding picture, a certain degree of group identification and a sense of being somehow validated by the film(s) they are the first to discover, or, in the case of retrospectives, re-discover. We might see the act of watching a film at the Festival as a sort of cult, as a kind of mass (i.e. 'religious' service), with its highly ritualistic conditions of presentation. In large measure, every film is conditioned by ritual since it takes place as a communal act, partitioned from everyday life. A film festival, as compared to a regular movie screening, is even more detached from the everyday experience: it takes place but once a year, it presents films 'for the first time' and has extras such as the presence of guests ('stars') and the creating of a more communal, more festive and, in many ways, more significant context by way of animation, presentation and the stimulation of a certain 'ambience'.

The central ritual of the film cult remains this formalised showing of the film, with its requirement of audience assistance or participation. In that context, viewers anticipate – and even help evoke – a certain emotional response. For, at the same time, viewers both are spectators and play at being spectators. One particular part of the audience, the group of subscribers (they even have their own website), are the ones that most obviously could be related to the notion of a cult. As every cult constitutes a community, a group that 'worships' similarly and regularly, and finds strength in that shared experience – it relies on a set of practices or conventions shared by the devotees. And the demonstrated knowledge of those things (the participatory action such as the shouting being the most evident example) certifies the initiates, binds them in their privileged knowledge to others – and even to another side of the self, a repressed self that longs to be known otherwise and to find expression.

Using the notion of 'cult' in regard to the Festival audience has another benefit: it effectively collapses the categories of 'art' and 'exploitation', eliding issues of both politics and aesthetics. What might previously have been distinguished according to the motivations of their makers is now rendered largely equivalent by the enthusiastic and loyal responses of audiences possessing different types of cultural capital. That leads us to the question of the film festival content, the different films which constitute the Festival experience and how they are selected and programmed.

## PROGRAMMING

Horatio Jackson:     He wont get far on hot air and fantasy.
>                    – *The Adventures of Baron Munchausen*, 1988

Programming is at the core of every festival. Programming is choosing. Programming is selecting. It is the romantic, heroic part, so to speak. The quest for the best, the worst and the most unusual. But then, of course, reality rears its ugly head. This film will not be ready for your festival, that film will cost you a thousand dollars per screening. Or: You can have this film if you take that one too. Better: I've just shot a medium-length horror film on DV, it would be perfect for your festival… Still: What's the name of your festival? Never heard of it…

The organisers look at hundreds of new films every year before making their choices for the Festival's next edition. A permanent team of about eight people operates around the year, each of them playing a small or larger part in the programming. The organisers dwell on film markets

(Cannes, Mifed) and festivals, talk to producers, negotiate with the Belgian distributors. The final result is always more of a compromise than one initially imagined. So, every year you have to start again. You may be dealing with the same organisations, but the people may change. You have to build up trust. Practically each film is a battle on its own, you are completely dependable of the whims of producer and distributor. Fortunately, after more than twenty years, Brussels has become a reference and there is hardly a distributor, a few exceptions notwithstanding, with whom we have not collaborated one time or another. Though with rapidly changing staff policies this is not a guarantee. What we do have is a firm reputation concerning the reception of the films presented, the very active and participative role of the audience, which from time to time is used by some professionals as a test case for their film.

Now, more generally speaking, film festivals operate in the field between art and commerce, between specialised film knowledge and commercial interest. That does not necessarily mean that one has to see a festival as a conflict of interests – commerce versus art, the worthy versus glamour, economics versus culture. It is just the intertwining of these opposites which will, overtly or more subconsciously, inform the programming and, as such, define the identity of the festival as a whole. As Janet Harbord points out, film festivals serve a global function in advertising cultural products, generating information about them and situating a point of information exchange.[9] They are a specific, intense and fleeting happening which generates expectation through its narrative of premiere screenings, prize winning, competition, different sections and creates a managed site of specialised knowledge. The organisation of festivals represents a management of cultural resources in the divisions and demarcations of spheres: of the market, exhibition venues, the criteria of entry, the categories of award, the creation of sections, the presence of guests or 'stars' and the press office. These are some of the parameters within which the programming, the choice of films, takes place and through which a festival tries to create its own distinctiveness. I want to discuss some of these parameters more in detail.

First of all, there is the basic notion of the premiere. Where first-hand experience is the premium value of the festival experience, this originality is instilled in the structure of the festival through the notion of the film premiere. Thus, the screening of a film at a festival is a transitional stage in the life of the film as commodity before it enters the flow of more dispersed channels of dissemination and as such the festival generates forms of knowledge prior to the marketing texts of general release.[10] This, of course, includes the notion of a festival audience as a kind of a cult, where the spectator gets a sense of being somehow validated by the film they are the first to discover. Additionally, it often leads to a competition between festivals, nationally and internationally, where festivals stipulate at least a national premiere and by extension a world or international premiere as a selection criterion, which on the one hand reinforces the prestige of the festival and on the other hand restricts the circulation of the selected films among and between festivals. In order to prevent this sometimes harsh rivalry, BIFFF was one of the founding members of the European Federation of Fantastic Film Festivals. Today it counts 14 members from 12 countries and forms a solid network of festivals, facilitating the circulation of films between its members and establishing itself, through the organisation of an inter-festival European Méliès Competition, as a tool for the promotion of the European fantastic film.

There are more selection criteria than the premiere. The most obvious, when we talk about a genre festival, is of course whether or not the film belongs to the genre. Consequently, the definition of what constitutes the genre becomes quite an import point of ongoing discussion in the process of programming. Far from giving an exhaustive definition of the fantastic, the Festival's dictum has been to present the fantastic in its broadest possible spectrum: from horror to slasher, from science fiction to fairytale to heroic fantasy, with the inclusion over the years of categories such as thriller, animé and the bizarre. The addition of these new categories has more to do with the evolution of the genre away from large narrative and interpretative cultural and historical communities ('the western', 'the horror film') to the notion of genre as an intertextual play of denaturalised and appropriated generic conventions ('a kung fu space opera with a bit of *Jaws*'), than with marketing or the following of certain trends.

Armed with such abstract guidelines as quality and innovation, the selection process turns out to be a sometimes very personal journey which ends in a confrontation of different aesthetic judgements and tastes from which the final programme is crystallised. In all this, the selection committee constitutes an 'interpretive community', a position from which the festival team as a whole and the individual programmers relate to each other and make meaning through texts/films. The committee consists of the four founders who were themselves first and foremost genre enthusiasts. The newcomers in the team are recruited in the Festival itself: all of them did, at one time or another, some kind of voluntary work for the Festival, which is an indication of their passion and commitment to and identification with the Festival. This team of eight different people, each with their own sensibilities and cultural capital, cuts across generations and different backgrounds. The result is a melting pot of popular and intellectual, younger and older assumptions, which guarantees the diversity of the programme.

The proliferation of the notion of genre led to a heightened awareness of the differences between audiences and of the importance of specialised constituencies such as fans and cultists. To meet their expectations, the Festival tries to establish a programme scheme where the different constituencies should more or less easily find their way. The films in competition and the big-budget productions, the most attended part of the Festival, are programmed at the most convenient hours, at 8 pm and 10 pm. The midnight screenings have their own, more die-hard, fan-based following. The films programmed at 6 pm are of a more familiar and less violent nature. And, finally, the opportunity of a new screening theatre with a smaller capacity, which during the rest of the year programmes films that do not find a distributor and film cycles that demand a different approach, attracts a very specialised public and helps, through way of a co-production, to outline the contours of a section apart, the seventh orbit, with films that flirt with the borders of genre and that through their semiotic diversity signal complex social messages (*Visitor Q* by Miike Takeshi, *Seul contre tous* by Gaspard Noe and *Of Freaks and Men* by Alexei Balabanov are some of the most successful examples).

The Festival programme, however inscribed in a cultural dynamic, cannot cut itself loose from a certain commercial logic. This results in a sometimes conflicting and heterogeneous mix between commercial and independent films. It is a fact that in a time when an independently produced film can become an overnight commercial success (*The Blair Witch Project*, for example) and 'independent' film has become a niche market for major companies, the separation between the two is not that easy to make. The fact is that of the 80 odd films in the Festival, only about 8 to 10 would normally secure commercial distribution in Belgium. Independent filmmaking, however relative this idiom, still makes up for a good two-thirds of the entire programme. While the choice is made to approach the fantastic in its broadest possible spectrum and a critical emphasis is placed on the value of the text/film, the resulting aesthetic practices align in opposition to a mainstream American film product. In other words, the Festival, in advancing a heterogeneous film culture with a focus on aesthetics, while concerned with the definition of film as a form, aims to broaden the categories of genre definition in contrast to the studio format of the Hollywood film. However, in terms of the Festival event, it is often the big-budget productions of major American studios that generate the most public interest. Together with the invitation of big names the universalised culture of international commodity inevitably flows into the Festival, while these films move out of the context of the Festival and into the commodity flow of major distributors.[11]

## CONCLUSION

As a conclusion we might append that, in addition to marketing and evaluating film, the components of training, education and a commitment to cultural diversity are crucial to the Festival. Our Festival remains committed to a range of activities and purposes, trying to keep a balance between art and commerce by way of a programming that tries to keep in line with the ever-changing evolution of genre. In making their selection and putting together the annual programme, the Festival takes into consideration not only the different sensibilities of the diverse programmers but, being themselves first and foremost genre enthusiasts, and thus seen as a sort of continuance of their economy of tastes, also the expectations of a heterogeneous, self-reflexive audience, consisting of different cult formations and groups.

**CHAPTER 19**
# THE ESPOO CINÉ INTERNATIONAL FILM FESTIVAL

Tuomas Riskala

The Espoo Ciné International Film Festival has been running for over 14 years and its growing popularity shows best in its increasing audience figures. Since 1997 the Festival has attracted way over 20,000 people each year, with over 23,000 attendants being our record so far.

The Festival has established itself as the primary showcase of contemporary European cinema in Finland. From children's features and gruesome horror treats, to small art-house efforts and major productions, the Festival's aim is to take a thorough look at the new cinema from the old continent. On average there are over 100 screenings during the six festival days in late August, which has been the calendar place for Espoo Ciné for all its existence. Over 80 per cent of the films shown are European productions.

Though clearly a European-cinema-driven event, Espoo Ciné's annual selection does not abide to geographical borders or to thematic boundaries. The ever-growing fantasy and horror sections will attract everyone hungry to stimulate their imaginations. The acclaimed US indies shown each year provides local film maniacs with the stuff Hollywood studios cannot come up with, and the occasional collection of third-world cinema showcases the best of the productions seldom seen in the West.

Espoo Ciné also arranges special screenings for schools (high and elementary) plus kindergartens. The spectacular outdoor screening is also one of the week's special treats worth mentioning. Variety and abundance are the secrets of the Festival's success. We also did a major 3-D series in 2000, including titles like Paul Morrisey's *Flesh for Frankenstein* (1973).

The audience of the festival is as wide as the variety of films been shown. During the six-day period you can find bloodthirsty gore hounds as well as cultivated art-house fans under the same roof. Espoo Ciné attracts people from almost every age group imaginable, with the clearly uniting element being love for the cinema, for its bright and darker visions.

The Festival has evolved towards more challenging, bolder and more ambitious directions each year. Still the quality of the titles, interesting guests and love for the alternative, marginal side of cinema, is the driving force behind the artistic vision of the event. As well as tempting our guests with the 'official refreshments' of sauna and Koskenkorva, we deliver an enthusiastic but respectful audience who loves to chat with the guests after the screenings of their films.

One of the main changes the Festival had the pleasure to cope with was becoming of a full member of the European Fantastic Film Festivals Federation (EFFFF). From 1999 Espoo Ciné has organised the Silver Méliès (Méliès d'Argent) competition for the best European fantastic feature of the Festival. The winner thus takes part in the Golden Méliès (Méliès d'Or) competition with the other silver winners from the federation festivals. Finally the golden winner is officially declared as the best European fantasy film of the year.

Espoo Ciné has established itself as the most important event to see contemporary horror and fantasy movies in Finland. The Festival has basically two main reasons for this. The most influential one is of course the Silver Méliès competition which has been organised now five times. Espoo Ciné's Silver Méliès winners so far are: *Zbogum na Dvadesetiot Vek* (*Goodbye 20th Century*, 1998) by Aleksandar Popovski and Darko Mitrevski, *Tuvalu* (1999) by Veit Helmer, *Thomas est Amoureux* (2000) by Pierre-Paul Renders (also Golden Méliès), *Fausto 5.0* (2001) by Isidro Ortiz and *Deathwatch* (2002) by Michael J. Bassett.

Some other titles which have competed in our Silver Méliès competitions include *Perdita Durango* (1997) by Alex de la Iglesia, *The Nine Lives of Tomas Katz* (2000) by Ben Hopkins, *El Celo* (*Presence of Mind*, 1999) by Antoni Aloy, *Nonhosonno* (*Sleepless*, 2001) by Dario Argento and *Beyond Re-Animator* (2003) by Brian Yuzna. European directors who have appeared as guests at the Festival's Méliès series have included the British director Ben Hopkins, the Spanish filmmaker Antoni Aloy and the living legend of American (and now Spanish) horror, Brian Yuzna.

Beyond the centrality of the Silver Méliès competition, the other reason for the growth of the Espoo Ciné Festival can be found in our traditional Night Series. This strand basically works as a free-screening platform for anything interesting, intriguing, bold and exceptional from fantasy/horror/exploitation cinema around the world. Some of the respected titles shown in the series include Jim Van Bebber's violence cult classic *Deadbeat at Dawn* (1988), Ole Bornedal's original Scandinavian scare-fest *Nattevagten* (*Nightwatch*, 1997), Michele Soavi's poetic zombie tale *Dellamorte Dellamore* (1994), Stuart Gordon's *Castle Freak* (1995), Julian Richards' award-winning *Darklands* (1997),

Alberto Sciamma's hilariously trashy *La Lengua Asesina* (*Killer Tongue*, 1996), Karim Hussain's ultra-controversial nightmare trip *Subconscious Cruelty* (1999), Michael Walker's psychological masterpiece *Chasing Sleep* (2000), Brad Anderson's chilling asylum terror-tale *Session 9* (2001) and Nicholas Winding Refn's dark drama *Fear X* (2003).

Espoo Ciné has also held major retrospectives of leading European masters of fantasy, horror and screen violence. These include Italian Dario Argento and Austrian Michael Haneke among others. We also did a retrospective of the American fantasy-film legend John Landis, who was our guest of honour in 1991, and we are planning to do the next one on Richard Stanley, the South African-born filmmaker of such cult classics par excellence as *Hardware* (1990) and *Dust Devil* (1992).

Espoo Ciné also arranges acclaimed seminars and panel discussions on topics concerning film both as an art form and as an industry. During the years the topics have included scriptwriting, sound editing, animatronics, CGI and special effects, just to mention a few. Some of the special guests we have had include Peter Parks, the special EFX designer who worked on *Alien* and *Excalibur*, and another great EFX designer John Richardson, whose work we can admire in such classics as Richard Donner's *The Omen* (1976) and Sam Peckinpah's *Straw Dogs* (1971). Some of the seminars are restricted to film and cinema professionals or students, but generally most of them are public.

Considering the ultra-strict film censorship law we had up until the beginning of 2001, Espoo Ciné has been one of the only places where cinema lovers have been able to see more dark and violent celluloid creations in Finland during the past ten years. This is because during the censorship era, film festivals had exceptional permission to screen titles which would have been otherwise banned or cut for normal commercial distribution in Finland. Through this unique position the Festival has actually contributed to a maturing interest in horror and exploitation cinema in Finland. These films are hungered after in the country, which clearly shows in the ever-stable popularity of Espoo Ciné's Méliès and Night Series sections. The end of cencorship era has not stopped the hunger, even though it has made the selection of the Festival little less exceptional. Violent celluloid creations are now easier to get your hands on, but of course with some titles the Festival works as the only place to see them on the big screen. The censorship law in Finland was very much targeted against 'video nasties', and was actually created during the late 1980s when video hysteria was at its highest in Finland.

While the Espoo Ciné Festival maintained a privileged position during this dark period of celluloid repression, it was still able to court controversy – even though it attained special permission to screen Europe's darker treasures. Some cinematic extremities, like the small-scale horror and exploitation series the Festival ran in conjunction with its now-dead collaborator, the Dark Fantasy Society, back in the early 1990s, included ultra-provocative titles that tested the very limits of artistic expression in Finland at that time.

Some golden memories are also attached to the Herschell Gordon Lewis retrospective we did in the early 1990s. People were not really expecting what they got, as our main venue's screen was suddenly filled with the screamingly bright gore colours of *Blood Feast* (1963), among other Lewis classics. The highly popular retrospective got us lot of attention, mainly positive reactions, but created also some huge controversy. To finish that dive to the waves of American horror with a red-blooded cherry on top, we also screened Frank Henenlotter's *Frankenhooker* (1990) and Jim Van Bebber's *Deadbeat at Dawn* (1988) in the very same year.

We will be attached to fantasy and horror even more in the future, as it will be our turn to host the prestigious Golden Méliès ceremony in just a few years. Without a doubt, in its scale it will be the single biggest international cinema event ever organised in Finland.

The ever-growing popularity of the annual Silver Méliès Competition also guarantees that the Festival tries to keep the selection on the level of high-quality and highly interesting titles. We do not wish to restrain the taste boundaries, and that is why you can see serious art-house flicks like Agustin Villaronga's *Aro Tolbukhin: En la Mente del Asesino* (*Aro Tolbukhin: In the Mind of a Killer*, 2002) in the same competition with hilarious black comedy gore-fests like Brian Yuzna's *Beyond Re-Animator*. We also treat lovers of high-quality gay and lesbian films every year with the annual Pink Zone series.

On the general and genre-pending level, Espoo Ciné also stays as the biggest film festival in Finland considering our admission rate per screening, which is still higher than that of the other local festivals. Also the place where everything happens is one of the most beautiful and architecturally respected areas in the joined map of Espoo and Helsinki (next-door neighbours): the Espoo Cultural Centre in the beautiful garden city of Tapiola. The location provides perfect surroundings for watching films and enjoying the festival mood.

The films are screened in three theatres, with two of them being inside the cultural centre. The third screen is located within a couple of minutes' walking distance from the cultural centre, and is the local cinema of Tapiola. The huge lobby of the cultural centre is the venue of the annual cinema fair, with all of the local distributors and film-related organisations present to exhibit their upcoming line-up and other intriguing activities. The garden city of Tapiola is also only 10–15 minutes away from the central heart of Helsinki – widely recognised as the ruling Baltic Party Capital, where the Festival throws occasional parties and other film-based happenings to boost the main event.

The attention of both local and international media is guaranteed for all the titles selected for the annual programme. The number of accredited journalists, local and international, attending the Festival every year is over 150. Espoo Ciné is also sure to attract at least as many industry professionals during the six-day event.

Moreover, as the number of films selected for the Festival's official selection has grown year by year, so has the number of films picked for commercial distribution from the Festival. To support this, we also give out an audience award for the best European film which still does not have a distribution deal in Finland. If the winning film, voted by our audience, is picked up after the Festival, we will give the distributor a money prize to support the commercial distribution of the film.

# CHAPTER 20
# THE FANTASTISK FILM FESTIVAL: AN OVERVIEW AND INTERVIEW WITH MAGNUS PAULSSON

Xavier Mendik

## INTRODUCTION

One key member of the European Federation of Fantastic Film Festivals is the Fantastisk Film Festival in Sweden. Over the last ten years the festival has established a reputation for programming an eclectic range of offbeat and unusual productions from Europe and Asia, while the dedicated band of organisers and assistants ensure the event good attendance by both the local audience and oversees guests. In the following interview, Magnus Paulsson, the founder of the Festival, offers an overview of the Festival's development, as well as providing an introductory overview of the Fantastisk Film philosophy.

Fantastic film is usually used as a collective term for film genres like science fiction, fantasy and horror. But the Fantastisk Film Festival does not set narrow limits for what can be screened. In short, fantastic cinema is about imagination, about stretching limits – between dream and reality, the ordinary and the extraordinary, the possible and the impossible. The aim of the Festival is to help stretch the limits of the imagination, and to reinforce the intrinsic value of imagination in films.

Since its inception in 1995, over 430 films from 34 countries have been screened at the Fantastisk Film Festival, including shorts, documentaries and feature films. Now, each year during 10 days in September, Lund, the idyllic university city of southern Sweden, becomes a meeting place for film-audiences, film-business and filmmakers from all over the world. Here everyone is offered a unique opportunity to get acquainted with the best and the latest within fantastic cinema.

In addition, the Festival offers lectures, exhibitions and other festivities in connection with fantastic film. Because of the international flavour of the Fantastisk Film Festival, the majority of the films screened also receive their Swedish premiere. Sometimes the Festival focuses on different directors (Shinya Tsukamoto, Peter Jackson, Brian Yuzna), interesting countries (Hong Kong, Korea, Spain) or specific themes (Japanese Animé, the tales of Astrid Lindgren).

Special focus, however, is always on the European continent, which contributes at least 70 per cent of the films, and the Fantastisk Film Festival is accordingly member of two important networks for the promotion of European cinema: European Coordination of Film Festivals and European Federation of Fantastic Film Festivals. Together with the latter, the Fantastisk Film Festival is hosting one of its several international competitive sections, the Méliès Competition.[1]

**Xavier Mendik**: *What was the original motivation behind the Festival?*

**Magnus Paulsson**: To create a festival for adults, as we already have a very good film festival for youths and kids – BUFF, here in the south of Sweden. We didn't want to start a 'normal' festival. We already have three of those in Sweden – Göteborg, Stockholm and Umeå. As all the founders were big genre buffs it was pretty easy to decide the theme of the festival. So we borrowed the word 'fantastique' from the French and created the first Swedish genre film festival – Fantastisk Film Festival in 1995.

*How has the Festival changed over the years?*

It is constantly growing, both in size and attendance. When I started it, we ran for just five days, now it goes on for ten days. We have started to run a 'best of FFF' just after the Festival at the Cinematek at the Danish Film Institute in Copenhagen to create awareness of our event. We are members of the European Coordination of Film Festivals and European Fantastic Film Festivals Federation – www.melies.org. We started from scratch and created a festival which has now grown into a big international thing.

*What traditions of the fantastic exist in Sweden?*

Not really very many! We totally lack the tradition of fantastic films in Sweden. We start from a position of invisibility, so we have always had to fight with the cultural establishment to get recognition of the genre films we love so much.

*The programming of the Festival seems to reflect both a European as well as a Far Eastern focus. How important are these differing traditions of the fantastic film to the Festival?*

We want to show a broad spectrum of the world of fantastic films to our audience. Our focus is to promote genre filmmaking in Europe, by showing some of the best features and shorts that have been produced over the last two years. It is also very interesting to show the audience here that there

233

are so many interesting film countries out there. One of the most interesting from Asia at the moment is definitely South Korea, so that's why we chose to have a special focus on that country.

*Those people not familiar with the Festival might presume that it is dominated by horror movies. But titles such as Il Mare (aka Siworae, 2000) and The Price of Milk (2000) that you have shown in recent years reveal the fantastic film as far wider than that. Would you agree?*

Absolutely! Once again we want to show people the breadth of the term 'fantastic film'. It doesn't have to just be horror or science fiction. It can also be a wonderful love story – with fantastic elements. In the case of *The Price of Milk* it just also happens to be surreal!

*The Festival is always marked by the strong entries to its feature film award category. Can you tell us about some of the titles that particularly interested you?*

For the past four to five years, the most interesting genre films have come from the East. When we here in the West seem to run dry on original ideas, they release a flood of very creative movies from Asia. Mostly these are really scary films like *Ringu* (*The Ring*, 1988), *Jian Gui* (*The Eye*, 2002) and *Janghwa, Hongryeon* (*A Tale of Two Sisters*, 2003). However, Asia is also producing amazing sci-fi films like *2009 – Lost Memories* (2002) and wonderfully wacky stuff like *Jigureul jikyeora!* (*Save the Green Planet*, 2003) – all these titles have been screened at FFF and all are very cool films.

*One of the Festival's more controversial movies was Bizita Q (Visitor Q, 2001), which was awarded a special prize by the jury in 2001. Were you surprised by this decision or do you think the film does have its merits?*

I wasn't surprised as I like the movie myself. It is a very hard and controversial film, but it is very well made and it hopefully gets you to think a little bit about if something like 'the perfect family' really does exist.

*The Festival has a particular focus on short films. What interests you about this filmmaking format?*

It is the perfect cinematic format. Many film ideas are not ideal for a feature length, so the short film format up to 40 minutes is often perfect. One discovers a lot of new talent among the short film directors and producers. We have a very tough selection, just picking the absolute best shorts out of the hundreds that are being submitted each year. Our short film programmes are very popular and the screenings are usually sold out.

*The Fantastisk Film Festival is a member of the European Fantastic Films Festival Federation. Could you tell us something about this organisation?*

The EFFFF was created in order to promote the production of genre films in Europe. We do this by arranging a competition among the European fantastic films screened at the member festivals. It is called the Silver Méliès. Then once a year the silver winners compete for the Golden Méliès as the best fantastic film of the year. Through the Federation you also get a lot of very good contacts that can help you to locate film prints and guests for your own festival. It's a great network for both festival organisers and film producers/distributors that want to show and promote their film to the right target group – the true film buffs!

*Sweden is a country that has experienced some censorship problems in the past. How has this affected the kind of movie that you are able to screen here?*

Well, we don't have a censorship problem any more. We used to have one of the strictest film censorships here until the mid-1990s (the last film being cut was *Casino*). Nowadays they just cut some pornographic films that go straight to video. They also cut a certain number of films per year because the film companies want to receive a lower age limit – the desirable 11 certificate (to reach a wider audience and earn more money). So, in order to get around these restrictions we can screen whatever we want at the Festival as long as we have an age limit of 15 years.

*Alongside screenings, the Festival also staged exhibitions as well as lectures and discussions. How important are these cultural activities to what you are trying to achieve?*

I find it very important to mix different types of projects in relation to genre cinema. I strongly believe that the entertainment value goes hand in hand with the educational when it comes to the fantastic film. I want the audience not to just go and see a movie. At the Festival they get a proper critical and contextual introduction to each screening, they also have the chance to meet the visiting guests – directors, producers, stars to discuss the meanings behind their movies. Festival-goers can also go and listen to related seminars and lectures given by visiting film theorists. These lectures occur at Lund University, with whom we work in tandem in relation to programming additional events for the Festival. We find this link very stimulating, not least because several of the Festival organisers studied film and related subjects at Lund University before taking up professional posts within our organisation, so the link between education and exhibition is very important to our philosophy. Beyond these lectures, our audience can also watch genre-related art at the Festival centre and listen to genre-related music at the Festival café. It is a festival that stimulates all senses! It remains a great meeting place for open-minded people and open, reasoned debate.

*Could you tell us something about your intentions for future Festivals?*

We want to continue to programme strong European and Far Eastern content to continue to create the total (sub)cultural cinematic experience. We also want to continue to develop the links between the exhibition and the critical and intellectual discussion of the materials that we screen.

*From a British perspective, the Fantastisk Film Festival would appeal to the film fan and theorist alike. What advice would you give for those patrons interested in attending the Festival from overseas?*

You're all very welcome! Lund is a great little city, with the largest University in Scandinavia. It's very easy to walk around the whole city centre (where all Festival activities takes place). There are numerous hotels, guest-houses and restaurants for all tastes and wallets. If you need more info about FFF and all our activities, just consult our website, www.fff.se.

I would like to offer my thanks to Glenn Ekeroth, Magnus Paulsson, Christian Hallman and all the staff at the Fantastisk Film Festival for their assistance and hospitality during the Cult Film Archive's 2001 and 2003 visits.

## CHAPTER 21
## THE TASKS OF THE EUROPEAN UNDERGROUND:
## A LETTER TO LUIS BUÑUEL

Benjamin Halligan

### INTRODUCTION: TIMELESSNESS OR CONTEMPORANEITY AS 'TRUTH'

My dear Luis,

Yesterday, something that Jean-Luc Godard once said came to mind. When asked, in late February 1968, what he thought of the New American Cinema, or the so-called 'underground' and 'is there an equivalent in Europe?', he replied:

> I'm aware of the existence of the underground cinema. … To me, however, the term 'underground' is silly, because the only true underground in the world today is North Vietnam. Instead of underground, I would prefer a term such as 'Third World Cinema'. Why? Well, because to me the underground is to the cinema of Hollywood what the new revolutionary politics is to the established order.[1]

I'm sure this was said in earnestness, even though it undoubtedly brings a wry smile to your lips. You, after all, had elucidated the lot of 'the wretched of the earth' in *Los Olvidados* (1950) and, most movingly with its naïve form and didactic tone, *Las Hurdes* (1933). Godard had articulated a notion of the use of the 'underground' long since implicit in your films. Today, looking at Godard's work and directions from the end of this turbulent period, a period in which he partially succeeded in aligning a cinematic 'underground' with the emergent geopolitical 'underground', one struggles to avoid a sense of déjà vu. I mean not only in terms of the questions and actions that gave rise to the 'new revolutionary politics' and its milieu; I'm thinking specifically of *Ici et Ailleurs*[2] and the urgent and sustained questioning of our relationship with the Palestinians. Let us note, pragmatically, that the occupation that concerned Godard continues, and that the historic failure to solve this has suggested an inherent weakness that has been eminently, and bloodily, exploited.[3]

But perhaps the perspective on the struggle for liberation has changed. Godard accused us of being unable to empathise with the reality of the Palestinians' struggles on a day-to-day basis whereas now, it has been argued, in general terms we find ourselves unable to empathise with our own – but can recognise a genuine and moral interaction with the realpolitik in the footage of the Palestinian militant resistance. The phenomenon of this déjà vu suggests *the very opposite* of the implications of Godard's contemporaneity ('in the world today') as qualifying his response to the question about a notional underground. Is it not the case that Godard rendered the seemingly transient timeless through abstracting ideas of struggle, revolution and emancipation?

Your films, however, are formally (that is, thematically, narratively, socio-politically) embedded in their specific periods. Your method, your analysis, is handed to us as a case study, to then be applied to other scenarios, to new questions and actions – a challenge it is difficult to avoid.

## THE EXPLOITATION OF PROBLEMATIC IMAGES

The difference is clear: you, Luis, often place your dispossessed within a wider sense of a world system – as the unfortunates who have found themselves, through no fault of their own, in a quarter of no use or interest to the imperialist powers of the twentieth century. They are the abandoned, the forgotten, they are those beyond the ken of any concrete bourgeois political system. It is here that the underground, in its preferential option for the poor, can remain naïve and didactic in form since it is in such quarters that imperialist death throes are blatantly manifest.[4] This form happily accommodated the 'exploitative' aspect of many of your films or, rather, the finding of such an aspect in the films in their 'exploitative' contents, presented, then, so as to shock (which then became a foundation for their promotion; I'm thinking of the wonderfully lurid posters advertising the films).

You need not disrupt the narrative or 'contaminate' the film form to invoke alienation and ambiguity. From the very outset, in a series of images that startled and offended (in *Un Chien Andalou*, 1928), you discovered that film was capable of delivering, straight-up, an impact sufficient to outrage the audience, to make them flinch, or even look away. In the context of the infinite underground of violence and oppression, as identified by Godard, it was always enough to simply allow the film to parade problematic images that seemed to resonate with outrage at the scandal of the twentieth century – a form of counter-terrorism. As Jean Vigo commented, in 1930, 'M. Buñuel is a fine marksman who disdains the stab in the back',[5] and as Dalí claimed, in the same year, about a man apprehended for an act of pornographic exhibitionism, that his action was 'one of the purest and most disinterested acts a man is capable of performing in our age of corruption and moral degradation'.[6] Your uncluttered film form also falls between these two notions.

Your interest in the dispossessed and the forgotten quarters of the world reminds me of Sokurov's preoccupation with the geographical and psychological limits of human existence. His film *Dni Zatmeniya* (*Days of Eclipse*, 1988) which seems to concern itself with such groups in a specifically backwater Eurasian context, and then in relation to a subtext of late Soviet Communism, is one such example. You both investigate and chronicle the 'underground' as a kind of subterranean annex to bourgeois society, an antinferno – something that is not an aberration in itself but a necessity for such a society. The expected method for such an endeavour (neorealism – also the cry that greeted *Los Olvidados* in the 1951 Cannes Festival) is rejected in favour of an evocation of the lineaments of the experience of such a zone. This is, in a literal sense, a 'cinema of exploitation' (an experiential evocation of exploitation) and, in this respect, attacks the collective faith in the ideological foundations of societies as being misplaced. So for you, unlike Godard, there was no surprise in the face of 'the world today', no earnest reaction necessary, and so no need for a call to arms via a realignment of, let's say, the practice of film. It is in this way that your work remained true to the spirit of surrealism rather than just acknowledging your first underground legacy via the occasional narrative flourish or visual motif. You disrupted in a literally radical way, attacking the very assumptions that are necessary to sustain normality, assumptions that failed perceptive Godard and so polemicised him.

This led Godard, Groupe Dziga-Vertov and others to the so-called 'Third Cinema', perceived as the harbinger of aesthetic solutions to political problems (and/or vice versa). Yet this too had already found expression in your ethnographic tendencies, many years before *Terra em Transe* (1967) and *Vent d'Est* (1969), Pasolini's 'Southern' tendency, Internationalism and 'Third Worldism' in general. And, by then, even the old enemy, the Roman Church, had partly recognised the need for some kind of convulsion, the necessity of an autocritique. Minor clerics, fired by Incarnational Theology, then discussed (no doubt with the same earnestness) moving the Vatican to a generic Third World country, so as to be on the new frontline of the third millennium of the historic mission. It inevitably brings to mind, if considered literally, the kind of scenes that could only be from the Buñuel lexicon: Papal splendour reconstructed in some far-flung subcontinental *faux*-socialist state – gloriously redundant, grotesquely outlandish (as if such scenes had been anticipated by the Mallorcan skeleton-bishops of *L'Age d'Or*, 1930).

## THE SUPRASENSIBLE IDEA AS 'TRUTH'

The 'underground' is not a transitory preoccupation for European cinema. Rather, it has historically possessed an oppositional political use, partly as the area in which societal norms were tested and challenged. If only this lesson was understood by our 'underground filmmakers' of today, by the avant-gardists of the last couple of decades (or, we could say, since the death of Rainer Werner Fassbinder). They have instead concerned themselves with a critique of form, a kind of relentless interrogation of their own language – in short, reformism masquerading as revolutionism, obscured by radical chic. They had ultimately subsumed their own alienated forms back into a framework that remained mostly agreeable for the audience.

Hence even the wildest excesses of the most furious films made for a kind of cohesive narrative sense, failing to induce the audience flinch. They were so busy accusing *themselves* that they forgot to accuse the *audience*, as you had done; the audience could be said to be entirely 'responsible', for example, for the anti-coherence of the waking spermatorrheoa-scape of *Belle de Jour* (1967). Here, the nature of the narrative shifts implicates the nature of the audience of such a film: those whose 'grip on reality' (to paraphrase Brecht) is easily prised open. Would you believe that so much of the confessional culture of the 1990s was to become a closed system of self-loathing and self-hatred, and therein was deemed 'underground'? How can such bourgeois self-criticism ever really constitute a worthwhile oppositional raison d'être in relation to a new European cinema? And I write to you, Luis, when the need for an oppositional front has never been more apparent.

Such thoughts occupied my mind after seeing a recent film by, it could be said, one of your disciples, Michael Haneke – *La Pianiste* (*The Piano Teacher*, 2001). It sketched out the customs and rituals of contemporary European bourgeois society, and held fast to these constructs as the film began to systematically defile any sense of decency within this civilised context (the Conservatory, family gatherings, quiet retirement, informal concerts, an 'old world' EU gloss to the whole thing). The net result was, in a way, classically Buñuelian: to render such rituals meaningful only in their enactments and repetitions, as a kind of neurosis – the veneer of respectability to offset the letting loose of the ego behind closed doors (pornography emporiums, hurried couplings, voyeurism, furtive self-harm, re-enacted rape scenarios). I wish Deneuve had essayed the protagonist – if only so that the film could play in a double-bill with *Tristana* (1970).

As I left the cinema, I wanted to feel that the 'sound and the fury' *had* signified something beyond the instinctive decimation of its own codes. But what? Even if this is a 'final word' on this subject (that is, an encounter with the extremities of the ability of bourgeois society to accommodate depravity), and it did seem to be the 'final word' for a few days afterwards – I was unable to furnish the film with the second viewing that it deserved – it still was a 'final word' and nothing more. It is akin to that Sartrean critique of blasphemy; that no matter how great the outrages uttered against God, in themselves a measure of an absolute rejection of God, blasphemy still presupposes that there is a God to be outraged – and so is essentially a conservative impulse. It also represents a mindset that Lukács would have recognised as 'ultra-radicals' who imagine that their anti-bourgeois moods, their – often purely aesthetic – rejection of the stifling nature of petty-bourgeois existence [etc] … have transformed them into inexorable foes of bourgeois society.[7]

Luis – we need to have moved *beyond* the final word, to have rejected the vocabulary altogether. Haneke's stalling of just such a dialectic is evident in his use of sharp edges that cut (a razor blade, shattered glass, a carving knife) in the film. How do these edges function? In narrative terms: in the first instance, the edges are utilised as weapons; in the second instance, to advance the dynamic of the story (the mutilation of the protagonist's vagina, for example – an act that radically rearranges our attempts to locate her within one of the two aspects of the film, 'civilised' and 'behind closed doors'). But do they function beyond this? Not really. One is tempted to say that such makeshift weaponry remains as redundant as a Hitchcock 'MacGuffin'. Yet in their centrality in the world of the film, the edges take on the role of the sublime, in the sense defined by Kant and considered by Žižek.[8] They 'intervene' in the world of the film, possibly even fatally in its closing moments. Yet in their failure to represent the 'Thing' (the suprasensible Idea: that the truth of the bourgeoisie is that the world 'behind closed doors' *is* 'the civilised world'), the limitation of the film itself is apparent. The edges do not even really achieve a denotation of their inherent failure to hint at that which they fail to represent. However, the suggestion of such a relationship is transcribed into the film elsewhere. During a party, the protagonist's mother is shown a violin (gingerly removed from a glass case – a historical piece, but also a fetish object) and a painting of some antiquity that includes this violin. The representation (the painting) and the object (the actual, historical item) are present in the same frame; we are confronted with the fascinating failure of the representation to capture the empirical-phenomenological 'truth' of the violin and the violin itself.

Perhaps, in this, Haneke was attempting to anticipate the sexual violence that will follow and its disconcerting double-nature. A rape seems to achieve the actual status of unwished-for forceful sexual battery within the context of role-playing, but the protagonist's compliance suggests that it is the actual unwished-for forceful sexual battery that allows her to reinvent rape as role-playing. Surely, through this, a dematerialisation of the empirical-phenomenological 'truth' is achieved. The item is removed – the empirical-phenomenological 'truth' of rape is dissipated across the ambiguities of the role-playing, reduced to a 'real simulation'. The item becomes the sublime; it is no longer afforded its empirical-phenomenological status since the context in which that status could be recognised is removed altogether. This is a fetishisation of the sublime.

Hence the presence of the item, becoming overwhelmed, is made redundant and is stripped of the epistemological value of its empirical-phenomenological 'truth'. Thus the violin is placed back in the glass case, now 'safe' behind a glass screen, in the manner of the previous fetish objects such as the performative aesthetics of hardcore pornography, viewed on a screen in a porn booth. The illogical frenzy of such a process – a kind of perversion of the sense of meaning – informs the nature of the deeply unsettling rape scene in which there is no point of reference for the real, or 'real simulation', or unwished-for or role-playing status of the events as they unfold. The return of the repressed (that is, the materialisation of an empirical-phenomenological 'truth' adjacent to the suprasensible Idea itself) occurs in the protagonist simply stabbing herself with a kitchen knife. 'Real simulation' or otherwise in intention, the injury is real enough in the context of the actions of the character. Yet rarely are weapons so commonplace and so blunt.

The oppositional suprasensible Idea seems to find a precedent in *Un Chien Andalou* and *L'Age d'Or* ('seems' since the films remain resistant to readings and fixed meanings). It is difficult to pinpoint in these early works but refractions of it can be caught later on – in *Los Olvidados*, for example, but throughout your 'Mexican Period' in particular. The theme is civilisation, in the widest possible sense. In all these films, it is addressed in a panoramic, observational fashion. Even in *Las Hurdes* there is a context of 'civilisation' in the way in which the modern world has failed to reach or, rather, neglected to encompass, the occupants of the villages. Here, the location is initially announced as being 'on the edge of Europe [where] there are still places underdeveloped', and the film ends with a call for 'workers and peasants' to align themselves with the international anti-fascist front – fascism, absent in the film, is, by default, identified *in the light of* having seen that which has been observed of this 'land without bread'.

*Los Olvidados* 'corrects' this absence of civilisation but retains the closing sentiment – 'the solution is left to the progressive forces of our time'. It opens, disconcertingly, with shots of cities (New York, Paris, London, Mexico) that, although they register as characteristically different are, we are informed, all characterised by the presence of 'unwanted, hungry, uneducated children … the criminals of the future'. From this vantage point, the city becomes generic – the locus of civilisation rather than a specific urban area. And so now the ills of the 'edge of Europe' are positioned *within* the city (that is, within the locus of an advanced Western 'centre') in a way that would be entirely familiar to contemporary critics of globalisation. Although the structure suggests a looking-on-into this area (as does the deceptively investigative tone of the voice-over, employed to 'justify' the preoccupations of the film, another exploitational tic), the reverse is achieved.

You do not allow us a critical distance from the horrors that are shown – rather, you position us squarely in front of them; for example, the final image of Jacobi's body rolling down into a rubbish dump at the city limits. It is delivered with such nonchalance, divested of all possible thematic meaning, that the viewer is forced to invest it with pathos (if of the left) or drama (if of the right). In this way, the perspective is now one of looking-at-from – an awareness of the position from which *we* view the film (as experienced too, in a partisan way, in *Las Hurdes*). The net result is that you force us into an area where, like the Blind Man of *Los Olvidados*, we are lost, disorientated and besieged by events around us – events that suggest meanings that we can only guess at. This is why, since our ideological framework is failing to provide interpretations for what is seen, the parade of problematic images encountered from the perspective of 'looking-at-from' represents a ferocious assault on us. In *Ensayo de un crimen* (*The Criminal Life of Archibaldo de la Cruz*, 1955) we are confronted with the same conundrum, albeit slightly higher up the social ladder – this time we try desperately to formulate an idea of the society, the type of civilisation, in which such acts can occur and do seem to be sanctioned. Herein is the assault on the fantasmatic foundations of such societies.

## THE UNACCEPTABLE IMAGE AS 'TRUTH'

I did not intend to wind up discussing the idea of 'blindness'. It would be too easy to cite a smoking starting pistol for such an endeavour in the slicing of the eye in *Un Chien Andalou*. And, moreover, my point is that the viewer may feel blinded by your films but, paradoxically, only because you deny the viewer the possibility of remaining within the true land of the blind: the ideological framework and its fantasmatic foundation, those within the First World 'sphere', blind to the meaning of the social ills that exist on the margins of their awareness, an awareness that itself is becoming eclipsed by the 'virtual'. And what is the virtual other than a 'real simulation', the fetishisation of the sublime which overwhelms the empirical-phenomenological 'truth'? In the light of this, your method represents a strong counter current.

I will reconsider this shortly, but first let me ask: what is the nature of the Buñuelian front against the virtual? It is more than just a didactic catalogue of 'social ills'. The waves of images that burn into the mind in the first third of *Los Olvidados* make for the lineaments of a nightmare – not of underdevelopment, but of a return to bestial, primordial times. The urchins seem more like a 'primal horde' than any Dickensian underworld mob, pre-moral rather than amoral. This, and the obscenity of the rubbish dump mausoleum, brings to mind the recollections of the disregard for human life that characterised those moments of the twentieth century which came to define historical periods of profound change (dying imperial monarchism to emergent totalitarianism) rather than the unrestrained capitalist ethos in general.

> Prof Dr W. W. Krysko recalls – towards the end of the twentieth century – a terrifying scene that greeted his ten-year-old self in the spring of 1920. As the snow melted in the field outside his father's factory in Rostov, mounds of corpses and skeletons appeared. Thousands of bodies had been dumped there for eventual burial. There were horses' carcasses too, whose rib cages became shelters for hundreds of wild dogs, wolves, jackals and hyenas. And among them lived bands of equally wild children, orphaned or abandoned.[9]

So can we conclude that this return to the bestial is not some accidental regression, but part of a wider system? The Scottish author Ralph Glasser, who chronicled a life not unfamiliar with the margins of civilisation[10] once told me that in *Los Olvidados* you had 'gone too far'; that you had spoken an unacceptable 'truth'. Let us take this speculative conclusion to be this 'truth'.

Remember the shot in which a boy is seen suckling a pig? Rather than dwell on this, or find critical distance from it, you blast the audience with it (an 'unacceptable' image, one that breaks rules of taste and decency), then a swish pan to the right and a rapid fade – leaving us to react to the *ghost* of the image as it vanishes. The way in which this moment is delivered underscores the way in which it counterpoints the scene of Jacobi's fate. In both instances you do not frame and deliver the image in a way that suggests a critique or judgment. Rather, you confront and shock us with the image and so force us to pass judgment. And the choice is clear – be reduced to the status of a beast or be eliminated. And why this imperative, of a rush towards a new prehistoric age? To prepare the way, outside the First World, for what we would now term globalisation.

To establish the historical precedent of your strategy, allow me to quote your fellow travellers André Breton and Diego Rivera, from the manifesto written with Leon Trotsky and published in 1938, 'Towards a Free Revolutionary Art'. This was written during a period in which 'Every progressive tendency in art is destroyed by fascism as "degenerate". Every free creation is called "fascist" by the Stalinists.'[11] And Trotsky, understandably, was drawn towards the dissident European intelligentsia:

> The communist revolution is not afraid of art. It realises that the role of the artist in a decadent capitalist society is determined by the conflict between the individual and various social forms which are hostile to him. This fact alone, insofar as he is conscious of it, makes the artist the natural ally of revolution. The process of *sublimation*, which here comes into play and which psychoanalysis has analysed, tries to restore the broken equilibrium between the integral 'ego' and the outside elements it rejects. This restoration works to the advantage of the 'ideal of self,' which marshals against the unbearable present reality all those powers of the interior

world, of the 'self,' which are *common to all men* and which are constantly flowering and developing.[12]

The meaning is not entirely clear; arguably, the passage is obscured by early brushes with the writing of Freud, and by a differing use of Freudian theory by Trotsky, Breton and Rivera. But a certain agreed praxis is evident: the artist, an individual particularly attuned to tensions in the day-to-day reality, experiences a profound sense of alienation (in the Marxist sense) in his interaction with society. This is the tension between the 'ego' and the 'outside elements'. Just as antibodies are generated by the body to fight physical illness, the mind attempts to dissipate this alienation through a process of overwhelming, engulfing and burying the tension ('sublimation'). The attempt is doomed to failure since the society that inflicts the psychic injury remains and continues to impinge upon the artist's sensibility.

Those who would find a process of displacement in the notion of 'sublimation' (and, subsequently, the circumstances for a repeated 'return of the repressed') then have a formula for application (the battle between competing tensions – the recognition of the world as it really is, and the devices to blind the subject to this recognition). This could be said for Haneke too, and it also suggests why there is, at base, a great humanism in *La Pianiste*; the protagonist battles against all odds to find equilibrium in a world that taunts her with indications of the way in which it refuses to allow her to restore the broken equilibrium. This puts her in a constant state of 'negative pleasure' – attempting to attain those very things that indicate the equilibrium that she is denied.

But sublimation suggests allowing the enemy in rather than shuffling him off into some 'safer' area for attempted neutralisation. So the problem is now embedded, perhaps so deeply that the artist is unaware of it; a kind of secular equivalent to the condition of 'original sin'. The reason for the impulse to tap into the subconscious to facilitate artistic expression is now evident. And anything that makes a kind of cognitive sense during this 'tapping in' process, no matter how spontaneous the process appears to be, should be rejected (as famously occurred between you and Dalí during the preparation of *Un Chien Andalou*: 'not to accept any idea or image that might given rise to a rational, psychological or cultural explanation').[13] This would make for unimpeded access to the turbulent, alienated subconsciousness – understood here to be a dialectical tension of alienation and sublimation – which could give rise to nightmare visions that, in themselves, come to represent the extent of psychic injury in the face of oppression. It is a case of 'the more you beat me, the more I see you, and resist you, in myself'. This, during the upheavals of the 1930s, would have represented the creation of a new front against fascism – a form of 'psychological warfare' against the enemy. And such visions, drawn from the subconsciousness, contain a progressive tendency founded in the 'self': the index for the kind of existence that is acceptable (that is, the kind of psychological balance that can and should be achieved) – so, not only critique, but also solution. And this process only strengthens the 'ideal of self'. In general terms, this solution is then related to emancipation and the 'spirit of history':

The need for emancipation felt by the individual spirit has only to follow its natural course to be led to mingle its streams with this primeval necessity – the need for the emancipation of man.[14]

In such a way, the surrealist work of the mid-1920s onwards, which had drawn on 'the world of the unconscious, irrationalism and psychical automatism, the transposition of oneiric images, planes and sequences without any apparent logical connection',[15] came to find a precise political context and use.

What was the counter-attack against such a front? Initially through controversy and bannings in the case of your films and others. And then, perhaps, in the subsequent readings of surrealism (roughly at the time that *Un Chien Andalou* and *L'Age d'Or* were properly back in circulation). Critical writing on your work did not help – the films are considered, and continue to be considered, in a fashion almost completely removed from their socio-political contexts. Linda Williams, in surveying the critical responses to this work in 1980, delineated two poles:

> (i) the psychoanalytical discourse of unconscious desire as represented by the dreamlike images of *Un Chien Andalou* and (ii) the broader, more distanced, anthropological discourse on the myths that animate social and political groups as represented by *L'Age d'Or*.[16]

The majority of critical responses have engaged with the first of these elements through a variety of psychoanalytical theoretical frameworks – the very area that was then to come under the scrutiny of 'post-theory'. Even the explicit instructions you left towards this (the final shots of *Le Journal d'une femme de chambre* (1964), for example, denoting the events as – literally and metaphorically – the calm before the storm) are mostly sidelined. Such a re-reading could be said to have been possible only in an era in which surrealism came to be seen as just another element of the film rather than *the* element. The 'levelling' effect of postmodernity as routing surrealism?

Perhaps it was simply a way of 'taming' your films – considering them through the lens of formal experimentation rather than as films that, in themselves, consider *us* in their assault on the fastasmatic foundation. (Of course, there is a new canon of films that are not afforded such privileges – formal considerations of *Triumph des Willens* (*Triumph of the Will*, 1935), surely a real contender for the European exploitation underground, remain forbidden in some parts of the Western world). Perhaps some of the blame must be pushed in your direction too. The glossy surface of *Belle de Jour*, the ease with which you transgressed societal norms against such an attractive portrait of such a disinterested society, invites a consideration of surrealism and your methods as a stylistic trait and nothing more. I would rather keep company with the audiences of your first three films than those of your late French period ones.

## CONTEMPORANEITY AND NEUTRALISATION

To return to the Palestinians and the question of perspective, allow me to revisit my claim of contemporaneity and relevance for your work (as oppose to timelessness for Godard's) in the light of the above so as to, in a final digression, articulate something of the use of such a method. In a previous polemic,[17] I invoked Walter Benjamin to provide a context for that substrata of counter-revolutionary work that utilised a surface radicalism – skimming off the outward appearance of the avant-garde for a variety of reasons (a process which would, followed to its logical conclusion, result in something akin to that mentioned above in relation to advertisements and surrealism). Benjamin diagnosed the way in which:

> we are confronted with the fact … that the bourgeois apparatus of production and publication is capable of assimilating, indeed of propagating, an astonishing amount of revolutionary themes without ever seriously putting into question its own continued existence or that of the class which owns it. In any case this remains true so long as it is supplied by hacks, albeit revolutionary hacks … I further maintain that an appreciable part of so-called left-wing literature had no other social function than that of continually extracting new effects or sensations from this situation for the public's entertainment.[18]

The routing of surrealism suggests that the revolutionary hacks had benefited from a rearguard action – that the radical elements they appropriated could only be used once they were first rendered ineffective or 'harmless'. Often now, we see similar strategies, in which the radical element is only defined by its radical action. By thus reducing anything radical to actions the radical element can easily be attacked from within; it is vulnerable to alteration. This, surely, is the most effective form of assimilating and neutralising the enemy and, as far as we can tell, a proven one too: it seems to have determined much of 'la strategia della tensione' in Italy across the 1970s, is suggested in the events of May Day 1977 in Turkey and in the state infiltration of the far-right in West Germany.

In a way these strategies aim at control over morality. By reducing the radical to 'improper' actions it becomes legitimate to neutralise it. In their study of 'Empire', in part as generated and sustained through 'the huge transnational corporations [that] construct the fundamental connective fabric of the biopolitical world',[19] so that corporations and communications become one and the same, Michael Hardt and Antonio Negri reconsider the old Marxist dictum that economics dictate ethics in the context of globalisation. Early on, they diagnose a pervasive subjectivity – the foundation for a rewriting of ethics at the behest of:

> The imperial machine … [which] demonstrates that [an] external standpoint no longer exists. On the contrary, communicative production and the construction of imperial legitimation march hand in hand and can no longer be separated. The machine is self-validating, autopoietic – that is, systemic. It constructs social fabrics that evacuate or render ineffective any contradiction; it creates situations in which, before coercively neutralising difference, seem to absorb it in an insignificant play of self-generating and self-regulating equilibria.[20]

This would suggest an institutionalisation of the system identified by Benjamin, and that this system itself has become an element essential to the defence of the fantasmatic foundation. Can we not recognise a facet or variant of the 'render[ing as] ineffective' in the tendency also apparent in the 'routing of surrealism'? This, then, is the rearguard action that allows for the construction of a 'social fabric' that neutralises radical elements – that *is* neutralisation.

## CONCLUSION

If *Ici et Ailleurs* is infused with déjà vu, is locked into a system of 'relevance' and so remains susceptible to this process of neutralisation even as it identifies it, your methods seem resistant. The Buñuelian underground continues to test, challenge and reject the norms. How can it not? The 'coercively neutralising [of] difference' can itself be sublimated, *heightening* the resultant critique of society. 'Go ahead!' you say, 'attempt to eradicate that which is problematic and unacceptable.' We can watch it coming; our vantage point is that of Simon, in *Simón del desierto* (*Simon of the Desert*, 1965): the visions, hallucinations and temptations are ultimately perceived to be just those things – and things drawn primarily from ourselves, in relation to society.

This vantage point offers a measure of pre-emption of the attack outlined by Hardt and Negri in the way in which the front of resistance now incorporates the battle for images and the limitations of the context from which we draw their meanings. We no longer live in an epoch defined by images, but one in which images continually attempt to define the contours of the epoch, as Baudrillard has argued.[21] So the battle is over the rematerialisation of meaning in the realm of the virtual – the fight for the suggestion of a suprasensible idea that works to explain. I take this state of affairs, in itself, as evidence of a crisis. And for this, you have equipped us with a weapon: the problematic image as a visualisation of the empirical-phenomenological 'truth', since it is 'looked-at-from' the position of an objective awareness of the incredible fragility of the fantasmatic foundation of the imperial machine. Since this fragility can no longer be directly manifest, it remains sublime – the element that continually suggests itself in the light of the necessity for a battle for 'meaning' in the first place, or suggests the failure of the attempts to invoke that element.

So, when we unavoidably encounter the systemic lineaments of a nightmare vision as evidence of the extent of psychic injury in the face of oppression *rather than* the given and apparent 'definition' of the enemy (by those who have infiltrated it), we are more inclined to believe the nightmare vision is a 'real simulation'. This Buñuelian 'underground' sensibility denies us the degree of blindness required to do otherwise. The Thing (the given suprasensible Idea) then fails to resonate since our standpoint remains closer to that of the impartial observer than the crisis-ridden oppressor. And in this way your work continues to represents a front of resistance in, and a model for, this emancipatory endeavour.

Yours fraternally,

BH

# NOTES

**INTRODUCTION**

1   Bourdieu, P. (1986) *Distinction: Social Critique of Judgement*. London: Routledge.

2   Sorlin, P. (1991) *European Cinemas – European Societies*. London: Routledge.

3   Dyer, R. and Vincendeau, G. (eds) (1992) *Popular European Cinema*. London and New York: Routledge, 2.

4   Forbes, J. and Street, S. (eds) (2000) *European Cinema: An Introduction*. Basingstoke: Palgrave, xiii.

5   Fowler, C. (ed.) (2002) *The European Cinema Reader*. London: Routledge.

6   Dyer, R. and Vincendeau, G. (eds) (1992) *Popular European Cinema*. London and New York: Routledge.

7   Ezra, E. (ed.) (2004) *European Cinema*. Oxford: Oxford University Press; Eleftheriotis, D. (2001) *Popular Cinemas of Europe*. London: Continuum; Holmes, D. and Smith, A. (eds) *100 Years of European Cinema*. Manchester: Manchester University Press.

8   Dyer, R. (1997) *White*. London: Routledge.

9   Sconce, J. (1995). 'Trashing the Academy: Taste, Excess and an Emerging Politics of Cinematic Style', *Screen*, 36 (4), 371–93; Hawkins, J. (2000) *Cutting Edge*. Minneapolis: University of Minnesota Press; Betz, M. (2003) 'Art, Exploitation, Underground', in Jancovich, M., Lazaro-Reboll, A., Stringer, J. and Willis, A. (eds.) *Defining Cult Movies: The Cultural Politics of Oppositional Taste*. Manchester: Manchester University Press, 202–22.

10  Mendik, X. (2000) *Tenebrae*. Trowbridge: Flicks Books; Mathijs, E. (2004) '*Les Lèvres Rouges/Daughters of Darkness*', in Mathijs, E. (ed.) *The Cinema of the Low Countries*. London: Wallflower Press, 97–108.

11  See for instance: Hutchings, P. (2003) 'The Argento Effect', in Jancovich, M., Lazaro-Reboll, A., Stringer, J. and Willis, A. (eds.) *Defining Cult Movies: The Cultural Politics of Oppositional Taste*. Manchester: Manchester University Press, 127–41; Grant, M. (2000) 'Fulci's Waste Land: Cinema, Horror and the Dreams of Modernism', in Harper, G. and Mendik, X. (eds.) *Unruly Pleasures: The Cult Film and Its Critics*. Guilford: FAB Press, 63–71.

12  See Bazin, A. (1975) *Le cinema de la cruauté* (edited by François Truffaut). Paris: Flammarion.

## CHAPTER 1

1   Luther-Smith, A. (ed.) (1997) *Delirium Guide to Italian Exploitation Cinema, 1975–1979*. London: Media Publications, 39.

2   Cruz, O. (1998) 'Tits, Ass & Swastikas: Three Steps Toward a Fatal Film Theory', in A. Black (ed.) *Necromonicon Book Two*. London: Creation Books, 93.

3   Wyke, M. (1997) 'Cinema and History', in *Projecting the Past: Ancient Rome, Cinema and History*. London: Routledge, 8–13; also see Sorlin, P. (2001) 'How to Look at an "Historical Film"', in Landy, M. (ed.) *The Historical Film: History and Memory in Media*. London: Athlone Press, 25–49.

4   Cruz 1998: 95.

5   Ibid.

6   Ibid.

7   Actually, cult film producer David F. Friedman.

8   Wistrich, R. S. (1982) *Who's Who in Nazi Germany*. London: Routledge, 143.

9   Lifton, R-J. and Hackett, A. (1994) 'Nazi Doctors', in Gutman, Y. and Berenbaum, M. (eds) *Anatomy of the Auschwitz Death Camp*. Bloomington: Indiana University Press, 304.

10  Karay, F. (1998) 'Women in the Forced-Labor Camps', in Ofer, D. and Weitzman, L. J. (eds) *Women in the Holocaust*. London: Yale University Press, 289.

11  Ibid.

12  Goldenberg, M. (1998) 'Memoirs of Auschwitz Survivors: *The Burden of Gender*', in Ofer, D. and Weitzman, L. J. (eds) *Women in the Holocaust*. London: Yale University Press, 332.

13  Karay 1998: 290–1.

14  Quoted in Williams, L. (1989) *Hardcore: Power, Pleasure and the 'Frenzy of the Visible'*. Berkeley: University of California Press, 127.

15  Lifton and Hackett 1994: 314.

16  Ibid., 303.

17  Ibid., 306–8.

18  Ibid., 305.

19  Ibid.

20  Ibid., 310.

21  Ibid., 309.

22  Sconce, J. (1995) 'Trashing the academy: taste, excess, and an emerging politics of cinematic style', *Screen* 36 (4), 386.

23  Hawkins, J. (2000) *Cutting Edge: Art-Horror and the Horrific Avant-Garde*. Minneapolis: University Press of Minnesota.

## CHAPTER 2

1   My thanks to M. J. Simpson for information about the production of *Queen Kong*. See also Fenton, H. and Flint, D. (eds) (2001) *Ten Years of Terror: British Horror Films of the 1970s*. Guildford: FAB Press, 245–7. *Queen Kong* was novelised by James Moffat (London: Everest Books, 1977).

2   The US region 1 DVD, with director's commentary, was released by Retromedia in 2003.

3   Erb, C. (1998) *Tracking King Kong: A Hollywood Icon in World Culture*. Detroit: Wayne University Press, 1998, 160–80.

4   Ibid., 160. For an insightful discussion of the allegorical subtexts of the original *King Kong*, see Carroll, N. (1984) '*King Kong*: Ape and Essence', in Grant, B. K. (ed.) *Planks of Reason: Essays on the Horror Film*. Metuchen, NJ: Scarecrow Press, 215–44.

5   On World War Two imagery in British science fiction films, see Hunter, I. Q. (1999) 'Introduction: The Strange World of the British Science Fiction Film', in Hunter, I. Q. (ed.) *British Science Fiction Cinema*. London: Routledge, 9–11; Cook, J. R. (1999) 'Adapting Telefantasy: The *Dr Who and the Daleks* Films', in Hunter, I. Q. (ed.) *British Science Fiction Cinema*. London: Routledge, 113–28. On *Gorgo*, *Konga* and *Behemoth the Sea Monster*,

see Conrich, I. (1999) 'Trashing London: The British Colossal Creature Film and Fantasies of Mass Destruction', in Hunter, I. Q. (ed.) *British Science Fiction Cinema*. London: Routledge, 88–98.

6   Hunter 1999: 6.

7   Berenstein, R. J. (1996) *Attack of the Leading Ladies: Gender, Sexuality and Spectatorship in Classic Horror Cinema*. Columbia: Columbia University Press, 160–97.

8   Ibid., 170–1.

9   Ibid., 171.

10  Peter Cook and Dudley Moore, *Derek and Clive Come Again* (Virgin LP 1977, CD 1994).

**CHAPTER 3**

1   Köster quoted in Herzog, D. (1998) '"Pleasure, Sex and Politics Belong Together": Post-Holocaust Memory and the Sexual Revolution in West Germany', *Critical Inquiry*, 24, 442.

2   Ibid.

3   Linke, U. (1999) *German Bodies: Race and Representation after Hitler*. New York: Routledge, 55.

4   Herzog 1998: 398.

5   Loiperdinger, M. (1993) 'Filmzensur und Selbstkontrolle: Politische Reifeprüfung', in Jacobsen, W., Kaes, A. and Prinzler, H. H. (eds) *Geschichte des Deutschen Films*. Stuttgart: Verlag J.B. Metzler, 496.

6   See Silberman, M. (1995) *German Cinema: Texts in Context*. Detroit: Wayne State University Press, 182.

7   Tohill, C. and Tombs, P. (1994) *Immoral Tales: European Sex and Horror Movies, 1956–1984*. New York: St. Martin's Griffin, 44–5.

8   Seesslen, G. (1990) *Der pornographische Film: Von den Angängen bis zur Gegenwart*. Frankfurt: Ullstein Verlag, 260.

9   Lenssen, C. (1993) 'Film der siebziger Jahre: Die Macht der Gefühle' [the chapter on West German film history in the 1970s], in Jacobsen, W. *et al.* (eds) *Geschichte des Deutschen Films*, 249–84.

10  Hake, S. (2002) *German National Cinema*. New York: Routledge, 152.

11  Elsaesser, T. (1989) *New German Cinema: A History*. Piscataway, NJ: Rutgers University Press, 69.

12  Foucault, M. (1990) *The History of Sexuality, Volume I: An Introduction*. New York: Vintage Books, 45.

13  Anderson, B. (1991) *Imagined Communities: Reflections on the Origin and Spread of Nationalism*. London: Verso, 204–6.

14  Berlant L. and M. Warner (1998) 'Sex in Public', *Critical Inquiry* 24, 549.

15  Foucault 1990: 62–3.

16  Mitscherlich, A. and Mitscherlich, M. (1975) *The Inability to Mourn: Principles of Collective Behavior* (trans. B. R. Placzek). New York: Grove Press, 25.

17  Ibid.

18  Speier, S. (1993). 'The Psychoanalyst without a Face: Psychoanalysis without a History', in Heimannsberg, B. and Schmidt, C. (eds) *The Collective Silence: German Identity and the Legacy of Shame* (trans. C. O. Harris and G. Wheelter). San Francisco: Jossey-Bass Publishers, 67

19  Speier 1993: 67.

20  Heimannsberg, B and Schmidt, C. (1993) 'The Psychological Symptoms of the Nazi Heritage: Introduction to the German Edition', *The Collective Silence: German Identity and the Legacy of Shame* (trans. C. O. Harris and G. Wheelter). San Francisco: Jossey-Bass Publishers, 4.

21  For a detailed discussion of these events in relation to the student movement see Thomas, N. (2003) *Protest Movements in 1960s West Germany: A Social History of Dissent and Democracy*. Oxford: Berg, 123.

22  Schneider, M. (1984) 'Fathers and Sons, Retrospectively: The Damaged Relationship between Two Generations', *New German Critique*, 31, 24.

23  Schneider 1984: 44.

24  Elsaesser 1989: 23; Seesslen, G. (1990) *Der pornographische Film*, Ullstein: Tubingen Verlag, 264.

25  Dyer, R. (2002) 'Entertainment and Utopia', in Cohan, S. (ed.) *Hollywood Musicals: The Film Reader*. London, New York: Routledge, 19–30.

26  Williams, L. (1999) *Hard Core: Power, Pleasure and the 'Frenzy of the Visible'*, 2nd edn. Berkeley: University of

California Press, 155–6; 270.

27 Geyer, M. (1996) 'The Politics of Memory in Contemporary Germany', in Copjec, J. (ed.) *Radical Evil*. New York: Verso, 177.

28 Geyer 1996: 186–8.

## CHAPTER 4

1 This chapter was first published, in a somewhat different version, in *Post Script* 20, 2. We thank the editors of *Post Script* for their generous approval to reprint it.

2 Borau, J. L. (ed.) (1998) *Diccionario de cine español*. Madrid: Alianza, 463.

3 Compitello, M. (1999) 'From Planning to Design: The Culture of Flexible Accumulation in Post-Cambio Madrid', *Arizona Journal of Hispanic Cultural Studies,* 3, 207.

4 Hopewell, J. (1989) *El cine español después de Franco, 1973–198*8. Madrid: El arquero, 458 (my translation).

5 Quoted in Hopewell 1989: 196 (my translation).

6 Smith, P. J. (2000) '*Open Your Eyes*', *Sight and Sound*, 10, 3, 48.

7 Arroyo, J. (1999) '*Perdita Durango*', *Sight and Sound*, 9, 3, 49.

8 Smith, P. J. (1994) *Desire Unlimited: The Cinema of Pedro Almodóvar*. London: Verso, 4–5.

9 Finney, A. (1996) *The State of European Cinema: A New Dose of Reality*. London: Cassell, 108–13.

10 Ibid., 121.

11 Alcón, A. S. (1998) 'Andres Vincente Gomez', in Borau, J. L. (ed.) *Diccionario de cine español*, 417.

12 Arroyo 1999: 49.

13 Torreiro, M. (1997) '*Perdita Durango*', *El País* (2 November).

14 Arroyo 1999: 49.

15 Kinder, M. (1996) 'Spain After Franco', in Nowell-Smith, G. (ed.) *Oxford History of World Cinem*a. London: Oxford University Press, 603.

16 Eleftheriotis, D. (2000) 'Cultural difference and exchange: a future for European film', *Screen* 41, 1, 94.

17 Hernández, R. J. (1998) 'La peliculilla del amiguete', *Dirigido*, 266, 38.

18 Rodríguez, M.-S. (2000) '*Torrente, el brazo tono de la ley* (Segura, 1998), o como reírse de las fantasmas', unpublished paper delivered at the 4th Conference of the International Society for Luso-Hispanic Humour Studies, Montreal, Canada, 28 September 2000.

19 Hernández, R. J. (1999) '*Muertos de risa*: Vanitas vanitatis', *Dirigido*, 277, 20.

20 Kinder, M. (1993) *Blood Cinema: The Reconstruction of National Identity in Spain*. Berkeley: University of California Press, 137.

21 Compitello 1999: 206.

22 Kinder, M. (1997) 'Refiguring Socialist Spain: An Introduction', in Kinder, M. (ed.) *Refiguring Spain: Cinema/ Media/ Representation*. Durham: Duke University Press, 1–31.

23 Maxwell, R. (1995) *The Spectacle of Democracy: Spanish Television, Nationalism and Political Transition*. Minneapolis: University of Minnesota Press, 5.

24 Martini, J. C. (1977) 'Introduction', in Sánchez Polack, L. and Coll, J. L., *Tip y Coll Spain*. Barcelona: Bruguera, 5–6.

25 'Entrevista: Alex de la Iglesia.' 'El humor es una cosa muy seria.' *Sala 1, Diario de cine*. <http://www.sala1.com/reportajes/alex.html>.

26 Fernández-Santos, A. (1999) '*Muertos de risa*', *El Paí*s (14 March).

27 Maxwell 1995: 45–6.

28 Rimbau, E. (1998) 'Raphael', in Borau, J. L. (ed.) *Diccionario de cine español*, 732–3.

29 'Raphael World Wide Site', http://www.galeon.com/raphaelwws/faq2.htm

30 Maxwell 1995: 35.

## CHAPTER 5

1 Mosley, P. (2001) *Split Screen; Belgian Cinema and Cultural Identity*. Albany: State University of New York Press,

24.

2 See Elchardus, M. (ed.) (1998) *Wantrouwen en onbehagen: over de vertrouwens- en legitimiteitscrisis* [*Distrust and Discomfort: on the Crisis of Trust and Legitimacy*]. Brussels: VUB Press; Eliaerts, C. (ed.) (1997) *Kritische reflecties omtrent de zaak Dutroux* [*Critical Reflections on the Dutroux Case*]. Brussels: VUB Press.

3 See Mathijs, E. (2004) '*Les lèvres rouges/Daughters of Darkness*', in Mathijs, E. (ed.) *The Cinema of the Low Countries*. London: Wallflower Press, 97–108.

4 In Temmerman, J. (1998) 'Een dode goudvis met bananensmaak (A Dead Gold Fish with Banana Flavour)', *De Morgen* (23 October).

5 De Coninck, R. (1998) 'We wonen blijkbaar in het grappigste land ter wereld [Apparently we Live in the Funniest Country in the World]', *Gazet van Antwerpen*, 21 October.

6 Didden, M. (1998) Flanders Image Press kit for *S*. Brussels: Europartners Film Cooperation.

7 Reviews in *De Standaard*, *De Financieel Economisch Tijd*, *De Morgen*, *Het Belang van Limburg*, *Knack* and *Film & Televisie* show a similar use of language.

8 Harvey, D. (1999) '*S.*', *Variety*, 28 June.

9 See: http://www.hollywood.com/movies/detail/movie/163563. Accessed 25 March 2003.

10 Anon. (1998) 'Interview with Guido Henderickx', *HUMO*, 14 October.

11 Kristeva, J. (1980) *Les pouvoirs de l'horreur*. Paris: Seuil. For a specific discussion of Kristeva's concept of abjection, see: Mathijs, E. (1999) 'Cultuur en het beest: het zondebokmechanisme en de filosofie van horror', in Baars, J. & Starmans, R. (eds) *Het eigene en het andere* [*Our Own and The Other*]. Delft: Eburon, 215–26.

12 Mulvey, L. (1975) 'Visual Pleasure and Narrative Cinema', *Screen*, 16, 3.

13 Lafond, F. (2003) 'The Life and Crimes of Ben; or, when a Serial Killer meets a Film Crew in *Man Bites Dog*', *Post Script*, 22, 2, 84–93; Lafond, F. (2004) '*C'est arrivé près de chez vous/Man Bites Dog*', in Mathijs, E. (ed.) *The Cinema of the Low Countries*. London: Wallflower Press, 215–21.

14 James, N. (2003) 'Murder in Mind', *Sight and Sound*, 13, 4, 24–6; Goodfellow, M. (2003) 'Liège Standards', *Sight and Sound*, 13, 4, 26.

**CHAPTER 6**

1 Lev, P. (2000) *American Films of the 70s: Conflicting Visions*. Austin: University of Texas Press.

2 Ibid.

3 Ibid.

4 Kael, P. (1996) 'Dirty Harry Saint Cop', in *For Keeps: 30 Years at the Movies*. New York: Plume/Penguin, 418–21.

5 Drake, R. (1998) 'Mythmaking and the Aldo Moro Case', *The New Criterion*, http://www.newcriterion.com/archive/17/nov98/drake.htm.

6 Ibid.

7 Ibid.

8 Ibid.

9 Jamieson, A. (2000) 'Mafiosi and Terrorists: Italian Women in Violent Organizations', in *SAIS Review*. Baltimore: Johns Hopkins University Press, 51–64.

10 Blumenstock, P. (1998) 'Men Before Their Time', liner notes – *Beretta 70: Roaring Themes from Thrilling Italian Police Films 1971–1980*.

11 Reid, D. (2001) 'The Historian and the Judges', *Radical History Review*, 135–48.

12 Godson, R. (1999) 'Crime, Corruption and Society', *The Journal*, 3, 3.

13 Ibid.

**CHAPTER 7**

1 Gorky, A. M. (1896) 'Beglye zametki [Fleeting Notes]', *Nizhegorodskii listok* [*The Nizhni Novgorod Newsletter*],182, 4 July, 3, cited in Taylor, R. and Christie, I. (eds) (1988) *The Film Factory: Russian and Soviet Cinema in Documents 1896–1939*. London: Routledge, 25.

2 Bowie, M. (1991) *Lacan*. Glasgow: Fontana Press, 162.

3   Woll, J. (2004) 'Exorcising the Devil: Russian Cinema and Horror', in Schneider, S. J. and Williams, T. (eds) *Horror International*. Detroit: Wayne State University Press, forthcoming.

4   Dobrotvorsky, S. (1992) 'Uzhas I strah v konze tisyachiletya [Horror and Fear at the End of the Millenium]', reprinted in Arkus, L. (ed.) (2001) *Kino naoshtup [Senses of Cinema]*. St. Petersburg: Seans Publishing House, 75 (translation of all references is the author's).

5   'The Russian Idea' is a synopsis of Kovalov's script for *Russkaya Ideya (The Russian Idea*, 1995), directed by Sergei Selyanov. It was the Russian entry of the British Film Institute project for the centennial anniversary of cinema. See Kovalov, O. (1996) '*Russkaya Ideya [The Russian Idea]*', *Seans*, 12.

6   Kovalov 1996: 12, 76.

7   Berdyaev, N. (1992) [1946] *The Russian Idea*. Hudson: Lindisfarne Press. http://www.emory.edu/INTELNET/four_thinkers.html

8   Hoffmann, S. P. (1995) 'Nicholas Berdyaev, the Russian Idea and Liberty', Taylor University, http://campus.houghton.edu/orgs/acad_dean/Hoffmann01_Nicholas_Berdyaev.htm

9   Berdyaev 1992.

10  Ronkin, V. (2003) 'Gorod-Sad [The Garden City]' http://kitezh.onego.ru/

11  Kovalov 1996: 76.

12  Laplanche, J. and J.-B. Pontalis (1964) 'Fantasy and the Origins of Sexuality', in Burgin, V., Donald, I. and Kaplan, C. (eds) (1986) *Formation of Fantasy*. London: Methuen, 19.

13  Laplanche, J. and Pontalis, J-B. (1974) *The Language of Psychoanalysis*. New York: W. W. Norton, 475.

14  Kovalov 1996: 76.

15  Ibid.

16  Turovskaya, M. (1988) 'I. A. Pyrev I ego muzikalnye komedii. K probleme zhanra [I. A. Pyrev and his musical comedies. On the problems of genre]', *Kinovedcheskie zapiski [Cinema Studies Notes]*, 1, 111–46.

17  Morris, D. B. (1985) 'Gothic Sublimity', *New Literary History* 16, 299–319.

18  Stojanova, C. (2004) 'Beyond Dracula and Ceausescu: Phenomenology of Horror in Romanian Cinema', in Schneider, S. J. and Williams, T. (eds) *Horror International*. Detroit: Wayne State University Press, forthcoming.

19  Stojanova 2004: forthcoming; T. Todorov (1973) *The Fantastic*. Ithaca: Cornell University Press, 41.

20  Stojanova 2004: forthcoming.

21  Foster, H. (1995) *Compulsive Beauty*. Cambridge, MA: MIT Press, 19.

22  *Encyclopaedia of World Mythologies [Mifyi narodov mira]* (1982). Moscow: Sovetskaya Enzyklopedia Publishing House, 29.

23  Stojanova 2004: forthcoming.

24  Schneider, S. J. (2001) 'Manifestations of the Literary Double in Modern Horror Cinema', *Film and Philosophy*. Special Edition, 51–62.

25  Freud, S. (1953) 'The Uncanny', in Strachey, J. (ed.) *The Standard Edition of the Complete Psychological Works of Sigmund Freud (vol. XVII)*. London: Hogarth, 219–52.

26  Berdyaev 1992.

27  For an explanation of the Latin phrase *mysterium tremendum*, see Varnado, S. L. (1974) 'The Idea of the Numinous in Gothic Literature', *The Gothic Imagination: Essays in Dark Romanticism*. Washington State University Press, 11–21.

28  For a description, see Leyda, J. (1983) *A History of the Russian and Soviet Film*. Princeton: Princeton University Press, 78. Also see: Youngblood, D. J. (1992) *Movies For the Masses: Popular Cinema and Soviet Society in the 1920s*. New York: Cambridge University Press, 2.

29  Varma, D. P. (1966) *The Gothic Flame*. New York: Russell & Russell, 49.

30  Ibid.

31  Berdyaev 1992.

32  Woll, J. (2004) 'Exorcising the Devil: Russian Cinema and Horror', in Schneider, S. J. and Williams, T. (eds) *Horror International*. Detroit: Wayne State University Press, forthcoming.

33  Dobrotvorsky 1992: 75.

34  Mantsov, I. (1998) 'Imitatsia Zhanra [Genre Imitation]', *Iskusstvo kino* 6, 3–4, http://www.kinoart.ru/1998/6/17.html

**253**

35    Horton, A. J. (1999) 'The Russian Soul Fights Back', *Kinoeye* 1, 1, 28 July.

36    Interview with the author, *Kinoeye* 2, 2, January 2002, http://www.kinoeye.org/02/02/stojanova02.html

37    Tsivian, Y. (1998) *Early Cinema in Russia and Its Cultural Perception* (ed. Richard Taylor). Chicago: University of Chicago Press, 6–7.

38    Bowie 1991: 162.

39    Romney, J. (2000) '*Of Freaks and Men*', *Sight and Sound*, 10, 5, 57.

40    Morris 1985: 299–319.

41    Berdyaev 1992.

42    Dobrotvorsky 1992: 75.

43    Morris 1985: 299–319.


**CHAPTER 8**


1    Lyotard, J. (1993) *Libidinal Economy* (trans. I. H. Grant). London: Athlone Press, 20.

2    Balun, C. (1988) 'Review: *The Horrible Dr. Hichcock*', *Deep Red*, 5 December, 29.

3    Martin, J. (1988) 'Review: *The Horrible Dr. Hichcock*', *Deep Red*, 5 December, 7.

4    Jenks, C. (1996) 'The Other Face of Death: Barbara Steele and *La Maschera del Demonio*', in Black, A. (ed.) *Necronomicon* Vol. 1. London: Creation Books, 88.

5    Ibid.

6    Lyotard 1993: 63–4.

7    From I. H. Grant's very useful glossary at the beginning of Lyotard, *Libidinal Economy*, xiv.

8    See Williams, J. (2000) *Lyotard: Towards a Post-Modern Philosophy*. Cambridge: Polity Press, 53.

9    Lyotard 1993: 21.

10    Deleuze, G. (1989) *Cinema 2: The Time Image* (trans. H. Tomlinson and R. Galeta). London: Athlone Press, 212.

11    Jenks 1996: 100.


**CHAPTER 10**


1    For a thorough catalogue of sexual images of nuns, see Fentone, S. (2000) *AntiCristo: The Bible of Nasty Nun Sinema & Culture*. Guildford: FAB Press.

2    Nun films from Italy (149) compared to those from Asia (Hong Kong, Japan and the Philippines, 40), Canada (34), France (66), Germany (24) and Spain (42). See Fentone 2000: 286–308.

3    See Fentone 2000; Zalcock, B. (1998) *Renegade Sisters: Girl Gangs on Film*. London: Creation Books; Bruschini, A. and Tentori, A. (1993) *Malizie perverse: il cinema erotico italiano*. Bologna: Granata; *Nocturno Cinema* (2000).

4    Bertolino, M. and Ridola, E. (1999) *Vizietti all'italiana: l'epoca d'oro della commedia sexy*. Florence: Igor Molino Editore; Spinazzola, V. (1985) *Cinema e pubblico: lo spettacolo filmico in Italia 1945–1965*. Rome: Bulzoni, 321; as well as in ads in trade journals such as *Variety* and *Film and T.V. Daily*.

5    Fentone 2000: 34–5.

6    Istituto Doxa (1976) *Il pubblico del cinema*. Rome: Istituto Doxa; Sorlin, P. (1996) *Italian National Cinema 1896–1996*. London: Routledge, 179, n.3; Della Casa, S. (2001) *Storia e storie del cinema popolare italiano*. Turin: Editrice La Stampa, 33.

7    Sorlin 1996: 178–9; Wagstaff, C. (1992) 'A Forkful of Westerns: Industry, Audiences and the Italian Western', in Dyer, R. and Vincendeau, G. (eds) *Popular European Cinema*. London: Routledge, 249; See also Della Casa 2001: 46.

8    Wagstaff 1992: 253–4.

9    Della Casa 2001: 87.

10    Caddeo, F. (2002) 'Incontro con Claudio Fragasso, un vero regista di genere', http://www.horrorcult.com

11    Fentone 2000: 31.

12    Gomarasca, M. (2000) 'Antinferno: lo sguardo laico', *Nocturno Cinema*, 18.

13    Mazzucchelli, M. (1961) *La monaca di Monza*. Milan: Dall'Oglio; Mazzucchelli, M. (1964) *Manzoni e la monaca di Monza*. Milan: Cino del Duca.

14  Russo, M. (1994) *The Female Grotesque: Risk, Excess and Modernity*. New York: Routledge, 53.

15  Foucault, M. (1990) *The History of Sexuality, Volume I: An Introduction* (trans. R. Hurley). New York: Vintage Books, 58–69.

16  Williams, L. (1989) *Hard Core: Power, Pleasure and the 'Frenzy of the Visible'*. Berkeley: University of California Press, 34.

17  Foucault 1990: 35.

18  Spinazzola 1985: 316–17.

19  Della Casa 2001: 73–5.

20  Foucault 1990: 6.

21  Ibid., 5.

22  Ibid., 4–5.

23  Russo 1994: 79–80.


**CHAPTER 11**


1   Crist, J. (1974) 'Emmanuelle', *New Yorker*, 16 December, 94.

2   Reed, R. (1975) 'Tsk! Tsk! How Boring', *New York Daily News*, 3 January, 56.

3   Cocks, J. (1975) 'Queen Klong', *Time*, 6 January, 6.

4   Oster, J. (1974) '*Emmanuelle* Glossy, Erotic', *Daily Variety*, 16 December.

5   Crist 1974: 94.

6   Hindes, A. (1995) '*Emmanuelle*', *Variety*, 6 November, 31–2.

7   Brown, M. (1980) 'Carry On (And On) *Emmanuelle*', *London Sunday Times Magazine*, 21 November, 21; and *Variety*, 4 September 1974, 35.

8   Columbia Pictures News (1974) 'This is *Emmanuelle*…', Press Junket for *Emmanuelle*, 1–6: 1.

9   Arsan, E. (1971) *Emmanuelle*. New York: Grove Press, 9.

10  Ibid., 221.

11  Ibid., 83–4.

12  Ibid., 114.

13  Ibid., 135.

14  Ibid., 145.

15  Ibid., 220–1.

16  Smith, H. and Van Der Horst, B. (1974) 'Scenes', *The Village Voice*, 16 December, 20.

17  Weiler, A. H. (1974) 'Screen: *Emmanuelle* Rates Columbia's First "X"', *New York Times*, 16 December, D47.

18  Schneider, P. (1974) 'Paris: Surprise Garden at Les Halles', *New York Times*, 11 December, D38.

19  Columbia Pictures News (1974) 'Who Is Sylvia, What Is She?', Press Junket for *Emmanuelle*, 2.

20  Ibid., 2.

21  Ibid., 4 .

22  *Variety*, 7 May 1975, 'Analyzing *Emmanuelle's* B.O. Impact On The U.S. Markets', 56.

23  Sterritt, David (1975) 'Other releases', *Christian Science Monitor*, 23 January 10.

24  *Variety*, 7 May 1975.

25  Weiler, A. H. (1975) 'Film Box-Office Receipts in '74 a Record $1.9-Billion', *New York Times*, 26 January, 17.

26  Ibid.

27  Ibid.

28  Ibid.

29  Winsten, A. (1974) '*Emmanuelle* Bows at the Paris', *New York Post*, 16 December, 47.

30  Brown 1980: 21.

31  Ibid.

32  *Variety*, 31 July 1974, '*Emmanuelle*', 18.

33  *Variety*, 27 February 1985, 39.

34  Cocks 1975.

**CHAPTER 12**

1   McClintock, A. (1996) *Imperial Leather: Race, Gender and Sexuality in the Colonial Contest.* London: Routledge, 22.

2   Tobing Rony, F. (1996) *The Third Eye: Race, Cinema and Ethnographic Spectacle.* Durham: Duke University Press, 7.

3   Ibid., 81–2.

4   Ibid., 7.

5   Ibid., 55.

6   Grant, B. K. (2000) 'Second Thoughts on Double Features: Revisiting the Cult Film', in Mendik, X. and Harper, G. (eds) *Unruly Pleasures: The Cult Film and its Critics.* Surrey: FAB Press, 19.

7   Williams, L. R. (2000) 'The Oldest Swinger in Town', *Sight and Sound*, 10, 8, 24.

8   Pinkus, K. (1997) 'Shades of Black in Advertising and Popular Culture', in Allen, B. and Russo, M. (eds) *Revisioning Italy: National Identity and Global Culture.* Minneapolis: University of Minnisota Press, 134.

9   Combs, R. (1978) '*Emanuelle V. Violence To Women*', *Monthly Film Bulletin*, 45, 532, 88.

10   Gomarasca, M. (1997) *To Emanuelle.* Milan: Media Word Publications, 4–5.

11   Pinkus 1997: 144.

12   Arsan, E. (1971) *Emmanuelle.* New York: Grove Press, 89.

13   Ibid., 95.

14   Ibid., 104.

15   Ibid., 88.

16   Ibid., 207.

17   Ibid., 208.

18   Ibid., 209.

19   Pinkus 1997: 149.

20   Tobing Rony 1996: 46.

21   Grant 2000: 25.


**CHAPTER 13**

1   René Magritte in conversation with Paul Waldo Schwartz (1967), quoted in Meuris, J. (1992) *René Magritte.* Cologne: Taschen GmbH, 112.

2   Callahan, V. (1999) 'Detailing the Impossible', *Sight and Sound*, 9, 4, 28–30.

3   Black, A. (1996) 'Clocks, Seagulls, Romeo and Juliet: Surrealism Rollin Style', interview with Jean Rollin in Black, A. (ed.) *Necronomicon Book 1.* London: Creation Books, 182.

4   Weiss, A. (1992) *Vampires and Violets: Lesbians in the Cinema.* London: Jonathan Cape, 85.

5   Black 1996: 178.


**CHAPTER 14**

1   Pomeroy, W. B. (1968) *Boys and Sex*, quoted in Simpson, M. (1994) *Male Impersonators: Men Performing Masculinity.* London: Cassell, 21.

2   Balbo, L. (1996) 'I Talked with a Zombie: The Forgotten Horrors of Massimo Pupillo', in Jaworzyn, S. (ed.) *Shock: The Essential Guide to Exploitation Cinema.* London: Titan, 18; 19.

3   Amazon.com Customer Review (2000), http://www.amazon.com/exec/obidos/tg/detail/-/B00004Y7HK/ref=cm_cr_dp_2_1/002-7005492-3951215?v=glance&s=dvd&vi=customer-reviews.

4   Lucas, T. (1994) 'Welcome to My Cutting Room Floor – The Crimson Executioner', *Video Watchdog*, 22, 55–7.

5   Heinenlotter, F. (2000) Liner Notes for *Bloody Pit of Horror* DVD, Something Weird Video.

6   Tohill, C. and Tombs, P. (1994) *Immoral Tales: Sex and Horror Cinema in Europe 1956–1984.* London: Primitive Press, 38.

7   Hardy, P. (ed.) (1985) *The Aurum Film Encyclopedia: Horror.* London: Aurum Press: 169.

8 Lucas 1994: 55.

9 Balbo 1996: 19.

10 Hardy 1985: 177.

11 Benshoff, H. M. (1997) *Monsters in the Closet: Homosexuality and the Horror Film*. Manchester: Manchester University Press, 36.

12 Hardy 1985: 169.

13 Ibid.

14 Heinenlotter 2000.

15 Hardy 1985: 169; G. Johnson (2000) '*The Bloody Pit of Horror*: DVD Review', http://www.imagesjournal.com/issue09/reviews/bloodypit/text.htm.

16 Johnson 2000.

17 Dumontet, C. (1998) 'Bloody, Scary and Sexy', in Dumontet, C. (ed.) *Ghosts, Vampires and Kriminals: Horror and Crime in Italian Comics*. London: National Art Library, 6–20.

18 Ibid., 4.

19 Ibid., 9.

20 Ibid., 12.

21 Elley, D. (1984) *The Epic Film: Myth and History*. London, Boston and Melbourne: Routledge and Kegan Paul, 20.

22 Bondanella, P. (1991) *Italian Cinema: From Neorealism to the Present*. New York: Continuum, 158.

23 Wagstaff, C. (1992) 'A Forkful of Westerns: Industry, Audiences and the Italian Western', in Dyer, R. and Vincendeau, G. (eds) *Popular European Cinema*. London and New York: Routledge, 245–61.

24 Ibid., 254.

25 Dyer, R. (1997) *White*. London: Routledge, 170.

26 Ibid., 165.

27 Ibid., 171.

28 Ibid., 176.

29 Ibid., 169.

30 Ibid., 165.

31 Johnson 2000.

32 Hardy 1985: 169.

33 Balbo 1996: 20; Johnson 2000.

34 Johnson 2000.

35 Simpson 1994: 30.

36 Ibid., 41.

37 Ibid., 23.

38 Ibid., 30.

39 Ibid., 38.

40 Freud, S. (1919) 'A Child is Being Beaten', in Richards, A. (ed.) [1979] *Freud: On Psychopathology*. Harmondsworth: Pelican, 161–93.

41 Marcus, S. (1969) *The Other Victorians: A Study of Sexuality and Pornography in Mid-Nineteenth Century England*. London: Corgi, 262.

42 Ibid., 263.

43 Benshoff 1997: 43

44 Berenstein, R. J. (1996) *Attack of the Leading Ladies: Gender, Sexuality, and Spectatorship in Classic Horror Cinema*. New York: Columbia University Press; Clover, C. J. (1992) *Men, Women and Chainsaws: Gender in the Modern Horror Film*. Princeton: Princeton University Press.

45 Heinenlotter 2000.

46 Ibid.

**CHAPTER 16**

1     Ward, M. Review of *Nekromantik* [sic], http://www.aboutcultfilm.com/reviews/Nekromantik.html.

2     Ibid.

3     See http://web.uvic.ca/geru/439/oberhausen.htlm.

4     *The Trend: Punk Rockers Speak About Their Lives* (1981–82) and *That Was S.O.36* (1984–85).

5     Jörg Buttgereit quoted in Kerekes, D. (1994) *Sex, Murder, Art: The Films of Jörg Buttgereit*. Manchester: Headpress, 52.

6     Elsaesser, T. (1989) *New German Cinema: A History.* London: BFI/Macmillan, 239.

7     Santner, E. (1993) *Stranded Objects: Mourning, Memory and Film in Postwar Germany.* Ithaca, NY & London: Cornell University Press, 39.

8     Kaes, A. (1992) *From Heimat to Hitler: The Return of History as Film.* Cambridge, MA & London: Harvard University Press, 68.

9     For example, films such as *Black Forest Girl* (1950) or *Green is the Heather* (1951).

10     Elsaesser 1989: 242.

11     Comar, P. (1999) *The Human Body: Image and Emotion.* London: Thames & Hudson, 87.

12     Franz Rodenkirchen quoted in Kerekes 1994: 40.

13     Barthes, R. (1993) *Camera Lucida: Reflections on Photography* (trans. Richard Howard). London: Vintage, 79.

14     Werner Herzog, interviewed in the *Guardian*, 24 November 1975.

15     Fassbinder, R. W. (1972) 'Six Films by Douglas Sirk', in *Douglas Sirk*, Mulvey, L. and Halliday, J. (eds) Edinburgh: Edinburgh Film Festival, 104.

16     Hake, S. (2002) *German National Cinema.* London: Routledge, 124.

17     Kerekes 1994: 39.

**CHAPTER 18**

1     Translation of the French phrases: 'Kill again!' 'Never again!!' 'Piiiigs In Spaaace!' 'Shut up'…

2     Corrigan, T. (1991) *A Cinema Without Walls: Movies and Culture After Vietnam.* London: Routledge, 77.

3     Bourdieu, P. (1986) *Distinction: A Social Critique of the Judgement of Taste.* London: Routledge, 56.

4     Watson, P. (1997) 'There's No Accounting for Taste: Exploitation Cinema and the Limits of Film Theory', in Cartmell, D., Hunter, I. Q., Kaye, H. and Whelehan, I. (eds) *Trash Aesthetics: Popular Culture and its Audience.* London: Pluto Press, 75–8.

5     Corrigan 1991: 139.

6     Ibid., 142.

7     Chibnall, S. (1997) 'Double Exposures: Observations on The Flesh and Blood Show', in Cartmell, D., Hunter, I. Q., Kaye, H. and Whelehan, I. (eds) *Trash Aesthetics: Popular Culture and its Audience.* London: Pluto Press, 89.

8     Hunter, I. & Kaye H. in the introduction to Cartmell, D., Hunter, I. Q., Kaye, H. and Whelehan, I. (eds) *Trash Aesthetics: Popular Culture and its Audience.* London: Pluto Press, 1–6.

9     Harbord, J. (2002) *Film Cultures.* London: Sage, 70.

10     Ibid., 68–9.

11     Ibid., 64.

**CHAPTER 20**

1     The description of the Fantastisk Film Festival philosophy is adapted from the organisation's mission statement and is used by permission.

**CHAPTER 21**

1     Sterritt, D. (1998) *Jean-Luc Godard Interviews.* Jackson: University Press of Mississippi, 11.

2     Brown, R. (1972) *Focus on Godard.* New Jersey: Prentice-Hall, 180.

3     Chomsky, N. (2003) *Power and Terror: Post-9/11 Talks and Interviews.* New York: Seven Stories Press, 111; Ali, T. (2002) *The Clash of Fundamentalisms: Crusades, Jihads and Modernity.* London: Verso, 324.

4 Durgnat, R. (1967) *Luis Buñuel*. London: Studio Vista, 13.

5 Quoted in Buñuel, L. and Dalí, S. (1994) *Un Chien Andalou*. London: Faber and Faber, xxvi.

6 From 'The Surrealist Conception of Sexual Freedom', in *Le Surréalisme au Service de la Révolution, No .2*, quoted in Nadeau, M. (1978) *The History of Surrealism*. Middlesex: Penguin Books, 305.

7 Adorno, T., Benjamin, W., Bloch, E., Brecht, B., Lukács, G. (1992) *Aesthetics and Politics*. London: Verso, 36.

8 Žižek, S. (2002) *The Sublime Object of Ideology*. London: Verso, 203.

9 Krysko, W. W., 'I Chose the Truth' (unpublished memoir), quoted in Thomas, D. M. (1999) *Alexander Solzhenitsyn: A Century in his Life*. London: Abacus, 38.

10 Glasser, R. (1999) *Gorbals Trilogy*. London: Lomond Books.

11 Siegel, P. (1970) *Leon Trotsky on Literature and Art*. New York: Pathfinder Press, 121.

12 Ibid., 118.

13 Camacho, E., Pérez Bazo, J., Rodríguez Blanco, M. (2001) *Buñuel: 100 Years*. New York: Instituto Cervantes/The Museum of Modern Art, 62.

14 Siegel 1970: 118–19.

15 Camacho *et al.* 2001: 52.

16 Williams, L. (1981) *Figures of Desire: A Theory and Analysis of Surrealist Film*. London: University of Illinois Press, 153.

17 Halligan, B. (2002) 'What is the Neo-Underground and What Isn't: A First Consideration of Harmony Korine', in Mendik, X. and Schneider, S. (eds) *Underground U.S.A.: Filmmaking Beyond the Hollywood Canon*. London: Wallflower Press, 150–60.

18 Benjamin, W. (1973) *Understanding Brecht*. London: New Left Books, 94–5.

19 Hardt, M., Negri, A. (2001) *Empire*. London: Harvard University Press, 31.

20 Ibid., 34.

21 See Baudrillard, J. (1995) *The Gulf War Did Not Take Place*. London: Indiana University Press; and Baudrillard, J. (2002) *The Spirit of Terrorism*. London: Verso

# INDEX

# Underground U.S.A.
## Filmmaking Beyond the Hollywood Canon

Edited by Xavier Mendik and
Steven Jay Schneider

Foreword by Lloyd Kaufman

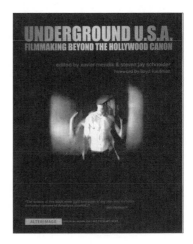

2002

£15.99 pbk

1-903364-49-3

256 pages

Whether defined by the carnivalesque excesses of Troma studios,
the art-house erotica of Radley Metzger and Doris Wishman
or the narrative experimentations of Abel Ferrara, Melvin
Van Peebles, Jack Smith or Harmony Korine, underground
cinema has achieved an important position within American
film culture. Often defined as 'cult', 'exploitation', 'alternative'
or 'independent', the American underground retains seperate
strategies of production and exhibition from the cinematic
mainstream, while its sexual and cinematic representations differ
from the traditionally conservative structures of the Hollywood
system.
*Underground U.S.A.* offers a fascinating overview of this area
of maverick movie-making by considering the links between
the experimental and exploitation traditions of the American
underground. This volume brings together leading film theorists,
critics, exhibitors and filmmakers who take as their focus those
directors, films and genres typically dismissed, belittled or ignored
by established film culture. The contributors thus consider the
stylistic, generic and representational strategies that have emerged
in the alternative American film scenefrom the 1940s to the
present.

"As vast and variegated as the American underground itself, this
exciting collection bypasses Hollywood for a wild intellectual
ride through Indiewood and beyond ... an unflinching guided
tour of cinema's least-explored caves and caverns, combining
sophisticated theory and history with unabashed affection for the
screen's most subversive, rambunctious visions."
– Prof. David Steritt, Long Island University

The writers of this book shine light into some of my own very
favourite darkened coreners of American cinema...
– Jim Jarmusch

Xavier Mendik is the Director of the Cult Archive at University
College Northampton, UK, and General Editor of the
*AlterImage* series. He has published widely on the topic of cult
and underground cinema, including *Fear Theory: Case Studies
in European and American Horror Cinema* (Wallflower Press,
forthcoming). Steven Jay Schneider has published widely on the
horror film and related genres and is author of *The Cinema of Wes
Craven: An Auteur on Elm Street* (Wallflower Press, forthcoming).

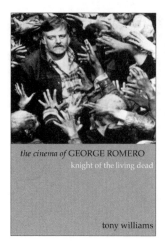

2003

£14.99 pbk   1-903364-73-6

£42.50 hbk   1-903364-62-0

208 pages

# The Cinema of Gerorge A. Romero
## Knight of the Living Dead

## Tony Williams

*The Cinema of George A. Romero: Knight of the Living Dead* is the first in-depth study in English of the career of this foremost auteur working at the margins of the Hollywood mainstream. In placing Romero's oeuvre in the context of literary naturalism, the book explores the relevance of the director's films within American cultural traditions and thus explains the potency of such work beyond 'splatter movie' models. The author explores the roots of naturalism in the work of Emile Zola and traces this through to the EC Comics of the 1950s and on to the work of Stephen King.

"This thorough, searching and always intelligent overview does full justice to Romero's *Living Dead* trilogy and also at last rectifies the critical neglect of Romero's other work, fully establishing its comnplexity and cohesion."
          – Robin Wood, *CineAction!*

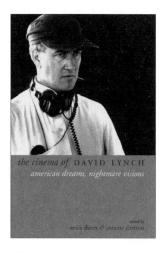

2004

£14.99 pbk   1-903364-85-X

£42.50 hbk   1-903364-86-8

208 pages

# The Cinema of David Lynch
## American Dreams, Nightmare Visions

## Edited by Erica Sheen
## and Annette Davison

David Lynch is an anomaly. A pioneer of the American 'indie' aesthetic, he also works in Hollywood and for network television. He has created some of the most disturbing images in contemporary cinema, and produced startlingly innovative work in sound. This collection offers a range of theoretically divergent readings that demonstrate not only the difficulty of locating interpretative positions for Lynch's work, but also the pleasure of finding new ways of thinking about it. Films discussed include *Blue Velvet*, *Wild at Heart*, *The Straight Story* and *Mulholland Drive*.

"A ground-breaking collection of new essays presenting a range of challenging theoretical perspectives on, and insightful  readings of, Lynch's work."
          – Frank Krutnik, Sheffield Hallam University

## The Horror Genre
### From Beelzebub to Blair Witch

Paul Wells

2000
£12.99 pbk
1-903364-00-0
144 pages

*The Horror Genre: From Beelzebub to Blair Witch* provides a comprehensive introduction to the history and key themes of the horror film, the main issues and debates surrounding the genre, and the approaches and theories that have been applied to horror texts.

"A valuable contribution to the body of teaching texts available ... a book for all undergraduates starting on the subject."
– Linda Ruth Williams, University of Southampton

## Science Fiction Cinema
### From Outerspace to Cyberspace

Geoff King and Tanya Krzywinska

2000
£12.99 pbk
1-903364-03-5
144 pages

From lurid comic-book blockbusters to dark dystopian visions, science fiction is seen as both a powerful cultural barometer of our times and the product of particular industrial and commercial frameworks. The authors outline the major themes of the genre, from representations of the mad scientist and computer hacker to the relationship between science fiction and postmodernism.

"The best overview of English-language science ficiton cinema published to date – thorough, clearly written and full of excellent examples. Highly recommended."
– Steve Neale, Sheffield Hallam University

## Disaster Movies
### The Cinema of Catastrophe

Stephen Keane

2001
£12.99 pbk
1-903364-05-1
144 pages

From 1950s sci-fi B-movies to high concept 1990s 'millenial movies', Stephen Keane looks at the ways in which the representation of disaster and its aftermath are borne out of both contextual considerations and the increasing commercial demands of Hollywood.

"Providing detailed consideration of key movies within their social and cultural context, this concise introduction serves its purpose well and should prove a useful teaching tool."
– Nick Roddick

# AlterImage

a new list of publications
exploring global cult and popular cinema

For further information about the AlterImage series, or any other of our publications across the field of film and media studies, please visit:

## www.wallflowerpress.co.uk

other series include:

Short Cuts  entry-level undergraduate introductions to film studies
Directors' Cuts  in-depth studies of significant international filmmakers
Critical Guides  comprehensive reference guides to thousands of contemporary directors
24 Frames  edited collections on the films of national and regional cinemas around the world

**WALLFLOWER PRESS**

LONDON and NEW YORK